Atavistic Tendencies

Atavistic Tendencies

The Culture of Science
in American Modernity

Dana Seitler

University of Minnesota Press | Minneapolis | London

An earlier version of chapter 1 appeared as "Freud's Menagerie," *Genre: Forms of Discourse and Culture* 38, nos. 1–2 (Spring/Summer 2005): 45–70; reprinted with permission from the general editor of *Genre* and the University of Oklahoma. An earlier version of chapter 3 was published as "Down on All Fours: Atavistic Perversions and the Science of Desire from Frank Norris to Djuna Barnes," *American Literature* 73, no. 3 (Fall 2001): 525–62; all rights reserved; reprinted with permission from Duke University Press. An earlier version of chapter 5 was published as "Unnatural Selection: Mothers, Eugenic Feminism, and Charlotte Perkins Gilman's Regeneration Narratives," *American Quarterly* 55, no. 3 (March 2003): 61–88; reprinted with permission of The Johns Hopkins University Press.

Published by the University of Minnesota Press
111 Third Avenue South, Suite 290
Minneapolis, MN 55401-2520
http://www.upress.umn.edu

Library of Congress Cataloging-in-Publication Data

Seitler, Dana.
    Atavistic tendencies : the culture of science in American modernity / Dana Seitler.
        p. cm.
    Includes bibliographical references and index.
    ISBN 978-0-8166-5123-8 (hc : alk. paper) — ISBN 978-0-8166-5124-5 (pb : alk. paper)
        1. American literature—20th century—History and criticism. 2. American literature—19th century—History and criticism. 3. Atavism—History—20th century. 4. Atavism—History—19th century. 5. Eugenics in literature. 6. Human reproduction in literature. 7. Biology—United States—History—20th century. 8. Biology—United States—History—19th century. 9. Science and literature—United States—History—20th century. 10. Science and literature—United States—History—19th century. I. Title.
    PS228.E85S45 2008
    810.9'36—dc22

                                                              2008034070

Printed in the United States of America on acid-free paper

The University of Minnesota is an equal-opportunity educator and employer.

15 14 13 12 11 10 09 08   10 9 8 7 6 5 4 3 2 1

Contents

Acknowledgments

I AM indebted to many people and institutions for helping to make this book possible. In the embryonic stages of the project I was lucky to have Lauren Berlant and Bill Brown as mentors; each helped me to realize the argument in these pages. From Bill I learned the pleasures of materialist thinking; from Lauren, a love for difficult ideas and the ability to trust myself. I also owe thanks to the many libraries, archives, and special collections in which this project was carried out: the New York Public Library, the Stanley Burns Artistic and Medical Photograph Archive, the rare books divisions at Duke University and the University of Chicago, Duke Medical Library, the Burroughs Memorial Collection at the University of Louisville Library (with special thanks to its curator, George T. McWhorter), the New York Medical Society, the New York Academy of Science, and the Wellcome Trust Medical Photographic Library in London.

Numerous people took the time to read or listen to the project in its multiple incarnations (either in part or whole): I thank Alan Bewell, George Chauncey, Katie Crawford, Cathy Davidson, Rita Felski, Jonathan Flatley, Sander Gilman, Debbie Gould, Miriam Hansen, Neville Hoad, Donna Landry, Deborah Nelson, Elizabeth Povinelli, Larry Rothfield, Greg Tomso, Priscilla Wald, and David Dario Winner. Of the many supportive colleagues, friends, and interlocutors I have had the fortune to encounter along the way, I thank Mikki Brunner, Sarika Chandra, Michael Cobb, Brian Currid, Van Hillard, Annie Howell, Kim Germain, Michael Gillespie, Elaine Hadley, Colin Johnson, Gerald Maclean, Steve Shaviro, Siobhan Somerville, and the graduate students in my "Time, History, Modernity" seminar at Wayne State University. The gang in Nyack has sustained me in more ways than they know (thanks Pebo, Julie, Kevin, Dave, and Alix). I owe particular thanks to Joe Harris for providing me with an encouraging first work environment and for the time and support afforded me by the Mellon Foundation Postdoctoral Fellowship at Duke University. I am greatly indebted to Richard Grusin, my former chair at Wayne State University, not only for enabling a supportive and productive professional environment but also for his thoughtful contributions to this book—and for his friendship. I also owe thanks to Brian Corman, Jill Matus, and Elizabeth Harvey for helping make the transition to the University of Toronto faculty as collegial as it was fruitful. Special thanks go to my mother, Joan Seitler, for her limitless care and support, my "in-laws," Jack and Zebe Schmitt, my sister, Kim Roma, and my aunt, Bernice Bernhard, who began sharing her love of literature with me before I could crawl.

Portions of the book appeared previously in *Genre: Forms of Discourse and Culture, American Literature,* and *American Quarterly;* I thank the editors and publishers who generously permitted me to republish the material here. I am also happy to acknowledge the funding that made this book possible: at Wayne State, I received several rounds of summer funding and the Josephine Nevins Keal Faculty Fellowship, which provided me with a semester of leave; at the University of Toronto, the Connaught Start-up Award provided funds to carry out the project's final stages. Thanks are owed to my editor, Richard Morrison, and his well-informed editorial staff, as well as to the anonymous readers at the University of Minnesota Press for their helpful suggestions for revision.

My greatest debt is to Cannon Schmitt for his acute intellectual participation, editorial expertise, unwavering belief in the project, and, above all, for being in my life. Beckett River Seitler Schmitt is my deepest joy: from him, I have learned the significance of the present tense, and to him I dedicate this book.

Introduction
Down on All Fours

The Beast had lurked indeed, and the Beast, at its hour, had sprung.
—Henry James, "The Beast in the Jungle"

Historical Atavism

MODERNITY IS an atavism. Its advent in Western culture led to and was given shape by political, social, and aesthetic developments that can be characterized by a recursive temporal subjectivity. This book provides a historical and theoretical account of that subjectivity by looking at late nineteenth- and early twentieth-century science, fiction, and photography. Theories and expressions of atavism in these representational spheres reveal the way modern thought oriented itself around a paradigm of obsolescence and return that structured the experience of modern time. If "modernity" designates itself in terms of its eternal up-to-date-ness, atavism—a theory of biological reversion emerging out of modern science—functions to regulate and upset that designation. In the context of the period of U.S. political and social life with which this book is concerned, the entrancement with temporality—the disorienting experience of modern time—gave rise to a paradox: modernity sought a break with the past, but that break necessitated the past's return. Atavism, this book argues, provides a privileged lens through which to grasp this paradox. *Atavistic Tendencies* thus explores how late nineteenth- and early twentieth-century social and cultural shifts, manifest in the discourses of human science, mass production in the context of industrialization, and social categories of gender, race, class, and sexuality, forced a reimagining of historical time itself.

At present, the word *atavism* is not much in use in our everyday vocabulary. But this was not the case in the late nineteenth and early twentieth centuries, when the term was a frequent placeholder for newly developing notions of human being in the arts and sciences. The *Oxford*

English Dictionary's entry on *atavism* shows it coming into vogue during the second half of the nineteenth century, appearing in popular science texts such as English journalist Walter Bagehot's *Physics and Politics* (1876) and later cropping up in works of modern fiction such as William Somerset Maugham's *Of Human Bondage* (1915), where the main character's actions are described as resulting from "some atavistic inheritance of the cave-dweller."[1] Derived from the Latin kinship term *atavus,* "great-grandfather's grandfather," atavism names a condition of "resemblance to grandparents or more remote ancestors rather than to parents." Secondary definitions include a "tendency to reproduce the ancestral type" and the "recurrence of the disease or constitutional symptoms of an ancestor after the intermission of one or more generations." As the *OED* definition indicates, the concept of atavism posits a notion of the individual self as constitutionally affected by the past. Indeed, atavism is a "reproduction" and a "recurrence" of the past in the present, a recurrence that is specifically one of ancestral prehistory. The key terms used to describe atavism in this definition— reproduction, recurrence, and intermission—all suggest something of the ideological and temporal aspects of the word's usage. We are constituted as individuals, the condition of atavism suggests, not just by way of the contents of the recent past, but in relation to a more distant biological past as well. Atavism brings the ancestral past into conjunction with the modern present, and given the post-Darwinian moment in which the widespread deployment of the concept occurs, this ancestral past was always understood as part and parcel of the course of evolution. Insofar as this understanding punctures the modern idea of the self as individual and autonomous, atavism can be said to open up liberal notions of the privatized subject to the genealogical record. Operating less by a process of continuity than by sporadic interruption, atavism skips generations: it requires a period of latency or "intermission" before it recurs in the present. It thus belies the conception of identity as direct and individualized and of time as an unbroken continuity, instead placing human being in a more inclusive and unpredictable history of biological origins and influences. Indeed, atavism is posed as a category of personhood that erases an immediate reproductive connection between parent and child, situating the locus of the individual's identity in a much earlier ancestral moment that is no longer secured in the past but destined to recur.

In this book, I read the various manifestations and functions of the concept of atavism in the ever-shifting terrain of modernity, when the term first begins to gain currency. Tracking the term and its various figurations enables a historical and theoretical engagement with the dramatic reallocations of self, body, and subjectivity underway in U.S. culture and politics at this moment. In the mid-nineteenth century, Darwin's theory of evolution, although most concerned with progress and development over time, made room for instances of reversal and retrogression as well. The fin de siècle biology this project attends to understood the evolutionary concept of retrogression not simply as a possibility, but as an actuality and a threat. Facing what physician Max Nordau in 1892 called "the horror of world annihilation," for instance, the human sciences posited a nervous question, one that transferred the realm of concern from the individual organism to the social world: if evolution makes thinkable the idea of infinite progress, doesn't it also raise the specter of an equally infinite regress?[2] The concept of atavism emerged as a signal response to this question, functioning pro-phylactically to ward off that specter. Examining post-Darwinian figu-rations of atavism, therefore, is not merely a thematic endeavor; rather, it is a historical one that allows an observation of how the language of science came to inform a new way of thinking about human identity, and how this new way of thinking, in turn, affected political movements, national policies, and narrative forms. I concentrate on the various usages and instantiations of atavism as a potent concept and an imag-ined condition, then, in order to anatomize the nature of the histori-cal situation of which it was a condensation and to which it was a response. History, in the sense that I deploy it here, is not a concrete, observable thing; it has no material existence outside its manifestations in culture. An ineffable source, history is only to be grasped by way of its various mediations, and even then imperfectly.[3] But as a situational aggregate, a collocation of discursive, aesthetic, and emotional changes and expressions at any given moment, history matters precisely because of its ineffability: it precedes and surrounds us, and for this reason en-gaging it means engaging how we come to know what we know about our lived lives.

As this reference to the question of knowledge suggests, another motivation for examining atavistic theory is fostered by an epistemolog-ical concern. As Lorraine Daston has argued, any account of scientific knowledge production necessitates an inquiry into particular knowl-edge projects at the time in which they occur. Daston calls this a practice of "historical epistemology," which entails rejecting the idea of science as producing an empirical, unchanging, and transcendental truth, instead exploring the practices, methodologies, and conceptual categories through which scientific knowledge comes into being and achieves legitimacy.[4] This demands not so much a refutation of scientific method as a sufficiently theorized approach to it. Daston's project is primarily a Foucauldian one insofar as the practice of historical epistemology that she advocates is in many ways akin to what Michel Foucault calls "genealogy," a way of performing historical analysis that deliberately cultivates "the details and accidents that accompany every beginning." This mode of understanding the dispersed origins of discourse demands the identification of "the minute deviations—or conversely, the complete reversals—the errors, the false appraisals, and the faulty calculations that gave birth to those things that continue to exist and have value for us."[5] I treat the emergence of the theory of atavism with the kind of detailed scrutiny and genealogical analysis encouraged by Foucault and Daston. Doing so means asking a series of related questions concerning what this theory tells us about the kind of ideas positing the nature of the human at this time, and how these ideas changed and shifted with each new incarnation. It also means taking special care in attending to the cultural forms by which the theory of atavism was postulated and made available for popular consumption, for it is in these places that "the details and accidents" of which Foucault speaks can be found. Indeed, they are among the only places where history can be grasped.

Key evidence for how late nineteenth- and early twentieth-century scientific beliefs lent particular shape to our knowledge of human being is distributed across a number of different archives. I focus on three of the most productive and central: biological science, visual technology, and literary fiction. I pay close attention to those branches of biology dealing with species reproduction, eugenics, and degeneration; to the photographic images of the human body so often deployed by the sciences to support their theories; and, finally, to literary texts informed by those theories, from Jack London's naturalist novel *The Sea-Wolf* (1904) to Djuna Barnes's modernist *Nightwood* (1937). As is the case with my own interest in London, many critics have turned to naturalist fiction as the genre that most exemplifies fin de siècle concerns about biological personhood, both in terms of its engagement with scientific discourse and its gender politics.[6] But while I engage naturalist texts and arguments about them throughout this study, *Atavistic Tendencies* deliberately moves across a diverse array of textual and visual forms and genres in order to address how scientific theories, literary texts, and emerging visual technologies alike combine in the service of a project to make the human subject knowable. Thus, one of the implicit arguments throughout this book is about how we treat cultural forms as sites of historical evidence. What we learn from atavism is that literary genres often taken to be in contestation, like naturalism and modernism, in fact can be quite complementary. By pairing texts like Frank Norris's naturalist novel *Vandover and the Brute* with *Nightwood*, and London's *The Sea-Wolf* with Eugene O'Neill's expressionist drama *The Hairy Ape,* for example, we can see how different generic conventions engaged the same nationalist concerns about reproductive futurity. Moreover, not only did diverse literary narratives from the period under scrutiny mediate and reinterpret the residing political, medical, and scientific positions of their day, but the sciences themselves consistently borrowed from established narrative and visual conventions to give their particular theories shape and coherence. It is precisely this mutual borrowing that helped regulate and define the status of human being at the time, and that continues to shape the way we understand our bodies in relation to our worlds.

I am particularly concerned with how, in the fin de siècle United States, emergent theories of human being functioned to organize modern political and social life. The human sciences were consistently called on by the state and allied formations to assess what it meant to be human after the advent of such disturbing concepts as evolution and the unconscious, as well as to enter into debates about immigration, family values, and women's roles outside the private sphere. In response, dire predictions of decline emerged from the scientific realm and led many to advocate state control of national biology. For example, in his elaborate book on racial hygiene, *The Passing of the Great Race* (1916), Madison Grant writes: "The state through sterilization must see to it that his [the degenerate's] line stops with him or else future generations will be cursed."[7] Individual bodies—criminal, sexually deviant, and racially "backward"—were cited, but it was American national subjectivity that was at stake. Thus, former notions of human being tied to divinity in religious doctrine, or of the autonomous individual envisioned by liberalism, increasingly came to be replaced by (socio)biological concepts garnered from Darwinian thought. With the publication of Charles Darwin's *On the Origin of Species* (1859) came the ascension of an anti-Platonic understanding of the human self. No longer a matter of essences or pure forms, the animal world, and by extension the human world, was a site of individual variation that formed not emblematic types but populations and species.[8] What ensued was a linking of the individual, biological body to the species body, what Foucault has variously called "biopolitics" or "governmentality," the modern forms of power and knowledge concerned with the management of the biological population.[9]

An array of literary and historical studies, from those by Nicole Rafter and Daylanne English to those by Laura Doyle and Russ Castronovo, address the juridical and punitive power of the nation-state in the nineteenth and early twentieth centuries, scrutinizing the institutional and discursive forces by which the United States engaged in a task of governmental, administrative modernization. As these works aver, the process of governmentality took place across a range of institutional practices: the project of eugenics as demonstrated by Rafter and English; an ideological system of "racial patriarchy" as demonstrated by Doyle; and the administering of death itself (or "political necrophilia") as demonstrated by Castronovo.[10] In the context of atavism, Castronovo's work is especially useful; the continued presence of death in life that he discusses is analogous in many ways to the continued presence of the past in the present that I take as my focus. In each case, the living present of the nation is obsessed with invoking and differentiating itself from a past that refuses to go away.[11]

In addition, as Castronovo also demonstrates, if the body more often than not failed to act as an uncontested site of resistance within the U.S. political economy, it certainly did act as a productive site for the visual mapping of national futurity and decline. This is, in fact, one of the things we learn from the rise of atavistic theory. Atavism functioned as a way to make visible, to exteriorize on the surface of the body, characteristics that might otherwise conceal themselves in the more undetectable realms of the body's interior spaces. Constituted by discernible signs of ancestral recurrence in a present-tense body, atavism made the past of the human present, and it rendered this past not only visible but material, figuring forth the modern human subject as a subject of the deep past. Atavism's most powerful material manifestations were understood to come in the form of the irruption of the animal on the otherwise human body, bearing out the influences of Darwinian evolutionary theory on the fin de siècle state of mind. Accordingly, the sciences investigated the human body for signs of animality in the form of skull size, ear shape, and the slope of the brow, and theorized the appearance of these signs as a reversion to some earlier moment of species history. Instead of a progression toward physical and intellectual superiority as posited by more ameliorative adaptations of evolutionary theory, atavism signaled a retrogressive animalism. Criminals were said to have ears akin to those of lemurs; prostitutes and lesbians, genitalia like that of orangutans; sexual perverts, the brows of apes. Dramatizing the human return to the form of an animal, like a dog or a wolf down on all fours, atavism thus imagines a present always troubled by the past.

If atavism operated in part as a policing mechanism that fixed the human body within readable signs of aberrance, it also served to change how the body was conceived. At the fin de siècle, new knowledges produced by science forced the reconsideration of such seemingly basic notions as self, life, humanity, and nature.[12] One of the most potent incarnations of this redefinition was precisely the image of a human becoming animal. That image was also a potent incarnation of some of the new pressures that inhered within these uncertainties and thus posed a potential challenge to some of the narratives modernity told (and tells) about itself. In particular, atavism offers up a notion of time as multidirectional and of the body as polytemporal. Indeed, atavism can be said to suspend the narrative of modern time as a continuous forward movement in which one event is thought to succeed and supersede another. Instead, it brazenly pushes the past onto the present, materializing the pressing force of history on our lives. The atavistic body thus connects the fibers of time: past (human prehistory), present (the body now), and future (the bodies it will affect). We can begin to grasp the complexity involved if we think about what view of human being such connection posits: atavism suggests not simply genetic continuity but historical and corporeal recursivity. The body, atavism indicates, is reversible, changing, and susceptible to decline; it is affected by an endless cycle of decomposition and recomposition, futurity and return.

Multiple examples are ready to hand. A 1905 photograph of "Unzie the Hirsute Wonder," to take one such example from the popular sphere, advertises one of the "freak" attractions of a traveling circus exhibit. In it, Unzie appears in a tuxedo and boasts an unruly head of

"UNZIE, THE HIRSUTE WONDER."
From a Photo. by Wendt, New York City.

"Unzie, the Hirsute Wonder" (1905). Courtesy of Wellcome Library, London.

white hair and a long, curled mustache. The caption that appears underneath the photograph describes it as of an "albino aborigine." In this example, the appearance of the animal on the human body—in Unzie's case, excessive hairiness (hypertrichosis, as the sciences diagnosed it)—indicates an evolutionary regression. In turn, this regression enables a point of contact with embedded ideas of racial difference, for it is associated with Unzie's designation as an "aborigine." Most curious about the photograph of Unzie, however, is the pairing of this "regression" with an instance of the iconography of modern civilization: a tuxedo. By coupling the ostensibly disparate signs of excessive hairiness and the tuxedo (or, for that matter, "albino" and "aborigine"), Unzie's image puts pressure on, perhaps even challenges, the idea of the modern. It poses this challenge by putting the modern body into direct relation with what modern culture claims to renounce: its roots in the past, and, as dictated by the photograph's own associations, its racial others. In other words, if the photograph of "Unzie the Hirsute Wonder" confirms modernity's understanding of itself as having surpassed an earlier stage of primitivism, it also suggests that the modern is constructed by way of the very things it has purportedly left behind and seeks to deny.

What can we learn from figures such as Unzie the Hirsute Wonder and others like him, including Wolf Larsen of *The Sea-Wolf*, who, with his "massive build . . . [,] partook more of the enlarged gorilla order"?[13] Or from Vandover of *Vandover and the Brute*, who goes down "on all fours," barking like a wolf, at the novel's end?[14] How does a character such as the creeping, crawling narrator of Charlotte Perkins Gilman's "The Yellow Wall-Paper" compare to Tarzan, the ape-man of Edgar Rice Burroughs's popular dime novels? Familiar arguments account for these literary figures as reflections of evolutionary discourse in that they seem to reproduce in literary form the impact of that discourse on the social and cultural world in which it resides. But this will not be my argument here, not least because these figures, when compared to one another, all operate differently within the spectrum of biological science that they can be said to mediate. Moreover, these figures are not Darwinian, but rather post-Darwinian, and that makes a critical difference in how we read them. Each confronts nineteenth-century classificatory systems separating the human from the animal and therefore blurs a series of boundaries between spirit and body, whites and nonwhites, men and women, reproductive virtue and sexual pathology.

Further, and this is one of the most important distinctions this book will make, these figures and the theory of atavism to which they give form are not symptoms of their cultural moment. In other words, atavism is not a sublimation of the collective psyche, a return of the repressed in the symptomatic form of literature, or a trace, and therefore simply an effect, of the tension between the historical repression of an originary trauma and its subsequent displaced expression. Rather, it is a specific discourse that participated in and enabled an understanding of the object to which it was ostensibly opposed—that is, modernity. Atavism, I argue, is not a symptom but an operation, an epistemological strategy for understanding and experiencing the modern world. At once ontologically prior to the modern and central to the modern landscape, the embodied existence atavism incarnates became a convention of both modern aesthetics and modern epistemologies of human being.

Thus, atavism cannot be confined to a singular definition or function. Accordingly, I treat atavism in three ways: as a biological category that emerged at the fin de siècle to designate various forms of human regression; as a historical category that emerged to (re)produce and negotiate social anxieties over the status of human being; and as a theoretical concept that enables an understanding of modernity itself. In thinking of atavism as a theoretical concept in this last sense, I mean to suggest that as a pervasive and constitutive feature of modern conceptions of life and being, it illuminates the discontinuous temporal relationships that characterize American modernity. Specifically, the predicament of atavism points to a layered temporal formation, one of biological past and modern present, that suggests a primary organizing principle of the modern world.

Other persuasive theoretical accounts offer readings of the contingencies of the modern similar to my own. Jacques Derrida's *Specters of Marx* perhaps comes closest to articulating some of the problems I work through in this book. The term Derrida uses to describe this discontinuity is *spectrality*, a process of paradoxical incarnation by which ideas (such as capitalism) are given a body. "For there to be ideas," Derrida writes, "there must be a return to the body, but to a body that is more abstract than ever."[15] For Derrida, this corporeal abstraction is an expression of the spectral nature of being, for being is always ontologically indeterminate; it occupies a space between absence and presence, appearance and disappearance. By building on his earlier notion of *différance* (the non-self-presence of being), spectrality asserts that there can be no ontology, only hauntology. What this means for Derrida is that there are always ghosts haunting the constitution of the subject: a plurality of temporalities, identities, and epistemological positions hovering over the certainties of being.

An often unacknowledged interlocutor for Derrida, and one whose thinking has informed the shaping of this book, is Walter Benjamin. Benjamin's theory of history is articulated against the idea of historical progressivism and its attendant ideologies of positive directionality and infinite perfectibility.[16] Conventional historicism, Benjamin charges, requires a coherent logic of time in order to endow the present with a sense of stability. Operating as a rationalizing narrative of the passage of time, the practice of historicism mediates between the twin desires for continuity and disruption: the need to understand how time progresses in a consistent and predictable way, and the need to understand the present as a distinct and autonomous period. In critical response to this practice, Benjamin's explanation of the irreducible temporality of modern existence suggests that modernity should be understood less as a historical period than as a dialectical sign, one that moves between the poles of cultural neglect and material repetition: each moment that constitutes itself as modern simultaneously carries with it a (fleeting, flashing) mark of the past. Thus, for Benjamin, modernity comprises both the perishable and the recurrent, is undercut by the detritus and phantasmagoria of its own history.

Derrida's notion of the paradoxes of self and being in terms of absence and presence, appearance and disappearance, and Benjamin's understanding of the dialectics of modernity each bear a resemblance to how I approach the concept of atavism, itself a term used to designate the temporary disappearance of the past and its reappearance in some new form on some new body. Although these theories are productive accounts for me, and ones that I make use of during the course of this book, they do not replace or repeat what we can learn from a study of the emergence of the theory of atavism at the fin de siècle. What is unique to such a study is its engagement with the particular ways in which atavism fleshes out the experiences of modernity—in other words, in what it tells us about how changes in the understanding of human being came about and how modernity was shaped by those changes. The capacity for the atavistic subject to embody the most salient features of a post-Darwinian modernity is what also allowed it to surface as a site across which to plot the trajectory of U.S. socio-political life. Rather than taking refuge in the abstracted notion of hauntology that we encounter in *Specters of Marx,* the present study argues that the specific and particular modes through which history unfolds matter in terms of what we can know about that history.

Fortunately, in Benjamin's work, we find attention to these specificities, and with it a methodology for approaching history. One productive location where Benjamin discounts the historicist conviction that history moves continuously and progressively along a chronological time line is in "Theses on the Philosophy of History." There he asserts that the past conjoins with the experience of the present. Only the practice of historical materialism can locate that forgotten or repressed past, and only in the present. "A historical materialist cannot do without the notion of a present which is not a transition," he writes, "but in which time stands still and has come to a stop. For this notion defines the present in which he himself is writing history. Historicism gives the 'eternal' image of the past; historical materialism supplies a unique experience with the past."[17] To avoid presuming historical knowledge of a fixed past, in other words, it is necessary to start from our experience of the present, from "now-time" (*Jetztzeit*), a methodology that in Benjamin's case focuses on the material objects of everyday life. Out of our relation to a specific material object arises a complex narrative composed not only of the object's immediate history (period, region, ownership) but also of the process of history itself. Building on Benjamin's understanding of historical materiality, I read atavism as a productive site through which to explore the specificities of American modernity and as a site through which to grasp the modern world's own understanding and experience of itself. Tracing the narratives accompanying and giving voice to atavistic theory, unpacking, in Foucault's words, "the details and accidents that accompany every beginning," instructs us on the discontinuities that lie at the center of our/modern fantasies of human being and the involvement of science in the construction and maintenance of those fantasies.

Atavistic Modernity

At the fin de siècle, atavism was imbued with such explanatory force in part because the temporal character of modernity was itself in flux. The very instantiation of the word *modernity* sought to establish a new time period and a new social system; *modernity* in this sense doesn't just refer to but acts as a rupture in time in an imagined opposition to an archaic, premodern past (thus we have the famous struggle or *querelle* between the ancients and the moderns).[18] The reassuring power of the word *modernity* and its vibrations of social progress, however, were always troubled in practice, both by the vicissitudes of modern experience and by dramatic changes in the understanding of human identity. In the aftermath of evolutionary theory, the past was viewed not as something that had passed but as a live category actively involved in the structuring of modern life. Both in connection with evolution and in other ways, a primary aspect of the experience of modernity involved coming to terms with one's connections to the past, including former living arrangements, economies, and geographical locations. Recent and distant pasts impinged on the modern present, and they still do.

After all, the desire for a connection to the past is a strong one. To verify this, all we need to do is look at the popularity of reenactment culture (restaging wars, famous journeys, and obsolete cultural rituals) or flip through our own scrapbooks and photo albums.[19] But the past can also be something we want to forget: the awkwardness of our childhoods, the time we pronounced *ignominy* incorrectly in conversation with a favorite college professor, the pain of memory. The past, in this incarnation, is scary. This is especially true when we want nothing to do with a certain aspect of our individual pasts or, in a more collective sense, when history seems so other that we cannot begin to imagine it as a constitutive aspect of our own lives, let alone bodies. Of course, when we think of the past, we don't tend to think of the figure of the animal. In part, this is because human history and natural history have been produced as overly distinct processes. The project of liberal humanism, and its principles of human sovereignty and rationality, has in many ways necessitated such a distinction, for it relies on the age-old separation of nature and culture, and thus animal and human, themselves grounded in largely unquestioned assumptions of species difference (most infamously in Descartes's animals-as-machines figuration). The Enlightenment idea of progress, moreover, has resolutely required a notion of time as a one-way street and history as motivated by unidirectional causation. With progress, the Enlightenment project avers, the world marches forward unstoppably, and we are separated forever from our premodern ancestry. At the fin de siècle, however, the return of the animal on an otherwise human body that atavism dramatizes emerges to trouble this notion of time. Atavism bodies forth the past of human origin—an origin that may not be fully or even consciously cognized but nonetheless constitutes who we are. Such is the encounter with the animal staged by so many texts, images, and novels during the late modern period.

Because this book is concerned with history as an instantiation of events that bring to light our sense of things at a given moment, designating the book's period, however clumsily, is necessary. Throughout the book, I make frequent use of both the term *modernity* and of the periodization *late modernity*. By using the term *modernity*, I mean to invoke the host of interpenetrating forces of change, transition, and upheaval that can be said to characterize the idea and the experience of the modern—forces of industry, technology, war, massification, and so forth. At those moments when I refer to *late modernity*, I mean to indicate the fin de siècle expression of these forces, and to distinguish this period, although not absolutely, from the early modern period and the time of the French and English revolutions usually called on to identify the rise of modernity. But *modernity* itself is a vexed term, and it must not be flattened out as a singular form or ideation. Rather, modernity, in its late modern formation, can be understood as an amalgam of old and new practices and institutional forms constituted by the disjunctures of old and new conditions of living and old and new forms of experiencing the world intellectually and emotionally. Understanding modernity as both a historical period and a conceptual formation thus involves grappling with a series of cognitive, social, and cultural transformations and with a set of persistent cultural, social, and political structures.[20]

Western modernity, the story goes, arose as a conjoined set of revolutionary acts and discourses in which an emerging bourgeoisie, in at least temporary alliance with the radical aspirations of the working poor, struggled against the ancien régime. The bourgeois ideal of modernity, or the instantiation of modernity as a bourgeois ideal, was therefore also an ideal of progress, one that among other things looked optimistically on the possibilities of science, technology, and reason as the means for a more fully democratic state and thus a better life for the individual. One antibourgeois response to this brand of optimism constituted what we have come to call modernism, a practice of resistance and criticism through aesthetic forms.[21] Industrial production and urbanization, and the systems of rationalization that subtended them, the story continues, also shaped a feeling of impending social dissolution and self-alienation.[22] Modernity is thus structured by a sense of progress but also by a sense of loss. Within the context of cultural and economic "progress," anxieties emerged concerning the newness of the modern and the restructuring of social relations that resulted from what Max Weber has characterized as the bureaucratic standardization of everyday life.[23] On the one hand, therefore, there existed the desire to rationalize the world through modern architectural planning, the mechanization of labor, and the instrumentalization of the production process. On the other, there was in response a privileging of the autonomous, contemplative life so sought after by the likes of Charles Baudelaire.[24] Further complicating the (double) narrative of Western modernity, recent projects have discussed how, for the colonial world, modernity was forcefully imposed and so its radical political elements limited. These projects point out the political inconsistencies wrought by global capitalism and seek to decenter Euro- and Anglo-centric epistemic perspectives on the impact of modern idealism.[25]

Fredric Jameson has called the various descriptions of the modern "narrative options" and "alternate story-telling possibilities," by which he means that modernity, like history, is not a thing in itself but a "narrative category" whose rhetoric has served to "indicate itself."[26] In these narratives, modernity is at once a period, an attitude, an experience, a temperament, and a mode of self. Untangling the different meanings that the term conveys, therefore, is clearly a project unto itself and not one this book seeks to undertake. Instead, the specification of the period under investigation as "late modern" serves to delineate some of the particular ways I approach the late nineteenth and early twentieth centuries in the context of U.S. politics and culture. This was both a time of enormous economic and technological development and a time of cultural dissonance brought about by these developments, as well as by the influx of migration and immigration to urban centers that they encouraged. Perhaps more than anything, though, it was a time of an acute awareness of time: days were no longer defined by season or sunrise, but by minutes and hours; lives were structured not by agricultural cycles but by work time and leisure time; bodies were no longer responding to the rhythms and cadences of the natural environment, but to the rationalization of the workforce and the methodical vibrations of machines.[27]

One of the enabling conditions of the construction of modern time as rational, progressive, and machinelike was, paradoxically but perhaps not surprisingly, the notion of antiquity. By way of the construction of disparate times (the ancient and the modern), modernity fashioned itself as a break. Jameson, following Bruno Latour's premise in *We Have Never Been Modern*, describes how modernity identifies itself by establishing a distinction between two historical moments: then and now, the ancient and the new.[28] This identification often requires a repudiation of the past and a celebration of the present. Indeed, the presentness of the modern is marked by the new and the newness of the new, a newness that, as Benjamin reminds us, is always endangered, destined to be obsolete, and replaced by the next new thing. For the modern subject to emerge as modern, everything that came before it, the premodern, the archaic, had to appear remote and distinct. Latour adds, of course, that the idea of the modern as a passage of time that designates a new regime is merely a convenient reference point to explain away variations that nonetheless exist and proliferate.[29] What this means for Latour is that the ontological stability of modernity may be premised on the basis of taxonomic boundaries (between old and new, tradition and innovation, one disciplinary practice and another), but the very imperative for absolute distinction results in the ontological interdependency of opposites and thus in the proliferation of hybrids: "heads of state, chemists, biologists, desperate patients, and industrialists find themselves caught up in a single uncertain story mixing biology and society."[30] Nonetheless, whether or not modernity actually constitutes a historical and epistemological break doesn't change its self-understanding as having experienced one.[31] The idea, false or not, of a division between old and new, past and present, forged the epistemic regime of the modern world.

The atavistic body is, in many ways, exemplary of this sense of a break between the past and the present. This is in part because theories of atavism worked to allay the instabilities of modern experience by producing a body that could act as a site of racialized and sexualized primitivism cordoned off from a "modern" body. The idea of an unstable or tarnished present is thus displaced onto the past by way of the figure of the aberrant criminal, the "savage" individual, the preevolutionary being. Producing the atavistic body as a knowable site alleviates some of the challenges posed by the modern world insofar as that body is capable of enunciating the disciplinary organization that enables the modern to be understood as distinct and distinguishable.

Simultaneously, however, the atavistic body incarnates the present as a temporal synthesis, for it instantiates the crossing of temporalities and personhoods that should, at least ideologically, remain discrete. Of time in this nonchronological, and therefore a-modern, sense, Gilles Deleuze writes, "There is a present of the future, a present of the present, and a present of the past, all implicated in the event, rolled up in the event, and thus simultaneous and inexplicable." For Deleuze, this means that the present is a coalescence of times that get organized into distinct frames at the moment of its occurrence: "Since the present is constituted not after the present that it was, but at the same time, time has to split itself in two at each moment as past and present."[32] Despite this splitting, Deleuze argues, time is a multitemporal totality, and it is as a totality that we must understand it in order to get a glimpse at how we live, move, and change.

To conceive of time in the Deleuzian sense requires a refusal of the narratives modernity proliferates to support itself and a rethinking of the definition and constitution of modernity itself. In taking on this project of redefinition, I join a number of scholars within the field of American studies who have undertaken critical work that explores the racial, sexual, and gendered political economy that informs American nationalism.[33] In addition, this project shares common concerns with science studies, especially its focus on teasing out the cultural logic of scientific construction. This scholarship has turned to a range of medical and biological sciences, including histology, primatology, bacteriology, and obstetrics, to explore how science, as a highly varied and productive discipline, has transformed our understanding of human life.[34] Contra the belief that science proceeds logically and rationally without any regard for the social or the cultural, this book explores how notions of rationality and objectivity are themselves products of science's social organization. This approach does not by any means have as a goal an endorsement of a full-scale rejection of scientific inquiry in its endeavors of observation, identification, and experiment. Even if the workings of the polio vaccine proceed from a paradigm of immunology as opposed to an objective truth, that paradigm is not one I am willing to give up. However, such an approach does mean taking into account what Latour has described as a practice of studying science "in action"—that is, as time-bound practices that are themselves functions of the cultures in which they operate and develop.[35] If science studies questions scientific objectivity by looking at it in action—

in the lab, in the text, in history—this is not the same as a rejection of scientific innovation; nor is it a denial of the existence of reality, as some detractors of science studies have anxiously claimed. Rather, understanding scientific knowledge production as neither monolithic nor immutable means paying amplified attention to its location in the real, insofar as we can understand this amplification as one that concerns thinking through the specifics of scientific claims and the "situated knowledges" of their authors in a given time and place.[36]

Finally, but in many ways most importantly for me, I take up political concerns about identity and the body that have been crucial areas for feminist studies, critical race theory, and sexuality studies.[37] Whether or not we are in a posthuman, postidentity moment, and whether or not posthumanity is a desirable thing that has the power to liberate us from the chains of the Enlightenment rationalist project, we cannot deny that the issue of what it means to be human has been and continues to be an operative question for science, philosophy, and literature. Nor can we ignore how the question of the human is shot through with ideologies of race, class, gender, and sexuality, ideologies that have worked to regulate people's lives in often damaging ways. The history of biological and medical scrutiny purporting to locate, deny, or control indicators of identity and social practice in discrete surfaces of the body continues into the present with an abundance of scientific studies (on reproductive technologies, "gay genes," "race genes," and cloning, to name only a few). Scientific experiment and study continues to walk the line between who gets to count as human and who seems less so as justification for the ethics of their practices (in clinical trials for AIDS drugs, for instance).[38] That so many primary fields of scientific endeavor, from biogenetics to pharmacology, persist in the reproduction of the idea of essences and identities in ways that feed popular belief systems and dominant political practices means that a project on fin de siècle biology is less about a fixed moment in our past than it is a genealogy of our present. Writing such a genealogy is an important part of understanding the role science has played and continues to play in our cultural and political histories. Elizabeth Grosz, for one, has called for a return to what she says we have forgotten: "the nature, the ontology, of the body, the conditions under which bodies are enculturated, psychologized, given identity, historical location, and agency."[39] Making this call for deeply political and ethical reasons, she writes:

The exploration of life is a fundamentally feminist political concern, not because feminists must continue their ongoing suspicions regarding various forms of (male-dominated) biological research, but because feminists, and all other theorists interested in relations between subjectivity, politics, and culture, need to have a more nuanced, intricate account of the body's immersion and participation in the world if they are to develop political strategies to transform the existing social regulation of bodies, that is, to change existing forms of biopower, of domination and exploitation.[40]

Grosz's call for a more intricate account of the body and its participation in the world is one that I take to heart, but I pursue such an account with a different methodological approach than her own. Grosz traces out an intellectual history of three major thinkers in Western thought (Bergson, Nietzsche, and Darwin), paying close attention to the temporal dimension of their theories. In contrast (but not opposition), I look at the material conditions of this intellectual history. I do not use the term *material* here as it is often defined, either as an indication of economic forces in the Marxian sense or as a signifier of the laboratorial spaces in which science is articulated in the science studies/Latourian sense. Rather, I deploy the term to mark out the concrete substance, expression, and experience of everyday life at a given historical moment. Focusing on materiality in this sense follows from the methodological belief outlined above that the development of a politics of transformation demands reflection on the forms of power and knowledge produced by the variety of historically instantiated practices that shape any particular present. For this reason, this book brings together diverse discursive formations and archives, including literary discourse (both in popular and intellectual formations), visual topoi, and scientific rhetoric. *Atavistic Tendencies* draws attention to the concept of atavism with this kind of specificity in order to address the simultaneity of the multiple domains of human experience and thus to read history not through the unfolding of intellectual ideas, but in the folds of the varied articulations out of which the lived experience of human life emerges.

The struggles that play out over the appearance of the body's retrogressions in the present—its atavism—have to do with the constitution of modernity itself, of which knowledge of human being is a central concern. On the one hand, atavism operates as a benchmark for how far we have come. On the other, it simultaneously undermines such progressivism by way of its appearance on a body that, by lingering

Enlightenment accounts, should be purely human. In this second sense, atavism insistently displays the "impurities" of the human body, for it posits a constitutive intermixture of past and present, prehistorical and historical (an intermixture figured forth as one between "impure" racial bodies as well). As a living embodiment, atavism incarnates the past in the present: it is a material, corporeal recurrence of the past, the past in the flesh. By way of such an embodiment, the gap between past and present, between history and prehistory, becomes bridgeable. Atavism thus marks a culturally central conceptualization of human being through which we can trace modernity's implications in what went before, its constitutional alliances with that which it attempts to deny. In the photographs, scientific texts, and fictions that I explore, atavism serves to incarnate the constitutive anachronism at the root of modern selfhood, materializing what could otherwise be understood as the metaphysical questions posed by the modern—questions of loss and presence, obsolescence and repetition, the archaic and the new.

Narrative Atavisms

Such are the questions that plague the central character in O. Henry's short story "The Atavism of John Tom Little Bear," which appeared in *Everybody's Magazine* in 1903.[41] John Tom Little Bear is "an educated Cherokee Indian" who has "graduated from one of the Eastern football colleges that have been so successful in teaching the Indian to use the gridiron instead of burning his victims at the stake" (35). An example of this success, John Tom even comes to look the part of the assimilated citizen: "But for his complexion, which is some yellowish, and the black mop of his straight hair, you might have thought there was an ordinary man out of the city directory that subscribes for magazines and pushes the lawn-mower in his shirt-sleeves of evenings" (43). More than "civilized" in appearance, though, John Tom has also the gift of language: "That redman . . . [h]is vocal remarks was all embroidered over with the most scholarly verbs and prefixes. And his syllables was smooth, and fitted nicely to the joints of his idea" (45). This is more than the narrator of the story, Jeff Peters, can say of his own prose, pointedly cluttered as it is with irregular verbiage and grammatical patterns. John Tom and Jeff Peters become friends and decide to put Little Bear's heritage to use. John Tom dresses in native garb and passes himself off as a medicine man, and the two travel about the Midwest selling "Sum-wah-tah, the great Indian Remedy made from prairie herb revealed by the Great Spirit in a dream to his favorite medicine men" (36). Along the way, they meet up with a young boy who has recently run away from home. They contact his mother, who later takes them out to dinner in thanks. John Tom falls in love with her, and instantly recognizes his love as futile: "There's an eternal wall between the races," he laments, "you've taught me to hate the wigwams and love the white man's ways. I can look over into the promised land and see Mrs. Conyers, but my place is—on the reservation" (48). That same night, Mrs. Conyers's abusive husband, whom she has left, comes to town and kidnaps their son, but not before whipping her in the face with his horse's reins. John Tom Little Bear, who has been on a drinking binge to drown his sorrows, immediately sets off on foot to find the boy. Along the way, he degenerates into a "disrespectable Indian": a "Cherokee Brave" traveling on a "warpath" (51). When he returns with the boy in his arms and Mr. Conyers's scalp dangling from his belt, Jeff Peters hardly recognizes his friend, for "the light in his eye [was] the kind the aborigines wear" and "the flowers of the white man's syntax had left his tongue" (51). "'Me bring,' says he. 'Run fifteen mile. Catch white man. Bring papoose'" (52). The next morning, however, one can see "the nineteenth century in his eyes again." John Tom explains to Jeff that his behavior of the night before was due to "the interesting little physiological shake-up known as reversion to type" (52).

I turn to this story, and others like it as the book proceeds, to demonstrate something of the pervasiveness of the concept of atavism at the fin de siècle. I also turn to it because it demonstrates the development of a literary idiom of human transformation beyond a mere symptomatic discourse. Instead of treating the fiction, science, and photography into which this project delves as reflections of their historical climate, I explore how these three spheres all actively participated in the production of the human as an object of knowledge.[42] In O. Henry's short story specifically, the construction of an atavistic character like John Tom Little Bear may be seen as a negotiation of the increasing anxieties over the fragile boundaries of race, sexuality, and class at the fin de siècle. In this sense, the narrative plays on the motif of the Native American as a quintessential model for the primitive. Figuring as the uncivilized, or barely civilized, inhabitants of an ex-primitive world, Native Americans were the living signs of the atavistic legacy of American soil: homeland primitives. Although the story helps to generate the Native American as such, it also calls into question this very generation by democratizing atavism as a cultural descriptor. After all, the whole premise of the story is that John Tom Little Bear has been civilized and is only playing the part of an Indian medicine man to make a few dollars. Appealing to the desire for the primitive in "civilized" culture, he puts his "nature" in a bottle to be sold. It is the midwesterners who are shown to be playing (stupidly) into the notion of the proximity between race and the healing powers of nature as they eagerly make their purchase of Sum-wah-tah (that is, "some water" in mock Native parlance). Sum-wah-tah, in this sense, acts as a counterrational appeal to what is represented as a ubiquitous (and lucrative) need, perhaps one that we can understand as a wish to return to an earlier stage of human being, for the midwesterners' desire to purchase primitivism may also be read as a desire to become primitive. The commodification of primitivism and its exchange, therefore, upsets the idea of the primitive as limited to certain racial types.

O. Henry also pays close attention to the brutishness of the civilized world through the figure of the abusive husband. Indeed, the husband's kidnapping of his son inverts the captivity narrative: John Tom Little Bear, now playing the part of "noble savage," goes after the brutish husband, and so the locus of the primitive gets swapped from one to the other. The love plot, however, complicates this husband swap, demonstrating, in John Tom's own words, the "eternal wall between the races." John Tom's reeducation ultimately cannot overcome the greater force and "fact" of his race. One way to read his "reversion to type" at the story's end, then, is as a confirmation of his earlier lament. His nature returns to corroborate what he already seems to know: "his place is the reservation." When it comes to miscegenation, the story avers, otherwise permeable relations become impermeable, and race reemerges as a fixed part of the story's cultural bedrock.

But the fact that O. Henry intended this story as a playful farce may provide us with another way to read it. To be sure, we are encouraged to find humor in the act of reversion itself. John Tom loses all ability to be civilized, and we are treated to an "actual" performance of his nature, replete with linguistic error: "Me bring"; "run fifteen mile." At the same time, the punchline of the story lies in John Tom's final utterance, itself a recovery of his linguistic prowess, when he describes his actions as resulting from "the interesting little physiological shake-up known as reversion to type." This diagnosis is "funny" because it demonstrates John Tom's ability to recognize his own atavism, and to do so within the terms of contemporary science, something he should not be able to do if he were in fact what his actions have shown him to be. The joke, then, can be said to have two parts. The first part declares hilarious John Tom's atavism; the second part, his civilized and erudite self-recognition of this "physiological" condition. Each part of the joke contradicts the other as the different possibilities of where the locus of humor can be found run counter to one another. The enabling assumptions we need to "get" in order to get the joke run counter to one another as well: as readers, we need to believe in the relative fixity of Native American types on the one hand and in the success of the "civilizing" project on the other. Indeed, the joke lies at the juncture of these two assumptions as they bump up against one other.

Characters like John Tom Little Bear speak to the operation of atavism itself and its postulation of a human subject dependent on and maintained by a corporeal and temporal indeterminacy. His character, in other words, dramatizes the vicissitudes of subjectivity in relation to modern time. If John Tom experiences an evolutionary push forward by way of the reeducational forces of the Eastern boarding school for Indians, he also undergoes an inevitable reversion backward to a former primitive self, only to return once more to his elocutionary capability. If, on the one hand, the movement of becoming educated, and therefore becoming civilized, is figured as a kind of progressive overcoming of self, it is also shown to be an incomplete becoming, one subject to reversal (and counterreversal). His civilized self may be just one alternative mode of being among the many that John Tom has at his disposal: medicine man, intellectual, Indian. His personhood is constituted by myriad possibilities and their blurring interpenetration. He is educated and primitive, an eloquent speechmaker and an Indian warrior. John Tom Little Bear's reversion—the recurrence of his tribal blood—is, therefore, not necessarily a sign of the greater "truth" of his primitivism, but of the interconnections of past and present he carries with him. Time, his character affirms, constitutes our lived lives; it saturates our mode of thought and action, it lends complexity to every "present" moment, and it leads us back and forth and back again.

As "The Atavism of John Tom Little Bear" also demonstrates, this notion of time is enmeshed with fraught conceptions of the modern family and ideas of race and sexuality that came to inform it. It is the family, after all, that is shown to be in crisis in the story: the little boy runs away from home to escape from the reality of his parents' sep-aration and his father's abusive nature. Even while John Tom Little Bear is shown to be the better, more civilized man, his love for Mrs. Con-yers proves impossible simply because he is of the "wrong" race. The O. Henry short story, as farce and fable, may seem far from the mate-rial conditions of everyday life, but in it we catch a glimpse of certain social realities that have consequences in the world. John Tom's edu-cation at an Eastern boarding school references an actual program to assimilate Native Americans through the process of education (General Richard Henry Pratt, founder of one such school, famously held the philosophy that one must "kill the Indian to save the man," believing that only with complete assimilation could Native Americans survive in modern America).[43] In addition, the story's skittishness over interracial coupling indexes existing anxieties concerning the future of the Amer-ican family. Part of what the story illustrates, in fact, is how deeply the category of race, not to mention sexuality, is bound up with a regula-tory conception of the family and concerns over its self-governance.[44]

As Rafter and English have shown, the intricate bindings of power within the family were supported and reinforced by state ideologies external to it, including the project of eugenics.[45] The focus on ata-vism helps bring to light another layer of this history, for if eugenics was the practice, atavism was the theory, one that emerged specifically to address the fear of familial, and therefore national, dissolution that the possibility of evolutionary reversal was thought to determine. It was through the concept of atavism that the sciences sought to cen-tralize in the seeming impalpability of being the foundational char-acteristics of the human. In this incarnation, atavism was the smoking gun of the refractory elements of our social and biological existence. As biologist and eugenicist Lothrop Stoddard argued in 1922:

Each of us has within him an "Under Man," that primitive animality which is the heritage of our human, and even prehuman, past. This primitive animality potentially present even in the noblest natures, continuously dominates the lower social strata, especially the pauper, criminal, and degenerate elements—civilization's "inner barbarians." Now, when society's dregs boil to the top . . . in virtually every community there is a distinct resurgence of the brute and the savage, and the atavistic trend thus becomes practically universal.[46]

As something already present "even in the noblest natures," atavism threatens a resurgence of the prehuman past and, therefore, an im-plosion of the modern world. It also produces a fundamental, at times eschatological, relation between time and the body, and thus between temporality and human progress.

By FOCUSING on these uneven concepts of human progress and regress, *Atavistic Tendencies* argues that the emergence of the idea of atavism marks a fundamental shift in ways of knowing and understanding the human. I chart the ways in which atavism is dramatized in visual, scientific, and literary productions and trace the interaction among those productions, which from the fin de siècle on became increasingly significant as a means to tell the story of the human. Visual, scientific, and literary practices of representation not only reconfigured the idea of the human but also established modern practices of interpreting and experiencing it. By centering on the atavistic body, I contend, we gain a fuller understanding of the fiction and drama of the period. Because no other study to date exists that catalogs the appearance of the atavistic and animalized human self in American literary fiction, science, and photography, and because atavism was not just a subtext of American culture but a manifold presence, such a cataloging is worthwhile in itself. But this book also makes a distinct argument. The literary and visual culture of the period did more than satisfy a proclivity for mimetic representation; it also contributed to the altering of people's perceptual approach to the world. The larger stakes of this project, then, reside in examining the spread of a scientific project of the human and what it might tell us about the prehistory of our own contemporary sense of self.

The six chapters that make up this book establish a link between epistemological questions about the status of humanness and the emergence of new narrative and visual forms in which concerns over corporeal ruination play themselves out thematically and formally. This is why I begin, in chapter 1, "Freud's Menagerie," with an exploration of the formal and tropological devices deployed by Freudian psychoanalysis to establish human sexual drives as atavistic and the desiring subject as a "savage" subject. The chapter takes up Freud's case studies "The Wolf Man" and "The Rat Man" to ask questions about how the persistent figure of the animal, operating as a sign of evolutionary precedent, establishes the psyche as a residue of the past and thereby figures the hermeneutics by which human sexual development could be comprehended. The trope of the animal in these case studies, I argue, illuminates a particular history in which the archaic, the evolutionary past, is deployed to orient the unfamiliar terrain of sexual modernity. Chapter 1 demonstrates that atavism is not just an abjected form of modern life, a sign indicating modernity's Other; rather, it is an *operation* that makes modernity possible. This chapter also serves as a methodological primer where I put into practice the theory of historical epistemology as a crucial method for unpacking the links between time, narrative, and the modern human subject that I attend to throughout the book.

I continue this discussion in chapter 2, "Late Modern Morphologies," by looking at the practices of medical photography. I argue that the increasing fin de siècle collaboration between new human sciences and new photographic technologies bound human identity to the visible body. As a technology of personhood, the photograph aided science in its will to visualize the human form. It thus provided science with a new ground of knowledge and an ostensibly objective medium with which to track the disturbances of late modernity. I focus on photographic images and medical illustrations of human aberrance and in particular on the showcasing of the atavistic body. The medical photograph, I argue, was particularly well suited to the paradigm of modernity and its division of past from present, and thus aberrance from normativity. This is because the photograph is itself a temporal practice. In the photograph, the body is frozen in time: secured in the past, quarantined from the present. At the same time, not unlike the atavistic body that it so often displayed, the medical photograph is a site where the past recurs in such a way as to reinforce and reinvent meanings of and in the present. Whereas in the first chapter I set out the methodological practice of the book, in chapter 2, I add historical and visual layers to that practice. In so doing, I forward two related arguments: I show how the photograph emerged as a social technology with some force in the late nineteenth century, and I demonstrate how, as such a technology, the photograph insists on the corporeal and temporal contingency of human being. I begin by examining how theories of atavism transformed traditional concepts of a stable, integral human identity by offering the spectacle of human bodies in various states of regression and animalism. I then track the ways in which new modes of imaging the body and formal methods of displaying it accompanied the modeling of identity in the human sciences. Finally, I enter into a discussion of how the collaborative exchange between scientific empiricism and photographic representation offered up a new, unprecedented epistemology of human being at this historical moment.

In later chapters, I look at the emergence of what I call "degeneration narratives" and "regeneration narratives," stories that either dramatize the decline of an atavistic body or that articulate the potential for bodily renewal. In chapter 3, "Wolf—wolf," I look at Frank Norris's *Vandover and the Brute* and Djuna Barnes's *Nightwood,* where sexual perversity as a form of atavism is literally enacted as a character's return to the form of an animal (a wolf, a barking dog). I argue that the atavism described as present within each character in these novels exists as the precondition for the expression of their sexual subjectivity. I explore how each text incorporates theories found in scientific culture concerning atavism to organize their narratives and to explain their characters' perverse meanderings. With every embodiment and narrativization of bestial perversity, however, science is refunctioned in very different accounts of sexual personhood. Although *Vandover* produces an atavistic body so multiply determined that there is no way of tracing an etiology of sexual practice, *Nightwood* imagines a sexual subjectivity sublimely mobile and capable of an exquisite shattering of fixed notions of identity. Becoming-animal in each, therefore, becomes the basis for locating desire in narrative. As a result, the novels demonstrate how formal procedures of defamilarization (of the human, of the body) enable the generation of models of sexual personhood as critical alternatives to the logos of science.

Chapter 4, "Atavistic Time," takes as its object the emergence of the popular dime novel, with a focus on the *Tarzan* and *Dr. Fu Manchu* series as exemplary of this genre. I argue that the serial dime novel emerged as an ideological incorporation and dissemination of the idea of modern time, and I define this ideology in two ways: as a principle of continuation that mass production encouraged, and as a structure of epistemic familialism requiring reproduction as its active principle. Just as the process of labor was broken down into rationalized operations such that the final product could be reduced to a series of mechanical repetitions, the mechanization of reproductive labor afforded the possibility of rationalized, and thus more efficient, kinship units. The mechanization of reproduction took the form of the science of eugenics, whose goal was to yield over time the most efficient product for national reproduction. In the *Tarzan* and *Fu Manchu* serials, we can observe the interchange between both aspects of this ideology. First, as an instantiation of the new capabilities of mass-mediated modernity, serial dime novels formally and structurally engaged the capitalist embrace of technical reproduction. Second, linking up with the new techno-logical capacity for infinite serialization, plots followed suit by taking place not simply over episodes but over generations. Accordingly, both the *Tarzan* and *Fu Manchu* series unfold by way of the growth of their hero's and villain's families. It is significant, in this respect, that each series features what I call the "return issue" (featuring the dramatic return of the main character after his obligatory flight in the previous issue) and the "reproductive issue" (dedicated to the birth of Tarzan's son in one series and Fu Manchu's daughter in the other). Not only does this demonstrate how ubiquitous was the discourse of heredity in relation to ideas of modern progress or decay, but it also shows how the convergence of ideologies of production in the workforce and ide-ologies of reproduction in the family was wrapped up in a cultural project to imagine the reproduction of the nation.

In chapter 5, "Unnatural Selection," I ask: if some of the greatest anxieties over cultural progress or degeneration in this period were organized around theories of reproduction and heredity, what kinds of pressures, urgencies, or appeals were placed on motherhood? How did women-authored narratives react to or participate in the genera-tion of these appeals? Charlotte Perkins Gilman's fiction exemplifies a mode of reaction and participation I call "eugenic feminism": the use of eugenics for a feminist agenda articulated on behalf of perceived sociosexual problems. Gilman deploys this agenda to construct "regen-eration narratives" that respond to fears of degeneration by fore-grounding the cultural primacy of women and their reproductive status. As Gilman herself avers, this agenda was propelled by the threat of ata-vism and her confidence that atavism could be vanquished by women's widespread participation in eugenics. She writes: "It has taken Mother Nature long, long ages to turn fierce, greedy hairy ape-like beasts into such people as we are; it will take us but two or three close-linked gen-erations to make human beings far more superior to us than we are to the apes."[47] Overall, this chapter demonstrates how issues of repro-duction and eugenics saturated early feminist thought in a manner unrecognized by prevailing readings of the period. I make the specific argument that the histories of our feminisms are fraught with a dialec-tic between possibility and harm in ways that have mostly gone unex-plored. I link this model for engaging the history of feminism with a model of reading narrative forms. In particular, I explore how biological discourses helped bring about narrative innovation, and I trace out, with Gilman's work as an example, the ways in which scientific ideas about the threat of atavism shaped and were shaped by political and aesthetic imperatives.

In chapter 6, "An Atavistic Embrace," I look at three texts: London's *The Sea-Wolf,* Eugene O'Neill's *The Hairy Ape,* and Richard Washburn Child's "The Gorilla." That each of these texts belongs to a different genre of writing (the naturalist novel, expressionist drama, and magazine short story, respectively) testifies to the profound and even invasive presence of the idea of atavism in U.S. culture. In each text, the main character is placed within a post-Darwinian discourse, illuminating modernity's dependency on not only the idea of the past, but on a past conceived of as animal and/or "savage." Indeed, the animalized human subject we find in each gives shape and substance to the modern subject as an atavistic subject. In *The Hairy Ape,* for example, the main character is a coal stoker on a commercial ocean liner whose body is described within a double discourse of the human/not-human binary: he is "hairy-chested, with long arms of tremendous power, and [a] low, receding brow above small, fierce, resentful eyes."[48] In my reading of these texts, I focus on a scene of embrace that occurs in each: in *The Hairy Ape* we witness Yank hugging a gorilla at the zoo; in "The Gorilla," a life-and-death embrace between a capitalist factory owner and his bestialized worker; in *The Sea-Wolf,* a similar embrace between the effete landlubber Humphrey van Weyden and his kidnapper-cum-ship's captain Wolf Larsen as they discuss the difference between spirit and matter. Each scene, I argue, stages the surprising intimacies an encounter with atavism affords—intimacies both between men and across species. This chapter raises pressing questions about the social and biological entanglement of human being that each scene calls forth and that *Atavistic Tendencies* as a whole seeks to confront. Thinking through this entanglement entails thinking about human being as a lateral relation of kinship, as a self constituted beyond and outside itself in connection and alliance to other human and nonhuman forms, temporalities, and spheres. The moments of embrace between human and animal outlined in this chapter and the representations of the human as animal discussed throughout the book help us to see this entanglement more clearly because the figure of the animal as a characteristic of the human provides a sense of temporal continuity with our past and a point of origin, a sign of the beginnings of human being. Opposed to the imagined sovereignty of the human, atavism, the eternal recurrence of the animal, erupts as a potent flash of natural history that insists on recognition of a more complex kinship web. The animalization of the human subject, in short, conjures up a synthesis of past and present in which the collective perception of human history obtains significance.

Other diagnostic "conditions" prevalent in the late modern period could have been a focal point for this study. Neurasthenia, hysteria, melancholy: each has been a noted aspect of the medicalization of personhood at the fin de siècle, and each in many ways is a potent expression of the experience of modernity.[49] What remains unique about atavism is its simultaneous incarnation as a biological condition, a mode of experiencing modernity, and a fundamental organization and perception of modern time. Atavism itself enables the temporalization of modernity, for the atavistic body provides one of the principal sites where human being is transformed into a naturalized function of modern time. And yet it is also a site of recursive temporality that *denatu*ralizes conceptions of modern progress. In the contingent social and biological forces encrypted in the figure of the atavistic body, finally, we can see how atavism stands as an allegory where the perplexing fusions of past and present, modern and archaic meet. If the idea of the modern, on this reading, comes into being by way of the shaping of human bodies, then it again proves ungraspable, though not only because of the body's recalcitrance but also because modern temporality, with which that body is coincident, is perpetually recursive and shifting, forever a space of definitional struggle and epistemological resistance. Atavism and its organizing trope of a human down on all fours should thus be thought of as nothing less than a productive instance of modern time.

1. Freud's Menagerie

Our Atavistic Sense of Self

And what gives us hope is something still to be found in ourselves—in some, if not in all, of us; vestiges of ancient outlived impulses, senses, instincts, faculties [. . .] in some exceptional cases are rekindled and operate so that a man we know may seem to us, in this particular, like a being of another species. They are numerous enough, and when collected and classified they may form a new subject or science with a specially invented new name.
—W. H. Hudson, *A Hind in Richmond Park*

In an aversion to animals the predominant feeling is fear of being recognized by them through contact. The horror that stirs deep in man is an obscure awareness that in him something lives so akin to the animal that it might be recognized. [. . .] He may not deny his bestial relationship with animals, the invocation of which revolts him: he must make himself its master.
—Walter Benjamin, *One-Way Street*

IN THIS chapter, I explore some of Freud's most famous case histories as foundational texts in the thinkability of the human. In particular, I take "The Wolf Man" (1918) as a locus classicus. Sergei Pankejeff, the patient who came to be known as the Wolf Man, was the son of a rich Russian landowner. He is described in the study as suffering from debilitating compulsions resulting from his sexual development having gone awry during childhood. While growing up on his parents' estate, Pankejeff developed an animal phobia and had the famous dream of wolves, which for Freud proved invaluable to his understanding of childhood neurosis.[1] In Freud's reading of the dream, the human psyche becomes indissociable from the sign of the animal. Such an indissociable relation emerges, I argue, as a primary ground for Freud's account of the constitution of human being. The Wolf Man's dream animals are interpreted by Freud as dispersed elements of a repressed and otherwise incoherent self in both an ontogenetic and a phylogenetic sense—that is, in terms of the growth of an individual and

the growth of the species. Deliberately extrapolating from the Darwinian theory with which he was so enamored, Freud yokes together human
and animal and thereby provides an interpretation of the human subject as embedded in a former primitive state.[2] Further, in calling on
this correspondence between ontogeny and phylogeny, Freud asks us to
interpret the Wolf Man's dream as a simultaneous resurgence, or return,
of the individual past and the species past. The unconscious is thus
assigned a layered temporal function. As Freud puts it: "The prehistory into which the dream-work leads us back is of two kinds—on the
one hand, into the individual's prehistory, his childhood, on the other,
in so far as each individual somehow recapitulates in abbreviated form
the entire development of the human race, into phylogenetic prehistory too."[3] Our present psychological makeup, we are to understand,
is constituted by a common "racial" genealogy as much as by events
generated by our past experiences.

The temporal relays between human and animal as well as prehistoricity and modernity elaborated in Freud's case histories hold steadily
visible the definitional problem of human being. Placing the modern
subject within the evolutionary logic of animality, Freud's animal case
histories trouble entrenched practices of classification that would insist
on strict species boundaries, and position psychoanalysis as a menace
to the boundary-dependent theory of liberal humanism, asking us to
reimagine how we think about our sense of self, identity, and body.[4] By
articulating the workings of the psyche as an expression of animalism,
case studies such as "The Wolf Man" perform a breakdown of the species barrier in such a way as to suggest the nondifference of human and
bestial extremes, challenging the illusion of human rationality and of
the sanctity of the human body. The Wolf Man case study, moreover,
not only invokes an understanding of bestial kinship but also upsets
ideas of the sovereign human subject, of our experience of ourselves
as coherent and autonomous beings in the world.

According to the logic of sovereign humanity, we are individuals
bounded as much by an innate capacity for thought as by skin, a capacity that separates absolutely the human from its surroundings. The
Wolf Man's psychic hybridity interrupts this logic precisely because it
challenges the modern structuring of time. If we take the bestial as a
sign of evolutionary precedent, and one that modern culture works
especially hard to suppress, then Freud's analysis of the Wolf Man
collapses distinctions between the bestial precursor and the human

finished product, and between the prehistoric past and the modern present. By bringing the past into proximity with our present, the possibility of human–animal connection bridges the ostensibly insuperable distance between our more primitive origins and the onset of our modernities. What haunts the production of the Wolf Man's hybridity, in other words, is the prehistory of modernity and the inevitability of that prehistory's recurrence. As a material reminder of the human past, the animal functions as the sign of a return not *to* but *of* the past, and so precisely enacts that condition with which this book is concerned: the condition of atavism.

Belying the notion of the modern as an absolute break with all things that came before it, atavism incarnates a synthesis of past and present in which the entanglements of human history and natural history cannot be undone. Bruno Latour discusses such an incarnation as the "double asymmetry" of the modern, the process by which the very appearance of the words *modern, modernity,* or *modernization* define, by contrast, something archaic, like the past. In other words, the modern, conceptualized as a complete epistemological and historical break from everything that came before it (the teleologically named premodern) is constituted by that conceptualization and thus also by the premodern from which it distinguishes itself. For Latour, two sets of practices are instantiated by modernity's double asymmetry: purification and mediation. The practice of purification "creates two entirely distinct ontological zones," the human and the nonhuman. The practice of mediation "creates mixtures between entirely new types of beings, hybrids of nature and culture." The paradox of modernity is that it is the practice of purification that makes the proliferation of hybrids possible: "The more we forbid ourselves to conceive of hybrids, the more possible their interbreeding becomes."[5]

Like Latour, Isabelle Stengers explores modernity's stabilized networks of nature and culture and attempts to go beyond their irreconcilable positions. She stresses what she refers to as "the dense copresence of multiple significations" in "nature–culture" (Latour's coinage for what he takes to be intimately related spheres).[6] For Stengers, the discoveries or "inventions" of modern science always produce "unsuspected distinctions," the effects of which are the production of "a multiplicity of interveners." By way of example, Stengers explains: "When Jean Perrin, in 1912, imposed on skeptics the vision of a world in which macroscopic phenomena can be interpreted in terms of events and movements of imperceptible atoms, he did not impose on them a world reducible to atoms . . . he imposed on them a multiplicity of situations." In other words, the atom did not reduce all matter to its smallest unit; it exploded the apparent unity of matter. Indeed, for Stengers, the atom *intervened* in the unity of matter. Thus, molecular biology became capable of opening up the material world to its multiple significations: "Retroactively, we could say atoms, molecules, genetic transmission are the given conditions of our history, but they only 'make history' by also becoming conditions for *other* histories, transforming what had to be explained in one 'case' in the midst of a variety of cases."[7]

In what follows, I want to engage both Latour's conception of the proliferation of hybrids and Stenger's related idea of the copresence of the multiple significations of "nature–culture." Not only will I speculate that animals and other forms and formalizations of atavistic beastliness supplement and challenge the already unstable Western definition of human being, I will also suggest that such a speculation might produce the conditions of possibility for a different kind of knowledge production about modern human identity.[8] I use the term *supplement* deliberately here, following Derrida's notions of supplementarity: in my usage, the animal acts as a supplement that produces no relief, but rather confirms the excess, and therefore lack, of meaning it is deployed to both display and conceal. As a supplement, the animal marks a deficiency of and an addition to the human self. Thus Derrida: "One cannot determine the center, the sign which supplements it, which takes its place in its absence—because this sign adds itself, occurs in addition, over and above, comes as a supplement."[9]

Posing such an inquiry has, at its base, a political desire to shift away from empirical or foundationalist questions about whether or how we are human and toward epistemological questions about how we come to know what we know about the species of being called human. Rather than entailing a search for facts about or evidence of the human, such a shift necessitates a historical inquiry into the particular knowledge projects concerning the concept of the human. As I discussed in the introduction, Lorraine Daston has called this a practice of "historical epistemology," which she understands to be "the history of the categories that structure our thought." This means, as Daston explains it, exploring not the history of this or that empirical, unchanging fact, but rather exploring "a history of the competing forms of facticity."[10]

Engaging such a practice of historical inquiry here, I hope, will not reiterate and reinforce the liberal subject as posited by nineteenth-century American and European discourses but rather enter into a space of inquiry about that subject and how its formal contours have shaped both ethical questions and conservative legalisms about so-called human bodies and human life.

Creature Comforts

If "The Wolf Man" provides a fertile account of human sexuality, it does so by producing a narrative at once academic and intimate. Arguably, it is the genre of the case study, Freud's preferred method of theoretical articulation, that allows for this duality. In its most basic form, the case study seeks to answer deep questions of the human subject in relation to the social world; as such, it could be considered a formal methodology coextensive with modernity: qualitative, individual, and descriptive, with an eye toward the "real." The early sociological and psychoanalytic case study, formulated as an intense inquiry into an individual or a small participant pool, fixated on an interrogation of the human as human, on the psychic or social traits out of which the human is constituted. Sociologist Robert E. Park, for example, who was influential in developing sociological case studies at the University of Chicago in the 1920s, encouraged students to get out of the library and into the streets to view human experience firsthand.[11] For psychoanalysis, and for Freud in particular, the case study offered a similar first-hand view of human experience, from the inside out.

Popularized Freudian psychoanalytic theories of the self as alienated consciousness in need of cognitive restoration (in the idiomatic forms of "finding oneself" or "getting in touch," for example) have become so much a part of the everyday lives and language of the Western populace (at least) that, almost without being aware of it, we think and speak of ourselves as functioning humans in post-Freudian terms.[12] In many ways, the Freudian psychoanalytic project stems directly from the very nineteenth-century mode of liberalism it sought to challenge in that it retains a congruent, even derivative ideal of what Elaine Hadley calls "embodied abstraction." Embodied abstraction is Hadley's neologism for liberalism's "desire for a political subject who is abstract (and capable of abstract thought) but also individual, abstract and yet concretely materialized." In particular, Hadley argues that the instantiation of a code of awareness of the self as an autonomous individual was a major effect of the liberal project and ushered in a new sense of the condition of being human: rational, disinterested, individuated, and above all self-present.[13] Cognitive thinking, in this view, is that which links both the individual to the collective (in practices like voting) and ideas to the body (thus ameliorating the problem of the mind–body split). The case study is itself a mode of embodied abstraction to the extent that we understand its primary aim to be the concrete materialization of the individual in an abstracted form. In the therapeutic process, the cognizant self-reflection that Hadley describes is figured as psychological inner directedness, a process of introspection that acts as a modality through which the embedded latencies of self and being can be made present, the unconscious made conscious. The Freudian critique of self-presence notwithstanding, psychoanalysis as a practice was intent on forging an immediate and palpable relationship between an individual and his or her primary repressions. It is in this sense that I see the psychoanalytic project as a continuing discourse in the enterprise of the modern liberal subject. Precisely by refusing enlightenment concepts of unmediated consciousness, self-identical personhood, and self-possession, the therapeutic process proffers itself as both the discoverer of the split self and the bridge between its parts, thus restoring the self to the self as a self.[14] And by positing the psychoanalytic subject as the transhistorical, transgeographical subject of modernity, Freudian psychoanalysis participates in the insistence of the universality of the human subject more generally.

In keeping with Stengers and Latour, we may understand the process of psychoanalytic restoration as part of the deep architecture of modernity. By perceiving the subject dually, psychoanalysis strives to complicate the episteme of human rationality. At the same time, and precisely by doing so, it institutes a standardized "network of interpretation," a modern strategy to explain (away) the destabilized subject.[15] Modern psychology, in other words, establishes itself as a site for the alleviation, and therefore "purification," of the instabilities of the human. However, as Latour might suggest, any such establishment also aids in the invention of ontological varieties of self. The instantiation of the modern human subject, then, is at least doubly narrative: a story of its emergence can only be told as a story of the knowledge projects that sought to inscribe it.

The strongest example of this instantiation in "The Wolf Man" case study can be seen in the Wolf Man's dream of the wolves, which Freud himself takes as the heart of his patient's neurosis. The Wolf Man recounts his dream thus:

I dreamt it was night and that I was lying in my bed. My bed stood with its foot towards the window. . . . I know it was winter when I had the dream, and night time. Suddenly the window opened of its own accord, and I was terrified to see that some white wolves were sitting on the big walnut tree in front of the window. There were six or seven of them. The wolves were quite white, and looked more like foxes or sheep-dogs. . . . In great terror, evidently of being eaten up by the wolves, I screamed and woke up.[16]

Later the Wolf Man added that the wolves "sat quite still and without making any movement. It seemed as though they had riveted their whole attention on me." Eventually Freud asked his patient to draw a picture of the dream, detailing the tree with the wolves perched in the branches (173–74). From the material provided by the images in the dream,

"The Wolf Man's Drawing of the Dream of the Wolves." From Sigmund Freud, *The Wolfman and Other Cases,* translated by Louise Adey Huish. Copyright 2002 by Louise Adey Huish. Original German texts copyright 1940, 1941, 1946, 1947 by Imago Publishing Co., Ltd., London. Reprinted by permission of Penguin, a division of Penguin Group (USA) Inc.

Freud reconstructs the contents of what he comes to call the Wolf Man's "primal scene": the young boy's possibly real but potentially fantasized witnessing of parental sex. Observing the principle of distortion operating in the dreamwork, the way in which dreams are occasions for "screen memories" that both evoke and obscure repressed material from the individual's psyche, Freud infers the "violent motion" of the primal scene from the represented immobility of the wolves. Their immobility, in other words, screens the image of the Wolf Man's parents in the active motions of sexual intercourse. From the wolves' intent staring at the dreamer, Freud infers the little boy staring at the scene, witnessing his parents' act of lovemaking after having awakened in the middle of a late afternoon siesta. From the wolves' whiteness, he reads signs of the original setting: his parents' bedclothes, the sheets on the bed. From the several wolves, Freud derives two parents: "as would be desirable," he asserts, "the dreamwork avoids showing a couple" (42). Finally, elements in the Wolf Man's retroactive description of the dream combined with his childhood memories lead Freud to suggest that what he had witnessed was his parents "having sex from behind," that is, *"coitus a tergo."* Elsewhere Freud characterizes the *coitus a tergo* position as *more ferarum* or in the manner of beasts, an association that also leads him to read the wolves in the dream as metonymic for the parents: the wolves are symbolic displacements of the parents in the primal scene (213). Down on all fours, here an explicitly sexual position ("the man upright, the woman bent down like an animal" [183]), the parents become animal.[17]

The "becoming animal" image of the parents down on all fours encapsulates what makes the Wolf Man's case such an effective story and such a classical account of the psychoanalytic method. This is not so much because of its prurient quality, or even because of its traumatic substance, but rather because the figuration of animal sex allows Freud to posit a binding relationship between animality and sexuality as one of psychoanalysis's most operative metaphors.[18] The parents on all fours forge an indelible, deep-seated, and, for the young boy, disturbing picture of the throes of lovemaking. Moreover, the parents' position of sexual satisfaction, as seen through the Wolf Man's eyes, crystallizes something akin to what Freud says of sexuality in general: that the experience of *jouissance* produces both a satisfaction and a disturbance, an intimacy and an alienation. Here, though, it is not the parents who are disturbed and alienated but the young observer, which is why, for

Freud, sexuality is a constitutively triadic and thereby oedipal relation: mommy–daddy–me. The now traumatized witness of this parental scene signals as much himself: he begins to scream. At the same time, though, and as Freud explains, "he was delighted to recognize that the experience was one of gratification" as opposed to violence. Importantly, then, Freud's emphasis is placed on what the boy sees and how he interprets what he sees. The primal scene, in other words, is figured as an image to be interpreted, initially by the boy and later by the analyst. The image itself acts as a semiotic substitute for the originary trauma, a trauma destined to reemerge in the realm of dreaming and in the analyst's office. The Wolf Man's therapy sessions and the subsequent case history culled from the sessions, in fact, are what produce the trauma as such.

Freud's use of the visual nature of dreams and memories as a therapeutic tactic displays with particular clarity what it takes for psychoanalysis to make sense of the human psyche. It turns out that at least one of the ways we learn about the modern subject, and the modern subject learns about him- or herself, is by way of the visual; we are transformed by what we see and come to new understandings of ourselves because of it. In the therapy sessions, this epistemovisual function works in two ways. For one, the Wolf Man's therapy serves to represent his innermost traumas in illustrative terms, giving them material, imagistic form. For another, the therapeutic discovery of the young boy's position as an unwilling eyewitness of his parents' sexual act moves Freud to interpret sexual acculturation itself as, at least in part, a visual crisis and, moreover, to rely on this iconicity of parental/animal sex as a universal framework of subject formation.[19]

The genre of the psychoanalytic case study establishes the individual as an object of knowledge by deploying tropological and formal strategies as modes of knowing. Indeed, Freud routes one of the most visual aspects of the Wolf Man's dream, the wolves in the tree, through a series of specific narratives (biological, evolutionary, and literary) and formal structures (iconic and linguistic). It therefore becomes necessary to interrogate and specify these narratives and structures. To do so means recognizing Freud's complicated system of techniques, conceptual figurations, and formal strategies as the hermeneutics by which he comes to establish a model of modern humanity. Because Freud's case history of the Wolf Man places such extraordinary emphasis on visualization, I would like to suggest that the therapeutic process, in general, operates within an ekphrastic tradition. Narrowly defined, the term *ekphrasis* names a minor literary genre that uses prose to describe works of visual art or other art objects. The best known in this regard is Homer's ekphrasis of Achilles's shield or Keats's "Ode on a Grecian Urn." But ekphrasis also indicates a more general application that includes what Murray Krieger describes as the principle of using language to bring an object, event, or action to the mind's eye; it is "language which makes us see."[20] Much along the lines of Krieger's understanding of ekphrasis, Freud and the Wolf Man shift from visual to linguistic horizons of meaning as a way to "see" the workings of the latter's psyche more clearly. In other words, the Wolf Man's enunciative manifestations of his latent psychic content act as verbal transcriptions of what could be described as visual perceptions in and of the mind.[21] The space of therapy, in turn, serves to translate the medium of dreaming into a coherent narrative, transforming the raw material of the dream into something readable.

According to Freud, to take one instance of this transformation, the Wolf Man's actual memory of his witnessing of the "primal scene" gets metaphorized by way of an existing story—a fairy tale—familiar to his patient as a young boy: "The Wolf and the Seven Goats." In this reading, the wolves are the goats in the fairy tale, all of whom are eaten by the wolf, except one who hides in a grandfather clock. The wolf is, according to Freud's oedipal schemata, the father, the escaped goat, perhaps the boy. Here Freud appropriates a familiar cultural narrative, a well-known fairy tale, as the means to make sense of (to translate) the unfamiliar terrain of the Wolf Man's dream. Subsequently, Freud requests that the dream be rendered in more material–visual form when he asks the Wolf Man to sketch out the wolves. In so doing, Freud suggests that the verbalized narrative of the dream be reconverted back to a visual representation, a kind of ekphrasis in reverse. The Wolf Man's drawing realizes graphically the repressed originary trauma of the primal scene of which the dream is itself the manifestation.

For W. J. T. Mitchell, ekphrasis "focuses the interarticulation of perceptual, semiotic, and social contradictions within verbal expression" in such a way that creates the art object, the visual representation, as Other, as an impossibility.[22] Ekphrastic poetry, in this light, can be seen as an attempt to demonstrate the superiority of the verbal arts to painting or sculpture, working to produce the art object as a site in need of translation, unable to express itself on its own terms. Krieger describes the pro-ekphrastic argument as "the semiotic desire for the natural sign, the desire, that is, to have the world captured in the word."[23] This desire for the word, however, also leads back to the visual in an attempt to get beyond the word to the object in question, what Krieger calls "our search for a tangible 'real' referent that would render the sign transparent"[24] and what Mitchell refers to as "the pictorial turn." For Mitchell, in supplanting the word as natural sign, the pictorial turn achieves a dynamic of interreliance between word and image: "The dialectic of discourse and vision, in short, is a fundamental figure of knowledge as such."[25] In the Freudian situation, the verbal expressions of the "talking cure" structure the dream vision into readable patterns, just as the drawing of the dream gives shape to language, formalizing these patterns of meaning into a spatial and framed array. From this perspective, the dialectic between discourse and vision (text and image) becomes a fundamental and mutually constitutive figure of knowledge that the ekphrastic scene of psychoanalysis stages and enables.

Although ekphrasis involves the translation of the visual into the verbal, it also involves the reconversion of the verbal back into the visual. Homer's ekphrasis of Achilles's shield, for example, translates the shield into a poetics of written representation and offers this representation to readers so that they can visualize the shield as acutely as possible. In "The Wolf Man," the act of translation gets literalized by Freud's request to his patient to produce a sketch of the dream material, but it is also a fundamental aspect of the therapeutic process in general. Dream interpretation, in this sense, stages an elaborate scene in which the visual content of the dream is the object of ekphrasis, the analysand, the ekphrastic speaker; and the analyst, the reader.[26] We can thus only understand the dream as an intersubjective translation. It is what Mitchell calls an "imagetext," a composite that combines image and text, and thereby exposes a gap or fissure in representation.[27] The dream as imagetext both displays and conceals its suturing of subject and object, self and other, and the seeable and the sayable as interanimating structures of knowledge. In terms of "The Wolf Man" case study more specifically, the self as speaking subject, the dream content/image of the wolves as object of the speaking self, and the analyst as interpretative agent of both subject and object become interdependent features; the "other" (the wolf, the father, the archaic) is a psychic generation of the self made readable by Freud's formalizations.

In a certain sense, each of these interpretative strategies (the talking cure, the fairy tale, the picture) reduces the multiplicity of the dream to more legible media, as psychoanalysis as an enterprise of decoding is wont to do; now the Wolf Man's psychic interiors can be both read and seen. As Deleuze and Guattari have it: "For Freud, when the thing splinters and loses its identity, the word is still there to restore that identity or invent a new one."[28] But the fact that Freud's psychoanalysis must proceed by way of these multiple forms is in itself significant. Out of Freud's unfolding layers of interpretation and narration emerges an assemblage of meanings that he uses to constitute the human subject as a psychoanalytic (and, because thus converted, therefore modern) subject. In particular, Freud locates the dream in an oedipal narrative whereby the young boy's jealousy of his father's sexual relationship with his mother plays itself out as a trauma. The oedipal narrative stabilizes a teleological understanding of the human psyche and its development, a process we may understand, via Latour, as one of "purification," an act of translation that invents a subject, an object, and a demarcation between the two. In other words, by way of Freud's formal strategies, the Wolf Man becomes "purified" of his interaction with wolves (read: sexual desire and the sodomitical parental scene for which the wolves are metonymic). When bounded by clear visual and narrative terms, the dream content, produced as object, protects the Wolf Man's personhood from the very things that comprise it. Deleuze and Guattari put it this way: "The wolf is the father, as we all knew from the start" because "Freud only knows the Oedipalized wolf or dog, the castrated-castrating daddy-wolf, the dog in the kennel, the analyst's bow-wow."[29] According to Deleuze and Guattari, the multiplicity of the wolves (there is not just one but five in the drawing, and six or seven in the dream) must be shut down; their existence testifies too strongly on behalf of generation without filiation, sex without procreation, reproduction by another means—the proliferation of hybrids. Running counter to Freud's attempts to stabilize the subject, the multiple potentialities of the Wolf Man's erotic investments across species lines strike at the foundations of the oedipal account of human reproduction as they reveal fantasies that cannot be reduced to biological reproduction.[30]

Animal Projections

If these are the many forms the dreamscape takes, what of their content? Specifically, what of all these wolves? Parents on all fours, wolves in trees, wolves in fairy tales, and, finally, the "Wolf Man" himself—given this moniker, of course, because of this multiplicity of wolves and his fear of them. What of the intensely affective power of the wolves and their amalgamation of meanings? Certainly, we can see that they operate in the case study as a sexual sign, but how and why? I think we can understand the semiotics of the wolves more precisely if we take into account that Freud's project was not simply one of individual treatment but one that wanted to propose a theory of human development. The case study itself is meant to stand in for a larger argument about human behavior, and Freud persistently turns to human prehistory as the ground and means of his theories, especially but not only in works like *Civilization and Its Discontents* and *Totem and Taboo*.[31] In these studies, Freud's interest concerns less what the individual may tell us about human prehistory than what human prehistory may tell us about our individual modern selves. In the case study, his definition of modern selfhood as composed of infantile sexuality, neurosis, the unconscious, repression, oedipal strivings, and libido is rooted in a particular prehistoric narrative for which the wolves act as both sign and referent. The acts of "purification" and "translation" that Freud performs, then, are not only on behalf of establishing the Wolf Man as a modern subject, but also on behalf of purifying our tenuous knowledge of human origin. The oedipal complex thus becomes a reassuring narrative of evolutionary progress, a sublimation of "primal," "bestial," and therefore sexual, incivilities. The wolf is a mark of atavism, the sign of the return, even more, of the constitutive reappearance of a prehuman past. The recuperable presence of the not-human in the form of the wolves in this instance is, therefore, a repetition of the subject's deep past, psychological and evolutionary both.

Although Freud insisted on the exemplary status of the single case study, the human–animal associations in "The Wolf Man" are not isolated instances, nor is this particular patient alone in his animalized suffering, as we can see from other case studies such as "The Rat Man," Little Hans and his horse phobia, or Frau Emmy Von N. (from Freud's work with Breuer in *Studies in Hysteria*), whom Freud diagnoses as suffering from "zoopsia, macropsia, and zoophobia."[32] In each of these cases, an understanding of the modern human subject is exercised through an atavistic relay. It is precisely Freud's effort to consolidate human existence into a manifest orderliness of developmental stages that allows for, and indeed requires, this relay. As a result, the accretion of animal meaning in his work disallows the parsing of the human from the animal, of modernity from its history.

As both Lucille Ritvo and Frank Sulloway have amply demonstrated, Freud was influenced by Darwin's theory of evolution; indeed, Freud mused that it "held out the hopes of an extraordinary advance in our understanding of the world."[33] Freud's oedipal structure follows Darwin in its assumption that an inherited characteristic has behind it the developmental and experiential history of the species. For Freud, this means that oedipality is the ontogenetic repetition of the phylogenetic experience of the race. As he claims in *The Interpretation of Dreams,* "Dreaming is on the whole an example of regression to the dreamer's earliest condition, a revival of his childhood. . . . [B]ehind this childhood of the individual we are promised a picture of a phylogenetic childhood—a picture of the human race."[34] By suggesting that infantile experience is prehistorical experience in the "Wolf Man" case study, Freud grants access to human (pre)history through the figure of the child, who can now also be read as a prehuman form—like his parents, an animal. Freud explains, "A child catches hold of this phylogenetic experience where his own experience fails him. He fills in the gaps in individual truth with prehistoric truth; he replaces occurrences in his own life with occurrences in the life of his ancestors" (386). In "The Wolf Man," by way of "prehistoric truth," sexuality comes into view as an animal category and an atavistic drive.

Similarly, "The Rat Man," another case of Freudian animalia, depicts a patient whose feelings toward his father were dominated by hostility and rage. The primary incident that triggered the Rat Man's "obsessional neurosis" occurred during his time in the army when a fellow officer, whom he called "the cruel captain," recounted to him a story of punishment practiced in the East in which a pot containing live rats was strapped to a man's buttocks (The Rat Man: "They . . . bore their way in." Freud: "'Into his anus,' I helped him out").[35] For Freud, the Rat Man's ensuing obsessions indicated both a homosexual attraction and revulsion that could be linked back to his patient's unsatisfied feelings toward his father. "There can be no question that there was something in the sphere of sexuality that stood between the father and son, and that the father had come into some sort of opposition to the son's prematurely developed erotic life. Several years after his father's death, the first time he experienced the pleasurable sensations of copulation, an idea sprang in his mind: 'This is glorious! One might murder one's father for this!'" (59).

The Rat Man's guilt, arising from these oedipally murderous feelings, led him to deflect his hostility onto himself in the form of suicidal thoughts. In an attempt to assuage the Rat Man of the sensation of guilt, Freud writes, "I pointed out to him that he ought logically to consider himself in no way responsible for any of these traits in his character; for all these reprehensible impulses originated from his infancy, and were only derivatives of his infantile character surviving in his unconscious" (185). The neurotic predicament of the Rat Man, in other words, is due to the endurance of infantile trauma, the persistence of the past in the present. What he wants from his father are things he can no longer remember in unrepressed form because they are desires that arise from earlier stages in his psychosexual development. In this instance, psychoanalysis aids the Rat Man's psyche by performing an interpretative recovery of the past.[36] For Freud, though, sexual instincts themselves may perform this recovery, or at least the desire for it. In *Beyond the Pleasure Principle,* he explains: "An instinct is an urge inherent in organic life to restore an earlier state of things."[37] If we can understand instinct as a fundamental precept of self here, then we can also see that the self is constituted and pushed forward by its own compulsive urge to restore the past. Put more boldly, if all instincts are atavistic, then the Freudian subject is itself an atavism.

With this reading, we can perhaps understand the retroactive interpretation of the Wolf Man's dream as a fantasy of origins: what Freud in "The Wolf Man" calls a necessary "detour to the prehistoric" designates the space of therapy as a practice and process of the recollection of human prehistory (290). The human–beast hybridization that takes shape as a result (this proliferation of wolf parents and wolf men) illuminates the ways in which the archaic, the evolutionary past, is deployed to orient the unfamiliar terrain of sexual modernity and the illegible category of human being. In Freud's interpretative scheme, sexuality itself is deployed as an archaic category or practice and therefore as a relay through which the modern subject can be at once established and deferred (that is, routed through the past). The wolves are expressions of how the residues of the past can be organized into knowledges about modern selfhood. In one sense, this means that modern sexual subjectivity becomes familiarized in the context of the prehistoric; but in another sense, it means that the Wolf Man case study figures the hermeneutic(s) by which sexual desire is stabilized and human prehistory apprehended.

"Screaming Like a Savage"

An account of the Wolf Man ought not fail to register the racial investments of the image of the wolf (or, for that matter, those of the Eastern provenance of rat torture in "The Rat Man"). To do so would be to ignore the ways in which contemporaneous understandings of race played an enormous role in shaping knowledge of human being at the fin de siècle. As scholars from Sander Gilman to Siobhan Sommerville have shown, twentieth-century conceptions of sexual desire surfaced out of a racializing context that formed the human body according to its logic.[38] Following such conceptions, Freud situates the Wolf Man's sexuality in relation to theories of racial difference, ones that also accompanied the premises and adaptations of evolutionary theory.[39]

From Ernst Haeckel's theory of biogenesis, of which Freud was a reader, we have received the "ontogeny recapitulates phylogeny" hypothesis that, as I have already discussed, influenced Freud's view of the human subject (a hypothesis that, of course, also influenced Darwin). In Haeckel's version, the individual, recapitulating stages of evolutionary development from its embryonic form on, follows the developmental path of the species on its way to individuation. American physician and psychologist G. Stanley Hall adapted Haeckel's theory for his own work on adolescence, claiming that young boys physically recapitulated the evolutionary process in their individual life span, and that "savagery" was a healthy part of a young boy's developmental process.[40] Freud's own allegiance to Haeckel's biogenetic law, and his knowledge of Hall's work on boyhood, informed his understanding of the developing psychological subject as constituted by progress through various stages.[41]

For Freud, the development of sexuality is neatly characterized as a linear progression moving through distinct pregenital organizations of the libido (oral, anal), culminating in the phallic. Fixation at any particular stage, a form of "arrested development," accounts for specific psychosexual patterns in adults. Although the oral stage and its corresponding erogenous zones of mouth, tongue, and lips relates to the evolutionary aim of self-preservation (nourishment through the mouth), the anal stage points to the sexual gratification that occurs by relieving the tension of the bowels and thus stimulating the anus. For Freud, these two pregenital stages correspond to and repeat the function of odor as the primary stimulant in the sex acts of early humans: "The anal–erotic disposition . . . is one of the archaic traits which distinguish that constitution [of obsessive neurosis]," a form of arrested development that occurs when an adult regresses to the anal stage. These pregenital dispositions in man, moreover, "should be regarded as vestiges of conditions which have been permanently retained in several classes of animals" (108). The *coitus a tergo* position that shapes the "primal scene" of the Wolf Man's neurosis, then, harkens back to this "earlier" or "archaic" form of sexual desire. Freud writes, "Indeed *more ferarum*— or copulation from behind—may be regarded as phylogenetically the older form" (185). This is what leads Freud to his diagnoses of the Rat Man and his heightened olfactory sense: he is stuck in the anal phase. Normative ontogenetic development, in Freud's theory, prescribes that taking pleasure in odor should become "extinct" in childhood, as he notes in "The Wolf Man": "The atrophy of the sense of smell . . . was an inevitable result of man's assumption of an erect posture" (247). In these examples, Freud constructs oral and anal desire as prehistorical, thus producing the distinction between anal and oral sexuality on the one hand and vaginal/penile sexuality on the other as an evolutionary one. As developmental phases, the oral and the anal are thus posited by Freud as anachronisms of the modern constitution of self.[42]

Freud's specific understanding of sexual development corresponds with contemporaneous currents in late nineteenth-century thought more generally. Nineteenth-century sciences such as ethnology and its attendant theory of polygenesis, craniology, and to a certain extent comparative anatomy as promulgated by Georges Cuvier understood racial difference as a function of arrested development during the phylogenetic process. In an attempt to legitimate claims that certain races were less evolved than others, these sciences often constructed a visual link between nonwhite populations and lower animal forms. A number of different instances in this history can be cited: Josiah Nott's argument in 1843 that mulattos are "degenerate, unnatural offspring doomed by nature to work out their own destruction," which he supports in his study *Types of Mankind* with images of primate skulls; Peter Camper's comparison of the facial features and cranial angles of a "coloured criminal youth" to a chimpanzee; Georges Cuvier's dissection of Sara Bartmann, the so-called Hottentot Venus, in which he compares

her external features to those of a monkey and an orangutan.[43] These
strategies grew out of the comparative method by which cultural conditions and practices observed among existing populations or social
groups were placed in a series that was taken to represent a process of
evolution. Étienne Balibar has described the techniques of the comparative method as "the systematic 'bestialization' of individuals and
racialized human groups." For Balibar, this means that "man's animality, animality within and against man . . . is thus the means specific to
theoretical racism for conceptualizing human historicity." By drawing
on "anthropological universals," what Balibar terms "theoretical racism"
interprets the conflicts within society and history as a synthesis of transformation and fixity, repetition and destiny. Humanity is thus an eternal leaving behind of animality and eternally threatened with falling
into "the grasp of the animal." "That is why, when [theoretical racism]
substitutes the signifier of culture for that of race, it has always to
attach this to a 'heritage,' an 'ancestry,' a 'rootedness,' all signifiers of
the imaginary face-to-face relation between man and his origins."[44] The
comparative method, in other words, in its most ameliorative form,
attempts to resolve the problem of human origin by distinguishing between temporal forms of humanity, forms either more or less marked
by the taint of animality.

We can see the bestialization that Balibar discusses in Freud's narrativization of the Wolf Man's ineluctable drift into neurosis as well as
in his own substitutions of animals for origins and savagery for sexuality. From the Wolf Man's narration of his childhood, Freud discerns
a shift in temperament from a good-natured boy to an "irritable" and
"violent" one who "screamed like a savage" (160). Freud reads these
screaming fits as attempts at seduction because they often provoked
beatings from his father, the Wolf Man's narcissistic love object via his
overidentification with him (172). Accordingly, the young boy experiences his father's beatings as a form of sexual attention; "screaming
like a savage" thus emerges as a language of desire. The young boy's
screams give voice to a form of expression unexplainable by a reproductive longing or function, or any other biological need. Instead, they
become the enabling condition for affective attachment, tendering
primitivism as the ground for human interaction and familial intimacy.

Even earlier in the therapeutic process, we are given evidence of
Freud's association of the young boy's sexual development with the
primitive. In one version of the *coitus a tergo* incident, after witnessing

his parents' lovemaking, the Wolf Man defecated in his bedclothes. In Freud's words, "The child interrupted his parents' intercourse by passing a stool, which gave him an excuse for screaming" (222–23). Freud describes this act as a direct response to the primal scene: "It is a sign of a state of excitement of the anal zone. In similar cases, a grown-up man . . . would feel an erection." By responding fecally, Freud explains, the Wolf Man "was making use of the content of the intestines in one of its earliest and most primitive meanings" (223). The "gift of feces," as Freud describes it, this "first sacrifice on behalf of his affection," acts as both infantile protest and sexual stimulant.

The boy's characterization as a screaming "savage" with "primitive" desires repeats Freud's comparison of the content of the unconscious to "a primitive population in the mental kingdom," thereby establishing the psyche as both a residue and an *Umwelt* or environment of the past.[45] As Akira Lippit aptly notes: "Unconscious ideas, like animals, remain alive through the processes of perpetual rejuvenation: the unconscious allows ideas to remain charged forever."[46] The unconscious mind is the space of the past; the past is a primitive beast; we are all just animals. What I am most concerned with in this chain of associations is the ways in which the figure of the animal, like unconscious ideas, obtains social specificity. By deploying the animal as a sign of atavism par excellence, Freud embeds his therapeutic subjects within a composite discourse of race and sexuality. Recourse to animality, in other words, enables a point of contact with embedded ideas of racial difference and sexual development, suggesting the simultaneity of the racial and sexual logic performed by the figure of the beast.[47]

Freud's postulations of various primitive forms and stages of sexual development through allusion to actually existing other peoples ("savages" and "primitives") is similar to what Cannon Schmitt describes as "savage mnemonics," "a form of and relation to memory that redefines what it is to be 'human' in relation to the past, and specifically in relation to those pasts—evolutionary, historical, cultural, personal—conceived of as 'savage.'"[48] We can read the zoomorphic energy animating the Wolf Man's psyche and his pathology, then, as just such a "savage mnemonic," as just such an invocation of racial memory. The return of (and to) the animal in Freud is the return of (and to) human prehistory, a prehistory understood in explicitly sexual and racial terms. Perhaps this, in itself, suggests another way to understand the figure

of the animal: as an aporia in the domain of the "purified" human subject and the discourse on "humanity" that supports it.

Nachträglichkeit; or, Bestial Returns

Summoning the anachronisms of self through the figure of the animal illustrates an implicit recognition of the contingency of human
being. Freud's use of the animal trope ameliorates the anxiety caused
by this recognition by translating animality into a literary register, an
ekphrasis of modern life that serves both to deny and to grant expression to human fears and desires that remain inarticulable. Ekphrasis
acts, in this sense, as Freud's own "screen memory." Yet the trope of
the wolf also performs the human–animal connection by deliteraliz-
ing it, producing it as sign and symbol. These hermeneutics instantiate
a new episteme of the modern human subject. "The Wolf Man" case
study introduces as constitutive what modernity must also disavow: atavism as an organizing tour de force of the modern subject. Atavism,
then, is not just an abjected form of modern life, a sign indicating
modernity's Other; rather, it is an operation that makes modernity,
and the subject of modernity, possible.

I have thus been asking that we understand Freud's case study as a
complicated literary enterprise, a project of reading and narration
that endows the modern human subject with an inexhaustible semiotics. But Freud constructs a chiasmic narrative; perhaps unwittingly, he
produces an inverted parallelism between the forms of his narrative
and their content—that is, between hermeneutics and meaning. The
narrative forms and relays Freud uses, such as the fairy tale, visual art,
verbal expression, and science, in one way work to exorcise the hybrid
from the human, to make the human psyche legible and distinct, something unquestionably modern. But in each specific formation, the
content works to undo this purification precisely because it relies
on atavism and animality, a proliferation of corporeal and temporal
hybrids, that upset Freud's otherwise linear developmental narrative.
Paradoxically, the content of Freud's narrative, as I have discussed it,
is also what attempts to "purify" the hybridity of the Wolf Man's vision
by placing his psyche within a developmental–evolutionary narrative,
while the form of this narrative functions as the proliferating agent of
modernity's productions. This can best be seen in the narrative's wayward progressions: Freud's endless deferrals throughout the therapeutic

process and in his relation of it to his readers, the Wolf Man's dream as a return to origins, the narrative's obligatory journey back to the Wolf Man's childhood, and, finally, the "detour" to human prehistory itself. Freud's formal "plot" structure, therefore, regresses as it progresses; or, rather, it progresses by way of its regressions.

Freud himself named that which ultimately directs his own narrative as the temporality of *nachträglichkeit* or "retrospective determination." *Nachträglichkeit* indicates the psychic process by which the meaning of a repressed trauma becomes established long after the initial events through forms of repetition and restaging. For Freud, mental trauma only gains significance through its continual deferral and therefore inevitable repetition. The cycles of *nachträglichkeit* that comprise the Wolf Man's psychic history also constitute Freud's interpretative strategies. The therapeutic scene, in other words, is a retrospective determination by which the dream content and everything it represents to Freud (such as human prehistory) gets repeated and revised. I therefore also want to suggest that *nachträglichkeit* may help name the process by which modernity constitutes itself as modern. The very interpretation of the wolves as signs of atavism is a method, and therefore enabling condition, by which modernity comes into being. In this light, atavism can be read as the materialization of the trauma of our inability to secure for ourselves the truth of ourselves: the anachronism of human identity, the destabilized relationship between the past causalities and present predicaments of the modern subject. In Freud's scheme, atavism is a necessary postulate (or intentional object) of psychoanalytic self-awareness. As such, atavism in the form of the animal in his case studies is an agent of meaning that defines the idea of self in late modernity.

Arrested Developments

To engage in such an exploration of a discourse of human science is to take a close look at changing notions of human identity and the constitution of late modern ways of reading it. Understanding more clearly the knowledge produced as a result of these reading practices may help us avoid approaching both modernity and the modern subject as preestablished positions or uniform entities; it may help us see them, rather, as a part of a dynamic map of power and knowledge in which human being is conceptualized, constituted, and translated, as well as racially and sexually inflected.[49] This kind of critical inquiry is a matter of grappling with the ways in which conceptions of human being are implicated in that which they exclude, and, following the lines of this implication, of gesturing toward future collectives that they might yield. For Latour, the modern human subject is rooted in an illusory ground of separateness that must be articulated in discrete opposition to other subjects (or objects). This formulation of modern subjectivity, accordingly, reproduces and reinforces the Enlightenment conception of the subject: the rational, stable self in distinct opposition to all things animal (and all things for which animals act as a supplement: the past, the archaic, the sexual, the racial). The modern human subject, as such, routinely reinstitutes difference in order to keep itself isolated—that is, modern. Such a routine neglects human contiguity with nonhuman collectives, with members of both natural and invented worlds.

Given the liberal political frame as I have described it, progressive political agendas organized around crucial attempts to obtain rights for those consistently treated as nonhuman are faced with a dilemma. How can we secure social equality without supporting the fetish of the human that produces these inequalities in the first place? A noted problem, for example, is the potential for progressive political agendas to be forced into a contrary or reactive position (insisting on one's or somebody else's humanity, for example), and thus perpetuating familiar ideological problems, rather than calling into question the system of the subjective, racialized, and sexualized enunciations and designations of the human and not-human binary. If it remains locked in this binary, the discourse on rights will fail to dismantle actually existing inequalities in the social world.[50] What is at stake here involves refusing to develop a politics that is organized around categorical norms where the aim is to be included within a privileged definitional frame, for this participates in the same taxonomizing imperative that constructs exclusionary concepts of human being to begin with.[51]

In the Wolf Man case study, atavism becomes the visible sign of modernity's loss (the loss of its own prehistory through the movement of time as posited by evolutionary biology, for example), but it is also the phylogenetic recapitulation of that prehistory, in which case there is something animal (that is to say, atavistic) about the modern subject. If the Wolf Man case study reveals anything, it is the hybridity of human and animal, past and present, which fractures the monolithic metanarrative of late modern culture that asserts that the two are always and inevitably different and unequal. Hence, one term (the human, the modern) is no longer always incommensurable with the other (the non-human, the archaic); the nonhuman is not always the abject result of the more civilized human. Just as the Wolf Man emerges as a subject out of the hermeneutic efforts of psychoanalysis, so does the atavistic subject of psychoanalysis emerge as the defining condition of modern subjectivity, producing as modern nothing less than our atavistic sense of self.

Throughout this chapter, I have asked that we understand the means by which this sense of self was shaped and given substance. In viewing psychoanalysis as operating within an ekphrastic tradition, as a method and procedure of translation between visual and linguistic horizons, I have treated it not only as a hermeneutic practice but also as a regulatory technology—in other words, as a method and procedure of the normative production of personhood. Conceiving of the modern subject as one forged historically, I have understood psychoanalysis as a component part of late modern social and political forces. Looking at psychoanalysis in this way, though, has also served as the means to think through what pressures arise and consequences result from these regulatory technologies. If psychoanalysis works toward the solidification of the human against the nonhuman (and therefore toward the separation of the present from the past in a correlated temporal hierarchy), it also insists on the proliferation of nature and culture and past and present as structurally interdependent categories and of modern subjects as entanglements of these categories.

As the next chapter demonstrates, other scientific, medical, and technological practices had the same object of modern personhood in view. The advent of medical photography, the increased usage of which coincides with the emergence of psychoanalysis, raises equally compelling issues about the effects of visual technologies on the understanding and shaping of modern personhood, which are effects that also delineate the features of modernity more generally. For Freud, the playing out of the traumatic event can be characterized by a time lapse that takes place between the original experience of the event and its subsequent effects on our psyche. We can only experience trauma as trauma, in other words, belatedly, through its return in some other form. In *Moses and Monotheism,* Freud suggests that this process of psychic belatedness becomes easier to comprehend "by comparing it with a photographic exposure which can be developed after any interval of time and transformed into a picture."[52] The photographic image, in Freud's formulation, is the unconscious mind; each is capable of recording and transporting events through time, events that can then be re-experienced at some, or any, future moment. This forges a significant, if obvious simile: modern subjectivity is like modern technology. Moreover, it is the belatedness of the photographic image, like the belatedness of early childhood trauma, that Freud marks as the chief organizing feature of both human experience and its representation. Framing the psyche within the language of the temporality of the photograph—indeed, producing the psyche as analogical to the photograph—Freud's comparison lays bare how that technology has seeped into the collective cultural consciousness as one of the most instructive means by which to explain and understand the workings of human being. It is precisely the emergence of the photograph as such a focal point of considerations of modern subjectivity to which I now turn.

2. Late Modern Morphologies
Scientific Empiricism and Photographic Representation

"Faith" is a fine invention
When Gentlemen can see—
But microscopes are prudent
In an Emergency
          —Emily Dickinson

IN 1870, attempting to prove that criminal behavior was hereditary, Italian anthropologist Cesare Lombroso performed an autopsy on a convicted criminal and purported to find that his skull possessed a number of atavistic features recalling an animal past. He described his discovery as "not merely an idea, but a flash of inspiration. At the sight of that skull, I seemed to see all of a sudden, lighted up as a vast plain under a flaming sky, the problem of the nature of the criminal—an atavistic being who reproduces in his person the ferocious instincts of primitive humanity and the inferior animals."[1] Lombroso's concern with atavistic criminals arose as one of a number of investigations at the fin de siècle, studies by well-known figures in medicine, psychology, sociobiology, criminal anthropology, and sexology who were convinced that certain social behaviors, practices, and other modern realities, including criminality, homosexuality, interracial relationships, and prostitution, were both causes and symptoms of an imminent and widespread cultural degeneration.[2]

When Lombroso describes his discovery as "a flash of inspiration," he rehearses a generic convention of scientific breakthrough, the "eureka!" moment that marks the emotive significance of a new understanding. He proclaims this understanding to be not merely "an idea" but an insight that "lights up as a vast plain," enabling him to "see" more clearly than before the traits of the criminal. Describing his insight in this way, he renders scientific inquiry a visual event whereby scientific clarity and visual clarity become one and the same thing. And by using the specific allusion of the flash, he places the body within the terms

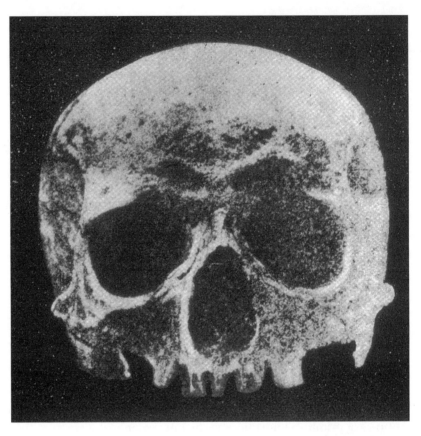

The skull of Charlotte Corday, from Cesare Lombroso, *The Female Offender* (1895).

of a new technology: the flash powder of a camera taking a photograph. Although his exclamation may also be read as a religious description, a moment of revelation signaled by the "flaming sky," the growing contemporaneous use of photography in both medical and criminological fields, as well as its mass appeal at least since Eastman's invention of handheld cameras like the Little Brownie in 1895, suggests there is something more at work here. Corresponding quite suggestively with the growing interest in visual technology, Lombroso expresses his discovery photographically. Lombroso was intimately familiar with the use of the medical photograph as a tool to investigate deviance and disease and he championed its use as such. His own immensely popular volumes on criminality, *The Criminal Man* (1911) and *The Female Offender* (1895), are filled with photographs of heads, skulls, and profiles of the subjects he studied. In fact, his texts, which offer medical, physical, and what he called "anatomico-physiognomic" descriptions of criminality and other forms of deviance, heavily depend on the visual archive he coordinates and displays within their pages.

In the previous chapter, we witnessed a similar epistemovisual constellation in the context of psychoanalysis, in which the "talking cure" afforded verbal expression of the visual aspects of images, dreams, and memories in the unconscious. There I argued that psychoanalysis operates within an ekphrastic tradition to the extent that the Wolf Man's therapy functioned to render in material form an otherwise inaccessible psychic activity. That is, by using language as a way to "see," the therapeutic situation created an illusion by which the subject's psyche appeared before the therapist in words. Psychoanalytic hermeneutics of this sort functioned as the means to grant access to the subject in language and beyond it, allowing contact with what at first might appear out of reach: the unconscious itself. The more purely visual technology of the photograph can be seen as another powerful device that many scientists believed granted access to the human subject. Lombroso's exclamation highlights the intimate relationship between the new sciences and the new visual technologies at the fin de siècle that, in turn, fostered an equally binding relationship between identity and visibility. If psychoanalysis makes interchangeable the self in language and the "real" self beyond language, medical photography makes interchangeable the representability of the visible body and the unrepresentable aspects of identity. In general for the human sciences, there was an increasing sense that attention to visual form confirmed their account of the human as both a social and biological being by virtue of the power of reference: if you can see it, it must be true. Human scientists posed the use of visual media as an epistemological advance precisely because they understood visual images to provide the scientist with an empirical, evidentiary starting point. This turn to ocular evidence inaugurated a particular and long-standing practice of understanding human identity as a visual entity such that it would soon no longer be possible to think of the category of the self outside the terms of visibility.[3]

Although it may now be a commonplace to state that we live in a culture saturated by images, Nancy Armstrong demonstrates that the relation between mass visuality and subjectivity is nothing new but dates back to at least the nineteenth century: "from cheap lithography . . . to further refinements of that process that came to be known as photography, people throughout Europe and the United Sates were confronted with an unprecedented number of images of the world and its peoples."[4] The late modern period and its attendant representational forms are therefore often characterized as coincident with the development of the camera and other emergent visual technologies. According to these characterizations, the new technologies of the cinema and photography in particular can be understood as products of, and reflections on, broader transitions characteristic of urban modernization that have shaped world culture particularly powerfully from the late nineteenth century to the present.[5]

For scientists, photographs in particular became key vehicles for gaining access to the workings of human being. Lombroso, for one, dedicated his life to the search for specific physiological anomalies that distinguished criminals from the rest of humankind. He argued that in order to unmask the atavistic criminal's "peculiarities," the observer needed to develop a scientific eye:

Many may find that after all these faces [in *The Female Offender*] are not horrible, and I agree, so far, that they appear infinitely less repulsive when compared with corresponding classes among the men whose portraits were reproduced by us from the "Atlas de L'Homme Criminel." Among some of the females there is even a ray of beauty . . . ; but when this beauty exists it is much more virile than feminine. To understand this at once, let the reader look at the lower profile in [two photographs], and then even the most inexperienced will see how hard, cruel, and masculine are these lines, which yet are not wanting in grace.[6]

Here Lombroso's theory of atavism requires vigilant observation to expose the female criminal's anomalies. "Less repulsive" than the male criminal, the female offender may even appear beautiful, skilled as she was in cloaking her underlying signs of atavism with makeup.[7] To see through her façade called for visual competence. The capacity to know the atavistic criminal, in other words, comes from the authority Lombroso attributes to the optical field, which makes his hard-to-read subjects recognizable.

This chapter introduces some of the methods, techniques, and images of the visual culture of human science on which hinges the status of the photograph as a social technology.[8] Responding to the dissolution of old certainties regarding human origin and the sovereignty of the self, modern science turned to technology as a stable site of truth and meaning. By way of this new investment, modern personhood

"The Physiognomy of French, German, and Russian Female Offenders," from Cesare Lombroso, *The Female Offender.*

became not only newly visible but newly knowable. Part of this chapter, therefore, will address how the photograph was used by science and medicine to give visual shape to their theories of human being. I will also suggest, however, that this collaboration reveals a fundamental paradox. Precisely because of the medical use of photography in the attempt to root identity in the body and the body in biology, the body emerges as a thoroughly technologized and thus unnatural entity. In what follows, I trace this paradox by attending to the medical photographs themselves, the texts in which they appear, and the "authors"—both cultural and scientific—of their meanings. Such an approach does not presuppose the body as a preconstituted category, a blank slate ready for social inscription, but instead aims to examine the ways in which the body itself is an effect of inscription that is discursively produced and maintained, whose demarcations are naturalized in order to produce a culturally coherent entity.[9]

Part of the genealogy of the body as a site of aberrant signification has been articulated by arguments positioned within the field of science studies. Sander Gilman and Nancy Stepan in particular have explored the fin de siècle obsession with theories of atavism and degeneracy. In their studies, atavism tends to be discussed under a rubric of anomaly and pathology. Accordingly, atavism is characterized as a coerced effect of a social structure working to consolidate itself. In a related set of concerns, modernity studies has focused on the ways in which visual technology emerged at the fin de siècle to constitute specific ideas and affective modes of personhood. Much of this work follows Walter Benjamin's argument about how the penetration of technology into art reshaped the aesthetic experience that can be said to be characteristic of modernity. Benjamin goes so far as to claim that modern visual culture led to a fundamental reorganization of human perception. On this argument, the newly emergent image culture of the late modern period is thought to have transformed our sense of self to the extent that visual technology allowed us to experience and understand the world, and our relationship to it, in new ways.[10] But there is still much thinking to do about the relationship between science and the body on the one hand and technology and perception on the other as new structures of modern social life. In the case of medical photography under exploration here, we see these issues converge, and we learn from this convergence that it is not photographic visibility and its forging of a new mode of perception per se that constitutes modern subjectivity;

nor is atavism merely a symptomatic discourse or effect of the fears and concerns of the modern world. Rather, the medical use of the photograph fashioned atavism as a category of visibility precisely by elevating the photograph as a form of seeing. It was this fashioning that bodied forth the modern subject as an atavistic subject. Although it is certainly true that atavism emerged within a locus of pathology, as Stepan and Gilman demonstrate, it did so only to the degree that, as pathology, it became a medium of expression for modern life normatively conceived. The collaborative exchange between scientific empiricism and photographic representation offered up a new epistemology of human being at this historical moment that can itself be said to be characteristic of modern subjectivity. Like Jacques Lacan's child peering at her image in the mirror and recognizing herself for the first time as a subject in the world, modern subjects, too, came to recognize themselves as subjects of, in, and through modes of visibility. Whereas Lacan's child saw in the mirror an image of herself, however much that identification was the product of misrecognition, the mirror of the atavistic photograph reflected back to its viewers the image of, in Lombroso's words, "the ferocious instincts of primitive humanity."

Degenerate America

Theories of atavism like Lombroso's were most forcefully articulated in the field of degeneration theory, whose power resided, in part, in its capacity to combine varying accounts of racial, sexual, and gender difference. French physician B. A. Morel brought the concept of degeneration to the medical profession by coining the term in 1857 in his *Traité des dégénérescenses physiques, intellectuelles et morales de l'espèce humaine (Treatise on the Physical, Intellectual, and Moral Degeneration of the Human Species)*. Morel described degeneration as "a morbid deviation from an original type" and posited just as morbid a theory of causalities and effects in human reproduction, a hereditary line that begins with a set of "defective" parents and ends in extinction.[11] According to this genealogy, the first generation, infected by any number of modern pollutants such as alcohol or sexual vice, passes its infection along to a second generation, which may be prone to epilepsy, neurasthenia, hysteria, and sexual perversion. The second generation, in turn, leaves a third generation convulsed with insanity and a fourth and fifth generation condemned to congenital idiocy and, ultimately, sterility. By the last decade of the nineteenth century, Morel's model gave way to one that awarded degeneration an even larger social etiology, with the capacity to spread like an epidemic throughout the unsuspecting population. In this model, an individual who may have inherited a particular degeneracy was considered highly contagious and thus could infect others who did not themselves have the genetic propensity for degeneration. If the individual body displayed signs of distortion or decay, therefore, the whole human enterprise could be in jeopardy.[12] As physician Max Nordau asserted, "We stand now in the midst of a severe epidemic; a sort of Black Death of degeneration and hysteria."[13]

By the 1890s, a vast number of figures in the sciences took up the study of degeneration, hoping to explain unsettling social changes and to provide insight into the question of human character. It was at this time that Lombroso's work was first introduced in the United States by Havelock Ellis, who translated Lombroso's findings for an English-speaking audience in his study *The Criminal*. In 1898, Nordau dedicated his own study of degeneracy to Lombroso. This study, a six-hundred-page rant against the "fin de siècle state of mind," extends Lombroso's physiognomic scrutiny to include not only "criminals, prostitutes, anarchists, and pronounced lunatics" but "authors and artists" as well (Walt Whitman and his "flowery prose" being one of the worst among them).[14] Although both Lombroso and Nordau met with criticism, their doctrines were influential and well known, each helping to characterize a general ethos of cultural deterioration at the fin de siècle—or "fin-de-race," as Nordau called it.[15]

Even while the discourse on atavism grew in popularity, scientists, physicians, psychologists, and criminologists disagreed about the exact nature of its workings. The theory to which Lombroso subscribed assumed degeneracy was a literal recurrence of primitive ancestral traits. Another, favored by Eugene Talbot, assumed that degeneration was a falling away from a more perfect evolutionary form—in other words, not the inheritance of an archaic characteristic but a devolution from an evolved state to an atavistic state. Many scientists also allowed for environmental factors as possible contributors to the decay of human character, relying on the Lamarckian theory of acquired characteristics, which held that a trait, habit, or physical illness acquired by social, cultural, or environmental means could be passed down to one's children. Psychologist G. Stanley Hall subscribed to yet another theory of degeneration informed by Ernst Haeckel: that of recapitulation and arrested development.[16] Atavism, in Hall's view, occurred as a result of the failure of an individual to complete his or her cycle of evolution. During the growth process, he claimed, certain physiological functions of the body would cease developing and thus disallow the individual to mature fully.

Regardless of these differences in supposition and argument, each account of atavism carried with it two primary conclusions. The first was that atavism was above all a quality of the body. As Thomas Speed Mosby, an American lawyer and criminologist, sums up, explicitly following Lombroso's lead, atavistic sites and indicators included

shorter statures, smaller heads, broader faces . . . deformed palates, disproportionate length of arms, prehensile toes, left-handedness, atavistic dental anomalies, prognathic jaw, facial asymmetry, cranial stigmata, small cranial capacity, retreating chin, pallor of skin, small and restless deep-set eyes, paucity of beard in the men, and masculinity in the woman, dark hair, deformity of hands—large and short in murderers and long and narrow in thieves, and various sexual anomalies.[17]

The second conclusion, a direct consequence of the first, was that atavism indicated a discrete temporal location. According to Mosby, for instance, the atavistic body constituted "the type of being, in general, of that of lower races or of the infantile period of our own race."[18] As Mosby's analysis makes clear, atavism operates as a structure of time in which "lower races" predate later ones. As such a racializing temporal implementation, one of the tasks of atavism was to designate which people had the capacity for modernity and which did not. It is not surprising, therefore, that the bodies that would become representative of the "primitive type" were not chosen arbitrarily, but with an eye toward producing entire populations as temporally backward.[19]

In particular, "questionable" racial bloodlines and sexual vice, widely conceived, became synonymous with atavism and were upheld as primary threats to Western civilization.[20] Dr. Prince Morrow, New York physician, founder of the Society of Sanitary and Moral Prophylaxis, and author of *Social Diseases and Marriage,* was a leading figure of the social hygiene movement that emerged to stem the spread of sexual disease and modern decay, and many followed his lead. Charlotte Perkins Gilman, for instance, was an avid reader of Morrow and urged young girls to read his books, for "the time to know of danger is before it is too late to avoid it."[21] Similarly, in an extended study entitled *Race Decadence: An Examination of the Causes of Racial Degeneracy in the United*

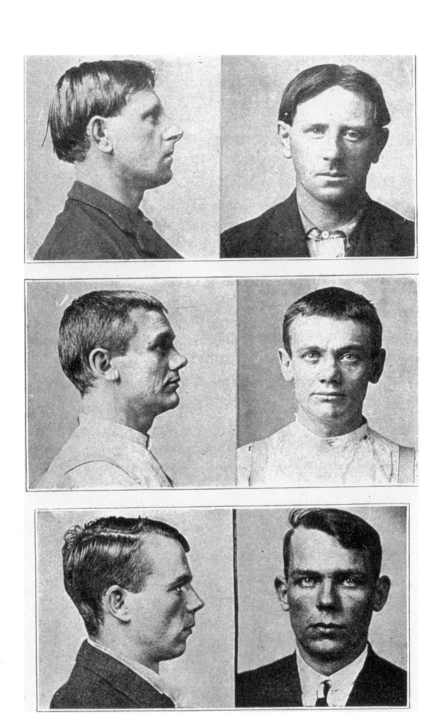

A group of "Sexual Degenerates" from Thomas Speed Mosby, *Causes and Cures of Crime* (1913).

States, physician William Sadler advised his readers that "the time has come when the American citizen should wake up and take a real interest in postponing his own funeral." In this "examination," Sadler claimed that "the negro is more subject to numerous diseases," and he called those who held and acted on desires for the same sex "a class of defectives who may be said to belong to and constitute the 'third sex,' in that they are so thoroughly abnormal that they can scarcely be classed sexually as either typical males or females" and who are "of a class belonging to the feeble-minded group as a whole, and who have directly inherited their brutal and perverted sex tendencies."[22]

In studies such as "The Relations of the Advanced and the Backward Races of Mankind" by James Bryce (1902), race was the sole focus. Bryce argued that when races "of marked physical dissimilarity" intermarry, "the average offspring is apt to be physically inferior."[23] William Benjamin Smith's 1905 pamphlet "The Color Line: A Brief in Behalf of the Unborn" warned that "race decadence . . . would follow surely in the wake of any considerable contamination by the blood of Africa."[24] Among the most pernicious of these accounts was biologist Lothrop Stoddard's book *The Rising Tide of Color against White World-Supremacy* (1920), where he promoted the importance of "race-consciousness" before American Nordics were overtaken by the increase of "less-evolved" immigrant racial populations.[25] He asserted that "not all branches of the human species attained the threshold of civilization. Some, indeed, never reached even the limits of savagery. Existing survivals of the low type savage man, such as the Bushmen of South Africa and the Australian 'Blackfellows,' have vegetated for countless ages in primeval squalor and seem incapable to rising to the level of barbarism, much less to that of civilization."[26]

Nancy Stepan's work has been crucial to the development of an understanding of these racial discourses, illustrating how, by the end of the nineteenth century, "racial biology provided a model for the analysis of distances that were 'natural' between human groups." According to this model, any crossing of the lines, not only by way of sexual relations but also by the literal crossing of geographical boundaries, would lead to degeneration.[27] Thus one organization of atavism in the racial science of the time was spatial, relying on tropes of distance and "proper place." But another, less often discussed mode of organizing atavism was by means of temporal tropes. Operating as a time claim that locates certain human beings as more or less advanced on the evolutionary scale, atavism scripts the criminal, racial, and sexual body as an aberrant throwback within the context of cultural and physical progress. Lombroso argued, for example, that "the atavism of the criminal . . . may go back far beyond the savage, even to the brutes themselves."[28] Atavism could thus be equated with "the reappearance of intermediate and indistinct fossil forms," what Lombroso would later call "atavistic morphological retrogressions."[29] In short, the atavistic body was an artifact, a "fossil," that incarnated in the present the temporal signs of a past ancestry. As a mixed temporal entity, the atavistic body was simultaneously read as a danger to the processes of modernization and as a signifier of modern decay.

The question that arises, then, is how the atavistic body can be both a site of repetition (that which signifies an archaic recurrence) and a site of newness (that which signifies the modern). As is clear from the temporal metaphors deployed by scientists like Mosby, Lombroso, and Stoddard—backwardness, decay, survival—the occurrence of atavism, a lingering vestige of primitive peoples and animals, draws a relationship between time and the body such that the modern body becomes distinguished and distinguishable from the primitive body. At the same time, atavism emerges as a mechanism for the constitution of modernity insofar as it illuminates modern subjectivity as ontologically dependent on atavism's significations. This produces modern subjectivity as less certain, less determinedly structured by the idea of continual progress, and, therefore, less distinct from the allegedly unenlightened, uncivilized, stateless time of human prehistory that the atavistic body also references.

John Frow's discussion of the relation between time and modernity is useful here. Frow describes how the disciplines of historiography and anthropology (he cites Eric Hobsbawm in particular) characterize the persistence of "tradition" in modernity as that of a performance of the past. In this argument, nostalgia for the past performs itself in various ways, such as tourism, the reenactment of cultural rituals, and the erection of monuments, in order to produce continuity with lost forms or events in history. In Hobsbawm's work, these performances are conceived as acts of recontextualization and, even more, of invention—what Frow describes as "stylized simulation(s)."[30] This is not the case with atavism, however, which neither recontextualizes the past nor performs a stylized invention of the past in the way that a repeated ritualized activity or monument might. Rather, as a living embodiment, atavism incarnates the past in the present: it is a material, corporeal recurrence of the past. Atavism, therefore, serves a different sort of binding function in the epistemological story of the human relation to time than those Frow and Hobsbawm delineate. The appearance of "morphological retrogressions" on the human body, according to the sciences that claimed to discover them, not only indicated the living existence of the human past but threatened to disturb the progress of the human future. Indeed, the atavistic body does not confer on the present a reassuring sense of a collective relation to tradition but disruptively impinges on the celebrated understanding of modernity as a wholly modern, progressing and progressive, period of time. The scientific claims supporting the notion of an atavistic body thus draw attention to the cultural and political doubts evinced by that body and the possibility of recurrence that it ostensibly evidences. What kind of difference does this difference make? How does the logic of atavism change how we characterize modern forms of subjectivity? How did the photograph, so often used by human science to stand as evidence for atavism, negotiate or mediate between these modern fantasies of progression on the one hand and regression on the other? Finally, what new forms of personhood did this mediation bring into being?

Visual Subjects

In an account of the role of the medical film in American culture, Lisa Cartwright evocatively argues that the motion picture was regarded as an apparatus uniquely suited to the study of physiology, the science of the living body. Cartwright's project describes how the optical dissection and penetration of the body in medical films coincides with the ascendancy of the term *life* as a core object of epistemological conquest in science.[31] By contrast, the static medium of the photograph was used by nineteenth- and early twentieth-century science as an instrument not only to document the human body, but also to reproduce it in a suspended state, more easily allowing for slow, methodical observation. We might understand the scientific and juridical investment in the photograph as opposed to the motion picture, then, as stemming from the camera's ability to freeze its subjects in time. Unlike the motion picture, the photograph promises to provide an image of reality that is not concerned with how the body lives (which, as Cartwright argues, requires representing the body in motion), but with the otherwise fleeting visual information an examinable body may provide. By freezing bodies in time as well as in space, photography, as Benjamin famously put it, "made it possible for the first time to preserve permanent and unmistakable traces of a human being."[32]

What made the practices of medical scopophilia so appealing was the enormous popularity already accruing to photography in every aspect of social life. Whether it was the obsessive aerial views of the city, the "Kodak craze" of amateur photography, or the social photography of Jacob Riis and Lewis Hines, photographic documentation was becoming a new, historically distinct way of seeing.[33] For instance, aerial views of urban terrain such as Eadweard Muybridge's 1878 "Panorama of San Francisco" fit in with a project to represent the city, both literally and ideologically, and thereby to remake it into a more controllable, more intelligible environment.[34] At the same time, "mole's-eye" views of urban slums and tenement halls were becoming increasingly fashionable, especially among the middle classes. These views of the city came in the form of tours of poor districts, pictorially illustrated texts of urban neighborhoods such as *Darkness and Daylight,* and photographic collections like T. H. McAllister Optical Company of New York's glass slides entitled "The Dark Side of New York," which offered "nearly 200 views illustrating the wretched conditions under which the lower 'other half' of our dense population live and die."[35] These various projects designated the spaces of urban poverty as both perilous and unknown, and in so doing encouraged a fascination with the urban underclasses. In a different way, the Riis and Hines photographs cataloged images of social injustice in their controversial attempts to document the growing urban immigrant populations of New York City. Whether it was mapping the city or representing the immigrant, the photograph played a major role in providing images of a world in a state of change. Perhaps this fostered in the minds of its spectators an assuring fantasy of control or, as Bill Brown argues, "a disturbing new sense of the condition of being visible."[36]

Although each of these photographic practices is unique and specific to its own context of production, use, and display, I review them to demonstrate that scientific visual culture emerged as a practice of studying the human body within a series of other visual practices and styles. Within this larger context of visual representation, scientific inquiry helped contribute to a paradigm of seeing in which visual

technologies functioned to organize a set of relations between identity and the body, and between the body and the population. That is,
the accumulation of images of individuals in specific environments or
under particular modes of scrutiny all corresponded to an emergent
historical paradigm in which the individual image was treated as index-
ical to the population at large. The central underlying feature of this
paradigm, as Alan Sekula explains, was how photographic technology
facilitated "a new juridical realism," a way to manage and to police
bodies more successfully.[37] This new scientific visual order sought to
produce a literacy of the body, a fixed grammar of the corporeal, which
privileges vision as knowledge.

As early as 1839, shortly after Louis Daguerre's invention of the
photographic process that bears his name, other technologies ensued
in the attempt to refine and enhance the medical and scientific ability
to examine the human body and its diseases more precisely. In addition to photography, technologies such as the zoopraxiscope, the pho-
tomicrograph (originally called a "microscope-daguerreotype"), and
the x-ray helped to facilitate what Foucault has termed "the clinical
gaze," a mode of perception that made visible hidden aspects of the
human body and "authorize[d] the transformation of symptom into
sign and the passage from patient to disease."[38] This transition was further augmented by set of transformations within the medical profession, of which the regularization of medical education, the new stress
on laboratory work, and the growth of the hospital system in the United
States are a few examples.[39]

In addition to the emergence of new technologies and medical institutions, a variety of scientific studies inspired by photographic technology emerged during this period. In 1872, for instance, Darwin used
the photographs of physiologist Duchenne de Boulogne in his work *The
Expression of the Emotions in Man and Animals* to explore his theory concerning the biological basis of emotional expression. H. W. Diamond,
a specialist in mental illness and president of the Royal Photographic
Society, stressed the diagnostic uses of photography in his work and
produced one of the first systematic photographic studies of mental illness at the Surrey County Lunatic Asylum in 1851. In 1867, the Paris
Medico-Physiological Society met to discuss how to apply photography
to the study of mental illness.[40] In Paris, at the instigation of Jean-Martin
Charcot, La Salpêtrière became a temple of photographic science when,
between the years 1876 and 1880, first Paul Regnard and then Albert

Photograph by Duchenne de Boulogne demonstrating the biological basis of human facial expression through the application of electric shock, appearing in Charles Darwin, *The Expression of the Emotions in Man and Animals* (1872).

Londe produced a series of images of "hysterical" women.[41] During this same period, Alphonse Bertillon emerged as a major figure in criminal science by inventing the first applied system of criminal identification. The "Bertillonage method," which was worked out over a period of time during the 1870s by the Parisian police, for whom Bertillon worked as a clerk, coupled mug shots with a series of detailed body measurements. According to Bertillon's book *Identification anthropometrique: Instructions signaletiques* (1893), specific aspects of the body needed to be carefully noted by the police, including ear size and brow width, as well as any distinguishing marks. All of this information was to be carefully calculated and entered onto an index card, and then filed along with a photograph of the criminal in question.[42]

Francis Galton's work is also characteristic of his era's fascination with recording and systematizing the human body. In 1883, he coined the term *eugenics* and advocated strongly for body measurements as the primary criterion for the scientific study of racial and criminal types. Intent on identifying the hereditary characteristics of social identity, Galton set out to discover "the biology of crime."[43] He wrote, "It seems clear that a scientific anthropology which is to cover the whole ground must deal with the idle, the vagrant, the pauper, the prostitute, the drunkard, the imbecile, the epileptic, the insane as well as the criminal."[44] The eugenics movement as championed by Galton sought to confirm social prejudices that people of color, women, and the poor occupy their subordinate positions by the dictates of nature. As David Green observes, "To eugenics the paupers, the unemployed, the criminal, the insane, and the inveterately ill were considered not as social categories but entirely as natural ones."[45] To aid his search for a science of human difference, Galton invented a method of composite photography by which successions of images were transferred onto a single plate. The result was a single photograph, blurred around its edges, that merged the images of at times thirty or more faces.[46] Through this method, Galton attempted to prove the physical similarity of different races, classes, and criminal types. The primary function of the composite photograph was to create facial maps of degeneracy and disease, and to visually stratify different populations into recognizable social and racial types.[47] Galton observed: "The individual faces are villainous enough, but they are villainous in different ways, and when they are combined, the individual peculiarities disappear, and the common humanity of a low type is all that is left."[48]

Francis Galton's composite portraits of "The Jewish Type," from *The Photographic News* (1885). Courtesy of the Galton Papers, University College London, Special Collections.

Both Bertillon's filing cabinet method and Galton's desire to "disappear" the specificity of the individual in favor of a "common" "low type" insist on what was to become a familiar and accepted claim: technologies for viewing and accounting for the body allowed for the possibility of both personal and typological identification. As Roland Barthes describes it, "The photomat always turns you into a criminal type, wanted by the police."[49] The asserted ability of these varying forms of representation to capture scientific "truth," moreover, ostensibly attenuated the mutability of human character by producing a fixed and direct relationship between the representation and the thing represented. As such, these new forms of visual inspection and assessment signal the onset of a new scientific as well as juridical reality in which mediation did not hinder but crucially aided an account of the real.

This new account of reality has its foundation in the codification of social statistics in the 1860s, for its underpinning ideology proceeds from the central concept of norms and standards first systematized within statistical practice.[50] Belgium astronomer and statistician Adolphe Quetelet, author of *Social Physics* (1869), was one of the first to popularize the idea that there were fundamental laws for social trends, and Bertillon and Galton followed suit (Bertillon studied under Quetelet and Galton was himself a statistician). As Ian Hacking describes it, "There [was] a particular obsession with 'analyse morale'—a statistics of deviance which produced and multiplied the categories of deviance through processes of classification (creating new ways for people to be)."[51] And as Susan Buck-Morss notes, "the statistical body" was one of the inventions of personal alienation in the nineteenth century: a body whose "behavior . . . can be calculated; a performing body, actions of which can be measured up against the 'norm.'"[52] The phenomenon that scientists like Galton and Bertillon enacted is one in which bodies and beings are transformed according to the dictates of scientific taxonomy. Corresponding with Foucault's description of "governmentality," regulatory institutions of science, medicine, and the law emerged to elaborate a new way of conceiving of the social world as a sphere of biological management. In this sphere, there were new bodies to be known and new sciences to know them.[53]

Theories of atavism played a primary role in the new rationalities of government because the atavistic body lent itself quite readily to the visible sphere. The atavistic body *was* a visible body; or, more precisely, medical photography produced it as such. The most common of physical stigmata, including irregular cranium, facial asymmetry,

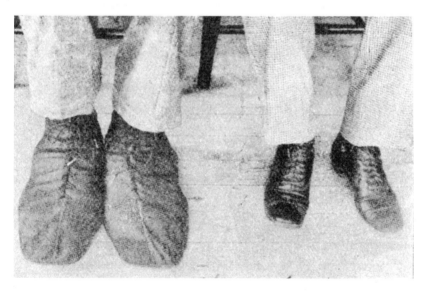

"Feet Degeneracies," from Eugene Talbot, *Degeneracy: Its Causes, Signs, and Results* (1898).

prognathism, receding brow, apelike physical features, were not only visually transparent, but also bespoke a savage and animalistic nature in need of state regulation. The visual display of the atavistic body demonstrated the visibility of atavism. A case in point is Eugene Talbot's 1898 study *Degeneracy*, which relies on medical images of various physical anomalies in an attempt to provide objective documentation of the visible character of human deviance. Talbot, referring to an image of atavistic feet, explains that "flat-footedness and other feet degeneracies have been found frequently among paranoiacs, moral imbeciles, and prostitutes." Here the physical attribute, what Talbot calls "the prehensile power of the foot," is both a symptom of degeneracy and a constitutive feature of the atavistic subject: the list of types, from "paranoiacs" to "prostitutes," comes into being at the moment their body parts can be named and classified.[54] The same can be said about Talbot's description of degenerate teeth, whereby "rapid decay of the teeth often leads to the discovery . . . of constitutional degeneracy."[55] In this example, teeth are external signs that help constitute Talbot's diagnosis of an internal disorder. In his use of both images, Talbot identifies the body as atavistic by creating an archive of atavistic features, a laundry list of anomalous corporeal signs. By using photographic images to display evidence of these signs, Talbot makes possible a constitutive look, an unlimited set of physical styles and exteriors of disease, for the atavistic subject to inhabit. Thus, the human sciences expanded not only the categories of deviance ("creating new ways for people to be," as Hacking has it), but also the categories of the visible body, creating new ways for people to *look*.

The sheer proliferation of images of the atavistic body testifies to the exorbitant and differentiated variations of this look. One need merely to glimpse any of the numerous popular medical texts from the period to note the excessive nature of medical culture's images. To qualify as atavistic, one's head or skull could be aberrant in hundreds of different ways; one's nose could be irregularly shaped with an equal amount of variation; one's arms could be of different proportions; one's eyes either too close together or too far apart; one's body could show signs of animality and decay anywhere and everywhere. This list could go on, and in medical texts it did. The medical photographs that so often accompanied these taxonomies were also highly differentiated. In fact, many of the images of varying atavisms existed indiscriminately among one another. For instance, in Mosby's book *Causes*

NORMAL AND DEGENERATE PALATES.

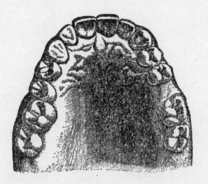

Fig. 1.—Normal upper jaw.

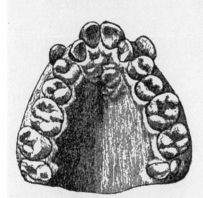

Fig. 2.—Abnormal upper jaw. "V" shaped.

Fig. 3.—Abnormal upper jaw. Saddle shaped.

"Normal and Degenerate Palates," from Thomas Speed Mosby, *Causes and Cures of Crime.*

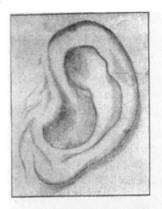

FIG. 40.

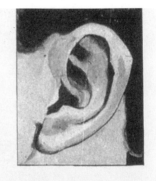

FIG. 41.

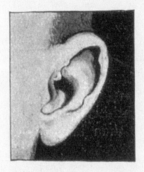

FIG. 42.

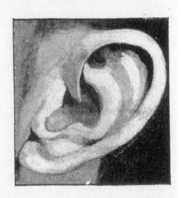

FIG. 43. EAR ALMOST HORIZON-
TAL AND AT RIGHT ANGLES
WITH THE HEAD.

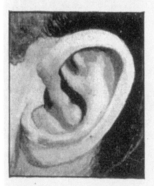

FIG. 44. EAR ALMOST
ROUND WITH THREE
DARWINIAN TUBERCLES
AT INNER BORDER.

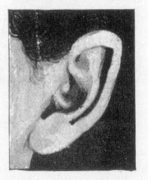

FIG. 45.

"Abnormal and Undeveloped Ears," from Eugene Talbot, *Degeneracy: Its Causes, Signs, and Results.*

and Cures of Crime, there are photographs of "sexual degenerates" and "sexual perverts" alongside "degenerate murderers" and "pickpockets and thieves." In his analysis, Mosby does not distinguish among these images; instead, he views them all with an eye toward their animalism, what he refers to as the different "conditions which induce reversion to savagery."[56] Mosby's analysis confirms what we have seen to be the case with the visualization of atavistic theory generally: an entire species of being emerged within the photographic frame that was made to act as an index for the existence of primitivism in the otherwise modern world. In his photographic portrayal of "epileptics" in *The Criminal Man,* for example, Lombroso draws connections between epilepsy and criminality by comparing facial profiles, placing both low on the scale of humanity. He concludes, "The criminal is a diseased person, an epileptic, in whom the cerebral malady . . . produces together with certain signs of physical degeneration in the skull, face, teeth, and brain, a return to the early brutal egotism natural to primitive races, which manifests itself in homicide, theft, and other crimes."[57] Lombroso's photographic plates attempt to produce the criminal as a legible entity and as a temporal category, where the image itself functions as a measure of racial advance or decline.

As with Lombroso's positing of "atavistic morphological retrogressions," Mosby's detailing of the "conditions which induce reversion to savagery," or Talbot's description of "prehensile feet," these photographs themselves became the measure of modern civilization, for they enabled a view into human prehistory as the means to shore up, by contrast, what could then be considered to be more purely modern. But like the condition of atavism itself, photographic representations of atavism simultaneously enabled the persistence of the past in the present, and therefore permitted an intermingling of ostensibly disparate temporal frames. We might even say that photographs are atavistic, composite spaces of perpetual return, sites of recurrence whereby the present is always also, instantly, an indication of the past.

By suggesting the atavism of the photograph so deliberately in my formulation here, I mean to put pressure on the ways in which the photograph operates as a temporal expression. To look at a photograph is always to look at a moment from the past. That is, in fact, the primary reason we take photographs: to remember a particular event or special occasion, to record a moment in time that will then serve to provoke enjoyment and sentiment in another.[58] But the *mechanical* operation of

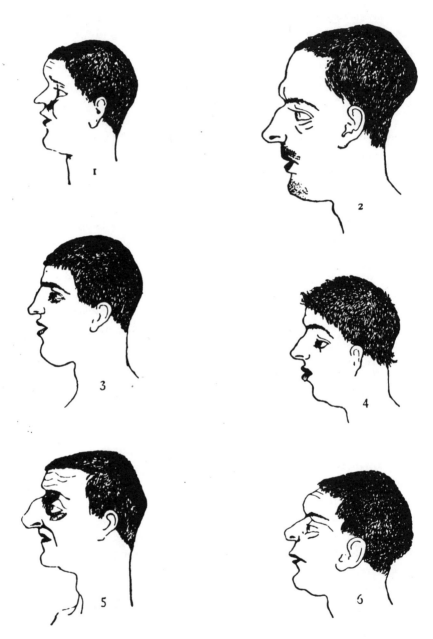

Criminal noses, from Havelock Ellis, *The Criminal* (1890). Reprinted by permission from Patterson Smith Publishing.

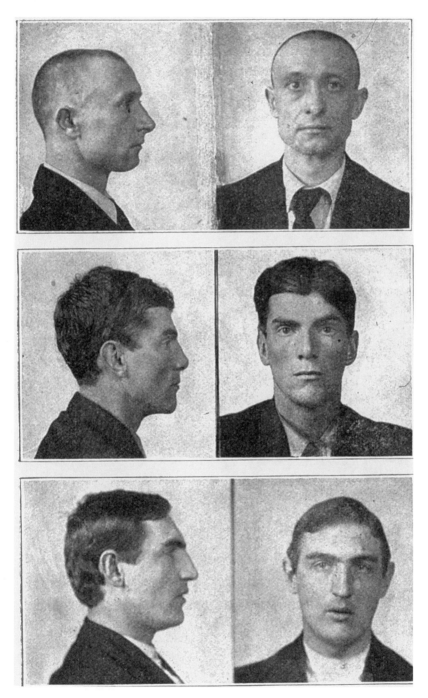

"Degenerate Murderers," from Thomas Speed Mosby, *Causes and Cures of Crime.*

Epileptics, from Cesare Lombroso, *The Criminal Man* (1911).

photography is also an expression of time. Photography, as a technology, has the capacity to excerpt an image from a temporal continuum and, in this manner, to momentarily impede the passing of time. The camera's ability to stop time also allows the photograph it produces to index other temporal moments, past times. Engaging how the photograph stops time and thereby projects the past into the future helps us understand the particular function of the medical photography under examination here. The increased use of photographic technology in science and medicine led to the full-fledged establishment of the practice as a primary form of representational proof for scientific claims. The photographic image thus operated as a structure of knowledge, an epistemological practice for understanding modern subjectivity that invoked an ideologically charged understanding of the temporal character of human being.

We can understand the photograph's choreography of being in time more fully if we compare it to other technologies of temporal organization such as the calendar or the clock. The calendar, for one, has the capacity to naturalize time and time's coordinates (like religious rituals and national holidays) by placing them within the temporal fabric of everyday life. The calendar freights the quotidian with ideological and political meaning, for it synchronizes forms of community—national, religious, social—according to such mundane things as the work week, the weekend, or Labor Day. As such, calendar time governs the practices of everyday life at the level of everyday life.[59] The clock functions in similar ways by segmenting the day into discrete minutes and hours instilled with ideological meaning (time to work, time to play, time to eat, and now back to work). But this is the time of modernity in its most progressivist (and capitalist) expression: linear, rationalized, forward marching. The photograph, by contrast, has the potential to disorder the routines of calendar and clock times, despite medical practitioners' attempts to the contrary. As a preservation of time that brings the past into the present, the photograph amplifies the experience of time as a polytemporal one. In the photograph, that is, the past is not sublimated so as to ensure the linear time consciousness of progress on which modernity depends. Rather, the photograph forges an alternative temporality resistant to teleological time.

The fact that medical photographs staged the body in contact with an archaic past, thus potentially threatening to reorient the experience of modern time, did not, however, prevent human science from relying on them as one of their central evidentiary mechanisms. On the contrary, scientists concerned with atavism found in the photograph an even greater opportunity to search the body for signs of the human past. By allegedly bringing the body's primitivism into sharp focus, the photograph aided science in its quest for proof of human animality. Moreover, to the extent that the atavistic body signals the specifically (pre)human past, medical photographs of atavism did more than defy modern progressivism; they also enabled a reexperiencing of the evolutionary past of human being. This is precisely Galton's point when he suggests that composite photography has the capacity to reveal "the common humanity of a low type." When the trappings of culture are stripped away, we are left with a baseline primitive self. The scientific management of human visibility, therefore, structures modernity through a double logic: the photograph performs a break with the past only to reenact that past. Put more boldly, the photograph serves to invent those visible features that can be taken as representative of the past and its recurrence. The scientific act of invention, in turn, ensures and proliferates the circulation of archaic forms as a central aspect of modern life, not just in the sense that specific scientific studies were responsible for the production of these photographs, but that in them practically every aspect of the body (eyes, ears, teeth, nose, feet) was interpreted as a potential sign of the past. Human sciences relying on photography thus produced what they had intended to control: atavistic bodies everywhere. The insistence on seeing atavistic signs in such abundance suggests that atavism was not just a containable occurrence to be read off aberrant bodies, but that the human body itself was an atavism.

Figures of Speech

I have thus far described the imagined accuracy of the photograph. Ironically, the method of presentation most often used by those scientists trying to publicize their findings in lectures, formal displays, or texts indicates a less than full commitment to the photograph's visual transparency. To buttress scientific argument, a detailed set of rationales, interpretations, and textual overlays (used to direct one's gaze to the appropriate sites of the body) were deployed to make visible what the photograph, despite its pretenses, could not fully display. For instance, although the argument concerning the medical use of the photograph supported the idea that the image taken possessed self-evident signifiers of the condition under examination, be it sexual behavior, intelligence levels, or emotional states, more often than not, that image was accompanied by any number of extraphotographic details illuminating what it was the spectator should be observing. These details and strategies came in the form of written explanations, accompanying interpretations, captions, charts, and other textual aids that penetrated the photograph, puncturing it with meaning that did not proceed from the image but rather entered into the image from beyond the frame.

As a result, the degenerate and atavistic body became the object of a variety of reading practices and the subject of an enormous variety of texts (medical, literary, photographic) through which human difference was explored, managed, and made—made public, made deviant, made up. Many of these images were published in medical texts that provided an important framework within which they could be read. In these texts, the displayed images of atavism were not wholly bounded by the photographic frame but rather surrounded by the interpretative devices of scientific inquiry that lent them their meaning. As was the case with Freud's case studies, in which interpretations shuttled back and forth between linguistic and visual horizons, in the medical photograph, we can witness a similar ekphrastic mode in which visual and discursive techniques were used with comparable frequency when neither one seemed to signify well enough on its own.

Only recently has attention been paid to the relationship between these textualities and scientific images of deviance by critics of visual culture or by those critics, like myself, interested in the cultural logic of scientific discourse.[60] Persistently, meaning has been attributed to the image itself as a bounded cultural signifier.[61] It is through attention to the mutually constitutive iconic and linguistic structures of medical representation, however, that we may be able to better understand the specific ideas emerging about the modern self at the fin de siècle. This attention also serves to complicate the all-too-structured distinction between text and image by stressing their necessary reciprocity.[62] The appearance of photographs in medical, biological, anthropological, and criminological texts suggests that text and image were not simply juxtaposed; rather, each mutually informed the meaning of the other.[63] Similar to the interpretative methodology with which Freud approached the Wolf Man's dream, by combining textual analysis, printed labels, and visual images, scientists created literary–visual tableaux, "image-text" portraits of modernity and its corporeal instabilities.[64]

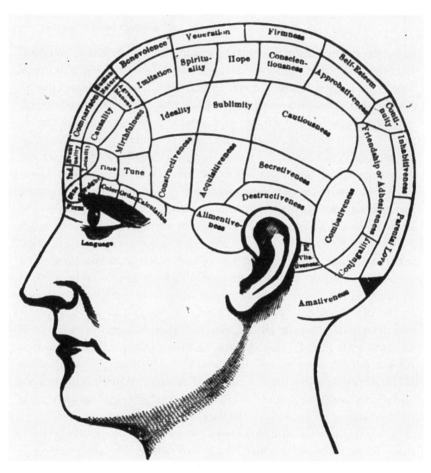

Model head, from Nelson Sizer and H. S. Drayton, *Heads and Faces and How to Study Them: A Manual of Physiognomy and Phrenology for the People* (1885).

At times, this took the form of a model head illustrated with various labels that described mental states, emotions, or intelligence levels in their corresponding locations in regions of the brain. At other times, descriptive labels were superimposed over photographs of medical subjects. The labels served to narrate the face, to coerce the subject into a medical story about a particular disease or degeneracy. In turn, the photograph served to visualize the medical labels, supplying an abstract theory with an accessible (because materializable) example. Captions appearing underneath photographs worked in much the same way, and they eventually informed Benjamin's own ontology of the photographic image in his "Little Essay on Photography." In one of his occasional less than optimistic comments about visual technology, he asks: "Will not captions become the essential components of pictures?" by which he means that the image comes into being only as a fragment, never complete in itself. As a consequence, the label and the caption become necessary features of photographic display to the extent that they function as the primary means of expressing the off-frame intent of the photographer, and in the case of medical photography, the scientist.

The virtue of photographic practice was its alleged ability to produce an objective standard by emptying the image of signs of human intervention, to alienate the body from imputed scientific claims, but, as Benjamin suggests, the image is nonetheless susceptible to deliberate, extraneous forces that shape and refashion it. Moreover, Benjamin's point seems to be that this is an inevitable feature of the photograph. And this, in medical texts that use photographic images as explanatory visual anchors, is precisely how the body was constituted. Indeed, text and image in these instances merged to form a collage of words and bodies. For example, Talbot uses the text/image format in order to argue that the "growth of the [negro] brain is . . . arrested by the premature closing of the cranial sutures and laternal [sic] pressure of the frontal bone," which, for Talbot, explains why "the intellect seems to become clouded, animation giving place to a sort of lethargy, briskness

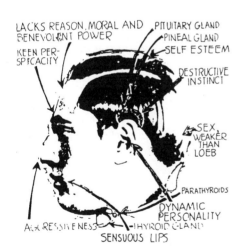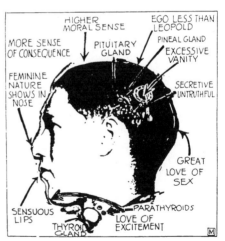

Physiognomic analysis of Nathan Leopold *(left)* and Richard Loeb *(right),* gay lovers and confessed murderers of fourteen-year-old Bobby Franks, from the *Chicago Daily Tribune* (1924).

yielding to indolence."[65] The format of the page asks readers to move between scientific explanations and visual examples that compare the head of a chimpanzee with that of a "coloured criminal youth" and of a member of the "Caucasic race," which has the more "evolved" angle of 75 to 80 degrees. In its attempt to legitimate racist comparisons, the formatting forces the reader into a diagnostic position. Readers encountering a text such as this one (which was at the time becoming exemplary of the science textbook) are asked to perform several tasks: they are to read the biological explanation typed on the page, they are to then map that explanation onto the three images presented on the page, and finally, they are to move back to the scientific explanation, now made more clear by way of the visual examples. Neither text nor image is privileged as the primary site of knowledge; each is necessary as a means of knowing the other. Talbot's analysis of an atavistic racial body thus only becomes possible through this specific method of representation; form gives way to content.

Lombroso's study of the "female offender" provides another instructive example of the merger between text and image in scientific arguments. Lombroso developed his system of anatomic-physiognomy by combining a number of materials, including statistics, comparative charts and graphs, and hundreds of photographs of female criminals. He also turned to anecdotal evidence to relate the details of the crimes and diseases behind the faces presented for visual analysis.[66] These anecdotes ranged from the efforts of prostitutes to hide their "masculine ugliness" to vivid accounts of the deeds of murderesses. Lombroso explains that the woman depicted in a series of photographs of convicted murderers "killed her husband with reiterated blows of a hatchet, while he was skimming the milk, then threw his body into the recess under the stairs, and during the night fled with the family money and her own trinkets." He adds that "this woman was remarkable for the asymmetry of her face; her nose was hollowed out, her ears projecting, her brow more fully developed than is usual in a woman, her jaw enormous with a lemurian appendix."[67]

Another anecdote tells the story of a woman who "was married against her will [and] ill-treated by her husband, whom she killed with a hatchet while he slept." Predictably, "her ears stand out; she has big jaws and cheek-bones, very black hair, and gigantic canine teeth."[68] Lombroso's anecdotes provide more than just a background for his scrutiny of female bodies, and the accompanying photographs provide more

FIG. 20.

of different species of animals, but also those which are found to exist between different races. The angle which the facial line or characteristic line of the visage makes varies from 70° to 80° in the race. All who raise it higher disobey the rules of art (from imitation of the antique). All who bring it lower fall into the likeness of the monkeys. If I cause the facial line to fall in front I have the antique head. If I incline it backward I have the head of a negro. If I incline it still further I have the head of a monkey; inclined still more I have the head of a dog; and, lastly, that of a goose."

This is excellently shown by the following illustrations. Fig. 20 is the head of Johanna, the female chimpanzee of Central Park, New York City. This head has (by Camper's method) an angle between 40° and 50°. The brain of this animal occupies one-third of the skull, and the jaws two-thirds. The negro criminal (Fig. 21) has an angle of about 70°. Here the brain is encroaching, while the jaws are receding. The Caucasic race (Fig. 22) has an angle of 75° to 80°. In many cases the

FIG. 21. COLOURED CRIMINAL YOUTH.

frontal development of the brain and resultant recession of the jaws produce an angle of 90°, with a general result not unlike the Apollo.

Although the general outlines of facial evolution as sighted by Camper are in accord with my own views, yet, as regards accuracy, this angle is not an ideal from whence to study face degeneracy, since the line does not fall low enough to include the chin, and also, as I have elsewhere shown, in the degenerate, the ear varies as much as one to one and one-half inches upon heads of different individuals. Frequently, in the degenerate classes, the ears of the same individual differ as much as one inch in height.

An ideal line, from whence to study a degenerate face, should be drawn perpendicularly from the supra-orbital ridge intersecting the upper and lower jaw and chin. While the chin of the Apollo Belvedere falls slightly inside of this line, yet this is hardly perceptible. Having now fixed a standard from which to study the degenerate face, it should be remembered that jaws which protrude beyond this line are atavistic, and those which recede are even more degenerate.

The angle between 80° and 90° may be accepted as an ideal by which to study degeneracy. This factor alone, however, can not be accepted; the

FIG. 22.

Page layout comparing the facial angles of a "coloured criminal youth" with the "Caucasic race" and a chimpanzee, from Eugene Talbot, *Degeneracy: Its Causes, Signs, and Results.*

than just illustration or evidence of an individual's atavism. The photographs, like the verbal descriptions, animate the story, give it shape, form, and tangible meaning. At the same time, the stories themselves work to redescribe the contours and representational vicissitudes of the bodies on display by providing them with a narrative in which they can be read. Significant in this respect is that the stories do not function to provide a theory of causality for the women's behavior. Lombroso does not bring into analysis the social conditions of domestic abuse, for example, that may have played a role in at least one of the women's turn to violence. Rather, the stories are selectively deployed to further consolidate the monstrosity of the female body, supposedly legible in the visual image but in actuality in need of textual support to make it so. I write "selectively deployed" because Lombroso's anecdotes seem deliberately to eschew a complete narrative of the individual under study. They are instead narrative fragments that stand in synecdochal relationship to the individual; they tell one part of a story in which a small piece of information stands in for the whole while eclipsing or foreclosing other potential or existing stories. This is much like the medical photograph itself, which forecloses certain realities or histories and inserts others in order to establish authority over its subjects. The photograph as synecdoche for the modern subject suggests that the fixity of identity scientists sought arose out of a disciplinary anxiety concerning the epistemological limits of science. Thus the space of the photograph became contiguous with knowledge production in such as way as to give rise to new forms and formats of representation. Lombroso's anecdotal evidence casts into high relief the particular opportunities photography afforded to scientists as well as the representational difficulties it simultaneously posed. Although the use of these images in medical texts helped to connect the morphological dots to the scientific "big picture" of human aberrance, at the same time, they could not help but foreground the image's (and by inference the body's) need for representational reinforcement.

Eugene Talbot clarifies the nature of this paradox of representation when he begins his own study on degeneracy by quoting Shakespeare. Talbot argues that in Shakespeare's dramatic work, we can find evidence of how the modern manifestations of "mental and moral defect" have a history. His interest in Shakespeare occupies the first five pages of his volume and ranges from the moment in *Richard III* when Margaret calls Richard an "elvish-marked, abortive, rooting hog" to Queen Margaret's words in *Henry IV* when she refers to Henry as "a foul misshapen stigmatic."[69] When Talbot invokes literature to explain scientific theory, he seems to recognize the rhetoricity of both the body and the science of the body. His inclusion of the literary in what is primarily a visual scientific analysis also indicates that photographic representation offered the potential not only for observing and identifying disease, but also for constructing narratives of disease that could best characterize the traumas and tragedies of modernity that they sought to manage.[70]

This is significant for several reasons. First, the use of the text–image format reveals the fallacy of the notion that the "human body" was an unmediated, self-present entity as it was conceived within the Enlightenment humanist tradition. Second, the representational abundance of scientific argument asks that we understand the construction of bodies in terms of their inconsistency and changefulness instead of their stability and integrity. Finally, the reliance on photographic practice exposes the fundamental paradox of fin de siècle human science: the more researchers attempted to secure the borders of "human identity," the more the body became available for new forms of subjectivity.[71]

The human sciences, then, were faced with a perpetual crisis. On the one hand, they sought to create an accessible literacy of the body, a democratization of scientific observation to aid everyday people in the detection of disease and harm. On the other hand, the body proved an unwieldy figure, one that required constant vigilance and (re)interpretation in order to remain a viable object of scientific knowledge.[72] This directly speaks to the problem of photographic representation. The photograph was thought to provide visible, material evidence of the substance of identity insofar as personal essence was defined in relation to physical attribute.[73] By capturing the body's "physiognomic details," the medical photograph came to function as a synecdoche of Being. Simultaneously legitimated by and legitimating the authority of science and medicine, the photograph represented the visible body as something true, certain, and complete: an objective sign of a human type. Yet thoroughly dependent on its formal structuring (layout, label, caption, storytelling), the medical photograph reveals the necessarily mediated nature of human identity, which comes into existence as a systematically technologized and therefore a-natural entity.[74]

Strange Gaze

Through the production of a series of corresponding narratives and images, the human sciences attempted to track the decline, or *degenerescence,* of individual bodies and thus to predict the epic ruination of the social body. The medical images in this archive illustrate the ways individual bodies were posed to fit the meanings dictated by a combination of institutional and social spheres. At the same time, the condensation of the atavistic body put productive pressure on the present to the extent that it preserved what modern culture claimed to renounce: its historicity, its animal origins, its rootedness in the pastness of the past. Both circuits of meaning are possible precisely because atavistic bodies were open texts that were constantly rewritten and reinterpreted; they could achieve no stable relation to a "core self," let alone a medical diagnosis, even if, inevitably, notions of disease and deviance were relentlessly rooted in the external contours of the body. Efforts to police the social body by way of quarantining individual bodies were constantly impinged on by the willful readings and writings of the body that the human sciences performed and inscribed. The will to visualize the body, then, resulted in a war of representation, a simultaneous reification and collapse of the past into the present and the present into the past, as if scientific visual culture had itself fallen prey to its own theory of recurrence.

Sigfried Kracauer, in his skepticism toward the photographic medium, argues that photographic technology has to do with the erasure of personal history, buried "as if under a layer of snow."[75] Kracauer begins his argument about the photograph by comparing the image of a "film diva" from a magazine to a photograph of a grandmother from a musty family album. The image of the film diva is safely secured both in the illustrated magazine and in the star system that has produced the image: "everyone recognizes her with delight."[76] But the figure of the grandmother references an identity for which there no longer is, or perhaps never was, any original: "the ur-image has long since decayed." The collection of traits that signify the grandmother in the memories of the children looking at her image fail to correspond to the "now darkened appearance" that is the photographic likeness of the grandmother.[77] The representation becomes not one of "grandmother," the woman the children knew, but an image of an archaic and unfamiliar past. "Grandmother" has been reduced to "an archeological mannequin which serves to illustrate the costumes of the period." And while the diva is more immediately recognized under the signs of star culture, the grandmother reduces to a historical type. "All right, so it is the Grandmother, but in reality it is any young girl in 1864. The girl smiles continuously, always the same smile, the smile is arrested yet no longer refers to the life from which it has been taken."[78] The smile has become a frozen performance of the past; it signifies a prototypical girl, but not a person, not someone with a life. The distinction between the evanescence of the image and the substance of her personhood is obliterated.

In *Camera Lucida,* Roland Barthes famously describes a problem that aligns with Kracauer's reading when he similarly encounters a photograph of his mother. While gazing at the image, Barthes experiences a disturbing sense of separation between his memory of his mother and the representation of her that he sees before him. His mother feels so unrecognizable, he reflects, because her photograph seems only to refer to an incomplete reconstruction of his memory rather than to a representation of her in relationship to her subjective agency: "straining toward the essence of her identity, I was struggling among images partially true, and therefore totally false."[79] The production of subjectivity in the photograph fails to correspond to the memory of the event of actually having known her. As a consequence, Barthes's quest for an image that would reveal some kind of truth about his mother appears as a wholly counterfeit one. For Kracauer and Barthes, in the space of the photograph the past becomes both memorialized and archaic, and thus the photographic medium produces a "separation of the image from real life."[80] And it is these signs of the past haunting the photograph that become instrumental in producing new and strained meanings in the present.

Following Barthes and Kracauer, we might understand how the photograph makes itself intelligible by reducing its social contingencies to optical signs: the bangs of the diva or the grandmother's chignon in Kracauer's example, and the shape of the ear, the sharpness of the tooth, the contours of the face in the examples of medical photography. What appears in the photograph is no longer the person "but the sum of what can be subtracted from him or her."[81] We might also say, as Miriam Hansen has argued in her analysis of Kracauer, that "the politico-philosophical significance of photography does not rest with the ability to reflect its object as real but rather with the ability to render it strange."[82] The strangeness of the atavistic body—its multiply registering meanings and discourses, its form misshapen by the conventions of scientific narrative, its sexualization and racialization—should point us toward considering how human science and its technologies, in their very surveillance of "out-of-control" bodies, authorized a proliferation of the forms of deviance. This is why Kracauer also gestures toward the potential for the photograph to disrupt the present arrangement of the world. By "warehousing the natural," the photographic archive can serve to disarticulate the elements that produce the illusion of nature. Photography thus allows for the analytic reconceptualization of the "provisional status of all given configurations" and presents an opportunity for the rearrangement of those configurations.[83]

In the atavistic body, intelligibility and unintelligibility are not posed in contradictory relation to each other where social phobias are concerned. Rather, social phobias shuttle between certainty and uncertainty in ways that constitute the meanings of the atavistic body and for which the atavistic body acts as a relay. In the medical photograph you can recognize "the type," but that recognition incites anxieties about the behaviors, practices, and contagions concealed and revealed in the body's display. The genealogy of late modern morphologies runs along these lines of knowing too much and not knowing enough. By producing irrational fears as rational forms of knowledge, the human sciences strategically parlayed the medical photograph into an epistemological practice. Photographs helped to visualize science, and in so doing, they firmly and irrevocably placed human identity in the optic field. The making present of the human as a biological being designated the production of images as an equivalence of reality, making reality an epistemological possibility with no aspect in excess of its representation. Yet the medical and technological construction of human aberrance also guarantees its own undoing. Repeated to the point where the image is fundamentally denaturalized, the human comes into view as a site (and sight) of impossible knowability. It is by way of these repetitions that human science articulated not only a new ground of knowledge but also a new ground of the subject, an articulation that ultimately brings the illusion of visual cognition into relief.

What I have found so striking in the archive I assemble here is how many of the sciences involved in exploring the epistemological structures of human being, regardless of difference in argument, turned to the notion of atavism as a core aspect of their work. The distribution throughout the culture of atavism as a key term demonstrates the centrality of the concept in the figuring of knowledge of the human. The overlay of the epistemological and the photographic, moreover, points to the strategies by which such knowledge comes to the fore. The change of experience that can be said to be characteristic of modernity was in large part a change effected by the new relationship between media forms and the modern sense of self. Photographic reproduction, specifically, was celebrated as the means by which to best gather objective evidence of the human, which, in turn, changed how self and body were to be thought. But with change comes transformation. Accordingly, photographic reproduction did not render the real so much as it altered it; it did not truthfully represent the person photographed so much as it transformed that person into a codified set of meanings. The result of fin de siècle medical photographic practice, therefore, was not that it offered an efficient model for the parsing apart of human type and character, but that it emerged as one of the defining conditions of modern subjectivity. After the advent of the photograph, the

Enlightenment idea of a humanistic subject that could exist in pretechnological, prephotographic terms became untenable, if not impossible.

If what it means to be human, as a result, is conceived as a concatenation of physical signs, temporal assignations, and modern technologies, how does this both iterate and undermine understandings of normative human nature? What we have seen is that photographic representation resulted in the proliferation of ways of being and looking in the world as opposed to a universalizing, progressive account of the modern subject. The function of the photograph in medical and scientific culture, therefore, perfectly articulates the paradox of modernity because it reveals the extent to which the desire to be modern requires the perhaps unwilling acceptance of human entanglement with representational forms, scientific interpretations, and disparate time frames, an entanglement (and here's the paradox) only fully realized by the decidedly modern technology of the photograph and the inauguration, more generally, of mass visuality.

Having examined the changes that the epistemological privileging of visual imaging in science wrought on conceptions of human being, in the following chapter, I want to shift attention to developments in literary fiction and its response to the status of the human as both a visible and an atavistic subject. In this chapter, I have asked that we recognize how the visual did not fail to fully represent the human so much as it required narrative and linguistic help to support and make more realizable its meanings. In the next, I will consider the other side of this problem: the affects on and meanings produced by literary fiction in relation to new visual epistemologies of the human. Responding to and negotiating ideas generated about the modern subject in more resolutely narrative terms, fiction writers retranslated the visual back into the verbal, making the body (more literally) into a text. And yet a similar paradox of representation emerges in these fictions in the attempt to narrate the density of human character and experience. I am particularly interested in how the literary fiction most involved in thinking through the nature of the human during this period invokes and attempts to overcome the limits of language and the problems of depiction—an effort that, like medical photography, ultimately produces the human as an atavism: a figure beyond words, an animal down on all fours.

3. "Wolf—wolf!"
Narrating the Science of Desire

[T]here is truly a brute brain within the man's, and when the latter stops short of its characteristic development, it is natural that it should manifest only its most primitive functions.
—Eugene Talbot, *Degeneracy: Its Causes, Signs, and Results*

A becoming-animal always involves a pack, a band, a population, a peopling, in short, a multiplicity.
—Deleuze and Guattari, *A Thousand Plateaus*

ATAVISM DEMONSTRATES, sometimes quite poignantly, that the body does not coincide with its present. It dramatizes the past as in communication with the present; it insists that the past and the present are temporal spheres fused in continuity. By making manifest a disordered temporality, the atavistic body demonstrates something of the nature of cultural preoccupations in late modernity. At the same time, the epistemological projects orbiting around this body demonstrate something of the nature of the formal procedures exercised in the scientific pursuit of corporeal mastery. If those procedures may be seen in psychoanalysis and medical photography, they also emerge with particular clarity in literary culture, which participated in the production and circulation of the concept and image of atavism. In this chapter, I look at two novels: Frank Norris's *Vandover and the Brute* (1895) and Djuna Barnes's *Nightwood* (1937), each of which takes as its focus the atavistic tendencies of their main characters. In their complex labors of documentation and transfiguration of scientific interest, we find a fashioning of subject positions by means of an animal.

In the final scene of *Nightwood*, we have the disturbing pleasure of watching Robin Vote imitate her lover's dog.[1] We find Robin, as does her lover Nora, in an abandoned, decaying chapel in the allegorical setting of the American woodland, wearing "her boy's trousers" and standing before the image of a Madonna (169). "Startled," Robin begins "going down" before Nora's dog "until her head swung against his; on all fours now, dragging her knees." Agitated by her actions, the dog begins "quivering in every muscle . . . his tongue a stiff curving terror in his mouth." Robin continues to imitate the dog, "whimpering" and running around the chapel floor on all fours until "she began to bark also, crawling after him—barking in a fit of laughter, obscene and touching." Their actions intensify simultaneously ("grinning and crying . . . moving head to head") until they both lie down, exhausted, the dog's "head flat along her knees" (169–70).

For readers of Frank Norris's novel *Vandover and the Brute,* whose main character ends up in a similar position, *Nightwood*'s closing scene may provoke a perverse feeling of déjà vu. In an equally "obscene and touching" fashion, after a series of homoerotic and dissolute sexual encounters, Vandover ends up on all fours barking like a wolf:

All in an instant he had given way, yielding in a second to the strange hallucination of that four-footed thing that sulked and snarled. Now without a moment's stop he ran back and forth along the wall of the room, upon the palms of his hands and toes, a ludicrous figure . . . imitating some kind of enormous dog. . . . At long intervals he uttered a sound, half word, half cry, "Wolf—wolf!" . . . Naked, four-footed, Vandover ran back and forth the length of the room.[2]

As in *Nightwood,* the atavistic brute within Vandover not only stages but also exists as the precondition for the ultimate emergence of his sexually perverse body. The "half word, half cry" of his bark, the "Wolf—wolf!" that constitutes both a noise and a noun describing his mental state, registers the in-between, hybrid status of this transformation. He becomes a perverse creature that resides somewhere between descriptive language and guttural utterance; he becomes a body "beyond words" (215). In its final scene, *Nightwood*'s uncanny repetition of *Vandover* suggests that these texts do more than dramatize the bestial decline of individual subjects in detached historical moments. The atavistic bodies they formulate, also on display in the discourses of evolutionism, sexology, and degeneration theory, not only haunted the temporal and epistemological structures of modernity, but also helped constitute modern conceptions of sexuality. In the narratives I explore in this chapter, this formulation of the atavistic body expresses itself in what I call a "degeneration narrative," a regressive "story." As with Freud's case studies, in the degeneration narrative the body is produced as an ekphrasis of sexual perversion—that is, as a lucid, self-contained animation of sex and sexuality in the modern world.

The science of degeneration, like other scientific inquiries at the fin de siècle, emerged as a culturally embedded practice at a time when traditional understandings of human identity were changing. Former conceptions of human origin within religious doctrine, or of the autonomous individual envisioned by liberalism as equipped with free will and responsible for his or her own actions, increasingly came to be replaced by the sociobiological concepts of social Darwinism and natural selection.[3] The loss of a stable sense of human being was expressed in a general fear of cultural deterioration. One account of this modern ethos of deterioration occurs in an 1897 article in the magazine *The Living Age,* when an author queries, "Is our race degenerating?" He concludes that while "[w]e are not yet a degenerate people," it is "beyond all question the classes which are the best endowed intellectually—and . . . physically—are passing into a relative and even an absolute decline."[4] Such popular magazine articles, which often included a "biological forecast" of the "future of America,"[5] provided a venue where biologists, social reformers, and politicians alike could make dire cultural predictions. One author, for instance, announces in a 1926 article in *American Mercury:* "It will only be a question of time, and not so much time at that, when the present moron majority will become an idiot unanimity."[6] During the same period that degeneration theorists worried about the possible collapse of civilization, a variety of sexologists (most famously Havelock Ellis and Richard Krafft-Ebing) defined same-sex desire within this framework. "[A]ntipathic sexual instinct," Krafft-Ebing claims, or "the want of sexual sensibility for the opposite sex," is a "congenital" and "degenerative" disorder that either results from "arrested development," as Eugene Talbot argues, or is "an episodic syndrome of a hereditary disease," as Ellis describes it.[7]

Thus, new fields in the human sciences emerged to provide documentation of the grievous effects of the perversities of modernity. As Jennifer Terry and Jacqueline Urla contend, however, the ultimate effect of degeneration theory was not the restoration of public health and social hygiene it envisioned, but the dehumanization of entire populations as well as the construction of new pathologies whose meanings rested on the belief that deviance manifests itself in the visible body.[8] As we observed in Freud's narrativization of the Wolf Man's neurosis as a form of sexual savagery, racial difference played an enormous role in shaping knowledge of human being at the fin de siècle. Indeed, the various images and representations of atavistic bodies that emerged helped to shape and were themselves shaped by historically and culturally specific ideologies of racial otherness. That is, the discourse around sexual perversion and homosexuality, and the very image of a human turning beast that *Vandover* and *Nightwood* draw on, intersects with U.S. constructions of the racial other as both diseased and less evolved.[9] As Siobhan Somerville argues, "[T]he structures and methodologies that drove dominant ideologies of race also fueled the pursuit of scientific knowledge about the homosexual body."[10] In narrating the processes by which sexual deviance assumes an embodied (sub)human and racialized form, both *Nightwood* and *Vandover* take up the biomedical arguments of their time. Each text stages the body in a state of ruination that bears the decaying effects of modernity and advances a bestialized human figure as a mode through which modern perversity expresses itself. Instead of stabilizing a "homosexual body," however, as Somerville's account of sexological discourse suggests it did, this model of perversion emerged within a number of multiple and unstable registers. It suggests more a queer physiognomy than a stable identity category. Queer physiognomies, in the sense I use the phrase here, name a construction of medical conceptual categories that yoke together what seem like potentially incommensurate modes of analysis. As I have demonstrated elsewhere, they are idiosyncratic composites of modern perversity that create the conditions for unique, newly imaginable binds of personhood.[11]

It is now a common practice in lesbian and gay studies to understand the sexological accounts of sexuality as evidence for the Foucauldian contention that sexuality in Western culture became a privileged object of social analysis at the fin de siècle, a development that produced medicojuridical sexual taxonomies and freighted sexual definition with a new set of power relations.[12] Foucault's genealogy of the modern sexual subject is simultaneously an account of power as a productive force proliferating sexual discourse and of the historical and cultural production of the modern body thoroughly permeated by these power relations. In this regard, the body is constituted as an "inscribed surface of events."[13] But Judith Butler, in an intervention that is useful for a reexamination of this modern body, asks: "[B]y what enigmatic means has 'the body' been accepted as a prima facie given that admits of no genealogy?"[14] When Butler critiques Foucault for theorizing the body as a "passive medium that is signified by an inscription from a cultural source figured as 'external' to that body," she means that the body is itself an effect of inscription, a permeable boundary rather than an a priori "being" that culture then appropriates and forces to signify.[15] Thus, the question of how sexual subjects were discursively produced and embodied in relation to this modern regime remains. What shapes, forms, expressions, images, abstractions, and positions did the body take on that made it a culturally coherent effect of the modern world? If the history of the body's construction is laden with binary determinations we have come to know by heart (disease–health, normal–abnormal, homosexual–heterosexual), there are still specific narrative formulations to explore, and stories to tell, about the multiple ways the body has come into formation in the context of its intense scrutiny, or in spite of it. What, then, are the particular forms of sexual perversion during this period? What narrative scenarios or embodied stories emerged around a struggle for epistemological certainty concerning sexual identity? What kinds of bodies took shape, or were disfigured, as a result? What do these representations reveal about our own perceptions of perversion and our present-day obsessions with the ontological status of "homosexuality"? In seeking to address these questions, I explore the work literature does to produce a set of signs for perverse bodies and sexual personhoods, and thereby engage how literature participates in the continual rethinking and remaking of sexual history.

This inquiry requires not only attention to the particularities of how the perverse body was made so, but also a closer analysis of the scientific discourses and cultural forms that mediated them. The human sciences at this time were far less stable than their representations tend to be; continually in flux theoretically, they produced a range of contradictory and contestatory versions of human identity. Moreover, the cultural forms that mediated these sciences—narratives like *Nightwood* and *Vandover*—did not provide a means for the resolution of scientific inconsistency. They did not, that is, as Amy Kaplan suggests of the realist novel, engage in "an enormous act of construction to organize, reform, and control the social world."[16] Nor did they, as Mark Seltzer proposes of the naturalist novel, "manage late nineteenth century 'crises' of production" by reformulating the double discourse of machine and body "within a single technology of regulation."[17] And they did not only, as Fredric Jameson understands the project of modernist literature, "'manage' historical, social, [and] deeply political impulses . . . [in order to] defuse them." Instead, I argue, they allowed new forms of sexual subjectivity to become imaginable.

Each of the literary historians cited above claims that literature is largely a practice of social control, regulation, and management, which is, as Jameson puts it, "the delicate part of the modernist project, the place at which it must be realistic in order in another moment to re-contain that realism which it has awakened."[18] The narratives under examination in this chapter, however, more often than not functioned to perform the incoherences of modern life. By incorporating "inac-cessible" and "fragmented" social realities, the degeneration narrative forges itself as an entropic genre that is aroused by the possibilities of becoming animal while convulsed by the anxieties of the modern world. By engaging in such an entropic practice, both *Vandover* and *Nightwood* demonstrate the potential for narratives to resist what Jameson terms "strategies of containment," not in spite of their incorporation of the "real" but because of it. It is precisely *Vandover* and *Nightwood*'s relation to social problems and anxieties that directs their plots and constitutes the chaotic regression of their narratives. Whereas cultural analysis tends to understand the literary as a mode of regulation and social supervision, then, these novels demonstrate something otherwise. In terms of both their content and their narrative strategies, they each capitalize on the inconsistencies within and among the human sciences. Restaging the multiple renditions within human and biological science of bodily signification and desire, as well as their gaps and argumen-tative failures, *Vandover* and *Nightwood* play with the uncertainties of sci-entific doctrine and extend their confusions into a narrative of modern chaos.

I turn to *Vandover* and *Nightwood,* therefore, as primary instances of the degeneration narrative, paying particular attention to modern-ism's relationship to earlier historical moments. In other words, as *Vandover* reveals, modernist fiction has a history.[19] The bestial, acting as a readily available metaphor for the expression of both sexual and racial indeterminacy, will guide my discussion. In both *Vandover* and *Nightwood*, sexual perversity as a form of atavism is dramatized literally as a character's return to the form of an animal in such a way as to perform the perceived unnaturalness of sexual alterity and to act as a persistent and threatening reminder of how far society could fall if perverse sexual activity were allowed to continue unhindered. Ulti-mately, and perhaps more powerfully, these atavistic materializations write and rewrite the "becoming animal" process as the moment when sexual identity breaks down and reformulates itself, "born of a sexual union that will not reproduce itself," as Deleuze and Guattari write, "but which begins over again every time, gaining that much more ground."[20] In discussing this process, I explore how it is through the incorporation of scientific discourse framing the perverse body as an object of modern knowledge that these narratives have the capacity to semiotically and rhetorically disrupt and reformulate that discourse, especially its attempt to identify and manage aberrance. Thus, rather than assert that these narratives simply reflect scientific culture, I suggest that they respond to biological theory in ways that recontextualize the history of scientific definitions of sexuality. Not only do they rewrite sexological narratives, they also inhabit the instability of their terms as new modes of sexual personhood.

Modes of Deviation

From the social Darwinism of Herbert Spencer to the eugenics movement of Francis Galton, biological determinism grew in popularity and influence in the late nineteenth and early twentieth centuries. Scientific taxonomies and their violent wrenching of certain social practices into binary categories of abnormal and normal became the central method of human science in its attempts to explain the changing social world. Sex acts, gender roles, and social behaviors fell under the scrutiny of a structuring process that organized whole populations in terms of their evolutionary progress on the one hand and degenerative decay on the other, with the effect of rigidly reinforcing racial, social, sexual, and political hierarchies. The medicalization of homosexuality, marking a historical shift from notions of sin within moral doctrine to notions of disease within criminal law, "transposed the amorphous qualities of social disorder into specific forms of sexual deviance," as Carroll Smith-Rosenberg explains. [21] Although complex debates took place at this time as to whether homosexuality was a congenital disorder or an acquired characteristic caused by social influences, many of the theories proposed by medical authorities, demonstrating the homophobia typical of the era, suggested that pathological drives led to homosexual practices. Sexologist Karl Heinrich Ulrichs, for one, describes the homosexual male as having the "soul of a woman trapped in the body of a man"; the mannish woman, it was believed, experienced this dilemma in reverse.[22]

It was primarily through the writings of Ellis and Krafft-Ebing that the twentieth century received its stereotypes of male homosexual and lesbian behavior. Drawing on both medical science and evolutionary theory, Krafft-Ebing divided those who express "antipathic sexual instinct," itself "a functional sign of degeneration," into categories on the basis of a combination of psychic and physical characteristics.[23] He described the female "congenital invert," for example, as possessing a masculine formation of the larynx, "short hair," a "rough deep voice," and "a strong preference for male garments," one who "[w]ould much rather have been a soldier" and would most likely "prefer a cigar."[24] Among the varying categories and descriptions of female homosexuality, "gynandry represents the extreme grade of degenerative homosexuality. The woman of this type possess [sic] of the feminine qualities only the genital organs; thought, sentiment, action, even external appearance are those of a man." In sum, she has a "masculine soul, heaving in the female bosom."[25] In this vein, sexologists drew attention to these bodies as examples of atavism, referring to them, as does U.S. physician Dr. K, as "a sign of the degeneration in the race."[26] The sexually disqualified populations that emerged out of this pandemonium of medical scrutiny became figures against which sanctioned sexual practices and gendered behaviors could then be measured.[27]

And yet the sheer replication of perverse bodies within these sciences, in the texts that imaged and inscribed them and in the juridical realities that surrounded them, from Ellis's photographs of sexual perverts to the infamous trials of Leopold and Loeb and Oscar Wilde, points insistently toward their inherent volatility. As Wilde's trial reminds us, medical explanations of male homosexuality existed alongside other cultural practices and (decadent) literary representations that placed the concept within a set of signs based on sexual style: homosexuality, in this arena of explanation, was overt and flamboyant, grounded in an aesthetic of luxury and sartorial excess associated with the dandy.[28] By contrast, medical study and sexological analysis literalized the notion that one could read homosexuality not through its cultural trappings but in visible signs of the human body. Accordingly, Eugene Talbot's analysis of male "feminism" claims that sexual perversity is signaled by sloping shoulders and a narrow waist, while Ellis extends this body to include atrophying genitals and the problem of "gynecomasty," or abnormal formation of breast tissue on the otherwise male body.[29] Never an untroubled or static phenomenon, the iconography of perversion was laden with aesthetic, social, and political tensions and subject to persistent conflict, both in contemporary debates within the human sciences and between and among their various literary mediations.

Like many authors of the period, including Jack London, Theodore Dreiser, and Stephen Crane, Frank Norris was an avid reader of the human sciences and a particular admirer of Italian anthropologist Cesare Lombroso, going so far as to write a short story, "A Case for Lombroso," about his theories. The main character of the story, like Vandover himself, slides down the scale of humanity to become "a brute" after having sex with Cresencia, a women tainted by the "red hot, degenerate blood" of her Spanish ancestry.[30] Authors such as London, Dreiser, Crane, and Norris read and grappled with the influx of scientific theory, which did not so much present them with a picture of a knowable nature as it fostered the idea of nature as an unknown quantity subject to scientific and literary reflection. Novels and short stories like *Sister Carrie, The Sea-Wolf,* "The Monster," and Norris's own *McTeague* belong to a literary grouping in which modern characters are gripped by recessional urges or become victims of a devolutionary turn. In the case of *Sister Carrie,* Dreiser accounts for the modern subject's potential for decline by exploring the determining and compulsive forces of life itself: "Our civilization is still in a middle stage, scarcely beast, in that it is no longer wholly guided by instinct; scarcely human, in that it is not yet wholly guided by reason. [. . . Man] is becoming too wise to always hearken to instincts and desires; he is still too weak to always prevail against them. As a beast, the forces of life aligned him with them; as a man, he has not yet wholly learned to align himself with the forces. In this intermediate stage he wavers."[31] Dreiser's Darwinian descriptions of struggle, survival, and extinction and his presentation of the coexisting stages of rise and decline thoroughly disengage with capitalist, laissez-faire notions of the autonomous self. Instead, the modern individual is at once stuck in an intermediate space of transformation and is part of a larger cosmos of unstoppable evolutionary change. Whereas for Dreiser this social and biological flux includes a progressivist vision of future perfection, the individual is just as unremittingly subject to corrosive descent. For Norris, the bestial, intermediary stage of modern humanity is physically evidenced on the individual's body. Thus McTeague: "His hands were enormous, red, and covered with a fell of stiff yellow hair. His head was square-cut, angular; the jaw salient, like that of the carnivore." Closely linking his atavistic nature with desire, Norris describes McTeague's attraction for Trina as an animal urge, "like some colossal brute trapped in a delicate, invisible mesh, raging, exasperated, powerless to extricate himself."[32]

Norris's familiarity and fascination with such themes as racial degeneracy and sexual atavism become a manifest presence in his novel *Vandover*, the story of a young artist who, after graduating from Harvard, settles in San Francisco and increasingly drifts into dissipation. As his brute desires manifest themselves in sexual vice, idleness, and self-indulgence, he loses those things that grant him respectability, including his fiancée and his social status. As his character weakens, the brutish "wolf" within emerges, scripting his social decline as biological in nature. At this moment, the novel relies on notions of human biology, rather than culture, to explain Vandover's sexual tendencies and to describe his perpetual decline, thus cleansing the social world of specific liability by casting its excesses as an individual's biological anomaly.

Sherwood Williams, in his account of Norris's text, places the narrative within the semiotic of decadence, which he opposes to the logic of naturalism, calling attention to Vandover as a "Wildean poseur, with his sybaritic passion for interior decoration, his 'veritable feminine horror' of finance, and his love of refinement that makes him 'as careful as a woman in the matter of dress.'"[33] We could add to this list Vandover's excessive passion for his "tiled stove with flamboyant ornaments" (182), where one could often find him lounging, "sit[ting] before it in his bathrobe, absorbing its heat luxuriously and scratching himself" (182). In this perhaps "decadent" moment, seemingly indebted to the scenes of idle lounging that Wilde made so popular as a sexual aesthetic, Vandover's body plays a central, and masturbatory, role, positioned practically nude in front of his "famous stove" (182) as he scratches himself "luxuriously." Williams, however, is more interested in detailing the aesthetic logic of decadence in the novel than its corporeal investments. In a similar dismissal of Vandover's body, but with a different aim, Mark Seltzer places the novel firmly in the tradition of naturalism and argues that during the early twentieth century two divergent cultural beliefs, emphasizing the natural and the made, resulted in a "double discourse" that blurred the divides between the natural and the constructed and recast nature as "a naturalist machine . . .

and individuals as statistical persons."[34] This leads Seltzer to read the stove in *Vandover* as a signifier of "the ethics of regulation and conservation that Vandover opposes to the brute." But in Seltzer's attempt to read this opposition through "the contradictory force that the brute represents," he, like Williams, neglects to attend to the chiefly sexual function of the stove.[35] More than a mere sign of sexual excess ("flamboyance"), the stove has the capacity to arouse Vandover. He experiences its "luxurious heat" not in utilitarian but in sexual ways; his naked body absorbs it, and he is inspired to "scratch . . . himself." Vandover's masturbatory response to his stove not only places him in a sexological narrative where such an activity is pathologized, but it also points to the autonomy of the body in this scene. The corporeal details of Vandover's appetitive desires surface here as equivalent to his degeneration. It is precisely the positions into which his body relaxes, slumps, or declines, as well as the desire and bodily need these positions express, that forge the novel's regressive plot.

I am suggesting, therefore, Norris's narrative should be read otherwise than for its decadent leanings or its regulatory machines. It offers its readers many more competing modes of deviation than that of the decadent or naturalist novel, recasting the homosexual dandy as the atavistic brute, thus shifting its terms from a case of "style" to a biological condition and offering, as I will discuss, contestatory medical diagnoses in its place. The narrative confuses any simple dichotomy between decadence and naturalism, and thus between conceptions of indeterminate, socially contingent sexual practices on the one hand and biologically rooted sexual identities on the other, which each genre ostensibly narrates. This confusion suggests the text's conflictedness concerning the nature of identity in general and of sexuality in particular. In fact, Norris's text works in such a way that it perpetually begins again, offering the reader an etiological array of the causes and effects of perversion from which to choose. It is to this array of choices that I now turn.

Neurasthenics, Syphilitics, Inverts, and Homosexuals

Vandover's exhausted state is multiply culled from a variety of sites and sources. He inherits neurasthenia from his mother, awakens to the pleasures of sexual vice from reading about sex in medical texts, apparently contracts syphilis from the various prostitutes he encounters, and is influenced and tainted by the debauchery of his all-male entourage, which constitutes the text's ubiquitous homoerotic flow. The opening scene of *Vandover* describes his mother within the terms of neurasthenia, and thus directly traces Vandover's own subsequent nervous condition to her, alluding to the inherited nature of his mental state. The scene of his mother's death, occurring when he is eight years old and in the process of migration from Boston to San Francisco in the summer of 1880, inaugurates the novel. "[L]ying back on pillows in a long steamer chair," his mother is "carefully lifted . . . from the car." She appears "very weak and very pale, her eyelids were heavy, the skin on her forehead looked blue . . . and tiny beads of perspiration gathered around the corners of her mouth" (3, 4). When she dies, "her face became the face of an imbecile, stupid without expression, her eyes half-closed, her mouth half-open. Her head rolled forward as though she were nodding in her sleep, while a long drip of saliva trailed from her lower lip" (4–5).

Vandover's memory of this scene lingers uncomfortably on a grotesque physical description of his mother, highlighting her humiliation in the throes of death. In her degeneracy, her very body, appearing "stupid" and like an "imbecile," advertises the wearying effects of the modern world. The embodiment of Vandover's mother as an "imbecile" corresponds with similar characterizations made by scientists from Nordau to Lombroso who linked "defective nervous organization" with, as Talbot puts it, the "congenital idiot" whose "animal type of brain" sometimes produces "animal traits and instincts."[36] But Vandover's mother is not only overcome with the nervous condition that had come to preoccupy medical specialists in the early twentieth century; her body also displays signs of the decay of the modern world, symbolically and actually liable to reverse cultural progress by contaminating those around her. Moreover, when Norris describes the eyes of Vandover's mother as "half-closed" and her mouth as "half-open," he aligns her with other "degenerates" in the text, such as Van's friend Dummy, a deaf-mute who makes peculiar utterances that are "half-noise, half-speech" (58), and Vandover himself, whose hysterical barking is described as "half word, half cry" (310). By coding each character with similar hybrid tags, Norris places neurasthenia, atavism, and "feeble-mindedness" in the same constellation of meaning; each medical condition resides somewhere between speech and noise, human and beast, virtue and perversion. In other words, Norris provides the outlines for a degenerate population, animating his text with deranged figures and multiplying the forms and embodiments of modern decay. Chiefly expressing themselves through the indeterminate indices of the human condition, his characters exist somewhere between their ultimate degeneration and their failure to evolve, between the primitiveness of a "noise" and a "cry" and the civility of a "word" and "speech."

George Beard was the first to use the term *neurasthenia*, a disease he claimed arose in response to the accelerating growth of large cities after the Civil War—"the vertigo and whirl of our frenzied life," as Nordau puts it.[37] Others, such as Herbert Spencer, supported this view and attributed neurasthenia primarily to women. This "hysterization of women," to borrow Foucault's phrase, belies the fact that many men were diagnosed with this condition.[38] But the phrase does reflect how both neurasthenia and hysteria were understood culturally as signs of feminine weakness. For instance, the hysteria transmitted genetically to Vandover by his mother is constantly represented as a feminine characteristic in the novel: when he paints, he is agitated by "feminine caprice" (228); when his father dies, he is overcome with a "feminine weakness" (158); and if he had "been a girl he would . . . have been subject to all sorts of abnormal vagaries . . . drifting into states of unreasoned melancholy" (8–9). By this logic, when Vandover is ultimately overcome by hysteria (the "strained, and unnatural condition of his nerves"), perhaps we are to understand his behavior, in part, as if he were a girl (228). Doing so means recognizing the similarities between Vandover's hysteria and Ulrichs's "trapped soul" theory of homosexuality, which, following prevalent views, claimed that men who were artistic and intellectual were weak and hypersensitive rather than masculine and mature. On this reading, the hysteric within Vandover is the woman trapped within the male homosexual body. Looking to other sexological accounts, we could consider how hysteria and other forms of "nervousness" were usually listed as symptoms of homosexuality in men, and at times, as in Krafft-Ebing, as one of its potential causes. Male hysteria, then, as a function of the misogyny and homophobia typical of the period, makes hysteria, femininity, and male homosexuality equivalent.

The text's preoccupation with the "hystericization" of masculinity, however, is further complicated by yet another mode of deviation: the sexual excitement Vandover experiences during the act of reading. Vandover first encounters reading as a causal locus of his deterioration during his adolescent years, when he is overtaken by "the perverse craving for the knowledge of vice" (11). Comically enough, his craving is initially satiated by the Bible, where he "came across a great many things that filled him with vague and strange ideas." Later an article on obstetrics in the *Encyclopedia Britannica* provides such pleasure; and later still, a dictionary entry, through which he experiences in "the cold, scientific definitions some strange sort of satisfaction" (10, 11). This movement from the Bible to the medical entry references the historical shift, to which I gestured earlier, from understanding sexuality in ecclesiastic terms to understanding it as medically determined. Further, Vandover's contact with medical knowledge, and by extension with the sexual definitions that later come to define his degeneracy, establishes a relationship between his affective bodily desire and his "medicalization." Here, reading about sex constitutes both arousal ("a strange sort of satisfaction") and contamination (Vandover catches sexual vice through his textbook knowledge of it).

We are also offered a third mode through which Vandover's degeneration can be understood: his multiple couplings with "loose women" and prostitutes. During his schooling at Harvard, for example, Vandover was "moved by an unreasoned instinct" into the bed of a girl who had previously "filled him with . . . deep pity and such violent disgust" (24). Although the girl with whom he shares this interlude is never directly named as a prostitute, she is characterized within those terms: she possesses "a hopeless vulgarity," wears "tawdry clothes," and uses "sordid, petty talk," "slang," and "miserable profanity" (23). But Vandover's initial repulsion and attraction to this nameless street woman also rests in the fact that she is wearing men's clothes, "a mannish shirtwaist, with a high collar and scarf" (21), much along the lines of sexology's description of the mannish lesbian popularized at this time by her "distinct trace of masculinity" and proclivity for transvestitism.[39]

Continuing its complication of any neat understanding of degeneracy as a contagious disease, a cultural "habitus," or a genetic condition, the narrative describes Vandover's contact with the prostitute-cum-mannish lesbian within each paradigm.[40] On one hand, Vandover is "infected" with sexual depravity by her in a model closely resembling theories concerning the transmission of syphilis (that is, through sexual contact). At the same time, Vandover, himself a sartorial aesthete, "as careful as a woman in the matter of dress" (26), shares, to borrow Bordieu's phrase, a "stylistic affinity" with his lady friend's cross-dressing tendencies, which indicates his shared, subcultural affiliation with the sexual invert. This interlude awakens a sense of regressive excitement that already dwells biologically within him, and by which he is plagued throughout the novel, as when he began to sense "the animal in him, the perverse evil brute, [that] awoke and stirred" (29). Although *Vandover* in part indexes the prostitute as the site and source of infection, as Sander Gilman has argued, Vandover's contact with prostitutes is only one of many activities of sexual debauchery that seem either to contaminate him or to signify his decline.[41]

Amid "the whiff of the great city's vice," Vandover walks hand in hand with his male friends, "as the desire of vice, the blind, reckless desire of the male, grew upon him" (79, 28). Migrating from bar to bar in drunken fits, "[h]e assumed the manners of these young men of the city, very curious to see for himself the other lower side of their life that began after midnight in the private rooms of fast cafes and that continued in the heavy musk-laden air of certain parlours." One night, Vandover "comes out" to his friends as they eat dinner in one of the "private rooms" of their favorite restaurant (28, 298). "[H]is breath coming short, his heart beating quick," he turns to Dolly, after asking him to "come down here close," and confesses: "[Y]ou know I'm a wolf mostly!" Afterward, Dolly replies, "You had some queer idea about yourself!" (301, 302).

The brutish, contaminating "queerness" of the spaces and populations of urban decay and male revelry perhaps foregrounds Vandover's desire for men, but even more, it foreshadows his eventual mental collapse, suggesting that *Vandover* is not simply the story of an individual's downfall but a narrative of modern decline. Vandover's whole world is chaotically strewn with sexual vice, from the books he reads and the mannish ladies of the night he encounters to the raucous all-nighters he pulls with his male comrades: "He rubbed elbows with street walkers, with bookmakers, with salon keepers, with the exploiters of lost women" (207). Norris's description of the city as a degenerate space teeming with degenerate populations shapes the novel's sexual landscape; he eschews a strict binary between healthy and diseased or deviant and normal to construct a social world in which illicit sexual and social behavior permeates everything and everyone who resides there. We might think, in this regard, of Vandover's otherwise virtuous friend Dolly, who contracts syphilis through an open sore on his mouth when he is inadvertently kissed by a prostitute, or of Dolly's young cousin Hettie, whom he fears will become "infected" with alcoholism by attending too many balls where her sisters overimbibe. Vandover, drifting ineluctably downward through this world, experiences the neurasthenic heredity that is his lot, becomes repeatedly contaminated by sexual vice, and in turn acts as a contaminating source of sexual disease. Unwittingly, he passes on his own degeneracy to several others, as when Ida Wade commits suicide after having sex with him, or when his father dies and he "could not but feel that he had hastened" the death (216). Thus he partakes of and contributes to the novel's proliferating logic of degenerate modernity.

Contagious Diseases and Inherited Conditions

If Vandover is a neurasthenic, a syphilitic, and an invert, how are we to understand the manifestation of his perversion? Physicians such as Krafft-Ebing, Nordau, and Lombroso asserted that homosexuality, hysteria, feeble-mindedness, neurasthenia, and atavism were all symptoms of the degeneration of the human race through the determinism of heredity. But their work just as persistently warned its readers of the possibility of contagion from other already existing degenerates. In Nordau's 1898 study of "the various embodiments which degeneration and hysteria have assumed" entitled *Degeneration,* he concludes that "we stand now the midst of a severe . . . epidemic; of a sort of black death of degeneration," the blame for which can be laid on "the effects of contemporary civilization" itself (536, 537, 42). According to Nordau's theory, the physiological afflictions of degenerate populations would eventually lead to their extinction, but a serious danger still resided in the threat the degenerate presented to nondegenerates: "Weak-minded . . . persons, coming into contact with a man possessed by delirium, are at once conquered by the strength of his diseased ideas, and are converted to them" (31). Even worse, acquiring a form of degeneracy through casual or intimate contact could affect later generations as well: "When under any kind of noxious influences an organism becomes debilitated, its successors will not resemble the healthy, normal type of the species . . . but will form a new sub-species, which, like all others, possesses the capacity of transmitting to its offspring, in a continuously increasing degree, its peculiarities" (16). According to this model, various modern diseases infect an individual, who then passes on the infection to his or her offspring, who in turn reinfect other individuals in the social body.

This threat is literalized in Norris's text when Vandover discovers the loss of his artistic ability. In the course of his devolution, he sinks into depravity "with that fatal adaptability to environment which he has permitted himself to foster throughout his entire life," thus crystallizing the reversal of evolutionary progress that Nordau predicts, "as if the brute in him were forever seeking a lower level" (317). When he tries to paint again after a long hiatus, the images he creates are "changelings, grotesque abortions . . . deformed dwarfs, [the brute's] own hideous spawn" (229). Here artistic production is figured as monstrous reproduction. Not only does Vandover's painting allegorize his potential threat to future generations, but it also manifests Nordau's (and Norris's) vision of modernity. Vandover's gaze is not unlike a scientific one that constructs, and then catalogs, the grotesque deformities and hideous bodies of urban vice.

If Vandover is capable of passing his degeneracy on through the process of heredity, however, we also know that the novel, like the human sciences that inform it, considers sexual vice to be highly contagious. This oscillation between heredity on the one hand and contagion on the other, in both scientific theory and in *Vandover*, allows atavism, as both a metaphor for modern decay and an actual disease, to operate as a relay, a two-way vestibule through which notions of intrinsic identities and acquired characteristics pass. Vandover's degeneration, in other words, does not establish a set of binaries between nature and culture, biology and environment, heredity and contagion, containment and communication. Rather, it brings them, strangely, together. This relaying function, rather than fixing degeneracy as a medically predictable object, indicates that scientific discourse places degeneracy in an in-between space that is both nature and culture, definitive and open, inherited and contagious, fixed and unstable, "half word, and half cry," like Vandover's bark in the novel's ending, and "half-open" and "half-closed," like his mother's neurasthenic face. So *Vandover* does not simply reflect scientific culture; it inscribes its subjects within an uncertain medical discourse that forces incommensurable meanings and incommensurable subjects into commensurability. If human science and its "civic managers," with their aim of identifying, classifying, and regulating deviance, act as "certified guardians of the normalcy of the nation," as Dana Nelson suggests, it is also clear that within its abundant inventory, sexual perversity is far from stable as either a concept or an operative category.[42] The perverse body, in its various incarnations, recapitulates scientific decree only to perform the instability of its terms and as a consequence suggests the irreducibility of the body to the regulatory regimes of human and subhuman taxonomy.

A Body beyond Words

If anything provides *Vandover* with a sense of narrative coherence, it is the incremental process of Vandover's decline into the form of a wolf, for his struggle with "the brute" repeats itself with ever stronger determination, so that his decline is staged as that struggle. At the same moments that Vandover gains knowledge about sexuality through medical texts, comes into physical contact with a prostitute, or succumbs to "feminine" hysteria, the brute—"huge, strong, insatiable"—emerges within him, surfacing more strongly on each return, "swollen and distorted out of all size, grown to be a monster, glutted yet still ravenous . . . groveling, perverse, horrible beyond words" (215). To be a body "beyond words" is to be a body which is excessively visible, "distorted out of all size," bigger than the space in which it resides, and larger than the economy of language within which it is formalized. Vandover's transformation into an unspeakable brute refers, in this way, to the degenerative process of becoming animal: "[H]e fancied that he was in some manner changing, that he was becoming another man; worse than that, it seemed to him that he was no longer human" (275). Words, we are made to understand, fail to capture the density of the problem of the inhuman. They are inadequate to the significations of monstrosity. Much like Freud when he requests that his patient draw a sketch of his dream, Norris turns to the visual realm as a curative method. What is unimaginable, or unimaginably obscene, is ascribed to the body, no longer a human body but an animal one made to stand in for the unspeakability of human perversion. Vandover's unspeakable body is thus deployed as a rhetorical trope (it is only made visual through the use of words) that negotiates the difficult terrain of representation at the limits of discourse and display, speech and spectacle: "Wolf—wolf." The sign of the animal here emerges to grant expression to something inarticulable, as a supplement that confirms the simultaneous excess and therefore lack of meaning attributed to Vandover's perversity.

As was also the case with Freud, Norris's recourse to animality indexes the racial logic of becoming animal. In the novel's description of perversion, race indeed forms a component part. This should come as no surprise given the novel's interest in heredity and the cultural climate of scientific racism out of which that interest emerged. In this climate, race and racial division were used by medical, judicial, and other discursive institutions to make room for normalization and disciplinary power—that is, to manage populations. The logic of race is most concisely revealed, if also somewhat abbreviated, in Vandover's unsettling encounter with Brann, a "deaf and stupid" "little Jew" (139, 124). During the prolonged storm leading to the shipweck that almost takes Vandover's life, the "little Jew" is omnipresent, sitting next to Vandover at supper, standing across the aisle from him in the ship's cabin, and finally "groveling upon the deck" as the ship is about to go under (132). "[T]he little Jew went into some kind of fit, his eyes rolled back, his teeth grinding upon each other" (134–35). Eventually Brann is beaten off the lifeboat that rescues Vandover and left to die in the ocean in order to secure the safety of the others. At this moment, the figure of the racialized other displays and predicts what the main character is to become. After their encounter, Vandover more forcefully enters a life of dissipation: "[d]runkenness, sensuality, gambling, debauchery, he knew them all" (207). And thus the "little Jew," placed into such deliberate and nagging (not to mention anti-Semitic) proximity to Vandover, confirms the status of Vandover's degeneracy.

Because *Vandover* cites degeneration theory so variously, it participates in the overdetermination of sexual perversion as a visual and iconic sign—a body beyond words—and also as a narrative, a story of the process of degeneration. In describing Vandover's excess, the narrative itself becomes excessive, forced to narrate competing models of degeneracy to the point that it makes no sense to refer to Vandover as either or only homosexual or syphilitic or neurasthenic. He exceeds a capacity to describe his pathology; he is "horrible beyond words." The contradictory accounts of sexual perversion in *Vandover* help to clarify what I have outlined as the unstable proliferation of the definitions and embodiments of perversity both within human science and through its cultural mediation, and the manner by which apparently conflicting diagnostic models break down into narrative excess only to reformulate themselves in visual terms: "the four-footed thing that sulked and snarled" (310). Vandover's transformation into something like an animal is elaborated in the narrative as a series of physical and emotional afflictions caused by opposed etiologies and contradictory prognoses. The narrative coordinates these conflicting accounts by embodying them within a single, albeit hybrid, body that has the capacity to express sexual perversion without the confusions and contradictions of language. But it is also language that enables this body to emerge. More specifically, it is the degeneration narrative that propels Vandover into lower, continually more monstrous depths. And so the degeneration narrative, like the Freudian case study, operates within an ekphrastic tradition; it deploys language to make us see what might otherwise remain beyond expression. This is not only a way of embodying modernity but also of formulating the variables of perversion into an unmanageable figure: a multiply produced, variously diseased, indeterminate body.

What I want to consider now is how *Nightwood* takes up this model of perversion in a way that continues to refunction degeneration theory and that illuminates some surprising connections between the allegedly separate projects of modernism and naturalism. Naturalism, usually considered one of the modes that modernism set at a distance, has been characterized as a unified narrative structure obsessed with the enabling conditions of human being, more often than not offering a deterministic vision ostensibly inimical to representations of the complexities of the subject. By contrast, according to familiar accounts, modernism evokes intricate verbal craftsmanship, a perspective of discontinuity, and a conscious and nuanced attempt to demonstrate the fragmentations of subjectivity and modern social life. Nonetheless, *Nightwood,* an exemplary modernist text, rather than hypostasizing naturalism as modernism's bad object, shares many of the concerns and narrative practices we witnessed in *Vandover,* including a fascination with scientific doctrine and a development of techniques that over- and underdetermine the conditions of sexual personhood. In *Vandover,* the excessive descriptive detail of naturalist narrative form fails to hold together as a structured whole and so, intentionally or not, produces effects of antitotalizing narration. Any absolute presentation of "objective reality" that Norris may have desired collapses into a discontinuous, overly abundant theory of sexuality. *Vandover*'s self-referential narrative construction of chaos and entropy, therefore, leads us quite readily to the project of modernism in which *Nightwood* participates. *Nightwood,* in other words, is not a break from this practice of narration, but rather its continuation.

Modernism, Sexuality, and a Doctor

In the years surrounding the publication of *Nightwood*, degeneration theory was still a prominent force in Europe and the United States, surfacing in a variety of forms, including Sadler's eugenic text *Race Decadence: Racial Degeneracy in the U.S.* (1922); Lothrop Stoddard's *The Revolt against Civilization: Menace of the Underman* (1923); George Henry's extensive two-volume *Sex Variant* study that, between the years 1928 and 1941, scrutinized the homosexual body for signs of pathology and heredity; and the English translation of Charles Fere's *Sexual Degeneration in Mankind and in Animals* (1932). Amid the flurry of scientific theory, Djuna Barnes, an American expatriate, journalist, and prominent participant in Parisian salon culture, wrote a letter to her longtime friend and unofficial editor, Emily Coleman. During her revision of *Nightwood*, Barnes experienced doubt concerning the title, which had originally been "La Somnabule": "I still do not think La Somnabule the perfect title—Night Beast would be better except for the debased meaning now put on that nice word beast."[43] This statement attests not only to the cultural climate in which Barnes was writing, a climate that associated perverse sexualities like the ones found in *Vandover* with animality, but also to her apparent disavowal of the cultural valences of the term *beast*, which she wishes to recuperate as a "nice word." It also suggests the centrality of *Nightwood*'s final scene, in which Robin "goes down" and devolves into a nonhuman, beastlike creature.[44]

Nightwood is a splintered, hallucinatory tale of an assemblage of degenerates of multiple nationalities, sexualities, and genders who come together to restlessly celebrate the decay of the modern. These characters couple with one another in degenerate solidarity amid the confusion and chaos of the stultifying and nocturnal landscapes of bourgeois modernity. Such a decidedly modernist text may make a strange bedfellow for Frank Norris's naturalism in *Vandover*, because modernism's heterogeneous style, refusal of narrative continuity, and antirepresentational politics are usually understood to be at odds with naturalism's fascination with "technological and biological ways of making persons."[45] As Andreas Huyssen points out, modernism "constituted itself through a conscious strategy of exclusion," especially from mass culture, literary realism, and naturalism, insisting on "the autonomy of the artwork."[46] This "absolute break" from literary tradition perhaps informs T. S. Eliot's insistence, in his introduction to *Nightwood*, that

Barnes's narrative is not "a psychopathic study" but a "great achievement of a style" that expresses "a quality of horror and doom very nearly related to that of an Elizabethan tragedy" (xxvi). For Eliot, *Nightwood* should be read for its modernist style, its vision of "universal" "human misery," and its "classical" themes, not for its reflection on historical and cultural specificities or social concerns, nor for its relationship to the perverse (xv).

Despite Eliot's advisory, Dianne Chisholm, in her perceptive examination of *Nightwood,* attempts to illuminate its investment in obscenity. Following Benjamin's historical materialism, Chisholm places the novel's "erotics of destitution" within the industrial postwar impoverishment of the 1920s and 1930s, and highlights Barnes's use of established modernist literary devices as well as her specific literary practice of "obscene resistance." In characterizing the tactics of and influences on Barnes's narrative style, Chisholm also describes the text's representation of obscenity as a uniquely modernist expression, "laboring in tacit solidarity with its Surrealist contemporaries" and distinctly at odds with a "naturalist presentation."[47] But *Vandover* and *Nightwood* are both in a suggestively similar conversation with the dehumanizing effects of modernization: both take on the aura and the atmosphere of modern decay, and both express perversity through the corporeal ruination of the human. These texts, positioning their main characters down on all fours, and thus producing equivalencies between animality and sexuality, point to a shared project of making social problems identifiable and resolvable in the body that extends beyond the limits of generic convention. Perhaps, then, we should reevaluate critic Theodore Purdy's observation when, in an ironic pastiche of Eliot, he characterizes *Nightwood* in a 1937 review as foregrounding "an atmosphere of decay" that despite its "Elizabethan pretensions stems from the fin-de-siècle."[48]

In particular, *Nightwood* relies on, even as it perverts, medical and evolutionary tropes to characterize sexual alterity. Although informed by a conception of the mannish lesbian that Smith-Rosenberg has described as a "sexually atavistic and ungovernable woman, associated with 1920s bar culture,"[49] Barnes's novel, like her investment in a "nice word" like "beast," also problematizes medical representations of sexual identity. In fact, Barnes takes much pleasure in ironically redeploying early twentieth-century sexual theories, sometimes through a series of hilarious gender inversions: Hedvig Volkbein has "great strength and

military beauty," while her husband, Guido, is a "gourmet and a dandy";
Robin Vote dresses in "boy's trousers"; and trapeze artist Frau Mann—
or Mrs. Man—appears to have no sex at all, or both: she is "muscular,"
"slight and compact," and "as unsexed as a doll" (1, 169, 12–13). Likewise, Dr. Matthew O'Connor carries in his heart "the wish for children
and knitting" and "never asked better than to boil some good man's
potatoes and toss up a child for him every nine months by the calendar" (91). *Nightwood*'s portrait of the "third sex" assimilates the scientific terminology by which an inverse relationship to gender signals
(homo)sexual identity (148). Sexual inverts, Dr. O'Connor explains,
are "neither one and half the other" (136). Although Barnes incorporates sexological discourse into her narrative, she does so with a twist:
she ironically and humorously reformulates such conceptions of sexuality into hyperbolic accounts of the self that are deliberately "profane," "debased," and "splendid" (142, 42, 11), determined as she is
"to never use the derogatory in the usual sense" (116).[50] In other words,
Nightwood willfully reimagines the terms of sexual inversion at the same
time that, like *Vandover*, it redeploys them in yet another degeneration
narrative.

   Nightwood provides particularly rich terrain for an exploration of
the contradictory narratives inspired by degeneration theory, both in
Robin's decline to a lower order of humanity and in the expertise of
the text's doctor-in-residence, Matthew O'Connor, who professes "an
interest in gynaecology" (14). Robin, as we shall see, carries out the
narrative's investigation of sexual forms and desires, but Dr. O'Connor
is always at hand to diagnose them. O'Connor is an eclectic authority,
"a doctor and a collector and a talker of Latin, and a sort of pteropus
of the twilight and a physiognomist that can't be flustered by the
wrong feature on the right face" (92). In fact, it is primarily and sometimes solely through Dr. O'Connor that the characters of the novel
obtain sexual knowledge and understanding, for they each go to him
"to learn of degradation and the night" (161). His near omnipresence and his readiness to provide insight into other characters' (and
his own) sexual behavior emphasize that the transmission of medical
knowledge depends on a master narrator in and through which sexual norms can be articulated and given cultural coherence. Yet if the
"pile of medical books . . . water-stained and covered with dust" or the
"rusty pair of forceps" and "broken scalpel" that litter his room are
any indication of the accuracy of the medical knowledge he wields so

freely (78), his diagnoses seem more like deranged pontifications than medical insights, warped as much by rusty science as by his own sexual degeneracy.

The same "appallingly degraded" room is glutted with "feminine finery" that "gave the impression [that they] had suffered venery," in the midst of which sits the good doctor himself in a woman's flannel nightgown and a wig "of long pendant curls" (79). Indeed, the description of the doctor resides within the terms of sexual science; his "venery" is what one nineteenth-century physician characterized as an "illegitimate perversion," which is "subversive and degrading" and can cause "hereditary weakness."[51] The doctor's room, strewn with revealing bits of medical effluvium, "each object . . . battling its own compression," microcosmically aligns with Barnes's image of modernity (79). The confused and layered characterization of the doctor's sexual proclivities and appearances, like the clutter of his room "brimming with abominations" (79), emblematizes the fragmentary, "abominable" sexual economy that describes and determines the novel's social world and its characters, who move, love, and suffer within it: the "dabblers in black magic and medicine" and the "sailors and medical men" (50, 87). The novel, then, points to a theory of sexuality that *Vandover* has already begun to suggest. *Nightwood*'s conversation with the pathologizing models of sexology does not reproduce a paralyzing binary between normal and abnormal, heterosexual and homosexual; rather, it characterizes a world in a state of ruination for which there is no "outside." Here, everyone is degenerate. In place of the static definitions of sexology in which sexual meanings become fixed as a physical set of signs, and in which gender and sexuality are conflated to make sexual practice readable, *Nightwood* offers several different modes for the expression and representation of sexual desire that, in the end, all emphasize mobility. Robin, we are told, "took to wandering" (48).

Homelessness

Robin, then, is partially informed by the medical diagnoses that Barnes's narrative incorporates. In describing her as an "invert" and "an infected carrier of the past," Barnes places her within the discourse of atavism (136, 37). Robin is not just perverse; she is perverse because contaminated by the past, which returns in her as a lethal kind of affection, threatening to spread impure and archaic traumas, memories, and ecstasies with her every move. She menaces the privatized individual, predicated on notions of temporal separation and personal autonomy, through her ceaseless replaying of a time already lost and her rupturing of a notion of modernity as domestic rootedness. Her persistent and nomadic desire, her investments in libido and loss, connection and solitude, and her promiscuous couplings ensure that her character is always in flux, changing along with the sexual and spatial shifts she enacts. Through Robin, *Nightwood* advances a concept of homelessness to expand the routes and journeys of Eros, forging an affinity to shameless desire radically distinct from the stasis of a sexuality grounded in the idea of the home and the modern family. I will turn in a moment to discuss the novel's atavistic bodies, which closely connect *Nightwood* to *Vandover.* But because Barnes eschews the heterosexualizing, reproductive couple form for a compulsive wandering of the individual, a digression on the concept of homelessness may help to articulate more precisely the semiotic and rhetorical function of the atavistic body in Barnes's degeneration narrative.

Although the world of Parisian nightlife, well known in the 1930s for its lesbian milieu, is a primary locale in *Nightwood,* its characters are nonetheless perpetually dislocated as they engage in a frenzied peripatetic mode determined by Robin's sexual adventures. Robin's marriage to Felix Volkbein lands her in Vienna; her love affair with Nora Flood leads her through Paris and the United States, then on a brief European tour; and her affair with Jenny Pretherbridge takes her back to Paris and then to the United States again, where Robin is finally reunited with Nora in the decaying chapel. These travels not only make the reader dizzy, they also enact a refusal of national definition and the structured identity that such definition would provide. Robin, Felix, Nora, and Jenny ceaselessly wander through social, geographical, and gendered territories, denying the inevitability of the enforced meanings of each. The novel favors instead the partiality of the domains that a degenerate and degenerating landscape allow. And because Robin engages in multiple relationships, because her very desire is mediated by the proliferation of sexual couplings, the novel seems more invested in libido as such than in object choice.[52]

One way that Robin's homeless meanderings may be understood, then, is as a series of deformations, uncoupling desire from object choice, dislocating identity from the time and space by which it is usually bound, and offering up instead a multiplicity of dialectical images and meanings, what Susan Lanser has called Barnes's "maxims of uncertain intent."[53] When Nora confesses to Matthew O'Connor that "the night does something to a person's identity, even when asleep," she gives us a little insight into these deformations. The night destabilizes the comfortable knowledge produced by the day about the visible signs of identity, in which "it's the face that you tell by" (81, 92). In the wood at night, everything changes: "The face is what anglers catch in the daylight, but the sea is the night!" (93). The night transposes identity, changes it, and renders it strange. It despatializes the structures through which identity forms and signifies. The dreamscapes the night affords, as Dr. O'Connor explains them, always occur "in a house without an address, in a street in no town, citizened with people with no names with which to deny them" (88). The night designates both an atemporality and an aspatiality in which categorization cannot maintain social order, thus leaving the citizen-subject free from notions of sexual civility, for when "given an eternal incognito, a thumbprint nowhere set against our souls," "we cease to accuse ourselves" and instead commit "all abominations" (88). Robin flees into the night in an unremitting quest to escape the monogamy of couplehood and persistently attempts to multiply her desires.

By contrast, the domestic spaces in *Nightwood* house and petrify the relics that come to signify "love" in the novel. The couple as a social form, which threatens to harness Robin to a stable life, thrives within a domestic zone devoted to memory and memorabilia. Although *Nightwood* is laced with spatial tropes from the circus to the chapel, it focuses particularly on the museum. Just as Robin is rendered a "fossil" in Nora's heart through the domestication of their relationship, so their home becomes "the museum of their encounter," where only collected objects come to embody their life together (56): "[E]very item in the house . . . attested to their mutual love. There were circus chairs, wooden horses bought from a ring on an old merry-go-round, stage drops from Munich, cherubim from Vienna, ecclesiastical hangings from Rome, a spinet from England" (55). If their travels across Europe and America upset and cross geographical and sexual boundaries, and thus expand the definitions of national and sexual subjectivity that those boundaries mean to contain, in their home, these journeys become memorialized as collectors' items that come to bear the definitional burden of stability the couple form requires. The trope of the museum throws into critical relief the spatial perimeters the couple form establishes and the fixity of sexual identity it denotes. Inside the domestic interiors of the museum, love becomes instantly dead, frozen, and past, memorialized through the objects that couples collect to support a fantasy of stability. Barnes, however, does not highlight the interiors of romantic love simply to critique (heterosexualizing) domestic norms. These interiors figure prominently in the novel as part of its cataloging of modernity's many atavisms. They are spaces that function to keep the past alive and thus expose the past as irretrievably dead; they distill with confused clarity the decomposition and recomposition of the modern: its "ruined gardens," "*detraqués*," and "paupers" (52). These emotionally overwrought interiors and the obsolete objects they house are contiguous with the larger landscape of an indolent and cumulative modernity, archives of a recurrent past.

But the novel just as insistently catalogs the perverse energies and animations of the modern, "its beauties and its deformities" (85). To this end, Robin's travels across space and through a series of relationships show the migratory nature of the subject and its perverse dislocatedness. An unpredictable being whose identity is mobile and as temporary as her relationships, she resists the determining descriptions of the science–culture dichotomy by ensuring that avenues for desire remain polyamorous and continuously shifting: "[h]er thoughts were in themselves a form of locomotion" (59). Refusing to produce coherence for the reader, she travels through a series of scenes, each of which reveals another problem, another degeneracy, another agony, the accumulation of which forces the reader into a diagnostic position. Of course, such a position proves impossible. The explanations for sexual identity that set up a fixed relationship between the body (and how it signifies) and gender (and its designation of whom one should desire) are loosened at the joints as Robin refuses to be tied down to a home, let alone a sexuality. If she produces a sense of loss and betrayal in her lovers as she leaves them all behind, it is at the service of disrupting comfortable and naturalized assumptions of couplehood, romantic permanence, and heterosexual life narratives on which both the modern family and social order are founded. *Nightwood* makes visible a model of sexual personhood that is constitutively homeless, irrational, and always moving. The novel shows its readers the places Eros may travel, how it may migrate and mutate in a stroll through the wood at night.

The centrality of Nora's love for Robin in the novel, and Barnes's own affair with Thelma Wood that this fictive relationship supposedly indexes, has led many contemporary readers and critics to claim that the novel is primarily about lesbianism.[54] But Robin's endless migrations, as I have been arguing, frustrate identitarian notions of sexuality, opening up the narrative to a range of erotic possibilities. *Nightwood* places less emphasis on the relationship between Nora and Robin than on the various relationships that intermingle throughout its pages. Barnes's text spotlights spaces of nocturnal addiction, intoxication, and circus revelry through which her characters circulate, bringing Felix Volkbein's closeted Jewish identity, Nora's lesbianism, Robin's sexual flexibility, Dr. O'Connor's transvestitic homosexuality, and the circus performers' "splendid and reeking falsification" into alignment as they all linger in the excremental dialogue, melancholic irrationality, and destitution of sexual modernity that both the city and the wood at night come to symbolize (11).

Nice Beasts

This narrative alignment chiefly occurs through the bestialization of most of the characters of *Nightwood*. The circus performers are all "cheap cuts from the beast life" (11), much like Robin, who is "beast turning human" (37); Dr. O'Connor, who carries his hands "like a dog who is walking on his hind legs" (32); Felix, who bows down to royalty "as an animal will turn his head away from a human" (123); and Nora, who is both "savage and refined" (50). All the characters who populate this unstructured landscape are figured as sexual subjects in a state of bestial devolution, "going down face foremost, drinking the waters of night at the water hole of the damned" like "an angel on all fours" (97). Most of Barnes's characters "go down," as even her chapter titles indicate: "Bow down," "The Squatter," and "Go down, Matthew." The repetition of the decree to "go down" invokes an erotic or (homo)sexual vernacular (although fellatio, defecation, courtliness, and prayer are all brought into suggestive proximity here) and acts as a prophetic metaphor for the fate of the characters of the novel, who all go down the scale of humanity and revert to some animal form. Indeed, the bestial comes to constitute one of the primary ways in which the bodies in *Nightwood* are visualized and positioned as deviant, and deviantly sexual, open and prostrate on all fours in a position of penetration (and excretion, holiness, and respect). If the bestial is the most clarifying index to what degenerationism seeks to police, the ironic reappropriation of this theme in *Nightwood* constitutes a very different kind of imaginary. It layers its representational economy with bodies that are not so much subversive as they are dialectical: vulgar and sentimental, "obscene and touching," public and private. These bodies are beasts "on all fours" and also like "angels," both "damned" and "sacred" (142), in a state of spiritual ascension as much as in a position of human-to-animal collapse.

Barnes demonstrates her enchantment with the animal most dramatically at the circus, which she imagines as a space brimming with perverse solidarity. It is here that the lonely Felix manages to reinvent himself, for the circus "linked his emotions to the higher and unattainable pageantry of kings and queens." Just as the rest of the circus members "seized on titles for a purpose," he too "clung to his title to dazzle his own estrangement," and it is this act that "brought them together." The circus recognizes identity as a self-selecting performance, inspiring its members to adopt false names and titles, from "Princess Nadja" to "Baron von Tink" (11). But the circus members also seem aware that their performance is in a sense real, or rather that there is no other reality aside from their own invention. This realization is echoed in the portraits of Felix's grandparents, which are really "reproductions of two intrepid and ancient actors," and in Frau Mann's leotard, which "was no longer a covering, [but] was herself" (7, 13).

Thus the masquerade of the circus, like the night's redescriptive power, does more than simply reverse one knowledge for another, as in the practices of inversion Mikhail Bakhtin describes in his analysis of Rabelasian celebration and medieval carnival. For Bakhtin, the medieval carnival's strength arose out of its place in class culture: a transgressive space, nonetheless acknowledged and permitted by the law, through which the resentments of class hatred could be acted out in ritual and metaphor.[55] One can see why both Bonnie Kime Scott and Jane Marcus have called Barnes's narrative worlds "liminal" in Bakhtin's sense, existing somewhere between time and space, the real and the imaginary.[56] Carnival glories in the lower parts of the body and bodily functions and inverts the normal experience of everyday life, celebrating pleasure and excess, debauchery and sex. But the liminal spaces that the carnival produces allow injustice to be represented in a period of controlled disorder that can easily be reversed back into order at the end of the day. *Nightwood*'s characters, by contrast, do not masquerade within a fixed set of temporal and spatial parameters; nor are their performances ever recontained. The wood at night, which refers both to the American woodland and to the Parisian urban terrain, is a continuous space for which there is no outside, either linguistically or materially.

Nightwood expresses this vision through the discursive excesses of its wayward plot: through Robin's unfocused prowling, the "decaying brocades" of the circus, and the repeated trope of the human–beast hybrid (11), which displays on the body the range of incoherences that constitute modernity. That trope also registers and obscures an unsettling relationship to the "debased meaning" of the word *beast* that Barnes means to reconfigure. For although there may be no outside to the social world that *Nightwood* scripts, there is an outside to Barnes's text. Her fantasies of the primitive, bestialized embodiments and affiliations that take place in the novel depend on a scientific conception of racial atavism as a vehicle for her complex series of alignments.

As Stephen Jay Gould, Sander Gilman, and Nancy Stepan have all argued in their carefully historicized accounts of the human sciences, nineteenth-century racial science constructed a visual link between nonwhite populations and lower animal forms in order to legitimate claims that certain races were less evolved than others. Louis Aggassiz, for example, in an 1850s study of human types, used a pictorial chart comparing the heads and skulls of different races to animals to demonstrate his theory of polygenesis, or the idea that the various human races were separate species and that nonwhite species formed an inferior group. Disturbing racist claims such as this one located the potential for Darwinian reversal in the body of the racial other.

The racial logic of degeneration theory coincides suggestively with Barnes's deployment of atavism in *Nightwood*. Felix's "impermissible blood" and his son "born to holy decay" (3, 107), Jenny's imperialist fancy for "tiny ivory or jade elephants" (65), and the startling reference to "Nikka, the nigger who used to fight the bear in the *Cirque de Paris*" (16) all constitute the narrative's uneven and fetishistic racial logic, providing a key to the corporeal rendering of its characters in perpetual states of decline. As with the diseased "little Jew" in *Vandover,* and much like the Wolf Man in Freud's case study, who "screams like a savage," Felix Volkbein poignantly registers the text's racial economy. Felix and his father, Guido, are ashamed of their heritage and struggle to hide their Jewishness by producing a false family history. They "adopted the sign of the cross" and claimed to be "Austrian of an old, almost extinct line" with a fake "coat of arms" to prove it (3). Like Felix, Nikka focuses this discussion: "There he was, crouching all over the arena without a stitch on, except an ill-concealed loin-cloth all abulge as if with a deep-sea catch, tattooed from head to heel with all the *ameublement* of depravity! Garlanded with rosebuds and hackwork of the devil—was he a sight to see!" (16). The weirdly exclamatory description of Nikka aligns with representations of the primitive African with which modernist art was so fascinated, from Rousseau to Gaugin. Hyperprimitivized ("crouching" in a "loin-cloth"), hypersexualized ("all abulge"), and hyperembodied ("a sight to see"), Nikka's overdetermining descriptive frames suggest something about the racial inflections of the other characters' perverse embodiments. We might recall, again, Vandover's gaze into the eyes of the diseased "little Jew" that transfixes and contaminates him and, even more, confirms his own state of degeneracy. The sexually perverse embodiments in *Nightwood* can be similarly understood as racially marked, reminding us that twentieth-century conceptions of sexual degeneracy, promiscuity, and desire surfaced out of a racial and racializing context that shaped and disfigured the body according to its logic. *Nightwood*'s particular relationship to this racial context is a difficult one, for if we are to take the word *beast* as a "nice one," as Barnes hoped we would, then we must also respond with irony to the racial inflections harnessed to this word. If we are to share in Barnes's investment in this "nice word beast," in fact, then we may well also need to acknowledge the potency of atavistic subjectivity in which her characters thrive.

Becoming Animal

In the novel's closing pages, after a long separation from her anguished lover, Nora Flood finds Robin Vote at the decaying chapel. But this is no happy reunion in any typical heteronarrative sense. When Nora sees Robin in the chapel, she falls to the ground: "her body struck the wood" at the same moment that Robin herself "began going down," barking on all fours alongside Nora's dog (169). Desire and love reunited is dramatized as a shattering experience, a destabilizing event that brings Robin to her knees and leaves Nora's dog with "his paws trembling under the trembling of his rump" (169). This canine reunion is marked by both sexual excitement, as the dog's tongue becomes "a stiff curving terror in his mouth," and sexual antagonism, which Robin emblematizes: "she who has eaten death" (170, 37). Barnes offers us a sexual aesthetic akin to what Leo Bersani has called the "pleasurable unpleasurable tension" that occurs when the self is disturbed in excess.[57] Robin, for example, possesses an "insane passion for unmitigated anguish," and Nora professes: "There's something evil in me that loves evil and degradation" (75, 135). The irrational, nonrelational activity that Bersani calls "sex" happens for Nora and Robin when their ultimate encounter is mediated by a dog; they are subsumed into and by the wood at night. In this ever-present landscape of sexual modernity, one "strikes wood"; the other begins to bark; they both become animal.[58]

Djuna Barnes, sketch from *The Book of Repulsive Women* (1914).

Nora, Robin, and the dog in this scene become bound up in a hybrid relation in which an endless set of couplings converges: something "obscene" and something "touching," something "sacred" (like the chapel) and something "decaying" (like the chapel), something human and something bestial, something utopian (like a reunion) and something dystopic (like a reunion). If the codification of sexual desire as atavistic typically characterizes the degeneration narrative, *Nightwood*'s inheritance of this codification rewrites sexological narratives as a conjunctural hybridity exemplified by both this hybrid body and Barnes's hybrid text.[59] Although her narrative is animated by the images and hypotheses of degeneration theory, it recodes them from within, poaching its terms for its own meaning productions. But again, this is not an uncomplicated refunctioning. Through its bestialization, the body becomes increasingly visible as an embodiment of sexual desire and a racialized body at once.

This moment of "becoming animal," however, also ironizes the relations between woman and animal, pervert and beast, raciality and primitivism, reformulating these terms into an unpredictable combination capable of transforming what each one means. To critique the essentializing tendencies of cultural representations of identity, Homi Bhabha argues that these constructions are always contradicted because they create an "interstitial intimacy" and thus an outcome that is "somehow beyond control." For Bhabha, this hybrid intersection, "linked through an 'in-between' temporality," is a way in which the identity form becomes fundamentally challenged, rather than inadvertently reified: "This is the moment of aesthetic distance that provides the narrative with a double edge . . . a hybridity, a difference 'within,' a subject that inhabits the rim of an 'in between' reality."[60]

When Robin "becomes an animal" in the novel's closing pages, she not only imitates or reproduces a primitive form, she also expresses the kind of in-between relation that Bhabha denotes. Along with the circus and its "unattainable pageantry of kings and queens" (11), "becoming animal" represents a sexual subjectivity equally unattainable, a practice of farce, pageantry, fallacy, and loss that takes place in the intimate interstices between the real and the performance of the real, between the flaps of the nature–culture, sex–gender binary, and through a series of spaces in which the characters of *Nightwood* gather and meet in nocturnal, degenerate, and wretched festivity.

Narrative Persuasions

Vandover and the Brute and *Nightwood* both engage a narrative and theory of atavism; both articulate modes of sexual personhood within a
scientific apparatus that stresses collaboration between the hypervisi-
ble (Robin and Vandover down on all fours) and the excessively nar-
ratable (the process of naming, classifying, and overdetermining that
lines up different people along an axis of meaning and places some
within a regressive "story"). In many respects, as in medical photography, this collaboration serves to construct and congeal a narrative
of subject formation within hegemonic perspectives. As each novel
shows us, however, from such epistemological efforts arises the potential for transformative energies that do not necessarily reverse the taxonomic violence of scientific rhetoric but that may have the capacity
to mobilize and rechannel its effects. In these novels, the degeneration
narrative, rather than resulting in the closure of the conventional heterosexual love plot, results in the regression of an individual to an
atavistic state. As we witnessed in Freud's case study "The Wolf Man,"
the degeneration narrative regresses as it progresses. As the narrative
increasingly sinks into the excess of its own interpretative frames, the
bestialized and otherwise degraded body emerges to reconsolidate and
realign meanings. Whereas *Vandover* produces a degenerate body so
multiply determined there is no way of tracing an etiology of sexual
practice, *Nightwood* imagines a sexual subjectivity that is itinerant and
homeless, as well as capable of exquisite sexual shattering. In both novels, the sexual degenerate is not compared to a more "healthy" social
form but circulates through the ever-deteriorating landscape of bourgeois modernity.

   Although both texts incorporate and deploy scientific theories to
organize their narratives and their characters' perverse meanderings,
in doing so, they express an etiological multiplicity that withstands the
logos of sexual science. With each embodiment and narrativization
of bestial perversity, sexual science is refunctioned in very different
accounts of the journeys of sexual personhood. This does not mean
we can lapse into some easy celebration of the possibility of resistance
in art. These narratives do provide examples, however, of artistic practices that can act in the service of new forms of subjectivity, putting
pressure on the boundaries of scientific rationality. Locating representations and productions of sexual perversity in texts such as these,

moreover, may well recontextualize the history of scientific sexuality, as well as offer up a history of contested, contingent, and contradictory narration in its place, one that poses a challenge to the unproductive oppositions between science and culture, structure and agency, essentialism and constructivism. Such a practice of reading history contributes to a project of rethinking how sexual meanings and perverse bodies come into formation—in what ways, in which stories, and in what positions.

In his rejection of scientific anthropology, Georges Bataille, Barnes's contemporary, embraces a perverse counterrevolutionary myth by which nature "transforms itself in a vertiginous fall in celestial space, accompanied by a horrible cry" and thus "burie[s] existence in the stench of the night."[61] We might understand Bataille's meaning to coincide with the hallucinatory pain and perpetual degeneration of the modern that the narratives I have discussed here describe. As Dr. Matthew O'Connor "goes down" on all fours, he too predicts just such a fall: "Now, the end . . . now nothing but wrath and weeping" (166)—to which Vandover responds in the distance, "Wolf—wolf."

4. Atavistic Time

Tarzan, Dr. Fu Manchu, and the Serial Dime Novel

Someday we will realize that the prime duty, the inescapable duty, of the good citizen of the right type is to leave his or her blood behind him in the world.
—Theodore Roosevelt

America must be kept American. Biological laws show that Nordics deteriorate when mixed with other races.
—Calvin Coolidge

There is no knowledge of the Other . . . that is not also a temporal act.
—Johannes Fabian

OUR EXPERIENCE of everyday life is always an experience of time: hours, days, months, dates, schedules, but also habits, rituals, memories. What Kath Weston has called the "time claims" of our world-historical moment dictate, in part, our sense of self, and our own sense of time shapes those claims in turn.[1] We act on time, and time acts on us. In Freud's case studies, discussed in chapter 1, this temporal function takes the form of a psychic recurrence whereby childhood trauma expresses itself as delayed consciousness, requiring a period of latency before its eventual return. For Freud, the return of the repressed makes possible a cleansing that allows for the elaboration of personal consciousness. But time also intensifies rather than lessens the trauma of the initial event as the return sets in motion the means of displacement that the trauma originally necessitated. Freud understands this temporal cycle as the primary motor of the development of the self and, therefore, of the social world. Reading the past of the individual as commensurate with the evolutionary past, he stresses that the progress of modern civilization depends on, and is in fact constituted by, an endless series of repressions, regressions, and returns. This double past drives the modern subject: only as a subject of the past can one be a subject of the present, a subject in and of time.[2] In Freud, the past–present of the subject materializes in the form of an animal: the dream of the wolves, the parents down on all fours, the Wolf Man himself. By embedding overlapping individual and prehistorical pasts in a temporal continuum, the animalized human body becomes at once the end point of a (perhaps failed) evolutionary trajectory—an atavism— and a rupture of the "master narratives" of the modern that dictate a more complete separation of temporal spheres.

Several major theorists have analyzed how modernity itself is all about time conceived as modern: time as progress, time as modernization, linear time, clock time. Part of the project of modernity, as Habermas has it, was an effort on the part of Enlightenment thinkers to characterize the central modes of rational thought and social organization as marks of temporal progression.[3] Enlightenment thought not only embraced the idea of progress, but, as David Harvey contends, "actively sought that break with history and tradition which modernity espouses."[4] The new economy of consumption at the fin de siècle, funded by Fordist organizational and technological innovations, was in many respects a fundamental expression of the project of modernity as Harvey describes it. The guiding principle of Fordism, Harvey continues, that mass production would lead to mass consumption, also fostered a new way for people to experience the world. Thus Miriam Hansen argues via her reading of Benjamin, "The impact of the industrially altered environment on the human sensorium" has resulted in nothing less than an "epochal restructuring of subjectivity and collectivity."[5] And as Adorno and Horkheimer famously contend, the penetration of mass culture into everyday life became a mode through which ideas and beliefs could be made popular, a way in which the personal and private realm could be accessed and managed. Indeed, Adorno suggests that forms of popular culture are media actively participating in the organization of social life.[6]

As a way to negotiate and explore these historical and affective changes, this chapter takes as its focus the serial dime novel, which emerged as one of the results of the new capabilities of mass-mediated modernity. I focus on two of the most popular dime novel series in the United States during this period: Edgar Rice Burroughs's Tarzan series (1912–47) and Sax Rohmer's Dr. Fu Manchu series (1913–49). The former features Tarzan, the ape-man, swinging through the African jungle and into the lives of his young boy readership; the latter, Dr. Fu

Manchu, one of the most virulent fictional embodiments of the "yellow peril" in the first half of the twentieth century. I argue that serial dime novels emerged as an incorporation and dissemination of the ideology of modern time, and I define this ideology in two ways: as a principle of continuation that mass production encouraged, and as a structure of epistemic familialism requiring reproduction as its active principle. The former definition may seem more obvious than the latter: it is not much of a stretch to see how serial dime novels are themselves both products and enactments of the conception of modern time as something progressive and progressing; nor is it difficult to place them within the celebratory matrix of mass production. But this chapter will argue that the structure of modern temporality was also entangled with the idea of biological reproduction, and that this entanglement lent itself quite readily to the serial form. I thus turn to the serial dime novel in order to think through how cultural forms emerging as a result of mass production enabled new categories and formats of storytelling that worked to produce equally new meanings about life, identity, and being in time.[7]

In the Tarzan and Fu Manchu serials, we can observe the interchange between the two primary aspects of the ideology of modern time. First, as an instantiation of the new capabilities of mass-mediated modernity, serial dime novels formally and structurally engaged the capitalist embrace of technical reproduction.[8] Second, linking up with the new technological capacity for infinite serialization, plots followed suit by taking place over episodes and over generations. Accordingly, both the Tarzan and Fu Manchu series unfold by way of the growth of their families. Shoring up the concomitance of this doubled ideology, each series features what I call the "reproductive issue," an issue dedicated to the birth of Tarzan's son in one series and Fu Manchu's daughter in the other, and the "return issue," which highlights the heroic or sinister return of the main character after a brief hiatus (in Africa or China, as the case may be). In one, the past always returns; in the other, the future is assured. Each prolongs the life of its characters and therefore the life of the series. By guaranteeing a revisitation (of the main character) or remanifestation (in the hero's or villain's progeny), the serial novel, like the mass commodity, promises to be both the same and different, new but familiar. This demonstrates how ideologies of production in the marketplace and ideologies of reproduction in the family were wrapped up in a mutually interested cultural project central to the imaginings of American modernity.

The technology that made books a mass medium was the large-scale production of cheap paperbacks. Book publishing, increasingly attempting to appeal to larger audiences and to establish a market niche within national mass culture, undertook its own practices of rationalization and production. The efforts of book publishers to increase sales also brought the production of the book into greater conformity with the workings of the modern culture industry and its marketing strategies: As Richard Ohman outlines, book publishers "acquired their own staffs of traveling salesmen . . . greatly increased the amount and the flamboyance of their advertising . . . [and] began to shape their product and create its market."[9] In addition, many paperback publishers relied on the already existing magazine distribution network, offering their wares in public venues such as train stations and newspaper stands. Similarly, to reach a wider market, book clubs relied on the postal service that an expanding railway system helped make more efficient and reliable.[10]

Thriving equally on these distribution strategies and on technical reproduction in general, serial dime novels ran over long periods—years, even decades. Their ongoing structure required a suspension of closure, for the end of each novel in the series gestured toward another adventure to come and offered to its readers the promise of an ever-increasing payoff of more excitement and pleasure than before. Keeping characters and story lines alive disallowed the possibility of an end or limit to the story. Serial novels thus ensured their marketability by ensuring their limitlessness, creating the reading experience as a practice of time, as something that must necessarily occur *over* time. Of course, this is true of any act of reading, but the serial novel extends the time of reading even farther into the future. Indeed, the structure and form of the serial dime novel emerged out of a principle of continuation that mass production encouraged. "The Return" issue, for this reason, is a staple of the genre, "I'll be back" the sine qua non of its articulation.[11] Serial dime novels, in this sense, are not a "timeless" form, as many have argued; that is, they are not fantastical tales transported out of the real to another place and time. Rather, they are timeful: they extend the life of a story to a viable eternity.

Therefore, the time of the serial novel is in part linear time, the time of (modern) progress, with one story appearing after another in a chain of succession and renewal. Deferring ends and outcomes to some future moment, serial novels play out in their pages the consumerist logic that there is always something more, something beyond, something just out of reach. But serial novels also repeat: their characters disappear in the distance, elude capture, and return, each time remanifesting themselves in greater acts of heroism, more sinister threats of cultural devastation, or by way of a new family addition. As a genre of repetition, the serial novel is also an expression of cyclical time, the time of recurrence. The serial novel instantiates as a generic convention an unavoidable reproduction of and return to its own past.[12] Serial dime novels are thus doubly temporal forms. Animated by the processes of perpetual arrival and transformation, they function as expressions of modern capitalist time, but they do so only insofar as they articulate that mode of time as a dialectic between progress and regress, linearity and recursivity.

The Tarzan and Fu Manchu series, which are exemplary instances of the serial dime novel, also have an exemplary status when it comes to the participatory forces and mass mediations of the experience of modern time in U.S. culture during the first half of the twentieth century. In the Tarzan series, the hybrid ape-man's body, centrally positioned in the African jungle, is bursting with musculature and therefore with imperialist power; in the Fu Manchu series, the bestialized Asian body, lurking in New York City's Chinatown, signifies "the yellow peril incarnate" of the Asian immigrant's perceived threat to the nation. Investigating this fiction, therefore, entails identifying a number of interrelated phenomena, not least of which are the ways it bears a marked relation to modern shifts in modes of literary production and distribution that I have been outlining. In addition, it mandates understanding the ways each series raises questions about how the United States imagined itself at a given time, including how the nation was embodied and from which bodies it perceived itself to be at risk. It is crucial to address these cultural forms not because they reflect their historical moment but because they provide a fuller purchase on newly mediated forms of personhood, predicated equally on mass production and theories of biology concerning the reproducibility of race. The fact that each series so deliberately foregrounds a bestialized figure as its main character points to how the generation of the subjectivity I call atavistic exists at the center of this conversation.

What Time Is It?

In 1918, certain that the United States was at a biological turning point, Charles Burr, professor of mental diseases at the University of Pennsylvania, asked, "What can be done to lessen the number of marriages between defective persons?" Answering his own question, he recommended state intervention: "Confinement for the life of the imbecile, the habitual criminal, with asexualization of a certain group of the insane."[13] A 1926 study entitled *Mongrel Virginians* shared similar concerns. The "specialists in eugenic research" that conducted the study investigated racial intermixture among related families in Virginia in order to support the state's 1924 Racial Integrity Law that required individuals to register their racial status and prohibited interracial marriage. The study concluded that the families they observed were "below average" and "mentally and socially represent[ed] a very crude type of civilization."[14] Earlier, in 1910, Charles Davenport founded the Cold Spring Harbor Eugenics Record Office, dedicated to compiling hereditary data and reducing hereditary disease in the United States. The Record Office soon after emerged as a central source for national policy making, particularly in connection with immigration acts. Harry H. Laughlin, Davenport's appointee as superintendent of the Record Office and eventually "Expert Eugenical Agent" to the House Committee on Immigration and Naturalization, was often called on to report his office's findings before Congress, and at one 1922 meeting, he covered the walls with charts, tables, and a gallery of Ellis Island photographs labeled "Carriers of the Germ Plasm of the Future American Population."[15]

In 1924, the Emergency Immigration Act was ratified by President Calvin Coolidge, who justified its passing with a racial logic previously made popular by Teddy Roosevelt. Coolidge made his stance on immigration clear when he announced in a public statement: "America must be kept American. Biological laws show that Nordics deteriorate when mixed with other races."[16] Such a statement follows on the heels of Roosevelt's infamous embrace of an imperialist policy of national and biological regeneration, as when he commented that "someday we will realize that the prime duty, the inescapable duty, of the good citizen of the right type is to leave his or her blood behind him in the world."[17] Roosevelt was basically advocating cross-racial sexual relations (needless to say as a potentially violent form of imperialist conquest, for it could quite easily be read as a sanctioning of rape), while Coolidge rode under a flag of isolationist nationalism. However, the poles of imperialism and isolationism, and therefore of expansion and containment, do not necessarily form an ideological contradiction. Roosevelt and Coolidge straddled two sides of the same agenda: they each understood national progress in terms of a racially based conflict through which they believed civilization survived or perished.[18] This belief led Roosevelt to embrace U.S. imperialism as a guarantee for national prosperity and culminated in his vision of Anglo-Saxon purity and masculine strenuousness. It later led to Coolidge's support of draconian immigration policies that were set up to protect the nation from "racial decadence."[19]

Roosevelt's and Coolidge's policies were drafted during a period of broad economic transition and technological advance characteristic of the urban-centric process of modernization in the late nineteenth and early twentieth centuries. In a world transfigured by modern technologies and events, for many, the body seemed intensely vulnerable to "exhaustion," "nervousness," and atavistic decline. As I have argued in previous chapters, the literary trope of atavism emerged as a potent incarnation of these cultural anxieties, for it served both to organize and to trouble contemporary understandings of the nature of human identity. I have also suggested that the concept of human identity that this trope generated was not equivalent to constructing a simple binary between two oppositional bodies or temporalities (human/savage or present/past). Rather, atavism fashioned an ambivalent subject, a subject produced by the convergence of bodies and times.

In the political arena, this temporally hybrid subject threatened the foundations of a nation-state dependent on clear-cut notions of progress and purity. In reaction to such a threat, Roosevelt and Coolidge based their policies of imperialism and isolationism on (pseudo)scientific notions of reproductivity similar to those informing the studies on and ordinances against interracial marriage and other "defective" couplings. The ideology of reproduction most powerfully took the form of a biological imperative that positioned women, as mothers, as the central site for the production of national health. It also required that legislative acts on state and federal levels become part of the juridical method to curb the unfettered reproduction of "unfit" generations. "Healthy" reproductive yields, by contrast, were encouraged as the primary means for national progress and imperial expansion. For these reasons, reproduction was not just a social or biological imperative, but also a temporal category that linked biological time with the time of the nation.

The belief in linear progress and rational planning by way of Taylorist and Fordist models of production lent itself quite readily to understandings of the social and temporal function of human reproduction as dictated by Roosevelt and Coolidge. Just as the process of labor was broken down into rationalized operations such that the final product could be reduced to a series of mechanical repetitions, the mechanization of reproductive labor afforded the possibility of rationalized, and thus more efficient, kinship units. At the fin de siècle, such mechanization took the form of the science of eugenics, a specialized theory of the optimal production of human being for an ideal social order.[20] The goal, of course, was to yield over time the most efficient product for the reproduction of the nation. Although ultimately indefensible in practice, the initial effects of the eugenics movement were vast, including the forced sterilization of at least 20,000 women between the years 1927 and 1930 (following the 1927 Supreme Court ruling that permitted the practice) and the drafting of the policies on immigration and miscegenation discussed above. Male and female reproductive bodies were seen as a function of time: the healthy body of the future, the unhealthy body of the past.

The modern process that Bruno Latour describes (the repudiation of hybrids and thus their inevitable proliferation) helps illuminate some key aspects of the eugenics movement and the government policies attempting to manage reproductivity on the national level.[21] Modern thinking, Latour claims, celebrates the distinction and an ability to distinguish between natural and social phenomena, denigrating those figured as incapable of making such distinctions as "premodern." In theory, this produces two distinct spheres: nature and culture, human and nonhuman. In practice, however, these spheres are not so easily separated, but are fundamentally intertwined. We don't live in a world of strict opposition; we live in a world of mixture, a network of associations of subjects and objects, natures and cultures, and much in between. Everyday life, as we live and practice it, is a mesh of relations, spheres, and time claims informed by and circulating through an amalgamation of materials, spaces, and architectures. This network of associations makes for a multiplication of reality. This is the proliferation of hybrids.[22]

In its own attempts to establish the modern world as something modern, as something progressive and progressing, eugenics sought to manage human life at its reproductive core. And yet, as Latour would have it, accompanying the eugenic management of life was an unavoidable proliferation of the discourse of life in all its combinations. In particular, the eugenics movement inspired a vast literature and an institutional structure for the study of the atavistic body. As a result, the idea and image of atavism flooded the popular sphere. The discourse on atavism thus brings into sharp focus the constitutive hybridity of modern subjectivity. In the atavistic self, we find a nexus of past and present, human and animal, connection and estrangement. The atavistic body, an ineluctable hybrid in the Latourian sense, confirms the hybridity of modernity, for it disallows the modern construction of time as a unity that can be distinguished from a stable, archaic past. As an instantiation of the past's perpetual return, atavism forges a state of hybridity in the present. The modern strategy of contrasting progress with backwardness, a strategy used to organize programs of economic modernization, thus also promotes a view of the modern subject as always potentially an atavistic subject.

In *Rudeness and Civility: Manners in Nineteenth Century Urban America* (1990), John Kasson, like Caroll Smith-Rosenberg in an earlier study, addresses the cultural anxiety that emerged as a result of the increasing hybridization of culture by detailing how the emerging middle class placed an intensified urgency on controlling the body, sexuality, and public habits. In particular, Kasson demonstrates the critical emphasis placed on physical and social hygiene that led to the production of a set of proper public behaviors and private manners in middle-class America. He draws on the work of anthropologist Mary Douglas, who argues that the female body, subjected to pollution rituals in various cultures, could be read as a displaced "image of society," and that this gendered control of the body is actually a symbolic attempt to establish social control. What we learn from both Kasson and Douglas is that at those times when the social body is experienced as chaotic and out of control, the individual body becomes increasingly subject to hygienic scrutiny.[23]

Although for Douglas this scrutiny was generally directed toward the policing of femininity, literary critics and social historians have demonstrated how the late nineteenth century also spawned a crisis in masculinity as public/private topographies asserted by the state no

longer seemed so firmly in place and as a "new heterosocial world of
commercial amusements" reorganized spatial and ideological conceptions of gender.[24] At least one response to these shifts was the emergence of new models of male solidarity at the fin de siècle, evidenced
in the establishment of all-male clubs, the organization of all-male ath-
letic activities at amateur and professional levels, the formation of youth
groups like the Boy Scouts of America, and the idealization of the active,
strenuous life that Roosevelt came to embody. The formation of these
new groups contributed to what Mark Seltzer has called "the topography
of masculinity" in America at the fin de siècle, a landscape congested
with images and activities centered on masculine physical display.[25]

Because young boys seemed more susceptible to modern perversity as images of masculine labor were increasingly replaced by "the
machine," various projects emerged to (re)generate an image of national virility and thus of a corporeally intact male citizen.[26] But regenerative masculinity, seemingly in symbolic opposition to degeneracy,
was also haunted by the specter of its own deterioration. David Starr
Jordan's argument in *The Human Harvest: A Study of the Decay of the Races
through the Survival of the Unfit* (1907) summarizes the prevalent cultural fears in the following terms: "In the red field of human history
the natural process of selection is often reversed. The survival of the
unfittest is the primal cause of the downfall of nations."[27] The dramatic reversal of progress that Jordan describes was the threat against
which the hypermasculine body was directed as a prophylactic, both
preserving and reconstituting a protected ideal of "manhood."[28]

In the United States during the early twentieth century, it was more
consistently than not black people migrating to the North, the working classes, prostitutes, immigrants, and "homosexuals" who were said
to be creating the crisis that left so many feeling under threat by moral,
social, and sexual disease. These are the populations that fell under
surveillance by the anxieties of the age of reform, an age gaining greater
authority through the increasing legitimacy of science as a profession,
even as the idealization of physical culture, health, etiquette, and masculinity strove to produce a more stable, less fragile middle-class world.
Thus the project of "making men" in the physical culture of what Donna
Haraway has called "Teddy Bear patriarchy" was freighted with a new
kind of urgency.[29] It had the responsibility of overcoming a fantasy of
national deterioration. Not surprisingly, the emergence of the craze of
physical culture was accompanied by the rise of the eugenics movement

I outlined above. Since its inception in 1883, when Francis Galton first coined the term, the eugenics movement spawned a large number of proposals that warranted coercive state intervention in reproductive choice. In support of these proposals, free-love activist Victoria Wood-hull wrote: "The best minds of today have accepted the fact that if superior people are desired, they must be bred; and if imbeciles, criminals, paupers, and otherwise unfit people are undesirable citizens, they must not be bred."[30] In 1911, Havelock Ellis echoed Woodhull with his own eugenic remarks: "We generate the race; we alone can regenerate the race."[31] G. Stanley Hall, in his well-known study, *Adolescence* (1904), advocated a rigorous physical education for young boys or else "our race is to degenerate again"[32]; and Ellen Swallow Richards, in *Euthenics: The Science of Controllable Environment* (1910), began her study by citing the Report on National Vitality, stating, "Human vitality depends upon two primary conditions—heredity and hygiene." She recommends that although eugenics provides hygiene for future generations and is thus necessary, euthenics, as a practice of improvement focused on education and environment, could additionally provide the "immediate opportunity" to develop "better men now" and thus "a better race of men for the future."[33] An equally anxiety-ridden call to arms came from more surprising quarters. In her feminist-anarchist monthly, *Mother Earth,* Emma Goldman writes that those who denied women access to birth control methods would "legally encourage the increase of paupers, syphilitics, epileptics, dipsomaniacs, criminals, and degenerates."[34]

If evolutionary advancement through the mechanism of natural selection gave rise to "civilization," the argument went, was this process reversible? Might the human race devolve into some lower animal order? Even more perplexing, if we are still evolving, are we all in some way atavistic—not yet fully human, still "beasts" ourselves? Many scientists imagined that "hereditary degeneration" could be evidenced literally in signs of animality appearing on the human body. Lombroso, for one, claimed that atavism was recognizable through certain bodily deformities: handle-shaped ears, for example, could be "found in criminals, savages, and apes."[35] Charles Caroll's toxic *The Negro, a Beast* (1900), which moves from racial science to full-fledged racism, insisted that Africans and African Americans "are not a part of the Adamic family" but a nonhuman species altogether. Caroll's text found pernicious confirmation in a 1931 study by physician F. G. Crookshank, who argued: "There seems a good deal of evidence that, anatomically, and functionally, primitive Black . . . races again conform to the goril-loid and chimpanzoid plans."[36] The tropes of bestiality, savagery, and atavism were thus deployed to simultaneously police the line between human and animal species, white and black bodies, and civilized and primitive societies.[37] Accordingly, both the animal and the racial other (and the animal as a trope of the racial other) functioned as an index for social and cultural decline, for they were each understood as mark-ers that distinguished the modern from the primitive. We might even say that the racing of the Other was a race against time.[38]

A study by William S. Sadler, MD, entitled *Race Decadence: An Exam-ination of the Causes of Racial Degeneracy in the United States* (1922), pro-vides an illuminating example. Chapter 1, entitled "What Ails Uncle Sam?" imagines the nation as a body under attack by polluting and degenerative forces:

Is the quality of American citizenship deteriorating? Has Uncle Sam admitted to our shores thousands—even millions—of immigrants who can never become typical, happy, and prosperous American citizens? Is it or is it not a fact that there are certain races and types of individuals who are so constituted by nature they can never reach an intelligent comprehension of American institutions? If these questions can be even partially answered in the affirma-tive, then the time has come—the hour has struck—for every real American seriously to take up the study of these fundamental facts of national health and racial hygiene, and seek to really understand what ails Uncle Sam![39]

"The time has come." "The hour has struck." Sadler's argument places ordinary citizens at the forefront of a national mission, calling on those citizens to diagnose and heal the national body. Time may be running out. By representing the nation as itself an ailing body, figured in the national-familial trope of Uncle Sam, Sadler establishes a set of relays between the health or sickness of the individual and the national body, and between individual responsibility and the future of the nation. The exclamatory utterance that concludes Sadler's command concentrates the tendency that I have been tracing in scientific and political thought during this period to be deeply, excitedly troubled by fears of cultural devastation. In urgent response to these fears, Sadler prescribes reme-dies to heal Uncle Sam's sick body before it is too late, thus under-scoring the temporal fragility of the nation-state. Sadler's brand of nationalism stakes its claims on its citizen-subjects through its ability to define and delimit the life and well-being of the people. Such a strat-egy attempts to produce and exploit social anxieties by placing them in narratives of collective national destiny. Inevitably, these strategies betray their ideological underpinnings and rely (almost banally) on a familiar cast of characters (heroes and villains) to support what seems always to end up as a series of highly racialized and gendered dramas of national emergency.

From Savagery to Civilization: Tarzan of the Apes

Edgar Rice Burroughs's novels are well known for staging his concern over the decadence of civilization compared with the virtues of nature.[40] As one character in the Tarzan series warns, the civilized world is filled with "deceit, and hypocrisy, and greed, and avarice, and cruelty" in contrast to the jungle's "noble beasts."[41] The original Tarzan series, published between the years 1912 and 1947, is filled with Burroughs's fascination with the theories of evolutionism, heredity, and ecology; they reflect, in particular, his self-proclaimed interest "in playing with the idea of a contest between heredity and environment."[42] Burroughs was influenced by the demonstrative national policy and physical regime of Teddy Roosevelt, and he was also a strong supporter of eugenics. He summed up the global condition in the following terms: "An inestimable fraction of the world's population will be fit to survive, and on the other hand, hordes of the unfit stand ready upon the slightest provocation to engulf and destroy the minority."[43] As if in response to his own diagnosis, Burroughs imagines a utopian future civilization in his fictional essay "I See a New Race." The story, told in flashbacks, describes the debauched conditions of a society before it began the regeneration process: "the stupefied multiplied without restriction" and "the whole world was constantly growing stupider." Advances in science and applied eugenics, including human breeding, forced intelligence tests, and "the sterilization of criminals, defectives and incompetents," resulted in the "rapid rise in the standard of national intelligence after two generations." Burroughs concludes his fantasy thus: "And so the life of the nation is filled with gaiety and action, and happiness and hope."[44] National progress occurs in the story through a controlled evolutionary process, resulting in the emotional well-being of the nation. Its "gaiety," "happiness," and "hope" is occasioned by an ideology of genetic progressivism.

Burroughs's vision in "I See a New Race" delivers up an account of the nation defined in terms of the genetic composition and reproductive activity of its citizens over time. In the Tarzan series, this national drama is displaced on to the African region, to be played out as an origin story of humanity itself. As many critics point out, an imperialist plot inaugurates the first novel of the series, when Lord Clayton Greystoke and his bride set sail for Africa in 1888, commissioned by the Colonial Records Office to investigate a competing power's activity there. Imperialist adventure goes awry when, shipwrecked, a tiger kills Tarzan's parents shortly after his birth. Kala, an idealized ape mother, finds Tarzan in his parents' abandoned hut and decides to raise him as her own. In fact, Western imperialist activity in Africa abounds throughout the series. For example, in *The Son of Tarzan* (1915), researchers scour the jungle for undisclosed precious minerals and zoological specimens commissioned by "European Corporations" and "Zoological societies," and ships "chartered by a syndicate of wealthy manufacturers, equipped with a laboratory and a full staff of scientists" are sent "to search for some natural product which the manufacturers who footed the bills had been importing from South America at an enormous cost."[45] The Tarzan series thus allegorizes the typical schemes of imperialist conquest and exploitation, not least because its publication is situated among a number of suggestive events. The series began, after all, in the wake of Roosevelt's celebrated account of his 1910 hunting trip in *African Game Trails* and was still going strong during the founding of Parc Albert (now Virunga National Park) in 1914, a conservation site in the Congo initially established for the purpose of African safari tours.[46]

Burroughs's interest in the African jungle was twofold: it allowed for the promotion of the imperialist fantasy of regeneration as advocated by Roosevelt's presidency, and it provided a lush atmosphere of human and animal life ready for a drama of "civilization."[47] In what is by now a familiar narrative trope of the adventure genre, the jungle becomes Tarzan's prerequisite training ground for the forming and masculinizing of his body, a training his son, by the fourth book, must also endure to "become a man."[48] At a time when the rapidly mechanizing urban industrial environment contributed to the production of a cultural ethos of "nervousness" and images of technology increasingly offered the promise of cultural salvation, rescue, and progress (of which D. W. Griffith's 1916 film *Intolerance* is but one incarnation), the hypergendered male body formed in the "training" sequences challenges the iconic imagery of the machine and makes up for what Sadler characterizes as Uncle Sam's ailing body. Indeed, the Tarzan books offer the "primality" of the African experience as a remedy for Western degeneration. Tarzan's physical training in the jungle guarantees the manifestation of what his heredity would allegedly predict but which "blood" alone could no longer fully ensure. Tarzan, it turns out, is a member of the aristocracy, but to activate his "natural" claim to social superiority, Lord Greystoke needs a good workout.[49] The training montage in the first novel, which includes Tarzan learning to wrestle, fight for food, and use jungle resources (vines, rope, and a knife he discovers in his parents' old hut), operates as a screen fantasy for cultural anxieties about the decay of modern manliness.

Along these lines, in *Tarzan of the Apes,* Burroughs's narrative continually seduces its readers with "the sinuous curves" and "enormous strength" of Tarzan's body (108). Its readers are asked to pleasure in "his straight and perfect figure," which "told at a glance the wondrous combination of enormous strength with suppleness and speed" (108). His body and physical skill awe Clayton, Tarzan's cousin: "The man before him was the embodiment of physical perfection and giant strength" (126). Jane, too, is fixated by Tarzan's "great muscles" and "huge biceps" (175). By entrancing both the female and male gaze, Tarzan's body distills the evolutionary and imperialist plot of the novel into a spectacle of male heroism. This allows the narrative to emphasize the dramatic effects of Tarzan's body while blurring the kinds of violent actions that he takes against the African and Arab populations living in the jungle.

Tarzan's "evolution" is thus staged as a series of conquests that are reminiscent of Roosevelt's call for masculine imperialism. At the same time, Tarzan's body literalizes the evolutionary process. As Burroughs explains, "the life of Tarzan of the Apes is symbolic of the evolution of man and the rise of civilization."[50] Tarzan's individual development is thus shown to recapitulate the stages of human development as outlined by G. Stanley Hall's theory of "savage boyhood," in which an individual follows the developmental path of his ancestors. Hall claimed that children physically recapitulated the evolutionary process in their individual life span and lamented that "overcivilized" men had lost touch with their savage boyhoods and primitive pasts, forgetting the "hate that makes men mad or bestial . . . love that is not only uncalculating but is stronger than life . . . the wage of battle where men fight beasts or each other with teeth and knives and spitting revolvers."[51] The physical prowess that Tarzan demonstrates in battling the jungle's inhabitants has a compensatory function: it refutes the "refined sensibilities" of modernity that scientists like Hall feared undermined manhood.

Many scholars from various disciplines have noted Tarzan's status as both a national icon and a figure of idealized masculinity. Gail Bederman describes the ape-man as "a powerfully appealing fantasy of perfect, invincible manhood" whose "cultural work was to proclaim that 'the white man's' potential for power and mastery was as limitless as the masculine perfection of Tarzan's body."[52] Marianna Torgovnick's work suggests that we understand Tarzan's masculinity within the context of modernity's obsession with the primitive, and that we "take Tarzan seriously as an attempt to imagine the primitive as a source of empowerment."[53] Tarzan, however, is implicated in his imperial adventure in ways neither critic acknowledges—namely, as a subject of hybridity. Tarzan promises the restoration of American manhood only by the prospect of interspecies relations. As such, his body functions as a recuperative model of sociocultural evolution only insofar as the sociocultural model engages a theory of cultural exchange, racial intermixture, and animal subjectivity.

Without a doubt, Tarzan is a national icon. His rugged individualism and his eventual interpellation into American culture through his marriage to the Baltimore-born Jane (herself imbued with the adventurous resourcefulness of the New Woman) all qualify him as an American hero. On the other hand, he is also a brute beast, for he incorporates the most vital characteristics of the jungle into his body and, even more, into his sense of self. Not only does he refer to himself as an ape throughout the series, he also acts and comes to look like an ape: he walks low to the ground, hunches his back, and swings effortlessly through the trees with the agility of a monkey. Of course, he also possesses qualities that "raised him far above his fellows of the jungle—that little spark which spells the whole vast difference between man and brute—Reason."[54] Tarzan resides in both material and metaphysical spheres; he is brute beast and "forest god" (122), a hypermasculine body and a reasoning mind. In the traditional story of Darwinian human development, at least in terms of its popular adaptations, reason stands at the summit of human faculties, and in turn, the most reasoning humans stand at the summit of civilization. This is a story of progress away from body and toward mind that depends on a system that subordinates matter to spirit. Thus, in one scene, as Tarzan bends over a book he has found in the remains of his biological father's tattered hut, Burroughs calls him "an allegorical figure of the primordial groping through the black night of ignorance toward the light of learning" (53). As such an "allegorical figure," Tarzan enacts a transition between two worlds, what Burroughs, in his racism, characterizes as the difference between "black ignorance" and "white enlightenment," or more broadly between "barbarity" and "civility," "bestiality" and "humanity." Here Burroughs, like the human and evolutionary sciences that inform his work, plays out the contest between human and animal as a contest between white and black populations. But this contest never comes to full narrative resolution. Tarzan, as both a human–ape figure and as a white man embracing black culture, keeps these divisions in play as they are continually reinscribed on his body. His body, moreover, converts the bestial and the human, the primitive and the civilized, the ability to wrestle and to reason, the earthly and the godlike, the atavistic and the evolved into one being. Certainly, that body displays an intense national virility, one that works to vault American masculinity over its continental others. But it also produces an epistemological crisis that disturbs the enlightenment notion of a bounded human self and the imperialist dogma of racial difference. This is what remains missing from cultural analysis of the Tarzan series, for critics too readily reduce the powerful meanings and contradictions of his body to a single narrative—one of masculinity, or primitivism, or imperialist allegory. Tarzan's body, however, resists the singularity of these readings and therefore resists the national and temporal narratives that would otherwise contain him.

Throughout the first novel in the series, Tarzan's evolution from baby to beast to "man" is accounted for in different ways. When Tarzan sees his reflection for the first time as he takes a drink from a lake, he is startled and appalled by his image. He can't understand why he doesn't look like an ape. He quickly attempts to cover his body with mud to hide "the ugliness" of his white skin. At this moment, Tarzan misrecognizes himself; even more, he misrecognizes his relations of kinship. His ape family, the only family that he has ever known, doesn't seem to make the same mistake. They name him Tarzan because it means "white ape" in their language (Tarmangani). They know what he doesn't: that he is both part of their family, an ape, and something else, white.

Later, Tarzan reads an illustrated children's primer and sees images of other humans for the first time. "A is for Archer" is printed underneath a picture of an archer, "B is for Boy" underneath a picture of a boy (43). After a few of these lessons, Tarzan undergoes a change: "No longer did he feel the shame for his hairless body or his human features, for now his reason told him that he was of a different race from his wild and hairy companions. He was a M-A-N" (56). The object of his shame shifts from his whiteness to the hair growing on his face. As a response, "almost daily he whetted his keen knife and scraped and whittled at his young beard to eradicate this degrading emblem of apehood" (109). His heart "beat with the great desire to cover his nakedness with *clothes* for he had learned from his picture books that all *men* were so covered, while *monkeys* and *apes* went naked" (65, Burroughs's italics). Tarzan's desire to see a reflection of his community in his own body, and of himself in others around him, can be read as a desire to achieve legible form. His desire finds fulfillment in a children's primer. In the pages of this book, Tarzan can gaze on and read about his body, thereby experiencing the identificatory power of words and images. As a result, almost instantaneously, he is interpellated into the text's prescriptive bodily norms; no longer darkening himself with mud like an "animal," he decides to wear clothing like a "man." This interpellation requires that Tarzan not only learn species difference ("archer" and "boy" versus "monkey" and "ape") but also that he learn the orthography of human evolution: he was a M-A-N.

Yet like many of the paradoxes in the Tarzan series, the clothing he chooses to wear in order to become "civilized," a loincloth made from the hide of a lion he has slain, is also what marks him as part of the natural world. That is, the loincloth produces Tarzan's second skin as that of a jungle creature. Although his status as a hunter (or "archer") produces a distance, and one violently conceived, between himself and the natural world, his bodily contact with the flesh of a lion closes in on that distance, enfolding his body in the animal's touch. Although his primer-book education and later his "rescue" from the jungle by Jane and her entourage take Tarzan out of nature, this does not mean that nature has been taken out of Tarzan—at least not in terms of his emotional ties, his love for the jungle and his ape family, and his sense of self. Tarzan remains a self-proclaimed "ape-man" throughout the entire series. In *Tarzan of the Apes,* he is "a young and savage beast of the jungle," "a hairless white ape" who "knew no fear, as we know it" (48). Even after his identity as an aristocrat is restored to him, he tells his new friend D'Arnot, "I am still a wild beast at heart" (265). Or, as he wistfully confides to his new love, Jane, "I see now you could not be happy with—an ape" (266). Tarzan thus has an additional skill. He coordinates and aligns opposing designations in one body. On the one hand, he is "a perfect type of the strongly masculine, unmarred by dissipation, or brutal or degrading passions." On the other hand, he is the ultimate brute: "a killer of men and beasts" with "the cry of a great bull ape" (182, 248).

Tarzan, ultimately, is a combinational entity, a hybrid figure who more than anything else signifies cultural ambivalence: "In his veins flowed the blood of the best of a race of mighty fighters, and back of this was the training of his short lifetime among the fierce brutes of the jungle" (48). Tarzan's physically overpresent body is "regenerate" because of his "blood," and it is "degenerate" because of his brawn. Through the distillation of the discourses of degeneration–regeneration, the archaic and the modern, the series sustains this paradox of interiors and exteriors. Tarzan is neither atavistic ape-man nor docile supporter of "Teddy Bear patriarchy." Rather, he is the overdetermined sign of both. Despite Bederman's claim, therefore, that *Tarzan* "suggests that 'civilization' was, indeed, a coherent and recognizable discourse," it seems to me that Burroughs renders "civilization" a highly conflicted construction.[55] The series hybridizes Tarzan's body in such a way as both to redeploy distinctions set up by human science (distinctions between mind and body as well as human and animal) and to reconfigure those distinctions as a hybrid intersection. By producing Tarzan as an enigmatic figure, one that is both apparently subcivilized and instinctually cultured, the Tarzan series dismantles one of the prevailing understandings of primitivism within American culture. The typical narrative within American cultural studies, one outlined by Torgovnick, explains how the West finds a means for its revitalization through contact with primal others, a contact that also works to guarantee the West's superior status. Tarzan, however, does not simply have contact with the primitive jungle. He is part of its landscape and its kinship units; the jungle and his much-loved ape family have shaped and constituted his very being, his very body. Tarzan, finally, never moves from invigorating primitivism back to the status quo. Instead, Burroughs keeps Tarzan's bestiality in play throughout the course of the series. Apishness, not aristocracy, is the fundamental way Tarzan is characterized even now.

"A New Tarzan Novel," cover of *Blue Book Magazine* 1/6 (October 1935). Courtesy of the Burroughs Memorial Collection, University of Louisville Library.

Tarzan's hybridity sheds light on the relationship between time and narrative functioning in the series as well, in particular on the way his body, in its apish civility, brings different time schemes into productive collision. In its future-oriented arch, the Tarzan series moves perpetually forward, dogged and determined by the modern notion of improvement—the idea that, as time passes, things should get better, people and places should continue to advance and develop. And so Tarzan not only advances and develops on an individual scale, but also continuously saves the day (from vicious ant men attempting to rule the jungle and the like), and in so doing, he works to civilize the jungle and to craft it into a better place to live—hence the imperialist project. Because the perilous encounter is the thematic élan vital of the Tarzan novels, in order to keep the series going, for it to *be* a series, Burroughs must continue to invent hazardous and horrifying situations that only an American hero like Tarzan can efficiently address. But by keeping the motif of the dangerous situation alive in both the individual narratives and in the expectations of readers, the series ensures that progress, in the modern sense, can't ever really happen; there will always be a threat in need of a response, always a problem in need of resolution. Serial novels by definition represent modern time as something in perpetuity, as something that always goes on but that also stays the same in such a way as to allow for a series without end. And this is also what Tarzan's body stages, for it is in itself a site of temporal subjectivity that I have been calling atavistic: a site of prehistoricity and return, the forgotten past of human origin and its insistent, inevitable recurrence. His subjectivity as atavistic is forged not just by way of the contents of the recent past (his upbringing by a troop of apes) but in relation to a more distant biological past that that upbringing signifies. Because Tarzan's atavism brings human prehistory into conjunction with the modern present, we can read his body as an allegory that stands in for the subject's deep past, a past that lies "behind the times" like a (premodern) beast crouching in the jungle and waiting to spring.

The Tarzan series, therefore, continuously reminds us of what threatens the modernity of the future, of what came before M-A-N (according to Burroughs's pop-evolutionary concerns), and of where we may also potentially go if the hybridity of Tarzan's body is allowed to roam unchecked: back in human time. What pressures are placed on Burroughs's own embrace of the idea of forward-marching evolutionary progress when we take into consideration the inevitable hybridities that occur by very fact of the formal procedures and enabling conditions of the serial novel? Because the serial novel's formal practice of time is ongoing, the ideology of evolutionary progress occurs over the span of an extended sequence, and thus over time infinitely conceived. And because dramatizing evolution necessarily requires the representation of its opposite—the primitive—we can also say that the Tarzan series allows for and produces temporal convergences that never get re-ordered into narrative teleology and its requisite components of fini-tude and closure. In effect, M-A-N may be evolving, but he never evolves (in the sense of completion that the term denotes). In other words, the series more precisely enacts the *experience* of modern time as a net-work of spheres and temporalities as opposed to the *belief* of modern thinking that time is essentially progressive and distinct from its pre-modern past(s).

At this point, it may be objected that I am reading utopian moments into what is essentially a conservative narrative. I would suggest in response that I am not so much reading against the grain of the Tarzan series as I am noting what already exists in the texts' formal and the-matic parameters: an enactment of the hybrid temporal and corpo-real structures of the modern world. If people of African descent have most often been depicted as the antithesis of Western modernity and modern subjectivity, here we have a network of associations between modern and primitive, human and animal, the Western world and the African world, where the conception of each is shown to be a struc-turally dependent and reciprocal feature of the other.

To point out how Burroughs conceives a landscape populated with the images of a highly mixed community is not to ignore, however, the way his representations of this community range from anthropological reconfigurations to all-out racism. Not only are the ant men in *Tarzan and the Ant Men* pejoratively characterized as "a physically degenerat-ing race," but Kerchak, king of the apes until Tarzan unseats him, is also shown to be physiognomically degenerate: "His forehead was ex-tremely low and receding, his eyes bloodshot, small and close set to his coarse flat nose; his ears are pointed and thin, even smaller than most of his kind" (*Tarzan of the Apes*, 30). The Arab tribes of the jungle are described as being "of the bestial, degraded type" (*Son of Tarzan*, 189), and the local African tribes have "bestial faces, daubed with color—huge mouths and flabby hanging lips—yellow teeth, sharp filed—roll-ing, demon eyes—shining naked bodies—cruel spears" (*Tarzan of the*

Apes, 198). Here we witness Burroughs's reliance on the premises and theories of scientific racism as a resource for his narrative. Specifically, he uses the authority of degeneration theory and the project of eugenics to lend credence to his own sensational plot structures.[56] In so doing, he uses race as an ideology in the Marxian sense: racial difference and division emerges in the series to legitimate the subterranean workings of a larger social system, acquiring, along the way, a seemingly autonomous power to shape identities. Étienne Balibar forwards this Marxist understanding of racist ideology and discusses how racism, as a system of classification, is what produces race, not the other way around. In other words, racism is what naturalizes race as a category of human classification; its various manifestations in culture work to produce subjects within the regulatory fictions of the nation-state. For Balibar, the function of racism also draws a relationship between race and time: "The symbolic kernel of the idea of race," Balibar writes, "is the schema of genealogy; that is, quite simply, the idea that the filiation of individuals transmits from generation to generation a substance both biological and spiritual and thereby inscribes them in a temporal community known as 'kinship.'"[57] From the vantage point of this "temporal community known as kinship," we can glimpse how the idea of the family as a racialized category is a site through which time is accorded relations of dominance and subordination. Produced as both a temporal and a racial category, in other words, kinship becomes the means to mark inequalities between social and racial groups based on the measure of each group's ability to progress over time in the evolutionary, reproductive sense.[58]

Perhaps it is partly because of the destabilizing potential of Tarzan's undifferentiated body—its potential to produce dichotomies as convergences—that the series erupts so antagonistically and hierarchically along the lines of race. The tribal cultures in the novel represent a backward temporal community as opposed to the civilized Westerners represented by Jane and company. The perceived inhumanity of the jungle's occupants serves as a rationale for subjecting them to the "humanizing" (and thus modern-progressive) process of colonization.[59] But Burroughs also launches aggressive critiques against the nature of the human world in general. In describing his intentions for the Tarzan series, for instance, he commented, "It pleased me to draw comparisons between the manners of men and the manners of beasts and seldom to the advantage of men. Perhaps I hoped to shame men into being more like beasts in those respects in which beasts excel men, and these are not few."[60] Thus, in *Tarzan of the Apes,* after several encounters with men, "Tarzan began to hold his own kind in low esteem" (45). In other instances, Tarzan's violent nature is attributed not to "primitivism" or bestiality but to his human traits: "He killed for food most often, but being a man he sometimes killed for pleasure; for it has remained for man alone among creatures to kill senselessly and wantonly for mere pleasure of inflicting suffering and death" (61). Conversely, Burroughs attributes some of the better qualities of "humanity" to the jungle's creatures like Tarzan's ape mother, Kala, who is physically and therefore socially evolved; her "round, high forehead, which denoted more intelligence than most of her kind possessed," explains her capacity for "mother-love and mother sorrow" (31). Although Burroughs invokes a romanticized, even patronizing vision of the animals and "noble savages" living harmoniously close to nature and thus imbued with transcendent morality, *Tarzan*'s narrative ambiguity also undercuts the dichotomy between human and beast as well as the racial hierarchy that dichotomy sets up, thus troubling the too-simple temporal opposition between what counts as the modern and what as the primitive.

This narrative ambiguity occurs obstinately throughout the novels, positing a series of unanswered questions: are humans beastly? Is the civilized world actually degenerate, while the natural world thrives? Is the modern subject in a state of evolutionary progress or atavistic decline? What time *is* it? The plot of the first novel echoes this ambivalent pattern and plays with the uncertainty of Tarzan's identity, holding out the answer to who he really is until the narrative's end. His "true" self is finally restored to him in a sequence that resonates as much with biological expectations as with acute cultural anxieties. In the final chapter, entitled "The Height of Civilization," D'Arnot submits Tarzan's biological father's diary, also found among the ruins of the shack, to the European authorities. He instructs them to compare the ink print of a small boy's hand contained in the diary with that of Tarzan's own fingerprint. Unfamiliar with this new technology, Tarzan asks:

"Do fingerprints show racial characteristics? Could you determine, for example, solely from fingerprints whether the subject was Negro or Caucasian?"

"I think not," replied the officer, "although some claim that those of the Negro are less complex."

"Could the fingerprints of an ape be detected from those of a man?"

"Probably, because the apes would be far simpler than those of the higher organism."

"But a cross between an ape and a man might show the characteristics of either progenitor?" continued Tarzan.

"Yes, I should think likely," responded the official; "but [. . .] I should hate to trust its findings further than to differentiate between individuals. There it is absolute. No two people born into the world have ever had identical lines upon all their digits." (251)

True to D'Arnot's hunch, the fingerprints in the diary match those of Tarzan, and his identity as an aristocrat is reestablished. Ascertaining Tarzan's familial heritage thus alleviates any anxiety over the possibility of intermixture in his blood.

Tarzan's conversation with the officer also pinpoints the potential trouble his body excites; he could be a mixed-race or mixed-species body. Allegorically, their conversation serves to clarify how the series's interspecies anxiety acts in relation to interracial anxiety, for an analogy is made in Tarzan's query between the fingerprint of the ape and the fingerprint of the "Negro," both considered to be "less complex" than that of a "Caucasian." These anxieties are resolved through the biological certainty of the fingerprint, which acts as the "absolute" guarantee of individual identity (if not racial or species identity). If the text produces the ape-man as a hybrid subject, animal and human, white and black, with brute strength and acute reason, in this moment, it refuses that production. Tarzan's status as a beast of the jungle and his self-reflexive, even proud, understanding of his bestiality are here replaced by a biological truth effect. The fingerprint is the deus ex machina of the first novel's plot, restoring to Tarzan his humanhood and thus replacing the possible interspecies/interracial story with the telos of evolutionary certainty.[61] Now, without shame or threat, Tarzan can marry Jane. So ends *Tarzan of the Apes*.

Tarzan's marriage to Jane (which occurs in the second novel of the series), however, summons a whole new set of problems that crop up in the series's third novel, *The Son of Tarzan*. As a young boy, Jack, Tarzan and Jane's son, is overcome with a desire to learn about the African jungle in such texts as "Carl Hagenbeck's book on men and beasts" (8) and to imitate the apes he sees among its pages by swinging from the chandeliers of his mansion or attacking his tutor, "going through the pantomime indicative of choking [him] to death" (9). Frightened by the possibility that her son may have inherited his father's jungle nature, Jane forbids Tarzan to tell young Jack about his past, going so far as to disallow Jack himself to visit the zoo. Nonetheless, the boy yearns for knowledge of Africa and is filled with a persevering "jungle lust" (11). Tarzan assures Jane that their son's "love for animals," such as his pronounced desire to see a trained ape at the zoo, is only natural in a healthy, normal boy of his age, and he argues that "just because he wants to see this ape is no indication that he wants to marry an ape, and even if should be, far be it for you Jane to have the right to cry 'shame!'" (10). At first, Tarzan characterizes their son's interests as the "natural" desire of a young boy, much in line with G. Stanley Hall's claim that "savagery" was a healthy part of the developmental process. But Tarzan also turns Jane's fears back on to their own relationship by pointing out that Jane married an ape of sorts herself. Tarzan thus clarifies Jane's fears concerning her son as a displaced apprehension about miscegenation, specifically a fear of the hereditary possibilities of racial intermixture. As the fingerprinting scene already began to suggest, the blurring of the boundaries of human and beast that Tarzan's body stages can be—and was—understood as a crossing of racial boundaries.[62]

Tarzan and Jane's son in this "reproductive issue" in the series serves to complicate the nature–nurture argument further. Afraid that his mother's restrictions will turn him into a "girl," or worse, "a mollycoddle" (9), Jack finds a chance to escape when he hears that the circus and their animals will be voyaging back to Africa by boat, and he decides to stow away on the ocean liner. He soon arrives in Africa and joins up with an old ape friend of his father's. Once there, he almost instantly and instinctively comes to embrace "the savage joy of living and of pitting one's wits and prowess against the savage jungle brood" (44). Invigorated by the jungle in this way, the newly named Korak (a moniker given him by his ape friends) learns the joys of his own nakedness and "revels in the freedom of his unhampered state" (46). "This was life!" he shouts from the treetops (43). Swinging "quite naturally" from the same branches his father once had, Korak experiences an "instinctive knowledge—a species of strange intuition inherited from his father" (46, 51). And like his father's, Korak's body is also a site of confused intelligibility. When Jenssen, a formidable colonizer of the jungle, encounters Korak, he is surprised to find "an intelligent looking European" fighting alongside a tribe of baboons. Although Jenssen notices "nothing of the imbecile or degenerate in his features or expression," he goes on to characterize him as a "wild apeman" and "a white savage" who "had allied himself with the beasts against the humans" (103). Korak's hybridity, Jenssen notes, makes him "infinitely more to be feared" than a mere ape (104).

In the most obvious sense, then, Jack/Korak's seemingly natural and instinctive affinity for jungle life suggests he has indeed inherited his father's apeish past through the process of reproductive heredity, thus bearing out the concerns, held within sociobiological and eugenic circles, about the eventualities of racial intermixture. His jungle affinity also metaphorizes, in truncated form, a more general evolutionary conundrum. His alliance with beasts and his instinctual knowledge about jungle life both suggest a kind of residual physical memory that floods the young boy's body as he returns to his animal origins. Burroughs intimates that it is precisely Jack/Korak's instinctive residualism that evidences both his father's past and the deep past of human being. The African jungle in the *Son of Tarzan* and throughout the Tarzan series, in other words, becomes a definitional space of human origin. This resonates with some of the familiar arguments about the discursive logic of imperialism. First, the representation of Africa as a space of the human past reinforces the notion that developing nations are a site of civilization's past more generally—that is, living forms of earlier moments in the timeline of evolutionary history. Second, Jack's near instant initiation into the "joy of living" that jungle existence enables plays out the fetishization of the primitive as a vital source for Western and masculine subjectivity. But there is a less acknowledged possibility offered by Jack/Korack's jungle experience of *racial alliance,* metaphorized as species alliance, whereby Africa emerges as the center of the human itself: the place where Tarzan feels at home, the place that allows Jack/Korak to experience the fullness of his doubled identity, the place where men and beasts fight and live side by side with shared and common interests.

Jack/Korak, like his father, exults in his affinity with the inhabitants of Africa. Tarzan himself decides that he is more comfortable living in the jungle than in the city, and so the whole family, Jane included, permanently relocates in the jungle in a safari-style manner of living. This return to Africa reinstitutes Western culture as a problem and maintains the characterization of modernity as a lesser choice in comparison to the jungle's attractions. The question then becomes: Does this also reinstitute the opposition between the modern and the primitive?

Does it then also reinforce the fetishistic portrayal of the jungle as a vital and vibrant antidote for Western emasculation? Or does it call that portrayal into question? Rather than erecting a strict dividing line between the modern and the primitive, Jack/Korak's inheritance of his father's atavistic tendencies establishes a dual subjectivity, at once human and beast, civilized and brutish, Jack and Korak, a confusion of alleged opposites. And to the extent that we understand Jack/Korak as simultaneously modern and primitive, and thus both present and past, we can also see how his subjectivity engages with and renegotiates traditional ideas of modern time. If the serial novel refuses teleological, narrative time, do its characters, in the example of Tarzan and his son, refuse racialized, reproductive time and the progressivist history out of which that notion emerges? If so, how can we characterize this more recalcitrant model of time? If not, how should we attend to the serial novel's interposing ideologies?

From Civilization to Savagery: The Insidious Dr. Fu Manchu

Tarzan is not the only dime novel series to raise these questions about the status of modernity, nor was Africa the only site of their narrativization. In 1914, the same year that *Tarzan* made its way into the book marketplace, an advertisement for Gouraud's Oriental Cream in a volume of *Vanity Fair* claimed that "the fashion of the day demands that the complexion of the well-groomed woman shall be clear and of snowy whiteness." The "regular use" of the cream, the ad assures, "will bestow the charms that are so admired in a fashionable woman," as it "whitens, softens, and clears the skin." In the advertisement, the well-groomed woman serves as a marker for consumer culture and for the presumed race of that culture, whose very whiteness is preserved and protected when the Orient is put in a package and sold.[63] As with Tarzan's Africa, the Orient has the capacity both to threaten and to regenerate Western civilization. Put another way, the Asiatic other heals the frailties of the feminine complexion and acts as a homeopathic opportunity to make it more pure. Gouraud's Oriental Cream promises to bestow on white womanhood a more ideal femininity in much the same way that Tarzan promises to compensate for the fragility of American masculinity. Of course, the popularity of orientalized consumer products did nothing to curb the racist treatment of Asian American immigrants in U.S. history up to this point, either in legislation such as the Chinese Exclusion Act of 1882, which disallowed Chinese laborers to become naturalized citizens, or in popular characterizations of them as "heathen Chinee."[64] Nonetheless, the celebratory commodification of the Orient and its representation as a source for the West's revitalization served a unifying function for U.S. culture. The Orient's status as an "ancient" culture, intermittently barbarous and healing, acts as a reminder of the West's prehistory from which it evolved. It therefore helps produce a more coherent self-definition of the West as the pinnacle of progress.[65]

East Asian immigration had been severely restricted by the Chinese Exclusion Act and by the euphemistic "Gentleman's Agreement" between Japan and the United States in 1907 and 1908 that reduced the number of Japanese immigrants allowed into the country. The American Eugenics Society and its various supporters formed one of the major lobbies for more restrictive immigration laws. Relying on Army Intelligence test scores and other "expert" testimony, they proclaimed before Congress that "biology" demanded the exclusion of most members of Eastern and Eastern European races. Congressman Robert Allen, Democrat of West Virginia, declared: "The primary reason for the restriction of the alien stream is the necessity for purifying and keeping pure the blood of America."[66] Allen's assertion illuminates the contradictory function of a simple advertisement for the whitening effects of Gouraud's Oriental Cream: representations of either disease or health guaranteed Asian exclusion by stabilizing the Orient as the constitutive other to the hegemonic Western subject and simultaneously allowed for the exploitation of Asia as a lucrative resource for capitalist consumer culture. Such advertisements testify to the strategic practices of American nationality, the contours of which are made intelligible not only through the racialization of certain people but the biologization of race as such.[67]

Sax Rohmer's novels, most notably those in the Dr. Fu Manchu series, offer exemplary terrain through which to explore some of the phantasmatic images on which the nation depended.[68] The series is filled with Asian criminal masterminds, most notably Dr. Fu Manchu himself, involved in various nefarious schemes to take over different parts of the world. For example, in *President Fu Manchu* (1936), a novel of "sinister drama," Fu Manchu, with his uncanny intelligence, aptitude for hypnotic mind control, inventions of never-before-known poisons, impossible surgeries, and vast knowledge of science, threatens to take

Perfect Beauty

The fashion of the present day demands that the complexion of the well-groomed woman shall be clear and of snowy whiteness. The regular use of

Gouraud's
ORIENTAL
CREAM

The favorite for over 65 years

will bestow the charms that are so admired in a fashionable woman.

Gouraud's Oriental Cream

is a liquid powder, far surpassing the dry powders that have to be applied so frequently to gain the desired effect. It whitens, softens and clears the skin. It is absolutely free from grease and consequently does not encourage the growth of hair.

Price, $1.50 per bottle

At Druggists and Department Stores, or direct on receipt of price.

Gouraud's Oriental Velvet Sponge.

should always be used when applying Gouraud's Oriental Cream. It is perfectly smooth and velvety, and will give you the most satisfactory results. Sent in a dust-proof box on receipt of 50c.

Ferd. T. Hopkins & Son

Advertisement for Gouraud's Oriental Cream, *Vanity Fair* (1914).

over the nation, "perhaps the world," at "a desperate period in American history."[69] Only Denis Nayland Smith and his colleague, Mark Hepburn, an expert in toxicology for the FBI, may be able to save America from "the yellow peril incarnate." By and large, the series revolves around plots to rule the world and the British and American police forces' attempts to thwart them. And although the police always manage to prevent global doom, they never actually catch the evil doctor.

Like Tarzan, Rohmer's representations of Asian criminals vacillate between extreme barbarity and fierce intellect. Although Rohmer's narratives do set up binary oppositions between the West and the East, the civilized and the atavistic, these oppositions become increasingly tenuous over the course of the series. Dr. Fu Manchu, for instance, is both depraved and ingenious, while the detectives that hunt him down are both stalwartly patriotic and utterly exhausted. Dr. Fu Manchu is presented as an animal-like and "uncanny being," but he also poses as a model of civilization; he is, after all, a doctor, and a highly advanced one at that. Similarly, the detectives are described as scientifically adept and resolute, but they are also prone to physical weakness, including occasional fainting spells.

Rohmer's narratives may be structured by a contest between Western civility and Asian atavism, but it is a fragile contest at best. The series's uneasy and unpredictable quality is incarnated dramatically in the alternately weak bodies and strong minds of the leading characters themselves. On the one hand, Rohmer's detective protagonists are smart, and they are usually medical practitioners of some sort. Detective Denis Nayland Smith of the Fu Manchu series, for instance, is aided by an entourage of doctors and scientists, like his friend, Dr. Petrie. In Rohmer's novel *Yellow Claw* (1915), a woman is mysteriously murdered and Detective-Inspector Dunbar, an authority in "criminal anthroposcopy," M. Gaston Max, and Dr. Cumberly, an "expert in physiognomy," are all on the case. Together, they uncover a global opium operation led by *"Mr. King,"* a Chinese villain.[70] Readers are equally entertained, however, by the various flaws of the detectives, who operate in these instances as something of the inverse of the hale and hearty characters in the Tarzan books. Dr. Petrie, for example, is often "in a condition closely bordering the hysterical"; he tracks down Asian evil with "quivering hands."[71] In one novel in the series, after enduring torture at "the hand of Fu Manchu," Petrie expresses his increasingly neurasthenic state in the following terms: "Some fine nerve of my brain, already strained to utmost tension, snapped."[72] In *The Return of Fu Manchu,* Dr. Shan Greville, another friend of Detective Denis Nayland Smith, describes his mental state in similar terms: facing imminent danger, he "uttered a sigh that was almost a sob" and felt "ashamed to confess that [he] was trembling" (98, 24). Other characters in the series are described in similar ways: FBI man Mark Hepburn is always "clammy with nervous perspiration" (*President Fu Manchu,* 162), while Smith himself cuts "a disheveled figure" (*Return of Fu Manchu,* 17) as he "feverishly" (*Return of Fu Manchu,* 21) and "frenziedly" (*President Fu Manchu,* 116) trails Fu Manchu in different parts of the world. Significantly, the series's protagonists often express these feelings of mental and emotional instability in terms that come close to the language of "savagery." In *The Hand of Fu Manchu,* at one point Dr. Petrie admits, "I turned with a wild, inarticulate cry, my fist raised frenzied above my head" (65); Smith nearly breaks down when "outraged emotion overcame him utterly" (66).

The various weaknesses of Rohmer's detectives and medical examiners evoke the culture's anxieties about American masculinity that characters like Tarzan served to attenuate. The series's detectives perform in their nervousness a metonymic relation to the ailing national body for which the enormous physical strength of Tarzan's body is compensatory; his hard and muscular surfaces provide a protective shield for their emotional frailties. Further enhancing the narrative's depiction of unstable masculine subjects wandering through an unstable social world is the fact that the detectives frequently change their physical appearances. They don a number of disguises when tracking down criminals, and racial cross-dressing seems to be a particular favorite. In *Yellow Claw,* for example, M. Max appears in one scene as a Jewish confidence man, Abraham Levinsky, and fools even his detective friends. In the Fu Manchu series, the detectives put on blackface and Asianface in attempts to disguise themselves as "criminals" so often that "an artificial stain still lingered" on Denis Nayland Smith's skin (*Return of Fu Manchu,* 309). This practice of disguise implies that there is a stable look to the criminal body, but it simultaneously bears out a sense of the constructedness of racial identity as something one can put on like a style of dress. But as Smith's "lingering stain" suggests, his flirtation with the racial other transforms his body into something else. Like Tarzan's loincloth that transforms his body into something part animal, Smith's lingering stain demonstrates the indivisibility of the self/other binary. The descriptions of the narrative's protagonists—their sensitive emotional states and morphing physical appearances—indicate their incoherent subject positions and point to the vulnerability of their own bodies. Who, in the end, is the "true" degenerate? The "insidious" Fu Manchu or the detectives in their perpetually nervous conditions? Is the invasion of a "foreign scourge" the site and cause of cultural degeneracy, or is modernity itself simply exhausted? Rohmer's narratives don't so much answer these questions as they deliberately, menacingly pose them.

We can read Rohmer's descriptions of the repeated failure of the police to apprehend their suspects as a function of his interest in producing an Asian supercriminal rather than an American superhero. Although Tarzan and Fu Manchu are both portrayed in bestial terms, there is a radical difference between the enormous totality of Tarzan's body (his "huge" and "perfect" form) and the fragmented body of the Asian villain in the Fu Manchu texts. Fu Manchu is variously described as "beetlesque" (*Yellow Claw*, 101), an "uncanny being" with "a cat-like gait" who possesses "a fleshless yellow skull" (*Fu Manchu's Daughter*, 308) and speaks with a snakelike "hissing voice" (*Insidious Dr. Fu Manchu*, 10). Supporting these descriptions is the emblem of Fu Manchu's head that appears on the frontispiece of each of the first editions of the Fu Manchu novels. The illustration emphasizes his vacant, hypnotic eyes, stereotypical Asian mustache, and elongated, clawlike hands. This bestial representation often makes its way into the book and chapter titles as well: *Yellow Claw*, *The Hand of Fu Manchu*, "The Questing Hands," "The Fiery Hand." In *Yellow Claw*, this imagery becomes the central focus of the text's affective mode of suspense when, at the novel's start, "a hand, of old ivory hue, a long, yellow, clawish hand, with part of a sinewy forearm," commits murder: "Two hands—with outstretched, crooked, clutching fingers—leapt from the darkness into the light of the moonbeam. Straight at the bare throat leapt the yellow hands. 'Oh God!' came a frenzied, rasping shriek—'*Mr. King!*'" (10–11).

To further aid in the production of readerly anxiety, Rohmer makes use of typography as a means to translate the anxious emotional experience of his characters. Look again at the above utterance: "'Oh God!' came a frenzied, rasping shriek—'*Mr. King!*'" Here, heightened emotional response is produced by way of the use of italics. This is no isolated incident. Whenever Mr. King's name is mentioned in the narrative, it is italicized. The use of italics signifies the cataclysmic effects of the

THE RETURN OF
DR. FU-MANCHU

By SAX ROHMER

McKINLAY, STONE & MACKENZIE

Original frontispiece of *The Return of Dr. Fu-Manchu*, by Sax Rohmer (1916).

Asian criminal on the characters in the novel. It also creates a pause in the narrative flow, thus producing a shock effect in the reader. As readers, we are asked to linger over the typographical figure and to charge that figure with meaning. In this context, italics function as a visual sign of difference in language. They produce racial otherness literally as a graphic figure. In their emotive substance and their visual form, the italics are a sign of both cultural nervousness and racial horror, each expressed in the shuddering and trembling features of language.

Similarly, as Dunbar, Cumberly, and M. Max all search for their villain, pseudoclimactic peaks in the series's plot structures are momentarily achieved by the mention of the possible race of the criminal, followed repeatedly by an exclamation point. Exclamatory remarks, such as "he was a chinaman!" (146) or "Asiatic!" (79) in *Yellow Claw*, occur throughout the series, as if the emphatic mode makes race readable as the site of fear and suspense without any further explanation (aside from the exclamation). As with the use of italics, the exclamation point registers the text's assumption of the shock of racial otherness, but it also points to the unrepresentable aspects of this shock. The criminal Asian body is so frightening and unreal, we are asked to believe, that its register of horror must take place in diacritical substitutes for the body. The repetitive focus, as in *President Fu Manchu*, on the Asian villain's "veinous, claw-like hands" (40) and "hideous yellow face" (78) are, therefore, given even more exaggerated emphasis when paired with these circumflexive signs. Throughout *Yellow Claw*, in fact, the identity of *"Mr. King"* is never revealed. Until the end, he remains a racialized, clawlike hand and a set of italics, never a whole body.

Rohmer's series hinges on this overparticularization of the racialized body; his Asian criminals appear only as a set of physically isolated features—ears, eyes, nose, skulls, and claws—or typographic valences—italics and exclamation points. The fragmentation and animalization of the Asian body and the diacritical strategies deployed to register its ghastliness are put to the service of Western productions of a racial type that bears the weight of group identity. As discussed in chapter 2, new technologies like the photograph, increasingly put to use in scientific and juridical culture, functioned to re-present the human form as a generalizable site of physical identification: the nose, ears, brow, and cranial formation of an individual became genericized and abstracted locales through which racial, sexual, and gendered difference ostensibly could be perceived. In a similar attempt, Rohmer uses visual and linguistic signs to stratify different populations into recognizable social and racial types. His description of the fragmented yellow claws of Fu Manchu and his minions, and the diacritical marks that represent the Asian criminal, function as synecdoches for an entire racial population. As we are told in *The Return of Dr. Fu Manchu*, Fu Manchu is invested with "all the cruel cunning of an entire Eastern race [. . .] the 'Yellow Peril' incarnate in one man" (10). This "cruel cunning" expresses the series's racial and racist logic: "This man's existence was a menace to the white race" (186). Very much like the medical photograph, typography in the Fu Manchu series functions as a technology of personhood with the capacity to yield a reality of its own, underscoring how mechanical media carry the individual across a regulated threshold of identity and identification, type and stereotype.

Like Burroughs, Rohmer also evokes suspense through the use of the serial form itself, which allows him to leave his individual narratives open ended. Throughout the Fu Manchu series, the bad guy gets away. The detectives are always too late to make the arrest, managing only to chase the supervillain they are after to another part of the world. In *President Fu Manchu,* for example, the evil doctor escapes down the waterfalls of Niagara. Typical of and necessary for dime novel series culture, this kind of villainous escape allows for the possibility of another book in the series, and along with that, more profit in the book marketplace. The inevitable escape of the villain also refuses closure to the threat of world domination by a nonwhite population, preserving the dangerous possibility of the imminent *Return of Dr. Fu Manchu*. The form of the serial dime novel itself—its capacity to continue infinitely—assures the escape of the supervillain and thus the lack of narrative closure and its jurisdiction over the finite and the certain, for without his escape and subsequent return, the series could not continue. By staging unrestrained criminal activity in this manner (and we see this in the Tarzan series as well as in Fu Manchu), serial dime novels do not and cannot resolve or manage cultural anxieties. Instead, they intensify them.

By redeploying the stereotype of the atavistic Asian genius as an uncontainable threat, Rohmer stabilizes the Asian other in which his books traffic as a site and source of national devastation. He also positions the imagined reader as always potentially vulnerable to this threat. He does so by drawing the reader into a performance of anxiety. What will Fu Manchu do next? Why can't the detectives ever catch him? Or perhaps more angrily: they've let him escape again! Not unlike the detective's anxieties, these emotions register on the body of the reader: we quiver and quake as we turn each page. We could even say that Fu Manchu functions as a form of emotional mimesis. The series inspires a heightened affective response to its stories that repeats and exaggerates the cultural anxieties of modern social life. Like the detectives we follow through the series, we are supposed to "sigh," "tremble," to become "clammy with nervous perspiration." The sense of anxiety that is transferred from detective to reader can be seen as another staple of the serial form, allowing for an uncontainable emotional flow between the text and its context of reception. As a species of sensationalism, serial novels use this flow to great advantage: the more repeatable the plotline, the more intense the reader's (pleasurable) displeasure in reading the individual novels. The serial dime novel form thus serves to produce a new type of anxious reader in mimetic relation to the anxieties of a culture.[73]

Part of what is supposed to frighten us is the character of Fu Manchu himself, who is never simply described as bestial or atavistic, but rather as combining bestial with civilized qualities. In fact, Fu Manchu's true threat to "the white race" seems to lie in his ability to be both physically degenerate and unusually gifted in the higher arts of civilization. He is endowed with "terrifying genius" and he is an archaic monster, "a very old man, emaciated to a degree hitherto associated only with mummies."[74] Rohmer often describes the Asian archvillain in these monstrous and animal terms: Fu Manchu is "a person tall, lean, and feline, with a close-shaven skull, and long magnetic eyes of the true cat green" (*Return of Dr. Fu Manchu,* 4), and he has "long, yellow hands with incredibly pointed nails" (*President Fu Manchu,* 76). Physically, Dr. Fu Manchu is an illusory figure whose body, like *Mr. King's,* never fully materializes, but appears only in dim outline. Rohmer just as often emphasizes Fu Manchu's mental capacity: "His skull—his fleshless yellow skull—was enormous," and he "accumulated in one giant intellect . . . all the resources of science, past and present" (*Insidious Dr. Fu Manchu,* 10). More than anything, therefore, Fu Manchu is a temporal and corporeal hybrid: "high shouldered, with a brow like Shakespeare and a face like Satan" (*Insidious Dr. Fu Manchu,* 10). To be both Shakespeare and Satan is to be both poetic genius and biblical evil; to be all the resources of science, past and present, is to be a living incarnation of the history of knowledge. As one character worries, "I thought such a brain must be that of a madman or of a genius" (*Fu Manchu's Daughter,* 308). Of course, Rohmer's point is that Fu Manchu is frighteningly all these things. He is a doctor, a scientist, and a lunatic who tries to "take over America" and turn it into a "dictatorship," and thus "torture and terror stalk the White House."[75] Posing as a counterpoint to Tarzan's brute strength, Fu Manchu's body is evasive, incomplete, and archaic. His mental capacity, by contrast, surpasses the greatest minds of civilization.

As a whole, the series conjures a disturbing vision of modern progress. As one character laments in *President Fu Manchu,* "Machinery has made men mad. [O]n the day machinery reaches up to the stars, man will have sunk back to the primeval jungle" (15). As progress progresses, humanity regresses. Moving forward in time fosters an inevitable reversion. But the series also embraces modern progress, for if anything comes to the aid of Rohmer's detectives, and thus to national security, it is modern science, itself operating as a site of futurity and advancement. Indeed, it is through the rationale provided by science that the detectives achieve partial control over their chaotic surroundings. Consequently, when Dr. Cumberly discovers his friend, Leroux, in an apartment with a dead women, he knows Leroux is not the murderer by looking into his eyes because "in common with all medical men, Dr. Cumberly was a great physician and a proportionally great physiognomist" (*Yellow Claw,* 13). Understanding the dangers of visibility, Soames, one of *Mr. King*'s criminal aids, attempts a disguise, but he is uncertain as to its efficacy because "he knew that [the police] judged likenesses, not by complexions, which are alterable, not by the color of the hair, which can be dyed, but by certain features which are measurable, and which may be memorized because nature has fashioned them immutable" (*Yellow Claw,* 190). The detectives and medical men's ability to "read" the body is not due to simple intuition, but to the essentializing devices of scientific culture.[76] Rohmer, like Burroughs, uses this science to direct the plot of his novels and to solve, at least partially, his narrative mysteries.

By writing the narrative from the point of view of medical men and expert scientists, Rohmer locates narrative control in the medical gaze. Thus, M. Gaston Max of *Yellow Claw* is eventually able to apprehend Soames by relying on the accuracy of scientific scrutiny:

Height, about four feet eight-and-a-half inches, medium build and carries himself with a nervous stoop. Has plump hands with rather tapering fingers, and a growth of reddish down the backs thereof. His chin recedes slightly and is pointed, with a slight cleft parallel with the mouth and situated equidistant from the base of the chin and the lower lip. A nervous mannerism of the latter periodically reveals the lower teeth, one of which is much discolored. His eyes are small and ferret-like, set very closely together and of a ruddy brown color. His nose is wide at the bridge, but narrows to an unusual point at the end. He has scanty eyebrows set very high, and a low forehead with two faint, vertical wrinkles starting from the inner points of the eyebrows. His natural complexion is probably sallow. His ears are set far back, and the lobes are thin and pointed. His hair is perfectly straight and sparse, and there is a depression of the cheeks where one would expect to find a prominence: that is—at the cheekbone. The cranial development is unusual. The skull slopes back from the crown at a remarkable angle, there being no protuberance at the back, but instead a straight slope to the spine, sometimes seen in the Teutonic races, and in this case much exaggerated. Viewed from the front the skull is narrow, the temples depressed, and the crown bulging over the ears, and receding to a ridge on top. In profile the forehead is almost apelike in size and contour. (334–35)

In a description that could have easily appeared in a textbook on atavism, Soames is described as a human–beast hybrid. He is covered with "reddish down," has a "receding chin," "ferret-like eyes," "high eyebrows" that seem to contradict his "low forehead," a sickly and "sallow" complexion, and vampiric ears "set far back" on his head with a "skull that slopes back at a remarkable angle." In short, Soames is "apelike." If *Tarzan* recuperates the body as the primary, if indecipherable, location of racial, national, and biological identity, Rohmer's detective novel proffers human science as a system of accurate identification of that body. As in the fingerprinting sequence in *Tarzan of the Apes*, science asserts itself in the Fu Manchu series to restore to the detectives what their bodies cannot accomplish and to act as a diagnostic remedy for what ails the nation. The authority ceded to science also serves to compensate for the fragility of the detectives' masculinity. That is, the medical sidekicks' scientific ability temporarily balances the failed masculinity of the main detectives. As the detectives' medical scrutiny expands, the criminal bodies they apprehend are reduced to their parts. This aids in the fragmentation of the criminal and racial body, forcing it to materialize in a way it otherwise refuses. As a result, the series's medical men emerge as masters of identification at least in some measure capable of controlling the subjects they hold in their gaze, and thus scientific knowledge helps to recuperate in their minds what has failed them in their bodies.

We can thus surmise that the nervous bodies of the Fu Manchu series act as a sponge for the nervousness of the nation, and it is this cultural anxiety on which Rohmer capitalizes. In Fu Manchu, he constructs the atavistic body in its most acute form, preserving it as a fixed site of contagion and alarming cultural destruction. Whether Fu Manchu is sending out deadly insects to kill his enemies in their sleep or force-feeding them opium, the Asian mastermind consistently spreads disease and addiction throughout the world, leaving those that he has touched either in "the ravages of sorrow or illness" (*Yellow Claw*, 4), tainted by "a sickly yellow tinge" (*Return of Dr. Fu Manchu*, 43), "limp, sallow-faced . . . and in a stupor" (*Fu Manchu's Daughter*, 71), or dead. All who come into contact with him are overcome by "the loathing inspired by a thing diseased, leprous, contagious" (*Yellow Claw*, 392). They are also made atavistic. *Mr. King*, for instance, lures politicians into an opium den named "the grove of a million apes" (*Yellow Claw*, 272), and Dr. Fu Manchu ensnares the unwitting detectives into "the tomb of the black ape" (*Fu Manchu's Daughter*, 51). By crafting an apish landscape such as this, Rohmer provides the details for an atavistic world at the hands of "the yellow peril."

And as was the case with Tarzan, Fu Manchu can pass on his atavism to his offspring, a capacity prominently featured in *Fu Manchu's Daughter*. In this book of the series, Fu Manchu has an evil daughter, Fah Lo Suee, who cuts as illusive and fragmented a figure as her father: her body is "a dim outline," she dresses in "shapeless black," and is a "she-devil" (64, 67). She, too, is a human–beast hybrid with "an unforgettable hand, delicious yet repellent, with pointed nails: a cultured hand possessing the long, square jointed thumb of domination; a hand cruel for all its softness as the velvet paw of a tigress" (63). Fah Lo Suee's characterization keeps the contradictions of Fu Manchu's body in play: she is highly civilized and a tigress, and therefore she is "the most dangerous woman living." In short, she is *"Dr. Fu Manchu's daughter"* (98, Rohmer's italics). The italicized appearance of Fah Lo Suee in the series not only allows for a fresh source of horror, but also confirms Fu Manchu's reproductive potency, dramatizing the troubling notion that criminality is hereditary. Readers of the series have seen this before, not surprisingly in *The Return of Dr. Fu Manchu*. In this book, Fu Manchu breeds human–beast hybrids, which he calls "cynocephalytes" (a fabled race of men with dogs' heads) in "glass jars." "Out from [the jar] peered a hideous dog-like face, low browed, with pointed ears and a nose almost hoggishly flat." The monstrosity had "gleaming fangs" and "a long yellow-gray body" that "rested on short malformed legs" (185). Fu Manchu explains that the creature "was a devoted servant, but the lower influences of his genealogy sometimes conquered" (185). Perhaps deliberately recalling the hybrid horrors of H. G. Wells's *The Island of Dr. Moreau* (1896), Fu Manchu's species of dog men, and other atavistic hybrids throughout the series, set the stage for a startling vision of modernity in which life itself, and power over its proliferation, is at stake.

It is by way of the "reproductive issue" in both the Tarzan and Fu Manchu series that we witness these stakes, which involve the mapping of cultural and national progress onto a post-Darwinian evolutionary model. Fah Lo Suee and Jack/Korak exist in their respective series not just as figures of narrative emplotment. Rather, they bring with them a sense of reproductive time. With their appearance, the series can go on, and by extension, so can the social world each series allegorizes; both series and society are now assured the ability to expand infinitely into the future. In the Darwinian model, human beings self-reproduce, with variation and natural selection as the mechanism for evolutionary continuance and change. Transmission and inheritance are the processes by which traits or characteristics are passed on to succeeding generations through reproductive variation of the organism. In both *The Son of Tarzan* and *Dr. Fu Manchu's Daughter,* race, character, desire, and tendency all become biologized entities that can be acquired through reproductive means. These traits, however, are not explained (à la Darwin's evolutionary gradualism) as adaptations to certain selective pressures over time, but as a more straightforward effect of reproductive choice. At least this is the case with Tarzan's son. In the case of Fah Lo Suee, we simply do not know the means of her generation because there is no mention of a human source for her birth. Fu Manchu is always a lone figure with no partner in sight, as if he himself gave birth to his daughter out of one of his chemical cocktails. In any case, each series engages the idea of reproductive time in that its temporal scheme requires the production of offspring as the means for narrative continuance. This is not the familiar heteronormative story where marriage and family resolve narrative and therefore social conflict. Quite the contrary. It is a story where social conflicts are not only exacerbated by reproduction, but where reproduction becomes the source of those conflicts.

The argument could be made that reproductive time, as I am describing it, parallels the time of mass production insofar as they both operate as tactics of narrative extension over the course of the two series. I am also inclined to argue that reproductive time and mass productive time are intertwined; each temporal paradigm relates to and reinforces the other. The temporal paradigm of reproduction avers that modern progress depends on the biological continuance of the human species. The temporal paradigm of mass production avers that modern progress depends on the technological massification of culture. But the two paradigms are really one; each participates in the idea of the managed producibility and reproducibility of the cultural and social world. As enacted by serial dime novel culture, machinic production and human reproduction converge as an ideology of modern time, an ideology that requires the attendant beliefs of reproductive regulation and rational management as the mechanisms of progress. As far as the conservative narrative goes, both forms of (re)production invoke a struggle of the present against the past in a determined march forward away from the destabilizing, threatening forms of premodernity. In this struggle, the modern nation-state is supposed to emerge intact, purified of its relations to the past. Yet if the past is what national and imperial projects like eugenics and its correlate scientific racism take on themselves to discipline, it is also what they produce. Both production and reproduction, as they are enacted in and by the serial dime novels at hand, lead us back (to human prehistory, to the product). Each series calls forth an injunctive politics of return, an allegorical reference to the inherent contradictions of late modernity whereby atavism, the embodiment and practice of historical recursivity, poses a challenge to progressivist notions of modern time.

Past–Present

A growing body of scholarship has argued that the American national subject is produced as white through a combination of symbolic representations of racial difference and political legislative acts and policies that subordinate or exile biologically and socially demonized underclasses. Of particular importance is critical work that explores how the political economy of the United States is entirely dependent on the internal racialization of the population.[77] The political and ethical urgency of these arguments resides in their attempt to release identity categories from their groundedness in scientific and other essentializing forms of representation. Animated by the same impulse, I have been suggesting the importance of a political and intellectual practice that looks at the cultural logic through which the body comes to be attached to biological explanation and discerns the corporeal and temporal contingencies of that attachment.

The Tarzan and Fu Manchu series present a picture of the nation haunted by multiple fears and desires. Stemming from these fears and desires, imperialist policies and national agendas established new forms of biological decision making. I have suggested that the concept of atavism and the trope of the atavistic body figure forth the ambivalences and ambiguities of a national body in sociocultural flux. Tarzan, as a national superhero, indexes a cultural desire to reinforce white masculinity as a symbol of the nation through the construction of male strenuousness and the display of human mastery over nature. Fu Manchu, as a national supervillain, indexes the ways in which human science rerouted anxieties of national decay onto the body of the racial other. In each instance, the trope of the animal emerges as the sign of the past's return and therefore as the nexus where the past and the present meet.

In *Primate Visions*, Donna Haraway argues that modern science uses nonhuman primates to remap Western notions of race and gender onto the boundary between nature and culture. Nonhuman primates, in this sense, function as "boundary keepers" between civility and chaos and simultaneously layer those boundaries with racial, sexual, and gendered value. In fin-de-siècle human science, this boundary was also mapped onto a template that separated out human species from each other, denoting races more or less adaptable to modern progress. Johannes Fabian, in his critique of anthropological discourse, has called this the "denial of coevalness," whereby the specifically racial other is refused entry into the ethnographic present of the anthropologist.[78] In other realms, this kind of thinking has relegated immigrants (in the context of the United States and other Western nations, for example) and people of "developing" nations to a temporal location prior to modernity. The texts I have explored, however, establish the animalized human body as a figure that breaks down these boundaries rather than holds them in place. Indeed, the atavistic body puts on display the incoherence of its cultural valuation.

If we can say at this point with some certainty that power is inevitable, that as subjects we are subjects of power, we can also see how the production of characters like Tarzan and Fu Manchu, as expressions and effects of power, are also hostile to ideas of modern selfhood predicated on liberal notions of the autonomous self and sociobiological notions of normative human and social relations. Not only do characters such as Tarzan and Fu Manchu cross out categorical distinctions like the human and the animal, they offer up competing narratives of modern personhood, which is also perhaps their utopian potential. This matters because it points to ways out of the more pessimistic argument that the subject, in and of power, is simply a passive result of the ebb and flow of the social tide. The two series I have discussed demonstrate the multiplicity of uses to which social structures—the regulatory forms of power that shape culture and cultural commodities—can be put, where the disciplined subject is potentially enlivened by its contradictions.

In *Degeneration,* his 1898 study of "the various embodiments which degeneration and hysteria have assumed," physician Max Nordau concludes that "degeneration is the consequence of the excessive organic wear and tear of nations" increasingly populated by "the senseless stammering and babbling of deranged minds" and by bodies pitifully overtaken by "the convulsions and spasms of exhaustion."[79] The Tarzan and Fu Manchu series bring to life the disturbing cultural hysteria resonating in Nordau's words. They do so, however, in a manner that undercuts the desire for a stable human subject implied by Nordau's lament. Instead of a unitary subject, instead of a legible human body, instead of the assurance of national futurity, the atavistic body reveals the contingency of the human, the potential beastliness of humanity, and the spectacle of a body fragmented by or laden with incompatible terms.

In *Time and Narrative,* Paul Ricoeur queries: "How can time exist if the past is no longer, if the future is not yet, and if the present is not always?"[80] I have asked that we read atavism as a trope that participates in such a question insofar as it challenges key narratives about modern time. The idea of modernity as a process of modernization depends on time conceived as a series of successive events in which each present moment determines the next. But it is the modern construction of time as linear and continuous that both undergirds a cause–effect understanding of history and subtends the notion of biological determinism that allows modernity to constitute itself as such. By contrast, atavism suggests that modernity's most influential temporal horizon is not the future but the past. In chapter 1, I referred to Latour's term *nature–culture,* which he uses to denote the intimately related and co-extensive production of nature and culture. His study of modernity as a project as opposed to an inevitable event in the unfolding of human history also concerns the modern organization of time. "The modern passage of time," Latour writes, "is nothing but a particular form of historicity." For Latour, this means that time, in and as modernity, operates "as an irreversible arrow, as capitalization, as progress." Just as Latour conceives of nature–culture as overlapping and networked materializations, he also asserts the nondivisibility of time. The temporality of modernity can be said to have existed only as a systematized idea, and therefore never to have existed at all. Fortunately, Latour professes, this is an idea we can reject in order to favor all those elements that elude the system, "since every cohort of contemporary elements may bring together elements from all times." Reimagining time in this manner means that "our actions are recognized at last as polytemporal."[81] The Tarzan and Fu Manchu serials, rather than assuming a division between nature and culture or past and present, posit their constitutive interpenetration. Allowing for the expression of a "past–present" in this way, serial novels challenge both the experience of the irreversibility of time and the progressivist belief in the inevitability of the future.[82] Each series forwards an understanding of the past not as something lifeless or inactive, but as a vibrant force that shapes and forms the modern world. The Tarzan and Fu Manchu serials move forward by falling back on themselves, formally as well as thematically. In them, time becomes cognizable as a progressive–regressive movement, an uninevitable, reiterative continuity.[83]

The temporal incongruities that converge in the animalization of the main characters of each series, and even more pointedly in their offspring, most dramatically perform the pull of the past on the present. With the rise of Darwinian evolutionary thought, views of nonhuman primates became firmly tied to an understanding of human evolutionary development over time. In the Western imagination in particular, the animal world became central to the iconography of the human past. The Tarzan and Fu Manchu serials can be read as an extended meditation on the aftereffects of Darwinian theory to the extent that we understand their concern with nation, generation, and reproduction to stem from that theory. The bodies produced by these serials are reiterations that engage a prior moment of species history; both Tarzan and Fu Manchu's offspring guarantee the repetition of the evolutionary/devolutionary cycle. In each, atavism functions to mark the past of the modern and becomes the means by which we locate ourselves in and as a part of modernity.

Because advanced civilization was the ultimate goal posed by eugenic adaptations of evolutionary science, the prominent inclusion of Tarzan's son and Fu Manchu's daughter in each series holds particular significance, demonstrating rather powerfully how pervasive theories of reproduction had become in the cultural project to represent or reimagine the nation. If I have been moving inexorably toward an engagement with reproductive discourses in the course of this book, this is because heredity hovers over the social and literary history of early twentieth-century culture in a way that demands serious attention. As anthropologist Lewis Henry Morgan wrote in *Systems of Consanguinity and Affinity of the Human Family*, "the permanence of species . . . [and] . . . the special creation of man" were "the question of questions in modern science."[84] Not only did new forms and legitimations of biological thinking instantiate restrictive immigration policies and violent imperialist actions, but they also worked to naturalize the relations of the modern family. The reproductive discourse through which ideas of kinship expressed themselves in the early 1900s posited a eugenic organization of the State, separating out the temporal confusions of the modern that, despite attempts to the contrary, nonetheless dangerously lingered. Reproductive transmission, therefore, becomes the motor for the reproduction of the nation-state, a motor that ensures the hegemonic concept of epistemic familialism.

In addition to Roosevelt's worry over and celebration of masculinity during this period, there is equally compelling evidence that femininity was experiencing its own sense of cultural jeopardy and national significance. Because of women's function as a reproducer of the social body, the figure of the mother in particular came to signify the potential for national renewal on the one hand or national devastation on the other. As Roosevelt put it, "the willfully idle man" was as dangerous as "the willfully barren woman."[85] This claim finds suggestive confirmation in the feminist reform movement of the period, which argued, in the words of self-proclaimed feminist Elsie Clews Parsons, that educated white women who "belong to superior stock" but refused to have children were committing "a crime against eugenics."[86] Clews's assertion raises important questions about the links between early feminism and the ideology of reproduction that I will address in the next chapter of this book.

5. Unnatural Selection

Mothers, Eugenic Feminism, and Regeneration Narratives

Not to go on all-fours; that is the law.
　　　　—H. G. Wells, *The Island of Dr. Moreau*

IN A 1915 short story in *Vanity Fair,* Anita Loos, the well-known author of *Gentlemen Prefer Blondes,* portrays a young woman in the grip of an unfortunate decision. In a story entitled "The Force of Heredity, and Nella: A Modern Fable with a telling Moral for Eugenists," Loos tells us that "twelve years had elapsed since Nella had promised her old mother that, come what might, she would always be eugenic."[1] In the duration of those twelve years, Nella moves to New York City, becomes a manicurist at a fancy hotel, and disavows "the teachings of her good old mother." In a rash, last-minute decision, Nella eschews her poor but "healthy" and "masculine" fiancé, Gus, for betrothal to the wealthier Sigsbee van Cortland, a Copper King, who also happens to have a wooden leg. Although Nella's true love is Gus, who was "as handsome as handsome is" with "a fine, sensitive mouth," the Copper King could produce the "tinkle," and so Nella set her fate.

In a chance meeting with Gus many years later, Nella lies on her chaise longue, weeping, miserable, and neurasthenic. On a walking tour of her home, we find out the reason behind her anguish as well as the moral of the story: "Together they wavered through one exquisitely furnished room after another and finally stopped before a door on which was a sign reading: NURSERY. Gus opened the door. Inside, hobbling pitifully around the room, were eleven children. Gus looked once again and recoiled. They had all been born with a wooden leg!" The intended humor, and horror, in Loos's fable depends not only on the way it plays on prevalent concerns about single, economically independent young women in urban areas, but also on how it glosses the premises of early twentieth-century eugenic theory, which argued that if the "right types" mated, a general evolution toward a more perfect form could be expected; conversely, imperfect unions would result in a degeneration from a more perfect form. According to Lamarckian conceptions, even acquired characteristics, like a wooden leg, could be inherited, and hence the joke of the fable. Although Loos lampoons and rejects Lamarckian premises, her story still raises intriguing questions about the popularity of the reproductive role of women in relationship to the threat of degeneration. If, as we saw in the previous chapter, some of the greatest anxieties over cultural progression were organized around theories of heredity, what kinds of pressures, urgencies, or appeals were placed on the category of motherhood, and how did women-authored narratives or feminist rhetorics react to or participate in the generation of these appeals? This chapter will focus on how the figure of the mother emerged with new meaning and significance at the fin de siècle as a privileged site of material and biological value. One of my central claims will be that eugenic conceptualizations of motherhood not only served certain white feminist goals, buttressing national expansion and concomitant nativist ideologies, but also brought about new narrative models through which reproductive ideologies were sedimented.

That "The Force of Heredity, and Nella" appeared in a magazine as popular as *Vanity Fair* suggests a more complicated social and literary history of the discourses of eugenics than tends to be acknowledged. In American literature, naturalist novels like Jack London's *The Sea-Wolf*, which frequently posed themselves as a form of scientific realism, and imperialist adventure novels like those comprising the Tarzan series, with their logics of race and civilization, are usually understood as the genres that most typify this cultural conversation.[2] In British literature, the gothic genre, in which the a-natural is often the central figure, best exemplifies the logics of degeneration by both producing and indulging fantasies of cultural instability and biological chaos.[3] But what goes missing in this loose generic history is fin de siècle "women's literature" (that is, fiction and nonfiction by and about women) and its mediation of these discourses. What gets lost, more specifically, is the significance of eugenic ideology for white feminist intellectuals and authors of this period. In this literature, it is not a monster but often a mother who negotiates, threatens, and ultimately restores a sense of cultural survival and national futurity to the social world.[4]

Although Loos's fable renders modern eugenic anxiety as hyperbole and farce, the work of Charlotte Perkins Gilman demonstrates how eugenic thought helped constitute a particular brand of feminism during this period. In *His Religion and Hers* (1923), Gilman makes an argument for the necessity of women, as mothers, to regenerate "the race." She writes:

Is the race weak? She can make it strong. Is it stupid? She can make it intelligent. Is it foul with disease? She can make it clean. Whatever qualities she finds desirable she can develop in the race, through her initial function as a mother. We should have conventions of young women gathered to study what is most needed in their race and how they may soonest develop it. For instance, far-seeing Japanese women might determine to raise the standard of height, or patriotic French women determine to raise the standard of fertility, or wise American women unite with the slogan, "No more morons!"[5]

Gilman fuses this edict with the rhetoric of feminist protest. It is a call to arms, a political battle cry that would send mothers into the streets, into the convention halls, to remake nations. But how should we understand the relationship between the feminist rhetoric of this argument and its eugenic impulses? Or, to extend this problematic to her fiction, how can we reconcile the feminist themes of Gilman's much acclaimed short story, "The Yellow Wall-Paper," with her eugenic thinking? How can we reconcile the gap that extends between the contemporary feminist reclamation of this text and the qualities of much of the rest of her fiction, such as the eugenic premises of the critically underexamined novel *The Crux* (1911)?[6]

These apparent contradictions pose a problem for how one might go about doing the history of feminism in relation to the biological theories of personhood I have been tracing in this book. The 1970s and early 1980s project of the reclamation of feminist texts, although marking a significant moment in feminist scholarship, suffered from the much-noted problem of presentism in which nineteenth- and early twentieth-century women-authored texts were often treated as confirmations of contemporary feminism, exciting proof of the ongoing fight for liberation. In response, many later feminist literary projects focused on the critique of early feminism. On the one hand, this criticism importantly offered a more detailed classification of nineteenth-century women's literature by understanding how "the cult of sentiment" at times could reinscribe various class and racial hierarchies—indeed, how sentimental narratives often depended on the subordinated labor of working-class women and women of color.[7] On the other hand, these reevaluations may have also generated a structural opposition between the problems of a feminist text from the past and the current project of feminist cultural analysis. The historical situatedness of a feminist text within dominant ideological discourses becomes something we can objectify and thus distance ourselves from, once again affirming and assuring, by contrast, what is "enlightened" and progressive about feminism now. Robyn Wiegman outlines these problems when she argues that contemporary political discourses often fail to attend to the continuity between the ideology in the text under scrutiny and our own politics and subject positions. Accordingly, she recommends that the rethinking of the historical shape of Western racial and feminist discourse should be a "vehicle for shifting the frame of reference in such a way that the present can emerge as somehow less familiar, less natural in its categories, its political delineations, and its epistemological foundations."[8]

In rethinking Gilman's work, then, I do not seek to maintain the "liberatory" aspects of her politics while repudiating her nativist ideology, nor, as one critic suggests, to understand her racism as part of "this extraordinary period of intellectual and political ferment" that should not "mar the importance [and] boldness" of her literary contribution.[9] Rather, I would like to employ Gilman's body of work as a useable history, a means by which to gain a fuller purchase on the contemporary inheritance of early twentieth-century feminism's campaign to free white women from masculine hegemony through a commitment to popular science, specifically eugenic discipline. I thus suggest that we reread Gilman's work not for its contradictions but rather for the coterminous ideologies of feminism and eugenics that she engages. Gilman herself uses eugenics for a feminist agenda articulated on behalf of current social problems, further demonstrating how feminism and eugenics during this period were not only compatible, but also mutually constitutive, each inextricably rooted in the other.[10]

Some recent criticism has begun to take the power of this coterminous relationship into account. Daylanne English's work traces how the mission of racial uplift deliberately borrowed from both eugenic and genetic theory to "bridge the gap between the individual and the collective."[11] Louise Newman's book, *White Women's Rights,* specifically analyzes how evolutionary constructions of racial progress and sexual difference were central to the ways in which white women activists in the late nineteenth and twentieth centuries conceptualized issues of equality, making it possible "for white women to overlook the ways in which white culture was implicated in systems of oppression that governed the lives of nonwhite women."[12] Along with Gail Bederman, who describes how, for white feminist reformers, "sexual equality was a racial necessity," Newman provides a nuanced sociological account of how discourses of "civilization" and "evolution" shaped the way feminists from the period positioned themselves in relation to large-scale social processes.[13] But a sociological analysis of eugenic rhetoric does not fully address the problem of how to view late nineteenth- and early twentieth-century women's fiction. As an empirical mode of analysis, it doesn't attend to representational technologies, and therefore it cannot adequately explain the ways in which scientific ideas shaped, and were shaped by, political as well as aesthetic imperatives. In particular, it cannot account for how these discourses helped bring about narrative innovation (new narrative forms that became a central device for the production and publicization of scientific rhetoric), and thus leaves unanswered many questions about the relationship between feminist literary production and reproductive ideologies. What follows is, in part, a reading of Gilman's *The Crux,* an overlooked novel where such relationships are negotiated and given voice. From *The Crux,* we learn that cultural forms do not just reflect the contemporaneous mood about nation, gender, body, and self, but also take part in the construction of their meanings. The aesthetic encounter with gender politics I engage may thus contribute to what we know about the shape and structure of American politics.

I am particularly interested in how Gilman fuses eugenics and feminism to constitute a new narrative form: a literary subgenre of feminist uplift that I call "regeneration narratives," or, more broadly, feminist regeneration literature. Unlike the degeneration narrative exemplified by *Vandover* and *Nightwood* discussed in chapter 3, the regeneration narrative acts as a curative to the ailing and atavistic body. As such a curative, it possesses two primary goals: the first is to forward the possibility of redemption from the vices of the modern world through an adherence to biological law; the second, to ensure that this redemption is understood as a specifically feminist project. Gilman's regeneration narratives thus deliberately inhabit and dramatically unsettle the "male" genres intent on producing masculinity as an index for national regeneration. Western and adventure novels such as those made popular by Edgar Rice Burroughs, Zane Grey, and Owen Wister responded to Teddy Roosevelt's call for men to "gird up our loins as a nation, with stern purpose to play our part manfully in winning the ultimate triumph."[14] Richard Slotkin has characterized these typically male genres as performing a "regeneration through violence" in which the articulation of male aggression assures American national superiority. In this sense, we can view novels like Owen Wister's *The Virginian* as "Social Darwinian laboratories" of masculine progress.[15]

By contrast, Gilman's regeneration narratives articulate a paradigm of white, middle-class motherhood as a model of social progress. Her work, like the regeneration scenario that Slotkin describes, in part depends on the narrative logic of the western or adventure novel that prescribes a separation from modern life and a temporary regression to a more "natural" state. Yet by simultaneously foregrounding the economic autonomy of women and their reproductive status, Gilman's regeneration narratives suggest that ideologies of national progress (indeed, of U.S. expansionism and the project of empire) have depended on the energies of motherhood at least as much as those of masculine contest. By substituting reproductive competence for masculine virility, Gilman attempts to remedy "the ills of modernity," which she characterizes in *Women and Economics* (1898) as a time in which "human motherhood is more pathological than any other, more morbid, defective, irregular, diseased."[16] Her fiction and nonfiction function together as an agenda for feminist rescue. By representing eugenic ideology as the source of this rescue, they racialize the language of feminism.

Such an argument constitutes a continuation of my discussion of the function and theory of atavism. I have already explored how the formal and tropological devices deployed by Freudian psychoanalysis establish human sexual drives as atavistic returns; how the photograph emerged as a social technology that insists on the corporeal and temporal contingency of human being; how atavism has functioned as the precondition for the expression of sexual subjectivity; and finally how atavism, in the form of the animalized human subject, emerges as a temporal designation that engages a dialectic of pasts and presents, what I call a "past–present." Here, I look closely at the ideological role of reproduction in consolidating understandings about so prominent an issue as the modern family, and the twofold role atavism plays as both a condition to be feared and a resource to be mined on behalf of the female citizen-subject.

Eugenic Feminism

The concerns over national degeneration in the fin de siècle United States may seem odd in a cultural climate that tends to be characterized by technological, urban, and economic progress. The reassuring grant of social progression, however, was always troubled in practice, not only by the vicissitudes of urban growth, immigration, and changing understandings of social identity, but also, and just as resolutely, by confusing shifts in gender norms.[17] As the rapid expansion and commercialization of the nation's urban centers facilitated women's entry into and circulation within a proliferation of publics as workers and consumers, tensions arose over the changing character of "femininity," over how to protect "innocent" youth from modern perversity, or how to encourage sociobiological responsibility in the face of competing sexual, social, and economic possibilities. Whereas the "new woman" was stretching the boundaries of gender definition, white middle-class feminist reformers were busy worrying over the destruction of the home through moral and social "contagion" in the form of prostitution, sexual disease, drunkenness, and the new public character of femininity. Because of what was understood to be women's capacity to pass down either health or disease to future generations, young girls, as potential mothers, became the focus of a campaign to stave off the degeneration of the nation.[18]

One of the more surprising aspects of feminist reform campaigns was the frequency with which self-proclaimed feminists like Charlotte Perkins Gilman, Margaret Sanger, and Victoria Woodhull advocated for sexual and economic freedom, reproductive necessity, and eugenic discipline simultaneously.[19] As Daniel Kevles points out, the eugenics movement was not simply upheld by a small element of radical conservatives, but also included progressives, radical liberals, and advocates of women's rights. Part of the feminist agenda was to push for legislation that would make prostitution illegal, resulting in the passing of one of the first laws directed against prostitution in 1917. Another part was to promote sex education at younger ages and to sponsor sexual purity literature, like "Hygiene and Morality" by Miss Lavinia Dock, a nurse. Other efforts involved the push for safe and legal birth control, and in turn a campaign to convince poor women to use it. Finally, more drastic measures included a program of "negative eugenics": legal segregation and sterilization of the "unfit." At stake in these efforts was the protection of the family from physical and moral contagion, and the protection of the nation from the onslaught of degenerate children. As Margaret Sanger succinctly put it in 1919, "More children from the fit, less children from the unfit."[20]

In agreement with Sanger, Victoria Woodhull, the suffragist and self-proclaimed "free lover" who famously ran for president in 1872, argued in a short pamphlet titled "The Rapid Multiplication of the Unfit" (1891), "The first principle of the breeder's art is to weed out the inferior animals to avoid conditions which give a tendency to reversion and then to bring together superior animals under the most favorable conditions."[21] In the view of both Sanger and Woodhull, women had to make the right choices in terms of marriage, avoid the danger of sexual contamination, and procreate the right types. If such procreation became impossible as a result of impoverishment, disease, racial intermixture, or hereditary defect, birth control would then be at their disposal to allow them to make the choice not to have children. If all else failed, sterilization programs would be in place to ensure the appropriate outcome.

Gilman's work embraced these concepts and helped generate them as part of the white feminist progressive agenda. Much of her nonfiction, in fact, is taken up with the twofold question of how to improve the social conditions of women and how women can improve the race. For Gilman, these questions were fundamentally related to one another. As a strong advocate for sexual and economic reform, she argued that it was a "human necessity" for "women as individuals to meet men and other women as individuals."[22] Her well-known theories of domestic efficiency sponsored the "kitchenless home" and socialized child care to remedy the conventions of housewifery, which she saw as part of a sexual economic contract obliging a woman to "get her living by getting a husband," or more pointedly, by exchanging sex for food.[23] To disrupt the regulatory connection between sex and subsistence, Gilman advocated that women obtain careers and establish communal eating arrangements for their families instead of doing the cooking themselves. Freedom in the domestic sphere rested on the principle, for Gilman a scientific one, that as mothers women were responsible for the care and regeneration of the race as a whole: "When the mother of the race is free, we shall have a better world, by the easy right of birth and the calm, slow friendly forces of social evolution."[24]

In a 1927 article for the *North American Review,* Gilman argued that birthrates of "many races" should be restricted for "sheer economic and political necessity." In an earlier essay that appeared in the *American Journal of Sociology* entitled "A Suggestion on the Negro Problem," she argued for the coercive removal of African Americans from the general populace, for their "present status is to us a social injury." Her "proposed organization" was to place them in an "industrial army" until such a time as they evolved to as high a level as whites.[25] Likewise, in the novel *With Her in Ourland* (1916), the main character, Ellador, criticizes U.S. immigration policy, which she thinks allows for "the crowding injections of alien blood, by vast hordes of low-grade laborers."[26] Whether addressing the need to regenerate the race or the imperative of sexual equality, Gilman summons the language of eugenic science. Her descriptions of African Americans and immigrants are fueled by nativist rhetoric, suggesting that each racial group carried in their biological makeup the capacity to contaminate the Anglo-Saxon race. At the same time, her feminist narrative depends on this eugenic viewpoint, for it suggests that white women's very identities (including their racial and class status) constituted a counterdiscourse, what she saw as an antidote, to the problem of racial contamination.

Eugenic theory allowed Gilman and other progressive feminists to imagine different configurations of gender and power in relation to the social body. The determinations of eugenics aided in the production of an idealized model of femininity, a realignment of gender with a set of moral and biological norms and a system of social value. Eugenics became a mode through which (white) women's social significance could be restructured. In this case, the mother appears as a biological subject organized not so much by a founding maternal identification as by identification with social and moral power, with a desire to participate in the civic-national sphere. In Gilman's work, this alignment of gender and power is developed and clarified in narratives that feature white women's assimilation to a system of social responsibility in relation to sexuality—what Foucault calls "governmentality."[27] In Foucault's formulation, "The individual delimits that part of [her]self that will form the object of [her] moral practice. . . . And this requires [her] to act upon [her]self, to monitor, test, improve, and *transform* [herself]."[28] But my need to revise Foucault's pronouns is telling. The self-governance he describes is an attribute of the modern subject, a moral agent, presumed to be male. Gilman's argument is precisely with this sort of rhetoric; her intention is to demonstrate how women, more properly mothers, need to be understood as the new moral and civic subjects. In Gilman's regeneration narratives, this transformation involves suturing women's sexual choices to a system of social hygiene such that female sexuality can be understood as, to borrow a phrase from Judith Butler, a "regulatory fiction."[29] In Butler's sense, Gilman's narratives do not so much strive to repress female sexuality as they do to compel the incorporation of female desire into the regulatory ideals of heterosexual reproduction in such a way that these ideals are experienced as part of the constitutive core of women's very essence. The regulatory fiction of sexual responsibility, then, is both a norm that manages female sexuality and a fantasy of female political agency, a fiction actively written and maintained within the obligatory frame of reproductive familialism.

We can, in fact, trace the beginning of these concerns to "The Yellow Wall-Paper," in which the female narrator takes up rooms in a "hereditary estate," which acts as a metaphor for both aristocratic decay and the degenerate state of the narrator.[30] Exhausted, postpartum, and neurasthenic, she finds it impossible to be a mother: "Such a dear baby! But, I *cannot* be with him. It makes me so nervous" (6). Instead, her physician husband recommends that she become a child. At his order, she sleeps in the "atrocious nursery" (5). This has the effect of infantilizing and animalizing her. In the yellow-wallpapered nursery, with its barred, cagelike windows and its nailed-down bed where the "bedstead is fairly gnawed" (17), whether by animal, child, or the narrator herself remains unclear, the narrator sees visions in the wallpaper of an animal-like woman "stooping down and creeping about" (11). "It creeps all over the house. I find it hovering in the dining room, skulking in the parlor, hiding in the hall, lying in wait for me on the stairs." Eventually, the narrator overidentifies with this preying image and metamorphoses into a creeping hybrid child–woman–animal herself: "It is so pleasant to be out in this great room and creep around as I please!" (18). As the metaphors of stooping down and creeping suggest, this transformation expresses itself as a kind of degeneration in which an individual, burdened with the traumas of patriarchal modernity or affected by a "hereditary e/state," reverts back to some earlier, lower form of humanity.

Gilman's language resonates with associations in the human sciences of the infantile with the primitive that were increasingly available with the publication of texts like G. Stanley Hall's *Adolescence* and Alexander Chamberlain's *The Child: A Study in the Evolution of Man*. Gilman was a reader of Hall, who, along with his student and colleague, Chamberlain, argued that in children, one could find both atavistic traits and an intense emotional life that tended toward repression in adults. Hall expresses the child–savage analogy in the following way: "The child comes from and harks back to a remote past; the adolescent is neo-atavistic, and in him the later acquisitions of the race slowly become prepotent."[31] In other words, according to Hall, children follow the developmental path of their forbears, and they physically recapitulate the evolutionary process in their individual life span. When the narrator of "The Yellow Wall-Paper" creeps about on all fours, she mimes a regression to the emotional intensity of the child–savage position that Hall describes. Borrowing from evolutionary discourse, degeneration theory, and Hall's theory of "recapitulation," Gilman dramatizes feminist concerns over female agency and eugenic concerns over the social body simultaneously. In "The Yellow Wall-Paper," in fact, feminism and eugenics appear structurally integral to each other. The argument essentially is that without sexual equality, the woman's body (and therefore her reproductive function) degenerates, thus disabling her role as a healthy reproducer of the social world.

The story also dramatizes even as it repudiates Silas Weir Mitchell's recommendation that nervous women undergo an actual process of infantilization/primitivization in order to redevelop into healthier individuals. Mitchell instructed women suffering from neurasthenia to practice balancing themselves on all fours, and then eventually to practice walking again in a literal drama of reevolution. Walter Benn Michaels has argued that the repetition of this treatment in "The Yellow Wall-Paper" imagines "the return to infancy as a moment of willed begetting" that "is the work of something like self-generation."[32] However, in her belief that domesticity made women "atavistic," Gilman structures the story as a narrative of degeneration that she wants to refuse. The narrator's crouching body stands in for an argument about presumptive (heterosexual) familial models in which women, as mothers, could only deteriorate. Gilman's critique of this model not only upset the sanctity of the family structure, but more precisely began to reimagine the constitution of a new kind of scientific familialism.

Fatal Kisses

In contradistinction to "The Yellow Wall-Paper," which, along with the novels *Vandover* and *Nightwood,* we might call a degeneration narrative, Gilman sought to create a genre that would reflect "the new attitude of the full grown woman, who faces the demands of love with the highest standards of conscious motherhood."[33] In "The Yellow Wall-Paper," the narrator finds it impossible to be a mother. She can only manage to be a degenerated child/animal who stoops and creeps. In *The Crux,* a young girl undergoes a continuous process of physical and metaphoric evolution which enacts a movement away from this kind of atavistic femininity and toward something like the work of socially responsible reproduction.[34] Published serially in *The Forerunner* in 1910 and then as a novel by Gilman's own Charlton company in 1911, *The Crux* tells the story of an intergenerational set of white New England female friends and relatives suffering from "arrested development" (71) and "arthritis deformans of the soul" (61) who relocate west in Colorado to start a boarding house because "the place was full of men who needed mothering" (164). These men themselves moved to Colorado to try to win their fortunes in the silver mines, a plot that rehearses the conventions of the male western. The women's westward movement to a more "natural" space, however, reconfigures the logic of a more traditional western plot, especially a novel like *The Virginian,* where an effete New Englander travels west in order to realize his own sense of "manliness." In *The Crux,* the women move west to rejuvenate themselves and to forge a "home"—a space of gendered care—within its open spaces.[35] The novel exemplifies a culture in uneasy transition, eschewing the vestiges of New England puritanism for what is represented as the enlightened sexual-civic discourse of the West. It is an important piece of work, for it complicates what we know about the feminist and eugenic writings of the period and allows us to view Gilman's entire body of work in a new fashion. *The Crux,* positioned between the 1892 publication of "The Yellow Wall-Paper" and the 1915 publication of her utopic feminist novel, *Herland,* asks that we reread these more studied works differently, and it points specifically to the development of the eugenic/regenerative rhetoric dramatized within them. It thus contributes to a conversation about early feminism's intersections with issues of citizenship, civic consciousness, and sex. Whereas "The Yellow Wall-Paper" represents medical men as misguided practitioners, *The Crux* characterizes its (pointedly female) doctors as the ideal citizens of a new republic; where the former text portrays heterosexual marriage as the breeding ground for female hysteria and bad mothering, the latter text argues that eugenic unions are the origins of a fit and vigorous national identity.

Significantly, the specter of sexual disease haunts *The Crux*. The central character, Vivian Lane, falls for Morton Elder, "a motherless boy" with "no good woman's influence about" (182) and who, unbeknownst to her, "has lived the bad life . . . [and] has had the sickness" (172–73)—in other words, syphilis. Dr. Jane Bellair tries to warn her good friend Vivian of Elder's illness, but her concern is not so much that Vivian will catch syphilis as that she may decide to marry and have children with a syphilitic and thus deteriorate the national "stock." She advises: "You must not marry Morton Elder. I know he has syphilis . . . one of the most terrible diseases known to us; highly contagious and . . . hereditary" (225). Here, the logic of syphilis has been borrowed to establish a domain of masculine sexual deviance in binary opposition to the healthy feminine regime that Gilman's work imagines.[36] Syphilis is not a dangerous disorder because of its effects on the individual bodies of the men who disseminate it or the women who catch it but because of its reproductive effects on and within procreative heterosexual unions. In other words, the novel codes syphilis as a danger not because it is a sexually transmitted disease but because it is a sexually transmitted disease that is also hereditary. Stopping the force of degeneration means that mothers, burdened with the cleansing of the future, must eschew sexuality for reproductivity; they must substitute for sexual feeling a desire to reproduce.

In *The Crux,* the threat to reproductivity is perilously hidden within a simple but fatal kiss. Indeed, the fatal kiss is one of the novel's central conceits, imposing itself on the text as a warning and thus signaling an intervention in typical heterosexual narrative form, and in the sentimental romance form specifically. The kiss is deployed, and ultimately deferred, not as a plot device that inspires either romantic suspense or heroic reward but as the site and scene of horror. In the typical fairy tale or romance novel, the kiss is a fundamental generic convention: with its consummation comes heterosexual union and thus narrative closure. In *The Crux,* however, the kiss is fatal. It is not the inevitable gift to the hero, who, after struggling with some tragic flaw, is rewarded by the woman in waiting; nor is it a precursor to the downfall of the sexually promiscuous woman who must be punished for her indiscretions. Rather, in *The Crux*, heterosexual romance itself is a dangerous funnel for social and sexual disease. For Vivian, "love had become a horror" (241).

The first kiss between Vivian and her hometown sweetheart occurs before he moves to the city and falls victim to urban degeneracy, and thus is described within romantic narrative conventions. In "the radiating, melting moonlight" among the "rich sweetness of flowers" on a "tender soft June night . . . he took her face between his hands and kissed her on the mouth" (28–29). The second kiss occurs years later at a coed dance. The encroaching Morton, trying to coerce Vivian back into a relationship with him, pushes upon her during another moonlit night, this one more like the setting of a gothic novel than a romance: he comes to her in the "sudden darkness" of the garden. Moving closer, "he kissed her white shoulder." His "coarsened complexion" (141) stands in obvious contrast to the "white purity" of young, untainted femininity that Vivian is meant to portray. "He was breathing heavily. His arms held her motionless." But, willfully, "she kept her face turned from him" (141). He lets her go, but not before extracting a promise for marriage. Underscoring the potential horror of this promise, the scene ends with Vivian glimpsing "the sight of Morton Elder's face as he struck a match to light his cigarette . . . [which] made it shine out prominently in the dark shelter" and induced in her feelings of "sudden displeasure" (205). The moonlight of her adolescence (romance's most hackneyed symbol) is replaced by the light of a diseased man's cigarette.

Taken together, the two kissing sequences provide the outline for Vivian's sexual development: it begins in a picturesque landscape of a small New England town and ends in a modern scenario of sexually transmitted disease. The lure of the fatal kiss transports Vivian from the sheltered knowledge of adolescence to the risky sensations of adult modern love. This developmental narrative both repeats and troubles the literary conventions of romance. It adheres to the romantic prescriptions for female sexual development in which the heroine must either overcome or fall prey to some sexual adversity. But it also interrupts a narrative of heterosexual closure, for Morton cannot rescue, only contaminate. This rewrites a social scene that tended to conscript disease and contagion onto the woman's body; instead, it relocates the site and circulation of disease in the body of a wayward young man.

Such a shift is particularly significant when we remember, as Elaine Showalter, Mary Douglas, and others have shown, that there is a long history in which women, represented as diseased and contagious, are made to signify national crisis.[37] Gilman reworks the narrative by which romantic bonds and family ties are consolidated and rearranges the traditional narrative patterns of late nineteenth-century family values. But herein lies the paradox of early feminism, for it is in its critique of the normative family that Gilman's narrative turns to conservative ideologies of social advancement. If a contemporary model of feminism typically positions itself against scientific renderings of identity, here, reforming masculinist structures like the family means embracing motherhood as a site of biological value. Positioning women at the center of national progress—at the center of the birthing of history—means corroborating the racialist impulses of national-patriarchal discourses.

Unnatural Selection

When Vivian defends her decision to stay with Morton by invoking that afflicted word, *love,* Dr. Bellair staunchly replies:

Will you tell that to your crippled children? Will they understand if they are idiots? Will they see it if they are blind? Will it satisfy you when they are dead? They may be deformed and twisted, have all manner of terrible and loathsome afflictions, they and their children after them, if they have any. And many do! Dear girl, don't you see that's wicked? Beware of biological sin, my dear, for it there is no forgiveness. (225–26)

Dr. Bellair censures love or sex without eugenic consciousness through the effigy of the deformed body of the future child, for love in this modern scenario can only result in the reality of "biological sin." Significantly, there are no healthy children in the novel at all, only potential mothers. The absent presence of the unborn child hangs menacingly over *The Crux,* shaming its characters to act on behalf of the national future and appearing only in horrific, disfigured form to disrupt the fantasies of heterosexual love and underscore the toxic effects of heterosexual vice. The potential horror of syphilis, then, is the traumatic center of the novel, the heterosexual crisis plot serving ultimately as a dramatic repository for anxieties over female sexuality.

After speaking with Dr. Bellair, Vivian turns for comfort to her grandmother, who eventually assuages her fears by carefully describing the beneficial role of eugenics in modern society. She explains that "the women's clubs and congresses have taken it up" and assures Vivian that "some states have passed laws requiring a medical certificate—a clean bill of health—to go with a license to marry," and that, most importantly, "we are beginning to teach children and young people what they ought to know." "Don't be afraid of knowledge," her grandmother affirms, "when we all know about this we can stop it! We can religiously rid the world of all these—'undesirable citizens'" (245–46).

The grandmother's advice hints at the collaborations through which eugenics found public support, intuiting, as she does, the state as a means of social control in combination with feminist reform. But her response is not at all the kind one may expect from a grandmother consoling her heartbroken, disillusioned granddaughter. Vivian's grandmother, who stands in as a kind of ur-mother in the novel, hardwires eugenics to motherly advice. She casts sentimental bonds not within the more familiar terms of domestic feeling but within the terms of eugenic prescription. In her role as Vivian's caretaker, in fact, the regulatory ideals of eugenic science register *as* domestic affect. This new affective register proposes a strategy for imagining collective feminist struggle and hygienic social progress simultaneously. It also points to the major function of this strategy: it is enacted at the service of the formation of a new kind of family, one consisting primarily of women and embedded in scientific decree. On the one hand, this augments an already epistemic familialism, whose function is to designate and maintain a quarantined and hygienic space for white middle-class culture. But as I have been arguing, it also rearranges conventional familial ideology in its attempt to configure the imagined feminine sphere (private and domestic) as a world of reproductive labor and responsible public life.

In a certain sense, this recalls Priscilla Wald's work on Typhoid Mary, a case of contagious disease that, she argues, formulated a "carrier narrative . . . that worked to contain dramatic changes in familial and social structure by linking transformations in gender roles to the fate of the (white) race and therefore the security of the nation."[38] As Wald describes it, the carrier narrative, "by using contagious disease as an explicit manifestation of the dangers of social contact," reconceptualizes the citizen in terms of their social responsibility.[39] For Gilman and eugenic feminists in general, the threat of contagion deployed in and by their culture's carrier narratives posed a central problem. Deflecting moral and actual manifestations of disease away from the unsuspecting family required a complete refashioning of the domestic sphere within the terms of science as well as a rigorous and conscious regime of differentiation between desirable and, to use Vivian's grandmother's term, "undesirable citizens." For Laura Doyle, whose book *Bordering on the Body* analyzes key novels in modernism and the Harlem Renaissance, this meant positioning the figure of the mother within a regulatory economy of "racial patriarchy."[40] As Doyle forcefully argues, "In these economies, mothers reproduce bodies not in a social vacuum" but rather function as "the cultural vehicle for fixing, ranking, and subduing groups and bodies" within a racially based kinship matrix.[41] Eugenic feminists were aware of the threats consolidated by the carrier narrative that Wald describes and of the patriarchalisms of the traditional kinship narrative, especially, for Gilman, the constricting and potentially dangerous predicates of the heterosexual couple (represented in *The Crux* by the syphilitic Morton). The eugenic family as conceived by Gilman, therefore, involves not only the repudiation of sexual feeling, nor only the invocation of the racial matrix that Doyle discusses, but in addition a deheterosexualization of the middle-class family. In this sense, white progressive-era feminists capitalized on the fear of contagion by emphasizing that the more incipient threat was to reproduction. This allowed them to position women at the center of debates about social progress. Gilman's narratives take this a step further by insisting on the disaggregation of reproduction from heterosexual and patriarchal authority. In Gilman's short story "Making a Change" (1911), for example, the main female character sets up a socialist child care facility on her rooftop and thus defines motherhood as a public identity and child care as a form of community labor.[42] Similarly, in *Herland* (1914), men are irrelevant to the reproductive process altogether. In that novel, the women become pregnant by their own will, not by intercourse, thus eliminating the conduit for contagion that might lead to degeneration.

As an avid reader of theories of civilization and degeneration, Gilman's work refunctions the Darwinian concept of natural selection into a theory of social evolution prescribed, in part, by Herbert Spencer, to whom she referred in her autobiography as the man who taught her "wisdom and how to apply it."[43] Spencer asserted that evolution created qualitative and quantitative differences between the male and female mind, and that when the body and brain were challenged, energy set aside for reproduction would be used up. In other words, if cerebral activity in women was too excessive, there would be losses in energy needed for "race-maintenance." For Spencer, the body was a closed and finite system, one that required a balance between physical or mental depletion in one area and preservation of energy in another, a process he identified as the body's need for "equilibrium."[44] According to Spencer, this process of economization and expenditure of bodily resources was differentiated by a gendered physiological economy: a greater portion of women's energy is designated for reproductive activities, leaving them with less strength for other forms of labor or intellectual pursuit. Of course, Gilman found his antifeminist characterization of women disturbing. But in the theories of Lester Frank Ward, an American paleobotanist turned sociologist who promoted the theory of "gynaecocracy," or the superiority of the female sex type, Gilman found a way to reinterpret Spencer's blind spots when it came to women's physiological nature. Relying on Ward's emphasis on the female sex as the primary factor of hereditary transmission, Gilman argued that although both sexes were vulnerable to the conditions of modern life, it was the women who, "as the race type," held the most immediate opportunity "through the immeasurable power of social motherhood" to "develop a race far more intelligent, efficient, and well-organized, living naturally at a much higher level of social progress."[45] (It should come as no surprise that Gilman describes Vivian as an enthusiastic reader of Lester Ward's theories at the start of *The Crux*.) Socially responsible motherhood thus required an evacuation of what Gilman calls "sex attraction" in order to mitigate the problems that could arise when young girls were poised for male interest. She writes, "The more widely the sexes are differentiated, the more forcibly they are attracted to each other . . . so as to retard and confuse race-distinction . . . and seriously injure the race."[46] In other words, unchecked female sexuality, and more specifically noneugenic sex, was what she perceived as one of the greatest problems of modernity. She argues: "We, as a race, manifest an excessive sex attraction, followed by its excessive indulgence; an excess which tends to pervert and exhaust desire as well as to injure reproduction."[47] For Gilman, via Ward, neither work nor education damaged women's reproductive abilities; rather, sexual pleasure did. For this reason, Gilman advocated against a model of reproduction based in desire and for a model of sexual sameness that she felt would do away with the problem of attraction. We can see this most of all in *Herland*, where all the women reproduce parthenogenetically. The all-female residents of this world dress in "sexless costume[s]" and are "actuated with a common impulse . . . [and] moved by precisely the same feelings, to the same end."[48] Throughout her work, Gilman provides an example of how conceptions of eugenic science offered feminist authors and intellectuals the means to redefine their relationship to heterosexual imperatives. This redefinition required a narrative that placed female agency within the parameters of familial social structures, rooting both the female body and the social body in biology.[49]

"The delight of mere ascent"

In many ways, Gilman's regeneration narratives repeat and complicate what Jackson Lears has described as the era's ethos of antimodernism. In *No Place of Grace,* Lears characterizes fin de siècle American culture as riven with a regressive antimodernist sensibility. This sensibility, Lears argues, was the result of a widespread recoil from overly consumptive modern existence and encompassed a search for more intense forms of physical and spiritual experience that would integrate all aspects of life and thus stand in opposition to the divided or discontinuous self of modernity. In her own way, Gilman was involved in a similar search, one that would allow for the more integrated selfhood that Lears describes as well as work toward the building of a better, less neurasthenic and less syphilitic social world. Lears, however, insists on a relationship between this search and the emergence of a "martial ideal." According to him, the violence of the warrior, or war hero, and his willingness to suffer serves as an antidote to overcivilization. Opposing the decadence and disorder of modern society, the figure of the warrior personifies wholeness and intensity of experience, and the concept of war promises social and personal regeneration.[50] But Gilman found the celebration of the brute warrior man troubling, conjuring up notions of masculine sexual dominance and even rape while simultaneously designating women as auxiliary attachments to social change.[51] As I have been suggesting, Gilman's regeneration narratives manage the problem of male violence by imagining a space of eugenic familialism that would safeguard women's reproductive resources against incursions by syphilitic men, where the disavowal of sexual energy, which for Gilman is the same as the disavowal of hypermasculine authority, becomes a means for the perpetuation of the Anglo-Saxon race. Nevertheless, in accordance with Lears's characterization of the antimodernist impulse, she locates the rejuvenation of young women's bodies and thus their ability to reproduce in the spaces of nature.

In *The Crux*, a climactic trip to the mountains most fully expresses Vivian's feminist regeneration, one that is both antimodernist and evolutionist in nature. She enrolls her students in a summer camp program in "the high lying mountain lake" (277) where Dr. Bellair owned "a piece of wild-rough country" (277). Here in the "untouched wilderness," Vivian would awake "to slip out for a morning swim," during which she would "glide, naked, in that water . . . and swim out . . . turn on her back and lie there—alone with the sky" (278). It is here that Vivian's body first comes into narrative view. *The Crux* thus imagines "the wild mountain country" as a regenerative space where her body emerges, or ascends, in a way that her New England routine would repress. And it is Vivian's body that becomes the vehicle for her grandmother's, Dr. Bellair's, and by extension feminism's eugenic yearnings.

Not surprisingly, race is the repressed sign of this process of ascension, for Vivian's new body, and thus her new self, takes shape in and through the mining of a frontier life rife with racial metaphor: she "learned to cook in primitive fashion" and "grew brown and hungry and cheerful" so that on her return, her grandmother remarks that she "is certainly looking well—if you *like* that color" (279). If Vivian's swimming ritual acts as a catalyst for an unmediated relationship to her body, her camping trip enables an unmediated relationship with the racially encoded spaces of nature. Vivian's racialization, evidenced in her new brown skin, reproduces the story of a hybrid body particular to American cultural forms that dates back to the colonial period and repeats itself within the new concerns of American modernity—that the restoration of self, health, and Anglo culture itself requires and is confirmed by one's proximity to and/or movement through a racialized space or body. In this cultural imaginary, primitive cultures and primitive landscapes are equated with nature and health and provide a means through which Anglo culture can experience both. (We witnessed this in the previous chapter through the character of Jack/Korak, who experiences the African jungle as a revitalizing source for Western subjectivity.) Nonetheless, while a flirtation with the "racial primitive" and their landscapes may be momentarily imagined and always seems metaphorically available as a therapeutic resource for white health, the derisive comment made by Vivian's grandmother suggests the anxieties over racial and cultural miscegenation that this new body may evoke.

Thus, in *The Crux,* anxieties over contact with white culture's primitive others are ultimately assuaged by reestablishing Anglo-Saxon civility in the form of a heterosexual union. The restoration of Vivian's self, the literal naturalization of her body, is quickly made hygienic through the staging of a last-minute, closing-chapter Anglo marriage, not to the syphilitic Morton but to a male doctor. Vivian's relationship to her female doctor friend finds a surrogate in a heterosexual marriage to Dr. Hale and thus shores up her interpellation into the space of hygienic medical culture. Not surprisingly, her marriage is based neither on "love" nor "desire"; the fact that Dr. Hale is nearly twice her age (more of an archetypal father figure than a lover) ensures this fact. Further, Dr. Hale himself has rejected typical heterosexuality. Having been used and discarded by a seductress in his youth, he distrusts most women and all sentiment. More than anything else, Vivian's marriage is a medical marriage; it replaces questions of desire with the eugenic rules that govern women's reproductive choices. It is the subgenre of evolutionary uplift, the eugenic–feminist regeneration narrative with its emphasis on physical health and its allegories of ascent, that creates the conditions of possibility for the emergence of both Vivian's eugenic consciousness and her "erect" (114) body and guides her away from irresponsible, indeed syphilitic, couplehood that Dr. Jane Bellair, along with her hard-boiled medical dogma, guards her against. The novel's telos of New England immobility ("arthritis deformans of the soul"), physical activity (going West), "erect posture" (114), ascent (climbing mountains), and, finally, the "right type" of marriage inscribes eugenic progress as feminist advance, and vice versa.

Gilman's regeneration narratives mean to derail the ideals of masculinity that the western and adventure genres tend to establish by replacing the typically male main characters with a series of college-educated, white, middle-class women. As in the western, many of Gilman's female characters go west to find themselves and regain their health, sanity, and bodies in open outdoor spaces where they engage in rigorous activity as opposed to rest. The transformation of these masculine genres seems to be a way for Gilman to expand the limits of her own and other women's domesticated social situations. These westward expansions act as an analog for the expansion of feminine identity. In turn, this new identity acts as an analog for evolutionary progress: Gilman's women do not only go west, they also go up. She often describes her female characters as dwelling in "upland valleys" surrounded by "steep canyons," and "the clean, wide, brilliant stillness of the high plateau," or even residing in sanatoriums called "The Hills" where they experience "the delight of mere ascent."[52] Geographical elevation is highlighted in Gilman's narratives not only as a representative aspiration in narratives that are inexorably conscious of women's domestic confinement, but also as a Darwinian allegory of evolution where one's physical ascent to a higher place guarantees the commensurate logics of superior social status, economic mobility, health, and moral well-being.[53] As in the male western, the emergence of this identity, the basis for its theory of progress, is predicated on racial ideologies and U.S. expansionism.[54] In Gilman's brand of eugenic feminism, the female crossing into "male" terrains and subject positions operates entirely in keeping with U.S. nationalist assumptions—that it is the duty of white people (male or female) to expand, extend, colonize, and reproduce. Gilman's narratives thus produce an unsettling territorial and regulatory regime; they operate as a map of sorts in which the rhetorical imbrications of time and location (of modernity and geography) reconvene the hierarchies of social categories one might hope feminist politics would disassemble.

The eugenic feminism that Gilman's work represents aligns with and mitigates typical anxieties of the period in which the body takes on the meanings and troubles of modernity, at times signifying its health, but more often signifying its degeneracy. We saw this in "The Yellow Wall-Paper" and its creeping, crawling narrator. In her later fiction, Gilman moves the body out of its crouched and degenerated position and mobilizes it within a narrative of regeneration that restages the crisis of modern personhood as a predicament of eugenic motherhood. In bridging the gap between female subjectivity and the body politic and between apprehensions over individual contagion and national health, the project of eugenic feminism fundamentally changed conceptions of each. Reproduction itself became a site of identity and a social imperative, a paradox of compulsory sexual agency. The conditions on which the regeneration narrative depends, and on which Gilman's social utopias are imagined, thus dramatize white women's identification with a power that requires an investment in the renunciation of their own sexual agency.

Mother May I?

If we could characterize Gilman's regeneration narratives succinctly, it might be to note how they are saturated with the longing to create compensatory feminist utopias as a means to solve the perceived problems of modernity, and how these "fictions of progress" seemed to secure white women's centrality to cultural evolution, allowing them to experience reproduction as a world-making practice. In turn, we might begin to unravel the participation of eugenic feminism in producing and stabilizing a distinct set of cultural meanings about sexuality, race, and gender that root identity in biology. Gilman inhabits scientific discourse as a mode of female agency; the centrality of motherhood represented, for her and her feminist counterparts, a dialectic between the constraints of biology and the capacity for self-transformation. Mothers emerged as a function in the formation of worlds enabling women to stake a claim in the struggle to define their bodies, making them "matter." This model of motherhood, in its accumulation of imperatives for self-management and in its racialist impulses, demonstrates how movements that we commonly take as radical or progressive (such as feminism) can engage or be constituted by other discourses (such as biology) to exert prohibitive functions. We might want to explore how this produces nonreproductive sexualities as waste and sexual pleasure as itself a sign and symptom of degeneracy. We could then join existing critiques of early feminism by authors such as Amy Kaplan, Louise Newman, and Michele Birnbaum that track how white female agency of this sort reinforces itself through rhetoric of empire and racial privilege. My point here, though, is not simply one of repudiation in contradistinction to the earlier feminist reclamation of Gilman's work. Rather, I seek to produce an account of how the histories of our feminisms are not politically transparent but fraught with a complex, and I would suggest dialectical, history of promise and damage. In this instance, the driving forces of white progressive feminism helped instantiate and inform what we might think of as a new version of liberal humanism in which the mother acts as ideal civic progenitor. In a move from an ideal of self-governance to an ideal of eugenic familialism, the public valorization of motherhood imposed and enforced regulatory limits on sexual agency that white middle-class feminists of the period pressed into the service of their own political campaigns. As a result, the mother's body emerged as atavism's counterpoint and thus as a location for the progressivist future.

Producing the future as the coveted site of the modern nation's success demands a teleological notion of time for which the past is a space of regression and loss, the future, progression and fulfillment. But the negative characterization of the past prevents recognition of how the present takes shape and how the future actually comes about. As it will be the object of the next chapter to indicate, recognition of the relatedness of past and present spheres may afford an alternative theory of the future. But in order to understand how narratives can generate alternative readings that identify the atavistic self not as the sign of the past's absolute difference but as modernity's constitutive feature, it will be necessary to turn away from Gilman's regeneration narratives and their negative valuing of human prehistory to those narrative moments that she and her feminist counterparts refuse to reflect on, in which an encounter with atavism enables surprising intimacies and political affinities that raise pressing questions about the social and biological entanglement of human being.

6. An Atavistic Embrace

Ape, Gorilla, Wolf, Man

Animals came from over the horizon. They belonged there and here.
—John Berger, "Why Look at Animals?"

When we . . . make love with someone of our own species, we also make love with the horse and the calf, the kitten and the cockatoo, the powdery moths and the lustful crickets.
—Alphonso Lingis, "Bestiality"

IN THE final scene of Eugene O'Neill's drama *The Hairy Ape* (1921), the main character, Yank, encounters a gorilla at the zoo.[1] As the two stare "intently" at each other, Yank admires the gorilla's body: "Some chest yuh got, and shoulders, and dem arms and mits!" (195). Inspired and awed by the strength of the figure before him, Yank breaks his new friend out of his cage, only to be repaid with "a murderous hug." Lying near death on the floor of the cage, Yank utters his last words "in the strident tones of a circus barker": "Ladies and gents, step forward and take a slant at de one and only—one and original—Hairy Ape from de wilds of—" (195) and then dies. Yank's initial attraction and attention to the gorilla's body mirrors his experience of his own body, described by O'Neill as "hairy-chested, with long arms of tremendous power, and [a] low, receding brow above small, fierce, resentful eyes" (141). But in his ventriloquism of the circus barker, he also seems to see his body as others have seen it, as a site of spectacle and exhibition. In the space of the cage, Yank intuits his classed and racialized status as the monstrous other. It is in this moment that he incarnates most acutely the subject/object duality that has come to characterize modern experience. He both embraces his identity and abjects himself: "I'm an ape," he mutters, "Come look at the ape." What this duality bodies forth is the question of how one acquires an identity in late modernity. In Yank's case, that acquisition depends on a fiction of resemblance and difference, what Lacan describes as the transitive and reflexive modes of subject formation. The double-voicedness of his utterance suggests his ability to be both self (the one that controls and calls attention to the ape) and other (the ape), both then and now.[2] In other words, Yank is an atavism.

The Hairy Ape was first performed in 1922 by the Provincetown Players, an experimental theater troupe made up of anarchists, socialists, and feminists.[3] Their production opened to critical acclaim and was moved to a theater on Broadway, where it continued to enjoy success. At its most basic, the plot follows Yank, a coal stoker on a transatlantic ocean liner, and his transformative encounter with Mildred Douglas, the rich daughter of an industrialist, who sends Yank into a confused rage when she refers to him as a "filthy beast." When his ship docks in New York, Yank wanders through Manhattan, at once seeking revenge against Mildred and trying to recover his sense of self. He painfully discovers he belongs nowhere: not with the socialites he encounters on Fifth Avenue, and not even with the labor organizers he meets on the waterfront. The only connection he forges is with the gorilla at the zoo, in whose embrace he dies.

Yank's bestialized figure belongs to the growing breed of "degenerate" populations that I have been discussing. Deployed to condense and sometimes to aggravate an unease, prevalent in the early twentieth century, over the conceptually vague distinctions between human and animal, mind and body, progress and regress, this population of degenerates in novels, short stories, dramas, and medical photographs deliberately positions the modern human subject in relation to its own evolutionary past. In the atavistic body, part human, part beast, human history fuses with natural history and thus (re)dramatizes the origins of modern human identity. In this redramatization, modern human identity surfaces as a fundamental hybridity that manifests the historical present's troubled relationship to its inheritance of the past.

Partly arising in response to the instabilities produced by vast demographic and economic changes, especially in American cities, the image of an animalized human figure conjured up the potential dangers of unrestricted social and sexual promiscuity within the larger community. The hybridity of the atavistic body, in other words, invoked the specter of cross-pollinization across class and racial lines. The atavistic body simultaneously functioned to put the experience of modern identity, deeply informed by rapid urbanization, technological innovation, and Big Business, back into contact with human origin, into tactile and visceral relation with the natural order. The appearance of the animal on the human body thus appeared as an indication of the core meaning of human existence, our evolutionary prehistory. In this sense, Yank's body operates as a metonym for our hominid progenitors. He is the brute against which modernity can measure its nonanimality. But he is also the condition of modernity: his character's crisis figures forth a larger ontological crisis (and paradox) of human being in the modern world. Put simply, the crisis concerns the fear that, despite the cultural trappings of civilization, we might still be just animals. The resulting paradox is that it is precisely this animality that enables the human to emerge as human at all. Both stem from the idea, following Darwinian theory, that we are part of the animal world, but also from the ideological cadences that attached themselves to the animal as a sign of human prehistory and atavistic reversion, cadences concerning sexual and racial aberrance in particular.

For Bruno Latour, modernity is a state in which we have never been; only modern thinking makes such a state seem real. Actual practices of the so-called modern world belie the epistemological divide between nature and culture that structure modern modes of living. One of the distinctions produced by modern thinking that accompanies that divide is the distinction between subject and object: the subject who can know and the object that is known. Latour argues, however, that in practice the world in which we live is fundamentally hybrid, a mixture of subjects and objects with multiple quasi-subjects and quasi-objects in between.[4] Yank's body performs a version of this "mixture" when he "becomes animal." By literally trading places with a gorilla, Yank exceeds and defies the injunction of the modern to be isolated from the natural world. And by transgressing the nature–culture divide set up by modernity, he brings to light the rules and regulations of that divide.

Prominent among the institutional discourses that asserted the uniqueness of the human was, of course, biological science. Perhaps not surprisingly, changing understandings of the human as part of, yet distinct from, the natural world within the sciences fueled a growing sense of uncertainty about what it meant to have a body in late modern culture. Yank's movement down the scale of humanity not only helps track this uncertainty, but also dramatizes the accompanying experience of racial, sexual, and class conflict that lent it its particular shape. Yank's human-to-animal collapse is predicted first by Mildred, when she calls him a "filthy beast," and again after he has been arrested for disturbing the peace. This second prophecy comes from a fellow prison inmate who reads aloud to Yank from a newspaper article about a U.S. senator giving a speech on the floor of Congress in which he characterizes the Wobblies (the Industrial Workers of the World) as "the devil's brew of rascals" who will "tear down society" and force civilization to "degenerate back to the ape" (186). At the drama's end, Yank has become the feral spectacle of these predictions, and thus he is forced to inhabit all that inheres in such a spectacle: subordinated personhood and social unease both. His incomplete final sentence taunts us with the multiple meanings we might understand this emblematic spectacle to generate. His origins are indicated by a dash: he's from "the wilds of—." Here the typographical mark functions as an indication of that which cannot be expressed; it, like Yank's own body, is an enactment of the ineffable. Yank, the dash tells us, originates out of mystery; he is a missing link.[5]

These indescribable origins have much to do with who Yank is: a deprivileged subject of modern labor. The narrative of his decline is shown to be inextricably connected to the effects of capitalist–industrialist modernity. At the same time, his body is marked as ontologically prior to modernity. He is an exploited laborer and therefore an atavistic brute—and vice versa. Amid a whirl of economic objectification, class resentment, and pain, Yank's story traces the catastrophe of a man doomed to extinction. His death is the death of inner life experienced by the modern laborer; his ineffability, his animality, dramatizes the impossibility of self under these conditions. In the final words of the play, from O'Neill's stage directions, we are made to understand that at the sight of Yank's death, "the monkeys set up a chattering, whimpering wail. And, perhaps, the Hairy Ape at last belongs" (198). One might wonder how these stage directions could be enacted in a performance of the drama, and how that sense of belonging might be conveyed to a viewing audience. But perhaps the impossibility of any such conveyance of belonging, like the dash of his origins, is the point here. Yank's journey through the streets of Manhattan to a New York City zoo is a search to belong, but given the conditions of capitalism that inform his existence, this belonging can only be found in the very stereotypes of animality and brutishness that came to designate, and deny, working-class subjectivity in the United States.[6] Yank's death among a community of apes leaves much room, in O'Neill's particular brand of dim irony, for making sense of his ultimate predicament as one of alienation.[7]

As much as this predicament points to the alienation of the working classes as the key motif of O'Neill's drama, Yank and the gorilla's
embrace suggests that this is not necessarily the only story being told
here. "Ain't we both members of de same club—de Hairy Apes?" (196),
Yank asks the gorilla. "Step out and shake hands," he continues, "We'll
knock 'em offen the oith and croak wit the band playin.' Come on
Brother" (198). A fleeting affinity, this, but one that calls forth a way
of thinking of ourselves "in relation," what Donna Haraway has called
a story of "co-habitation, co-evolution and embodied cross-species
sociality."[8] While Yank's body is indisputably an image of class distinction, it is also more, and I am interested in the myriad interpretative
stories that generate and are generated by that body. In his atavistic
downfall, Yank does not simply become an image of the working classes
in the 1920s, nor just a figure through which O'Neill could critique the
stereotyping of the working classes as subhuman. He is also a figure
that calls into question the production of categories of personhood
that structure late modern thought.

The work of French phenomenologist Merleau-Ponty may help us
to read *The Hairy Ape*'s final scene more fully, for it allows us to see
Yank's embrace with the gorilla as a site of unrealized promise in which
the complexities of human and nonhuman worlds offer up new forms
of subjectivity. Merleau-Ponty advances a theory of mutual access engen-
dered by the kinship among things and bodies in the world. He explores
the ways in which human consciousness interacts and exists in conjunction with nonhuman subjects and objects, suggesting that this conjunction contains the means for constructing worlds for ourselves.
For Merleau-Ponty, the nonhuman is a forceful and dynamic aspect of
and in our lives, and it has everything to do with how we experience
them. Merleau-Ponty's concept of a materially embedded self puts pressure on enlightenment rationalist claims of human sovereignty, claims
that assume a self-present human individual as the central, defining
figure in cognition.[9] By contrast, Merleau-Ponty asks that we reframe
the analytical categories of human experience that have heretofore
held sway. Instead of an objective "human individual," Merleau-Ponty
produces an account of the human as "a network of relationships."[10]
Yank and the gorilla's embrace enacts this network of relationships in
such a way as to call into question the modern human individual as cut
off from both things in the world and their historicity. "I am thrown

into nature," Merleau-Ponty writes, "and that nature appears not only as outside of me . . . but it is also discernible at the center of subjectivity."[11] If we remind ourselves that the return of the animal in the form of atavism is a figuration of the past in the present, we can see this point more clearly. Instead of a self modeled on an amnesiac present (a present without precedent), animal encounter points toward the inescapable past of human being. To the extent that this model requires grasping the contiguity between human history and natural history, it also points toward the nondifference of these taxonomies. To paraphrase Merleau-Ponty, we always meet time on our way to subjectivity.[12] Perhaps, then, the meanings and effects of Yank's atavism are not as unambiguous as they may at first seem. If the animalization of the human subject had by this time become a convention of social control, what were the consequences of this disciplinary process?

In this chapter, I continue to look at a variety of fictions written within different generic modes and formal conventions: O'Neill's expressionist drama *The Hairy Ape,* Richard Washburn Child's popular short story "The Gorilla," and Jack London's naturalist novel *The Sea-Wolf.* I begin by exploring how *The Hairy Ape* deploys atavism (the recurrence of a prehuman, animal past in a present-tense body) as a site for and sign of the corporeal and temporal constitution of modern subjectivity. I then extend this analysis to "The Gorilla" and *Sea-Wolf* in order to demonstrate the pervasiveness of the atavistic body in the first half of the twentieth century.

John Berger, in his essay "Why Look at Animals?" suggests that the zoo is a central site demonstrating relations between humans and animals: "With their parallel lives, animals offer man a companionship which is different from any offered by human exchange. Different because it is companionship offered to the loneliness of man as a species."[13] Berger's narrative is fundamentally one of loss, a loss that occurs when humans isolate themselves "as a species" from the natural world. For Berger, the caged animal in the zoo can be seen as the mark both of that loss and of that strategy of isolation. In the atavistic body, however, the animal returns. Insofar as this return refuses an isolation from the natural world, it might be appropriate to add to Berger's claim that the experience of loss he tracks (loss of connection to the past, loss of history, loss of self) is precisely what contact with the animal both stages and sates.

The Ape

In the cramped forecastle of a transatlantic liner, the set on which O'Neill's drama opens, Yank, an irreverent and brutish figure, is a prominent member of the ship's coal stokers, all of whom are represented as laboring machines. O'Neill's parenthetical stage directions describe the stokers as speaking in a chorus with a "brazen metallic quality as if their throats were phonograph horns" (145). They jump up "mechanically" to work (152), "handling their shovels as if they were a part of their bodies" to feed the furnace with "a mechanical regulated recurrence" (160). Despite these metaphors of mechanization, O'Neill also situates the stokers' bodies within an evolutionary discourse by describing them as "crouching in the inhuman attitudes of chained gorillas" or as "Neanderthal men" who "cannot stand upright" (141). Paddy, the oldest of the coal stokers, and the most romantic, provides readers with a succinct description of their condition: "caged in by steel from a sight of the sky like bloody apes in the zoo" (149–50). The men are beasts and Neanderthals, but they are also analogs for the machine, forming what Mark Seltzer has called a "body–machine complex," a "double discourse" that blurs the divides between the human and the technological.[14] In the stokehole, hypermodernization, figured by the omnipresence of the machine, is juxtaposed to animal chaos figured by the workers' bodies. To a certain extent, such a juxtaposition follows a Marxian understanding of the uneven development of capital: for progress to exist as a temporal cutting edge, it requires a primitive outside, a constitutive precapitalist space that allows for the production and reproduction of the modern.[15] But it can also be said that the hypermodern machine and the precapitalist animal inhere in one another in this space. The workers are, after all, both Neanderthals and machines. Their corporeal constitution, then, is both prehistoric and contemporary. In their bodies we find a constellation of the past and the present.

The collision of temporalities enacted here can perhaps be understood as what Walter Benjamin has discussed as the ideological fusion of nature and history in late modern culture. When Benjamin defines "the modern as the new in connection with that which has always already been there," he means in part that a temporal dialectic between obsolescence and recurrence is a fundamental aspect of the workings of modernity. The modern, in other words, is a time-space continuum in which the past exists in conjunction with the present. "Belief in progress, in endless perfectibility and the conception of recurrence are complementary."[16] As for Latour, modernity for Benjamin is hybrid: "The moments of nature and history do not disappear inside each other, but break simultaneously out of each other and cross each other in such a way that what is natural emerges as a sign for history, and history, where it appears most historical, appears as a sign from nature."[17] Nature and history here are intimately interlocking terms; they can neither be identified with nor hierarchically subsumed by each other. When deployed within a teleological conception of historical progress, the two terms work to mystify one another so that they may function as terms at all. Nature as the sign of history and history as a sign for nature; each allows the other to exist as a naturalized and inevitable form of truth. For Benjamin, though, the temporal designation that we call "the present" is not a series of continuous points on a teleological line through time but a montage of disparate times, an imbrication of shifting and contestatory temporalities. Not only does this posit a present never identical with itself, but it also suggests the necessary recurrence of the past at the root of modern identity. The coal stokers' bodies enact precisely this temporal complex. They perform the discontinuous relationships of the ordered states of nature and history. If a Marxian understanding of the social and economic spheres of labor and culture can be characterized by "uneven development," then we can extend this view to the "uneven" terrain of modern personhood as well. And it is Yank's personhood that is most at stake in O'Neill's drama.

Indeed, Yank insists on retaining a sense of personal power in a system that would otherwise render him an inconsequential cog in the machine. He prides himself, for instance, on having become an industrial champion of sorts, the composite of energy and end product thriving in the inner workings of the capitalist apparatus. He boasts, "I start somep'n and de woild moves! It—dat's me!—de new dats moiderin' de old! I'm de ting in coal dat makes it boin; I'm steam and oil for de engines; I'm de ting in noise dat makes yuh hear it; I'm de ting in gold dat makes it money!" (151). As he sees it, Yank not only supplies the energy for the action, but he also comprises the elements for fueling the motion; he is both matter and process: "I am steel, steel, steel!" (151). His tremendous brawn provides him with this illusion of power and control; he's the new that's murdering the old, modern progress itself. But his body is also trapped between matter and process; he is source material for capitalist exploitation, a necessary resource for late modern civilization: "the thing in gold that makes the money."

Yank, however, is not so much unaware of his split position as both subject and object of capital as mistaken about what the consequences of that split might be. Reveling in the strength of his own body, he enthusiastically enters into a sexualized relationship with the machine. O'Neill describes him constantly "stripped to the waist" as he shovels the coal into the ship's furnace while "rivulets of sooty sweat trace maps on his back." With "his voice rising exultantly," he rhythmically shouts, "Dat's de stuff! let her have it! Shoot de piece now! Call de toin on her! Drive her into it! Feel her move! Watch her smoke! Dere she go-o-es" (161). Yank, quite plainly, is sexy: an agentive desiring machine. It is in moments such as these that his desire seems temporarily capable of reconfiguring working-class alienation through appetitive and lustful identification with the means and processes of production, with a deliberate eroticization of his work.

But when later in the drama Mildred Douglas, the daughter of the ship's owner, a man who is a corporate giant of the iron and steel industry, makes a slumming visit to the stokehole, everything changes. Mildred is appalled by the grimy atmosphere and faints at encountering Yank's unashamed nakedness, but not before calling him a "filthy beast" (164). Although Yank had been completely adapted to his environment, he now finds out that there is a world in which he is not considered human. He is stunned and shattered by this new "identity": "You tink I made her sick, huh? Just lookin' at me, huh? Hairy Ape, huh?" (171). When Mildred, in her "ghostly white dress," tags him with this beastly moniker, Yank is devastatingly stripped of his already misrecognized relation to technology and his place in capitalist culture. At the moment she names him, Yank's experience of self is jeopardized. He is transformed not precisely into Mildred's referential epithet (a filthy beast) but into something slightly different: a hairy ape. Yank thus performs a semantic reinterpretation of Mildred's appellation: filth and beast, for him, turn into the metonymic associations of hair and primate. His misconstrual testifies to the power of evolutionary discourse as an interpretative rubric even as it also attests to the kind of misprision central to the identity form in late modernity.[18]

In O'Neill's implicit critique of this scene of identification, however, we see not only Mildred's horror at Yank's appearance, but also Yank's horror at the specter of Mildred's whiteness. Earlier, in scene 2, Mildred's Aunt calls her "a natural born ghoul" who was "even getting to look like one" (155), echoing O'Neill's stage directions, which describe Mildred as "fretful, nervous, and discontented, bored by her own anemia" and "looking as if the vitality of her stock had been sapped before she was conceived, so that she is the expression not of life-energy but merely of the artificialities that energy had won for itself in the spending" (154). Unlike Yank, who is "steel," life energy itself, Mildred is the lifeless effects of the capitalist process, yet another kind of degenerate.

Yank explains his bewilderment at Mildred's unexpected appearance in the stokehole to his friends thus: "And der she was wit de light on her! Christ, yuh coulda pushed me over wit a finger! I was scared get me? Sure! I tought she was a ghost, see? She was all in white like dey wrap around stiffs" (169–70); "She was all white. I thought she was a ghost, sure" (168). Mildred is thoroughly saturated in a symbolic of spectral whiteness, which is itself represented as degenerate and degenerating. She is a leftover effect of light and ghostliness in the world of iron progress, her body atrophying as her industrial empire expands. There is a specter, Mildred's ghostly appearance tells us, haunting capital, an absent presence of inertia and waste. Indeed, Mildred resignedly and apathetically describes herself as "a waste product in the Bessemer process" and goes on to lament, "I inherited the acquired trait of the by-product, wealth, but none of the energy, none of the strength of the steel that made it" (156).[19]

Mildred's aunt, continuing this class critique, a well-known stance of O'Neill's despite his own middle-class status, tells us that her niece's favorite activity is "slumming" in New York's Lower East Side, doing "social service work" and seeing how "the other half lives" (155). Not surprisingly, Mildred's destination on her father's ocean liner is a visit to a famous mental institution in London. Such a Riisian interest in "seeing how the other half lives," in fact, is what brings Mildred to the ship's stokehole. Escorted by the ship's engineers into the "fiery furnace," she ends up standing directly behind Yank. At first unaware of her presence, Yank continues to shovel coal. The stage directions explain: "He brandishes his shovel murderously over his head in one hand, pounding his chest gorilla-like with the other" (163). Mildred is "paralyzed with horror, terror, her whole personality crushed, beaten in, collapsed, by the terrific impact of this unknown, abysmal brutality, naked and shameless," this creature with a "gorilla face" (163). Mildred, in other words, encounters the animal, which is another way of saying that she encounters the contingencies of modern capital, a place where, as Hamlet, in another classic moment of narrative confusion, avers, "The time is out of joint."[20] As such, her encounter performs not only a destabilization of two selves (hers and Yank's), but also stages the cognitive dissonances of modernity of which this destabilization is a product. Before her visit to the stokehole, Yank feels "in place," perhaps even in control of his destiny; after her visit, he is pushed "out of place" and "out of time"—that is, out of the time-space continuum he once recognized as his own. By calling Yank a "filthy beast," Mildred transforms him into a categorical site of the past, into a figure of natural history that disturbs her (and his) vision of modern progress.[21] This process of bestialization places Yank at the crux of a modern strategy: he becomes a sign and site both of a collective desire to leave behind human origin (the animal) and of the perpetual recognition of the past as an operative feature of the present.

Significantly, the scene after Mildred's encounter begins with stage directions that describe the stokers: "Their faces and bodies shine from soap and water scrubbing," but "around their eyes, where a hasty dousing does not touch, the coal dust sticks like black make-up, giving then a queer, sinister expression" (165). All the stokers appear in this way except Yank, who has not washed at all and "stands out in contrast to them, a blackened, brooding figure" completely covered in the "black make-up." Disturbed by his dark presence, his mates remind him to wash, which Yank refuses to do: "to hell wit washin'" (165). Persisting in their concern, they warn him that the coal "makes spots on you— like a leopard," and finally call him a "piebald nigger," literalizing the simultaneity of Yank's animalization and racialization (165). Lest the readers or spectators of the drama forget Yank's blackened appearance, O'Neill emphasizes in his stage directions how "the black smudge of coal dust continues to stick to Yank like make-up" throughout the play; he also reminds us of Yank's "not shaving for days" (173). In short, Yank is presented to us as both black and hairy, "nigger" and "leopard."

As his shipmates stare at him, "half-apprehensively," "half-amusedly" (165), they dramatize the uneasy relationship between fear and interest, threat and amusement, which is a hallmark of spectacles of blackness in the United States. By 1922, the year *The Hairy Ape* was written and first performed, freak shows, dime museum curiosities, not to mention blackface minstrel performances, were a staple of American amusement culture, each spotlighting racial difference as its own sort of peculiarity. Bill Brown characterizes these forms of American popular culture as an "amusement/knowledge system." Such a system, for Brown, designates the apparatus of exhibition as "a visibility machine that produces 'knowledge' in convergence with, and *as* the convergence of, pleasure and horror."[22] This history of exhibition and spectacle informs O'Neill's characterization of working-class otherness. O'Neill infuses his drama with the language of amusement culture (the circus barker, for instance) as well as a persistent recourse to blackness as a major aspect of this culture (the black makeup).

The character of Paddy, who more fully characterizes the relationship between the spectacle of amusement and the spectacle of blackness, describes the scene that transpires between Mildred and Yank in the following terms: "And there she was standing behind us, and the Second pointing at us like a man you'd hear in a circus would be saying: In this cage is a queerer kind of baboon than ever you'd find in darkest Africy" (168). Paddy, as the resident wise man of the stokers, summarizes the scene of their encounter with Mildred quite succinctly: the men are spectacles of the other-than-human, figures of amusement and horror on display that fulfill a collective need (which Mildred's slumming desires represent), to know the human, to see how the human lives. But what Mildred learns is more about the fragility of her own belief system than anything else. In his racialized bestiality, Yank inspires both fear and ridicule; Mildred cannot imagine that a human could be this way, and so she turns him into both a racial other and an animal. In other words, she invents the necessary difference that distinguishes self from other.

By producing this difference, Mildred also reproduces the constitutive outside of the modern (the animal, the African primitive, the laborer in the precapitalist space of production). As a result, Yank becomes an unspecifiable being: a filthy beast. More strange than the strangest of baboons, more remote than darkest Africa, Yank's body—sooty, brawny, trembling with rage—resides in what Homi Bhabha describes as an "enunciative space" between the archaic and the modern. For Bhabha, such a space of enunciation "problematizes the binary division of past and present, tradition and modernity, at the level of cultural presentation and its authoritative address" to the extent that it preserves what it claims to renounce: the pastness of modern life.[23]

As Bhabha puts it: "It is the problem of how, in signifying the present, something comes to be repeated, relocated and translated in the name of tradition, in the guise of a pastness that is not necessarily a faithful sign of historical memory but a strategy of representing authority in terms of the artifice of the archaic."[24] By drawing an equivalence between minoritized subjects and the trope of the beast in her assessment of Yank, Mildred operates in the mode of social control that Bhabha describes, a mode that guarantees the haunting presence of the past as an organizing force of modern social life.

A persistent reminder of this presence, Yank's body emerges within a double discourse of the human/not human binary: animality and raciality not only converge on his body but also jointly descend from what Étienne Balibar has called "theoretical racism." In this sense, the animal, as an intrinsically racialized figure within U.S. history (for instance, as a sign of the "subhumanity" of racial others in nineteenth-century sciences from criminal anthropology to social Darwinism) conjures up, again to borrow from Balibar, "a racism that continues to effect the imaginary 'fusion' of past and present in which the collective perception of human history unfolds."[25] Much like Balibar's description of theoretical racism and Bhabha's theory of enunciation, O'Neill's depiction of Yank's body enacts the imaginary fusion of two incommensurable time schemes in such a way as to question their irreducible difference. Shifting from the capitalist space of production to the space of natural history and back again, that body emerges as both overdetermined and beyond understanding.

Earlier in the play, Mildred mockingly comments: "Purr little leopard. Purr, scratch, tear, gorge yourself and be happy—only stay in the jungle where your spots are camouflage, in a cage they make you conspicuous" (156). She issues these words as a response to her aunt, who strongly disapproves of her niece's slumming sensibility. She is thus ironically referring to herself. Outside of her social milieu, in all her outrageous whiteness, she becomes a conspicuous spectacle of her own sphere of consumption. But she might as well be referring to Yank, whose natural habitat is disturbed by her visit precisely because she exposes it as an a-natural space of capitalist production. Under Mildred's gaze, his own leopard spots, like the black makeup that sticks to his skin, become a conspicuous sign of the spectacular effects of modernity.[26]

A subsequent scene from *The Hairy Ape* further elucidates this point. When Yank's ship docks in the New York City harbor, he sets his mind to confronting Mildred. He suspects he may find her on Fifth Avenue, home to the rich. As he walks along, he gazes into the many storefronts that line the avenue. O'Neill's directions explain: "the general effect is of a background of magnificence cheapened and made grotesque by commercialism" (173). Yank becomes transfixed by a shop window where he sees a monkey fur "bathed in a downpour of artificial light" as "electric lights wink[ed] out the incredible prices." The fur propels him into a rage. He "clench[es] his fists . . . as if the skin in the window were a personal insult" (173). Yelling at the store window, he acts as if Mildred herself had created this display in mockery of his personhood: "Trowin' up in my face! I'll fix her!" (176). This display and the emotional response it invokes serve the play's anticapitalist stance. The monkey fur puts on view the laws of commodity fetishism whereby the reality of the production process is replaced by a selection of images and products that exist above it, as if autonomously. As we have learned from Marx, the products of human labor have a life of their own, a natural value apparently detached from their conditions of existence. The fetishism of commodities, as Marx would have it, is a necessary illusion that veils the social relations of production and the production process. Accordingly, the space of the stokehole where Yank works appears as if wholly separate from the window shops lining Fifth Avenue. The monkey fur, a commodity that mystifies the process of production for which Yank's own body is synecdochal, reflects back to Yank not only his alienation from the commodities his labor helps produce, but also Mildred's reduction of his personhood to a fetish of the capitalist process. The monkey fur is the visual object of the marking of the subject. It does not merely mystify Yank's labor in the process of production; it represents the fetishizing ideologies of capital that prove so injurious to his sense of self. The monkey fur, moreover, is not just any commodity (a table, say, in Marx's famous example), but a commodity literally connected to animality; not just its relation to production is mystified, then, but also its relation to the animal and everything for which the animal acts as a supplement, which in this case are the mutually constitutive constructs of race and class that comprise Yank's laboring body.

There is also a significant temporal dimension at work in commodity fetishism insofar as commodities, in their normative operation, necessitate a special relationship between the consumer and time. That is to say, in the world of commodities, our experience is organized around the rhythms of consumption, or more precisely of buying. Commodities, like the fur coat winking at us in the window, seem to beckon to us from an eternal now, a present that is perpetual precisely because the time to buy is always *right now.* There's an affective urgency built into the fabric of buying. This suggests that the ubiquity of the commodity form creates, as it were, a temporal structure of presence for our subjective experience, for in this scenario, the time of the commodity is always the present. This, however, is not the case for Yank. The monkey fur for him is a visual cue pointing to his own place outside of present time. It signals to him his own classification as a site of the past. In the fur coat, therefore, as much as in Yank's body, we can see a different, nonnormative temporal dialectic emerging, one between human and animal, present and past, subject and object. The fur is a product of modern industry and a sign of the natural world; it is at once the human past and the human present. Yank is produced as just such an anachronism: modern laborer and filthy beast, he has been transformed into a spectacle of racial and classed otherness and as such serves to support and reproduce the ideology of capitalist relations and modern subjectivity of which his body is an effect.[27]

And yet this "will to visualization" of Yank's body stands in stark contrast with Yank's encounter with the gorilla, his brother. Their embrace closes in on the space between man and animal, which we can read also as the space between self and other. Mildred's spectacularization of Yank's body produces, so as to confirm, the distance between them. In opposition, Yank's embrace of his animal friend collapses their spatial as well as ideological distance so as to suggest their proximity. Can such productions of proximity, we might ask, also produce new forms of subjectivity?

The Gorilla

In Richard Washburn Child's short story "The Gorilla," published in 1915 in *Harper's Monthly Magazine,* we get a different view of what one of Yank's coal stoker mates, Long, calls "the Capitalist clarss" (146).[28] The story tells the tragic tale of a ruthless giant of the iron and steel trade who learns too late the lessons of humanity. John Wolf, owner of the Fish-Plate and Metal Tie Company, is a man from the "Middle West" who was "wild for commercial power" (225). Quite pointedly, the animal moniker here (Wolf) refers to the uncontrollable and "wild" greed

of the capitalist. The story begins at the end, with John Wolf oversee-
ing an irrigation project being built in Gorgon Pass.[29] He relates his
tragedy to the two men who survey the area with him. Like Yank's dual
role of circus barker and ape, Wolf is both the author and the subject
of his own narrative. A few months before, as Wolf tells it, one of his
workers was injured at his iron plant in Ohio. Much like Yank and the
coal stokers of O'Neill's drama, this particular worker was "one of the
nameless immigrants out of the nameless mob that come and go," and
as such, he is inscribed within a discourse of animality. "From his low,
concave forehead short-cropped, wiry hair grew backward, as hair grows
from the face of a chimpanzee . . . his eyes were small and buried deep;
his ears were large and attached to the flat sides of his enormous skull;
his shoulders stooped, and his arms, with huge hands at their extrem-
ities . . . reached below his knees . . . head and neck and body were
bent forward as if it would be easy for the man to move off in the next
moment on all-fours" (226). Wolf often refers to him as "half man,
half animal" and mockingly names him "the Gorilla" (226). In the acci-
dent, the Gorilla lost an arm and a foot. John Wolf refuses any financial
settlement with his worker ("business is business" [226]) and terminates
his employment, even after the Gorilla comes to see him to plead his
case: "I no understand. I work for you—me. Now—I no can work.
You—Meester Wolf, eh? I no understand" (228).

In a predictable twist of fate, Ohio is hit with a major flood, and
John Wolf and his wife are caught in the middle of it. The forces of
nature prove to be greater than the forces of industry: their limousine
overturns on a bridge, throwing Wolf into the water below. Just at this
moment, "fate played her trick—the creature with the huge hand, the
long corded arm," the man that Wolf calls the Gorilla, is there to save
him. Wolf and the Gorilla, in fact, are locked in a death grip; the Gorilla
clings to a dislocated bridge cable with his one good arm, while Wolf
clings with "interlocked fingers" to his former employee's "thick neck"
(230). After hours in this position, Wolf can hold on no longer. Just
as he loosens his grip, the Gorilla "snapped like a dog at the wrist-
bones of John Wolf, and buried his teeth in the flesh" (332). Holding
onto Wolf thus, the Gorilla keeps him safe until the rescue workers
arrive. They save Wolf first, and by the time they realize there is another
man at risk, the Gorilla has plummeted to his death. "The unnamed
creature, out of nowhere, going into nowhere—he wasn't there" (232).
Deeply affected by this event, John Wolf slowly tells his story with a

"lifeless, expressionless face . . . tragic with the suggestion of power gained at the sacrifice of soul" (223). "Nothing but the spirit counts," Wolf ends, "accumulate what you will: if when you go, that is all you have left, you have left nothing" (232).

As with O'Neill's play, Child's story carries with it a message, albeit a more sentimentalized one, about class systems in the United States. Each text avers that we live in a society dominated by the capitalist mode of production based on consumption and exchange. Such a system affects the subjective side of the production process through its debasement of human relationships. In particular, the rise of big, organized industry (in each narrative encapsulated by the business of iron and steel) has led to the degradation of the working classes, figured forth as animals, and to the destruction of human ethics, "the sacrifice of the soul."

If from one point of view *The Hairy Ape* and "The Gorilla" display Marxian premises, from another they reveal the unpredictable intimacies struck up as a result of the business of capital. As Yank hugs his gorilla friend at the zoo and Wolf hugs his in the midst of a murderous storm, each scene performs an exchange between men and across species. The intimacy of the exchange in each instance allows for a transference that brings with it a significant renewal: identity and a sense of belonging for Yank, moral rebirth for John Wolf. The traversal of the distance from one body to another via direct and tactile contact is precisely what enables these renewals. In these scenes, the tactility of entangled bodies serves to translate both Yank's and Wolf's lack of a sense of self into substance in such a way that, at least momentarily, demystifies the process of capital whereby laboring bodies are alienated from the commodity objects that they themselves produce and the leaders of industry are affectively distanced from the exploitation and disavowal of their workers. Even more, it enables a material communion of sorts outside of the dehumanizing sphere of commerce. In "The Gorilla," specifically, the worker that saves his life incarnates as a corporeal value what John Wolf calls "spirit." In their embrace, the Gorilla transfers that spirit to Wolf. The physical contact between these two men's bodies thus serves to expose and disrupt the process of capital's alienation. Human–animal exchange materializes their condition under capitalism in such a way as to bring a new, hybrid quasi-subject to the surface: part man, part beast, an entanglement of bodies.

Addressing the encounter between human and nonhuman spheres,

Merleau-Ponty imagines a mutual exchange or kinship between bodies and things in the world that upsets an ideology of body and self as epiphenomenal to, or as positivistic referents of, language and history. For Merleau-Ponty, we live, think, and feel interdependently with both human and nonhuman forces through voluntary and involuntary connection with them, what he terms our "intercorporeality." The body is not isolated from the world around it but rather is "a knot of living meanings."[30] The corporeal self experiences the world through the body as it is lived. Merleau-Ponty's emphasis on embodied experience allows for a tactile theory of being-in-time that puts pressure on and enhances interiorized articulations of subjectivity such as those posed by psychoanalysis. It also opens up a space for thinking the self as a relation to the world outside of the binary catch of self/other. For him, tactile experience "adheres to the surface of our body; we cannot unfold it before us, and it never quite becomes an object."[31] Rather, these experiences become part of who we are and how we think. The people and things we encounter and touch and that in turn touch us cannot be separated or conceived apart from our bodies and thoughts; once they enter our sphere of existence, they cannot be removed. In fact, they come to constitute what we are at that moment and from that moment on. In "The Gorilla," the sensuous, somatic, and tactile forms of subjectivity enabled by human–animal embrace present to us something different from the othering phenomenon that Mildred's meeting with Yank sets forth. In both *The Hairy Ape* and "The Gorilla," in fact, the atavistic dramaturgy of human–animal encounter proffers a vision of human/not-human interaction without a subject–object dichotomy, a vision of noncoercive engagements of subjectivity that opens up and expands the self to objects, subjects, and experiences outside, and thus within, itself.[32]

Out of the encounter with animality arises a deeper knowledge of the modern human subject as posited by Western culture. With that knowledge, something is returned that formerly had been disturbed: a sense of the past, a sense of a place in history, a sense of self. The animal intimacy dramatized in both O'Neill's drama and Child's short story sensualizes this newly acquired awareness by enabling an intercorporeal exchange that presses beyond the boundaries of isolated individualism. In these cases, the collision of men and beasts (and men as beasts) is not a refusal of the modern, a nostalgia for a simpler evolutionary time. Rather, human–animal exchange constitutes an intimacy that works to unsettle and defamiliarize the human self and thereby to refamiliarize it as something else altogether. From the perspective of this exchange, we can glimpse the limits of the subject as posited by bourgeois liberalism and perhaps also feel the potentiality we have yet to be or know.

Whereas Merleau-Ponty conceptualizes perception of and interaction with the body of the other as a part of the field of the self, Deleuze and Guattari recharacterize the body as a desiring machine interacting with planes of existence outside of ourselves: "The breast is a machine that produces milk, the mouth a machine coupled to it."[33] Merleau-Ponty's phenomenological concern with the details of the "life world" fosters an ineluctable link between subjects (of the world) and objects (in the world). Deleuze and Guattari engage with phenomenology to insist on a more complete emptying out of the subject–object relation. Merleau-Ponty's view of the self as constituted by several sites of consciousness becomes, for them, a view of no subjective consciousness whatsoever. This shift removes the self from the realm of a centered subjectivity to one of a machinelike series emanating from a molecular infinity, the fractal multiplicity that "undermines the great molar powers of family, career, and conjugality."[34] It is with the concept of "becoming" that Deleuze and Guattari forge couplings, flows, and connections with other bodies and other things in the molecular sense, where bodily encounter performs a transformation that refuses and reformulates the dualistic categories between subject and object, mind and body, that we have inherited from Descartes: "Every object presupposes the continuity of a flow; every flow, the fragmentation of an object."[35] Deleuze and Guattari are interested in planes and surfaces, not interiors and depths. Within their planar paradigm, desire does not constitute a longing for the attainment of an impossible object (the "lack" of psychoanalytic theory), but rather forms a surface interacting with other surfaces that produce other interactions and assemblages. Replacing the concept of a distinct and distinguishable self, the assemblage specifies the indiscernibility of being and matter, what Deleuze and Guattari characterize as the forging of an alliance.

Perhaps the best example of Deleuze and Guattari's theory of alliance occurs by way of their reading of *Moby-Dick*, which they describe as "one of the greatest masterpieces of becoming." An irresistible desire to "become-whale" and forge a "monstrous alliance with the Unique" drives Ahab on his journey through the sea.[36] Deleuze and Guattari contend that it is only through such an alliance with an exceptional individual, the Anomalous (in this case, the great whale, Moby-Dick), that Ahab can become whale and thus part of the multiplicity of the pack of whales. They are quick to point out that the Anomalous has nothing to do with the individuated animal, such as, for example, the oedipalized, domesticated pet. This distinction is crucial insofar as it challenges a more conventional reading whereby Melville's novel seems to dramatize a human desire to conquer and thus control nature. "Moby-Dick is neither an individual nor a genus; he is the borderline." Ahab needs "to strike him to get at the pack as a whole, to reach the pack as a whole and pass beyond it."[37] In so doing, Ahab engages in "a phenomenon of bordering." Rather than reinforcing a man-against-nature ideology, Ahab's encounter with the great white whale instantiates a deterritorialization of the self and forges in its place "a symbiosis of or passage between heterogeneities."[38] For Deleuze and Guattari, the theory of alliance describes neither a binaristic nor a dialectical relation between two opposites (man and animal, for example). Instead, the potency of alliance lies in its ability to cut across the knot of social and corporeal multiplicities in such a way as to decouple and deform the illusory divisions of late modernity whose dualistic structures form its social topoi. In the sense that Deleuze and Guattari put forth, human–animal encounter serves as a reconsideration of the boundaries that constitute modernity. Read in this light, the animal encounters experienced by Yank and John Wolf do not fabricate a dead past over which the human has triumphed. They imagine the past as a palpable, living force. The animal, then, does not function as an emotional cushion to mitigate our anxieties or to prop up our beleaguered sense of self; it generates an opportunity for collective experience.

The Wolf

In O'Neill's drama and Child's short story, atavism serves as a medium of cultural critique. In each, the writers use the figure of the animal to voice their repudiation of capitalism and to challenge late modernity's categorical assessments. Thus atavism, the nexus established between human and animal, generates a literary expression of modern subjectivity that goes beyond a symptomatic discourse. Atavistic characters like Yank, the Gorilla, and ultimately John Wolf are not simply effects of the increasing anxieties over the fragile boundaries of race, class, and sexuality at the fin de siècle; they are also expressions of a new kind of modern subject. Perhaps we can see this most explosively in my final example, Jack London's novel *The Sea-Wolf*.[39]

At its most basic, the novel's plot follows the effete, overcivilized idealist, Humphrey Van Weyden (called "Sissy Van Weyden" by his school chums), in his acquisition of a more brutish masculinity while hostage aboard a seal-hunting schooner. The newly named "Hump" falls under the tutelage of the ship's captain, Wolf Larsen, a brute materialist who "partook [. . .] of the enlarged gorilla order" with "a strength savage, ferocious, alive in itself . . . the elemental stuff itself out of which the many forms of life have been molded" (16). Wolf is "a magnificent atavism" (78) who educates Hump in the ways of animal masculinity, brute competition, and corporeal swagger. An enthusiastic reader of Darwin, Haeckel, Spencer, and the school of social Darwinism in general, Jack London allegorizes Hump's education in masculinity as one in evolution as well: from Wolf, Hump learns "to stand on his own legs" (23).[40]

At the same time that Hump becomes more erect (pun intended), he also becomes more animal. Indeed, London deploys animality as a signal trope of the masculine, and thus as an antidote to what he sees as civilization's effeminizing influence. If at the novel's start Hump is "hysterical" (6), "with no sensation in [his] lower limbs" (7) and who "shriek[s] aloud as the women had shrieked" (8), by its end, he has "found [his] legs with a vengeance" (164). For Wolf Larsen, and Jack London, this means he has tapped into the primality of his masculine self. As Hump comments: "I was becoming animal-like" (78). His metamorphosis comes about as a result of his time amid the ship's crew of "human beasts" (41), whom Hump describes as a "half-brute, half-human species" (117). They are men who sleep in bunks "that looked like the dens of animals in a menagerie" (38). From them Hump received "repeated impressions from the die which had stamped them all" (110).

Although we could understand "the die" referred to here as the harsh sea environment that stamps the men with its brutality, the repeated references of the impressions of the animal on Hump's otherwise "civilized" body can also be read as a riff on Darwin from *The Descent of Man*. In his concluding remarks, Darwin writes: "We must acknowledge, as it seems to me, that man with all his noble qualities, with sympathy which feels for the most debased, with benevolence which extends not only to other men but to the humblest living creature, with his god-like intellect which has penetrated into the movements and constitution of the solar system—with all these exalted powers—Man still bears in his bodily frame *the indelible stamp* of his lowly origin."[41] No matter how hard we try to rise above the animal, Darwin seems to be saying, no matter how great our accomplishments or system of ethics, the mark of our "lowly" evolutionary origins will stay with us. Surprisingly for Darwin, this utterance draws a noticeable distinction between the "noble qualities" of Man and the "lowly" animal. Not only does this contradict Darwin's claims earlier in *The Descent of Man* that animals, too, have moral systems, but at least nominally, it makes his case for the sharing of a common ancestor by both humans and animals appear more disconcerting than he himself believed it to be. Perhaps we might read this as a momentary lapse from science into culture on Darwin's part? As the above passage makes clear, while the sharing of human and animal traits has not prevented the advancement of the human species to a more "noble" "god-like" state, such nobility does not and can not erase the stamp of our animal origins, and even for Darwin perhaps, this presented somewhat of a dilemma. Such a claim, for some, was not only new but traumatic, for it implied an ongoing struggle for the human to overcome its baser instincts. Further, there is always the danger, as some interpreters of Darwin had it, of our baser instincts becoming too strong and thus overwhelming the rational, social instincts to which we had become adapted. As Darwin himself noted, the appearance of "bad dispositions" in family members may be a sign of "reversions to a savage state, from which we are not removed by many generations."[42] Throughout *The Sea-Wolf,* London plays with Darwin's notion that we are but stamped impressions of a former self, and the characters of Wolf Larsen and Hump embody the possibility of an always potential reversion to it.

Nonetheless, Hump is unwilling to give up his idealism to brutishness so easily, and his ideological opposition to Wolf's materialism comes to a head in yet another scene of violent embrace. In one of their nightly intellectual exchanges, Wolf rejects Hump's belief in the transcendence of the soul: "You have talked of the instinct of immortality. I talk of the instinct of life, which is to live, and which, when death looms near and large, masters the instinct, so called, of immortality." To prove his point, he renders it in physical terms:

If I were to catch you by the throat, thus . . . and begin to press the life out of you, thus, and thus, your instinct of immortality will go glimmering, and your instinct for life, which is longing for life, will flutter up, and you will struggle to save yourself. You beat the air with your arms. You exert all your puny strength to struggle to live. Your hand is clutching my arm. . . . [y]our chest is heaving, your tongue protruding, your skin turning dark, your eyes swimming. "To live! To live! To live!" you are crying; and you are crying to live here and now, not hereafter. (98)

That such an intellectual discussion erupts in violence may seem surprising, but it shouldn't. London's point seems to be that only through the kind of visceral experience that Wolf offers can Hump develop a relationship to his body and thus to himself. As another kind of human–animal exchange (in keeping with the novel's titular metaphor), it is this violent embrace that allows Hump to value his life beyond the hypocrisy of his intellectualism—at least so London suggests. Life, Wolf Larsen demonstrates, is embodied; even more, it is felt—heaving chest, protruding tongue, swimming eyes. In this moment of embrace, any sense of hierarchical opposition (mind over body, human over animal) vanishes. In a death grip, Wolf and Hump relay between the physical violence of the animal and the intellectualism of the human, up and down the gamut of atavism and evolution.

Here and elsewhere, London suggests that Wolf Larsen's violence is motivated less by pure aggression than by scientific philosophy. As I have already begun to suggest, there is a strong element of Darwin in Wolf's beliefs; similarly, he embraces the thinking of Ernst Haeckel, who made a strong impression on London when he read him in 1901. Wolf's philosophy of life, in fact, is indebted to Haeckel's theory of "materialistic monism," the belief that human being emerged and continues to survive as an effect of what Wolf calls "an eternity of piggishness" (65). For Haeckel, the truth of existence is to be found in the lowest forms of life: Monera, the most basic, protozoic, unicellular entities. Haeckel described this truth as "the law of substance," asserting "man is separated from other animals only by quantitative, not qualitative, differences."[43] Thus, according to Haeckel, all life could be connected in a genealogical tree with Monera at its root. Wolf Larsen's ruthless materialism is derived from this theory, which he uses in his heated physical discussions with Hump as a justification of his equation between the complex operations of human being and "yeast." "I believe that life is a mess," Wolf avers. "It is like yeast, a ferment, a thing that moves and may move for a minute, an hour, a year, or a hundred years, but that in the end will cease to move" (45–46). All one can do is struggle to survive in the midst of other living forms in the mess of life: "The big eat the little that they may continue to move, the strong eat the weak that they may retain their strength." Gesturing toward his crew, he concludes: "They move; so does the jellyfish move" (46).

One obvious way to read Wolf Larsen's materialism is as transparent social Darwinism insofar as he evinces an ideology of the survival of the fittest in the most brutish of terms. But another way to read his philosophical investments, perhaps beyond Wolf's own intentions, but not necessarily London's, would be to note the nondiscriminatory, nonhierarchical frame that the theory of yeastiness affords. Wolf uses this theory to demonstrate that human life has no transcendent value beyond itself: We move, and so does the jellyfish move. He thus also theorizes a space of possibility in opposition to the predicates of modern civilization and its attending classifications (the divisions of labor as much as the divisions of human being). That is, he insists on a kinship web between human and animal that refuses to privilege one over the other. Instead, the human and the animal coexist in a complex and interconnected plasma of life. To be sure, the seal-hunting schooner is no utopia; its environment is merciless and violent. But it is also a space that permits unexpected connections and alliances across class lines, between men, and with the natural world.

The scene of Wolf and Hump's embrace may be viewed as an exchange that asks whether humanity is not deceiving itself through its attachment to an unnatural order whose soul-over-body assumption dismisses or negates an understanding of the human body in relation to its "others" in the world. But the scrupulous reader cannot help asking in turn: Where might human ethics reside in Wolf's world of gross corporeality? For Wolf, the nondifference between bestial and human extremes means that "life is the cheapest thing in the world" (61). But Hump admonishes: "You have read Darwin, but you have read him misunderstandingly when you conclude that the struggle for existence sanctions your wanton destruction of life" (62). Hump is referring to a prior incident in which Wolf has sent Johanssen, an inexperienced crew member, to fix a tangled line in the rigging and unnecessarily endangers his life. Wolf characteristically replies, "There is plenty of more life demanding to be born. He [is] worth nothing to the world. The supply is too large" (63).

Brutal, yes, but, London suggests, perhaps also true, especially when understood in the blunt terms of capitalism that Wolf links to evolutionary theory. His harsh summation points out that capital trades in bodies: the cheap sweat and blood of the "disposable" workforce. What makes *The Sea-Wolf* such an ideologically ambivalent narrative, however, is the fact that London asks his readers to identify with both Hump and Wolf. He attempts to demonstrate the stigmata of overcivilization and uses the character of Wolf Larsen to campaign against it. He turns to Haeckel, via Wolf's interpretation of his work, as a reminder of our material existence, our basic human drives and needs. But like O'Neill in *The Hairy Ape* and Child in "The Gorilla," London is also invested in a critique of capitalism to the extent that his narrative points out that it is modern civilization that produces the violent taxonomies that work to minimize the value of human life ("the supply" for such life as a lowly worker's is "too large"). At the same time, there is an obvious anxiety in the narrative over the cost of Wolf's pure materialism, as the incident with Johanssen also demonstrates. To this end, London seems to want to preserve Hump's belief in human ethics as an unconstructed element of being, as a thing essentially human. Citing Herbert Spencer, Hump declares, "The highest, finest, right conduct is that act which benefits at the same time the man, his children, and his race" (73). But Wolf Larsen's acute remarks throw the hypocrisy of Hump's system of ethics into critical relief: "Why, you who live on the land know that you house your poor people in the slums of the cities and loose famine and pestilence upon them, and that there still remain more poor people, dying for want of a crust of bread and a bit of meat, (which is life destroyed), than you know what to do with. Have you ever seen the London dockers fighting like wild beasts for a chance to work?" (62).

Ultimately, London offers no easy answers to the dilemmas he raises. The narrative winds its way to greater and greater incoherence, as many critics have pointed out and attempted to resolve. Hump's heterosexual romance with Maud Brewster, for instance, appears as a deus ex machina that allows for closure to his adventure at sea, but not to the narrative's criticism of capitalism that heterosexuality would seem to support, and not to its conundrum over the human condition. Are we akin to protozoic forms trudging around in the yeastiness of life? Are we capable of ethical behavior despite our animal instincts? If London's novel raises an unanswered question about ethical responsibility, the fact that it posits a space for the conjecture of such responsibility should not be undervalued. For such a space of conjecture affords a discussion, precisely, of the illusion of the transcendent morality that Hump represents. It is, in part, the illusory basis of modern civilization as embodied by Hump that reinforces modernity's taxonomic violences (its class systems and social norms). Atavism in *The Sea-Wolf* (and *The Hairy Ape* and "The Gorilla," for that matter) thus functions to enhance an understanding of the interlocking social and biological mechanisms that comprise the human. Thinking through this entanglement entails thinking through the irreducibility of the human to the ethical questions that inform and continually remake it. It entails thinking about human being as a lateral relation of kinship, as a self constituted beyond and outside itself in connection and alliance to other human and nonhuman forms, things, and spheres.[44]

Man

Atavism becomes in late modernity a conventional means of understanding the modern self, linking up human and animal as the most predictable of relationships. Throughout this book, I have posed a distinct argument: literary characters such as Yank, Wolf Larsen, and the Gorilla illuminate modernity's dependency on the archaic; their animality gives shape and substance to the modern subject as an atavistic subject, an anachronistic being constituted by the fecund resources of the past. The figure of the animal as a characteristic of the human provides both a sense of temporal continuity with our past and a point of origin—a sign of the beginnings of human being.

The animal encounters posed in *The Hairy Ape*, "The Gorilla," and *The Sea-Wolf*, then, do not enact an opposition, nor do they suggest a simple integration in which opposites are reconciled. Rather, the respective moments of embrace in each narrative (between man and animal, capitalist and laborer, captain and mate) enacts an instance of eternal recurrence, what Benjamin might call a "rupture." That is, the self/other, past/present, nature/culture distinctions on which the idea of the modern seems to depend are shown by these moments of exchange to be impossibilities. Instead, by enacting a rupture in Benjamin's sense, such moments bring the present into critical time. In "Theses on the Philosophy of History," Benjamin distinguishes between historicism and historical materialism as methods of inquiry. He aligns historicism with the "eternal," the "universal," and with "progress."[45] Historical materialism, on the other hand, "blast[s] open the continuum of history" by discarding historicism's "homogeneous, empty time" in favor of "time filled by the presence of the now."[46] The presence of the now is a collision between past and present, when one can "seize hold of a memory as it flashes up in a moment of danger."[47] This moment of danger realizes a powerful instant in which an image of the past ignites a sudden recognition in the present. What Benjamin goes on to characterize as messianic time has the ability to reorganize relations between past and present and thus "blast open the continuum of history." The past, then, in Benjamin's formulation, is not an object to be known, but is rather an absent cause that can only be experienced in some material image or the sensation that image arouses. In his example of Proust's *Á la Recherche du temps perdu*, it is the taste of a madeleine that has the capacity to transport the narrator back to a forgotten moment in his childhood in Combray. In Benjamin's reading of this scene, and along the same lines of Proust's intent, the chance engagement with a singular and palpable sensation or image causes something (like a feeling or a memory) to erupt and thus to intervene in the continuity of time. The pastry suspends the temporal fiction of chronology and linearity, connecting perceptions in the present with those of the past.[48]

We can read the moments of atavistic embrace in the three examples explored above as representations of the blasting open of the continuum of history in Benjamin's sense. The eruption of visceral, embodied personhood in each unmistakably brings evolutionary time and modern time into salient accord. Such accordance disorients and reorganizes the sterile oppositions on which modernity depends. Opposed to the imagined sovereignty of the human, atavism, the eternal recurrence of the animal, erupts as a potent flash of natural history that insists on recognition of a more complex kinship web and a much more expansive life-world (here in Merleau-Ponty's sense). "Shake," Yank proposes to the gorilla, "the secret grip of our order" (198). Atavism, as a mesh of corporealities and temporalities, thus funds the possibility of compassionate and ethical comportment toward and in alliance with the unknown, not just with the "unknown" sphere of the animal, but with everything I have been arguing the animal is deployed to represent within modern culture: the classed, racialized, and otherwise subordinated subject. To be sure, such comportment carries with it attendant dangers, for it is the gorilla's embrace that kills Yank: "He got me, aw right. I'm trou" (198). But I am also suggesting that their attachment to one another might produce something other than the tragic and lamentable death of the subordinated individual, something like an ethicopolitical model of intercorporeal interrelationality. In part, then, animal encounter does metaphorize the fraught and painful misrecognitions of modern culture; but it also points toward the sensuous connections and haptic relations that forge the possibility of something otherwise.

Throughout O'Neill's drama, Yank continually questions where he belongs. Neither fully modern nor merely animal, Yank remains out of place. His out-of-place-ness performs the alienation of the working-class subject, but also of the modern subject more generally. What we learn from Yank's predicament is the predicament of modernity: in the megacomplex of industrialization, rationalization, and urbanization, what makes a subject is not merely the assignment of categorical difference, nor only the condition of alienation brought on by advanced capitalism, but also the politics of ineluctable contact, of propinquity. The stress point here is on encounter itself, which can be rethought via Yank's atavistic plight not as a cause–effect relation of othering, but as an event in itself of tactile perception. Yank's encounter with the gorilla, along with the emergence of his atavistic body, performs the promise of the animal, the animal's promise, that is, to push us toward a space of sensuous conjunction, connection, and transformation. Although *The Hairy Ape* does not fully provide the answer to the question of belonging, perhaps we can read Yank's atavism as a staging of the collision of past and present and thus as an opportunity to shape an ethics for the future. The atavistic trace of the animal in Yank, after all, reminds us of the materiality of our sense of self, and it further reminds us that it is in this materiality that anything we might call an ethics is grounded. As such, it offers the possibility of a theory of alliance, bringing incommensurable temporalities and corporealities into conjunction. O'Neill's tale is also a cautionary one, then: it warns us that if we continue to disregard the lived interconnections that constitute our being-in-the-world, we might be crushed to death.

Coda
Being-Now, Being-Then

Time, said Austerlitz in the observation room in Greenwich, was by far the
most artificial of all our inventions, and in being bound to the planet turning
on its own axis was no less arbitrary than would be, say, a calculation based
on the growth of trees or the duration required for a piece of limestone to
disintegrate, quite apart from the fact that the solar day which we take as
our guideline does not provide any precise measurement, so that in order to
reckon time we have to devise an imaginary, average sun which has an
invariable speed of movement and does not incline towards the equator in
its orbit. [. . .] Could we not claim, said Austerlitz, that time itself has
been nonconcurrent over the centuries and the millennia? And is not human
life in many parts of the earth governed to this day less by time than by the
weather, and thus by an unquantifiable dimension which disregards linear
regularity, does not progress constantly forward but moves in eddies, is
marked by episodes of congestion and irruption, recurs in ever-changing
form, and evolves in no one knows what direction?
—W. G. Sebald, *Austerlitz*

WHAT IF Robin Vote and Felix Volkbein met Yank? What
if they all ran into Tarzan one day, or had coffee with Dr. Fu Manchu
and asked Wolf Larsen to join them? And what about the Wolf Man
and the Rat Man; they would have a lot to talk about, no? These aren't
academic questions, I know. But I pose them because this book, in part,
has been about putting this cast of characters in the same room together. Meeting them, and having them meet each other, has meant
asking and trying to answer all sorts of questions about history, narrative, and the production of knowledge. And in a certain way, meeting them has meant encountering and querying our own sense of self.

We like to think of ourselves as *being-now*. We are ourselves because
we exist at this very moment. At the same time, we know we feel and
experience being-now by way of our memories of and experiences from
the past—*being-then*. Even the events we don't remember affect us in

some way, and we "know" this, even if that knowing itself is an invention, an imaginative willing of self. And what about tomorrow? What meetings do we have scheduled? What plans, tasks, or other habits and rituals that structure our lives will occur? Time is who we are, but time is also ephemeral. Its multidimensionality and multifunctionality ground and elude us. So too for the characters and persons in the pages of this book, who all, like us, endure time and therefore exist as one of its potent incarnations. What connects each of these characters to one another is indeed the venture of time: time rendered strange and dialectical, time as recursive, as a mutual enfolding of memories and events, pasts and presents. The variously atavistic bodies of the characters I have discussed are places where the past confronts the present and each teeters on the precipice of futurity. Those bodies are places where the ineffable concept and experience of modernity forges itself in skin. Their subjectivities index nothing less than modern subjectivity itself, shot through with the emotional turmoil of the new and the physiognomic contortions of the archaic.

Henry James, in *The Portrait of a Lady* (1881), his ekphrastic homage to the modern woman, insists that suffering is the common, perhaps even universal, feature of modern life. For Isabel Archer, there are no fairy-tale endings. She must learn to suffer because suffering is living. Lord Warburton, figure of romance that he is, cannot suffice: he is a leftover from an effete past. Isabel must experience pain, failure, and a sense of unending loss—"must" because in James's vision such is modern life and the lot of the modern woman Isabel is meant to represent.[1] The cast of characters in view in *Atavistic Tendencies*—Robin Vote barking like a dog, Yank dead in a gorilla's cage, Vandover on the brink of brutish psychopathology, the Wolf Man painting his psyche out on large canvases, and other figures too, like James's own John Marcher, who, in the thralls of the exquisite pain of suddenly knowing, throws himself down on all fours at May Bartram's grave at the close of "The Beast in the Jungle"—have all suffered, and they all have a story to share about the emotional and epistemological structures of modernity.

The Jamesian experience of modern time is of a Proustian sort, composed of regret for what can never be and nostalgia for what has come to pass. As the angst-ridden narrator of *À la récherche du temps perdu* laments at the end of the first volume: "The places we have known belong now only to the little world of space on which we map them for our own convenience. None of them was ever more than a thin slice, held between the contiguous impressions that composed our life at that time; a remembrance of a particular form is but regret for a particular moment; and houses, roads, avenues are as fugitive, alas, as the years."[2] Subjectivity is "housed" in the space of memory, a fallible and "fugitive" space that enables a narrative or "map" through and by which we can plot our lives. These maps and narratives are "convenient" but also remote and out of reach; in their shadowy, untouchable presence, we are reduced to melancholy. Melancholy thus emerges, for Proust as much as for James, as the overriding and undergirding state of the subject, as the place from which the subject moves, breathes, and comes to knowledge.

Atavism, however, is not a memory of things lost and therefore is not a melancholic reverie of a past experience. Nor is it a structure of memory, like Proust's houses, roads, and avenues, whose cracks and fissures and worn patches mark the passing of time, touched as they are by the passing through of the many bodies that use, inhabit, and travel over them. Nor, finally, is atavism something erected as a memorial to the past—something erected, that is, as a national or dedicatory monument to carry history into the future.[3] Rather, atavism is a relentless recurrence. It is a corporeal recognition that the past has never passed, has not ceased to shape and form our sense of self in both psychic and material ways. As a reminder of the coextensive interanimation of temporal schemes, atavism stages the contingencies of both modernity and the modern subject on the human body itself. An allegory for the modern as much as an invention of modern science, atavism materializes the past in the present, disallowing the past to remain past, keeping it alive as a constitutive feature of the modern self. Atavism, therefore, doesn't allow for the melancholic distance that Proust forwards as the fundamental relationship between the modern subject and her history. It closes in on the space between past and present; it is the past in present form: gorilla eyes, wolfish teeth, the mark of the animal.

If the modern world can be said to be characterized by an acceleration of history (industrialization, technological innovation, modernization), it can also be said to be characterized by perpetual return. Any amnesiac response to the imperatives of modern progress is balanced by the nagging presence of our own prehistories. Atavism in its most potent forms stands in for these prehistories and stages their reiteration. Within the theory of atavism, our very bodies become shrines to and enshrined as human prehistory; the folds, wrinkles, and ear slants of our physiognomic makeup, testimony to and traces of the genealogical record. Of course, this is just the opposite of what the scientific discourse on atavism intended. That discourse was meant to cordon off the modern body from anything that might disturb the ideology of the subject as always forward marching and self-governing. Nonetheless, in the narratives and images I have asked us to engage through the course of this book, we discover a coexistent story about the muddled time claims and combinatory structures of modern subjectivity. In chapter 1, for instance, we witness this temporally messy theory of the subject in the project of psychoanalysis. Freud names the temporal position of the subject *nachträglichkeit,* the psychic process by which a repressed trauma becomes reestablished in the present. For Freud, the idea of repetition correlates to the desire to redirect old events toward better conclusions, although it also ultimately condemns us to a relentless replaying of the scene of trauma. On this reading, atavism stages and repeats the "scene of trauma" that is human origin itself, our place within the evolutionary matrix.

But as Freud's work also demonstrates, atavism is not only a psychic and material repetition; it is also a theory of time. Eschewing the progressivist notion of modern time, or time as a rational unit, as calendrical time, or as clock time, atavism posits the time of human being as *Jetztzeit:* the Benjaminian understanding of the time of the now. Like Freud's *nachträglichkeit,* and deliberately so, Benjamin's *Jetztzeit* is a form of repetition compulsion, but of a decidedly material sort.[4] *Jetztzeit,* or now-time, consists of the points at which objects, activities, and actions from the past may be cognized as of the present, as shaping forces of the now. For Benjamin, these points come in the form of dialectical images: a phonograph, an arcade, Proust's madeleine. These dialectical images manifest knowledges uniquely available to a specific present moment. They are cognitions of the past that "flash up" in the present by way of the image and provide a new purchase on both history and subjectivity. These objectival cognitions, or knowledges through object attachments, are thus not limited to the material field as much as they are invoked by it, and so also have psychodynamic effects on those who experience them. Now-time thus counters the presentist notion of *being-now,* the notion that the present time has privilege and priority, even superiority, over all other times. Following Benjamin, we can instead recognize how the experience of being-now simultaneously also always means being-then.[5]

This book has addressed the question of being (now and then) as it manifests itself in the remarkable overpopulation of the animalized human form in the culture and society of fin de siècle United States, in its science, fiction, and photography in particular. The various visual and literary representations and scientific studies of the human as animal, I argue, conjure up a countervailing understanding of time to that of modernity as its own distinct time frame ideologically predicated on ideas of progress, innovation, and historical autonomy. Atavism, revealing as false the notion of the modern as a historical and epistemological break, makes evident a synthesis of past and present. Tracing atavism as a condition of regression imagined by modern science, therefore, has not just been a myopic study of a singular theory; it has also made possible a prying open of the conditional and dependent temporal structures of the modern world. If, at the level of intention, the scientific quest for signs of animality on the otherwise human body was meant to create temporal distance between primitive subjects and modern ones, the desire that animates that quest reveals a pervasive self-consciousness about the temporal uncertainties of modern subjectivity.

The double notion of time as both an invention of the modern world and an impossible entanglement of pasts and presents is the primary rumination of W. G. Sebald's *Austerlitz* (2001), a novel in which we find a stunning choreography of Proustian and Benjaminian thought. In *Austerlitz*, time emerges as not only an artificial and arbitrary invention, but as an invention that, in its artificial and arbitrary nature, works against the possibility of authentic experience, against the possibility of knowing either history or oneself. The narrator and the focal character, Austerlitz, while walking through the Royal Observatory in Greenwich, have an intense discussion about modern time, and specifically about how time is installed and imposed by such structures as the prime meridian. "Time, said Austerlitz in the observation room in Greenwich, was by far the most artificial of all our inventions." "Could we not claim," Austerlitz continues, "that time itself has been non-concurrent over the centuries and the millennia? And is not human life in many parts of the earth governed to this day less by time than by the weather, and thus by an unquantifiable dimension which disregards linear regularity?"[6] The prime meridian, which was instituted as the center of global time by international ruling at a conference in 1884, became the declared site of the starting point of each new day, year, and millennium. Much as Fordist and Taylorist principles sought to regulate the use of time, the decree of global time as something one could locate on the map sought to make time both imaginable and usable (for mercantilism, imperialism, and industrialism, among other things). Time became usable precisely by being reified into tangible, universal units: clock time, the work week, assembly lines. Once time is stripped of its illusions, Sebald's novel meditates, all that is left is an affecting and unsteady relation to the world, expressed by the viscerality of emotion experienced by Austerlitz in his search for his origins.

As readers of the novel come to learn, those origins reside in the time of the Holocaust. To save him from the concentration camps, his mother places him on a *Kindertransport* to Wales, where he is raised by a Calvinist minister and his wife. Austerlitz, having forgotten the first four years of his life but always feeling culturally and psychically displaced, as an adult, attempts to rediscover his childhood. By way of his various attempts, most poignantly expressed, perhaps, by a reencounter with his childhood caretaker in his original home of Prague, emotional contact with the past is presented as a space of if not recovery, then at least of emancipation from the amnesia of modern time. And this is what "real" time (as opposed to invented time) is in the novel as well. Like the impalpability of emotion that nonetheless feels so searingly "there," time is something "unquantifiable"; it organizes our lives into coherent temporal blocks, but in actuality is something "non-concurrent," something that "disregards linear regularity, does not progress constantly forward but moves in eddies, is marked by episodes of congestion and irruption, recurs in ever-changing form, and evolves in no one knows what direction."[7] And as is the case with time, the subject in time is posed by the novel not as an autonomous, unmediated, and self-conscious being but as an unpredictable mesh of temporal associations moving in "no one knows what direction." The problem for Sebald, then, becomes a historiographic one: how do we produce history in a significant way without falling into the pitfalls of reification and teleology? How do we tell stories and create narratives of the past, of violent pasts especially, without adhering to the historicist command to be "factual" and "objective"? How do we remember what we have been made to forget? One way is to make sure time itself is treated as an amalgamation of experiences and perspectives, as something polychronic in nature—that is, as a multidimensional, multiply informed, and above all uncertain predicament.[8] Understanding time and thus history (a narrative form that serves to organize time) in this way does not so much destabilize the more conventional practices of historiography as offer up a more realistic version of the unfolding of history. I say "more realistic," as problematic as that may sound, because more willing to be provisional, more willing to risk the incoherence of a multidirectional force. In the context of *Atavistic Tendencies,* atavism has emerged as a theory of time as such. The human as a fundamentally atavistic being posits the body as a site of temporal recursivity that defamiliarizes and denaturalizes the claims of modern progressivism. Under the rubric of atavism, human being can be understood not in terms of the inevitable teleology of origin and advance but as a polychronic social and material relation. And this is not only because our memories are unorganized and dispersed, or only because our psychological lives unfold in wayward directions, but because our very bodies are comprised by the deregulating flows of time that Austerlitz so aptly explains.

To bear out this claim, I have adhered to three distinct aims. The first has been to explore the thick history of atavistic theory as postulated by fin de siècle human science in the American context. Reading closely a variety of scientific studies, I have shown how the idea of prehistoric and ancestral recurrence functioned not in the more utopian ways I ruminate on above but as a practice of violent taxonomy. The tropes of animality and savagery that accompanied the theory of atavism functioned to establish certain racial, sexual, and gender populations as less evolved than others, to place them outside of modern time. Atavism was thus pressed into the service of maintaining the temporal boundaries of modernity. The scientific narratives examined in this book, therefore, served as pivotal documents that have helped to foreground late modern modes of subordination. The assertion of scientific sovereignty at the fin de siècle was made in the hope of bringing the traumatic effects of progress under the control of a new system. This served both to racialize time, as discussed in chapter 4, and to racialize specific discourses concerned with the time of progress, as with the eugenic feminism discussed in chapter 5.

Atavism, in this historicized view, can perhaps be seen as a mere component part of modernity, and an epiphenomenal one at that. It might even seem that atavism should be characterized as some fairly small offshoot of the late modern period, a justifiably discounted episode in the history of pseudo-science. And from a certain perspective, it is that. The historicist impulse of this project has been, undeniably, to flesh out the specificity of a now-forgotten discourse as it existed at the time. A second aim of the book, however, has been to understand atavism as a damaging discursive regime and simultaneously as an allegory of modernity. Atavism, on this reading, is not just a curious episode in U.S. history, but a privileged vantage point from which to view the project of American modernity. The advent of the modern world may well be understood as a fantasy of historical autonomy, but modernity was never actually autonomous, either in practice or ideology. Rather, this book has shown it to be a binding collage of the archaic and the new, and it is the discourse on atavism that so markedly sheds light on the modern experience as such.

At the same time, though, I have concentrated not only on the disruption of the idea of modern time, but also on the alternative possibilities generated by such disruption. For this reason, a third aim of the book has been to engage the concept of atavism as expressive of a temporal plenitude, and therefore as productive of a new theory of the subject in time. From Émile Benveniste or Jacques Lacan to Michel Foucault, from structuralism to poststructuralism, the "subject" has emerged as one of the more embattled terms of art for cultural and social theory. Though they are substantially varied in focus, one shared thrust of these theories has been to trouble the idea of the coherence and unmediated presence of the subject, thus shifting the grounds on which the subject can be thought. For the past few decades, the category of the Other has been a prime tool in the struggle waged against the Enlightenment-sponsored idea of the individual as unmediated and ontologically stable. The Other, and the subsequent lowercase corrective "others," has been used as a theoretical lever to pry open the subject to its conditions of possibility and thus to reveal its ontological interdependency on ideological constructions of cultural difference. In Benveniste's influential understanding of the constitution of persons, for instance, subjectivity emerges in language when the "I" located within utterance remains transcendent to the "You" or the "not-I" it simultaneously posits.[9]

This may seen like old hat, but critical discussions of identity continue to be understood along similar lines of the self/other binary, even in more Derridean-inspired accounts of the non-self-presence of the "I." Crucial work in feminist theory, queer theory, and critical race studies has usefully problematized this understanding of subject formation, pointing out how, as ontological categories, both "self" and "other," and "subject" and "object" have operated more often than not as placeholders for the complexities and contradictions of social and subject formation.[10] But this isn't the only problem with an uncritical adherence to the self/other binary within critical discourse. Risky, too, is how the theoretical use of the self/other binary may potentially prevent other theories of social and subject formation from emerging. The proclamation of the death of the subject, of which I am unquestionably a proponent insofar as this has meant the death of the subject as unified, stable, and centered, has unfortunately not altered the centrality of the self/other binary. Rather, it has guaranteed its longevity in critical discourse because we have to keep addressing the question (perhaps unwillingly) of why the subject is in fact decentered, and what forms the "constitutive outside" that the (universal) subject takes, so stalwart and repetitive is the discourse on humanism. This has prevented a discussion of thinking otherwise about subjectivity, from approaching it as something other than an encounter with an other. It has also assured the very construction of an Other that liberal, even radical, discourses intend to resist. No matter how important the critique of the universalizing tendencies of liberal humanism may have been (and still are), a limit has been produced, and it is a constraining, falsely consoling thing to be always limited to two opposing identities and/or groups: I and you, outer me and inner me, colonizer and subject of colonization, and so forth.

In part as a response to this dilemma, this book has called for and articulated a theory of subjectivity and subjectivization that is less a set of oppositions than a never-ending process of active formation. By following the method of historical epistemology, I have located the coming into knowledge of human being not as an individual or institutional subject or object that itself could be known, that could operate as a truth effect for what really happened, but as occurring across and within a number of archival and institutional discursive regimes, treating these regimes as dynamic and provisional, as forms of knowledge production that conjure different ideas about the past and countering ideas of subjects in the past. The very notion of a knowable subject, as Wendy Brown has argued, can then be conceptually pulled out of a neat temporal ordering, thereby expanding the possibilities for subjectivity.[11] If the time of the subject is without a forward-moving, future-oriented logic, then no predictable inference can be drawn from it about where the subject may go, or how subjects may change, or with whom subjects may ally themselves.

Put simply, atavism proposes a lateral, directionless relation of subjects in time. Unimpeded by the command of rationality, it calls into question some of the most widespread and traditional ideas about human identity as teleologically ordained. More interesting than simple exposé, though, is how and what atavism produces, namely a new relation of self. Such a notion of being and existing in relation (with other objects, nonhumans, animals, and things) allows for a different way of thinking of ourselves in the world. Atavism, to press hard on the term, may even be thought of as a new ontological category, but one that does away with the dualities of the subject–object relation. This is not to reify the term into a concrete thing that we can take up, inhabit, or become. Rather, it is to see the history of atavism as usable. If part of what we do, as scholars of culture and history, is not only to interpret significant objects and events but also to understand the multifaceted ways these objects and events shape our own experience and understanding of the world, then atavism has during the course of this book granted access to alternative experiences and expressions within the narrative of modernity. If it can be recuperated out of the violence and racism of the conditions of its emergence, it can also point us in the direction of a different ethics of subjectivity, an ethics that does not rely on sovereignty and human exceptionalism as its guiding principles but that conjures the idea of a subjectivity moving in "who knows what direction."

This last of my aims may well garner all sorts of (perhaps deserved) accusations of utopianism. For those of us concerned with the politics of the present moment and the U.S. government's total disregard, under George W. Bush, of an intersubjective sense of being in the world, articulating a theory of subjectivity in such esoteric terms may seem more like intellectual musing than significant political engagement. Nonetheless, I would argue that no disciplinary or social change can occur without a struggle to clarify models that make sense of the institutional structures that rationalize forms and forces of power and that search for alternatives to and within those rationalizations. Moreover, if we can take as a given that time is one of those categories that structures everything around us, including ourselves, then addressing the subject in time offers a valuable practice of addressing the coexistent energies of any given moment.[12] It does not necessitate, as many programs of social change do, waiting or longing for some future moment of liberation, or seeking a utopian horizon somewhere out there. Nor does it nostalgically mourn a political past now deemed to be over. Rather, it seeks spaces and conditions of possibility at the very moment of any discursive regime's articulation, conditions that act productively on behalf of the subordinated subjectivities of those regimes.[13] This is what I have been referring to as a polychronic understanding of the subject in time and of the relation of subjects and times. I have therefore examined the devices—the therapeutic situation of psychoanalysis, photography, and scientific and literary narrative—used to delineate and order persons and things into sequentialized frameworks.[14] Through these devices, temporal notions of progress and regress, primitivism and civility, became the justification for treating certain bodies and persons in one way and others in another. I have looked at how these notions have stabilized accounts of modernity, at the ideological valuations placed on these pasts and presents, and finally at the openings within these frameworks for concurrent frames, practices, and persons.

I would like to conclude by going back in time to look at one final case of atavism out of which all three of the aims of this book emanate. In James Huneker's 1895 short story, "Nosphilia: A Nordau Heroine," a young man named Odin marries a woman whose "ears showed the lobe undetached" and who had "the nose of a predaceous bird."[15] After several months, Odin began to notice "his wife's curious taste for odours." She "filled their rooms with scent-bottles and spent the day arranging and fussing over them," and she had the curious habit of "plung[ing] her face into his neck," taking "long . . . passionate inhalations" (30). Increasingly concerned with this behavior, which "stifled" and "repelled him" so that he "feared bedtime," Odin decides to read Max Nordau's "ponderous, tiresome tome," *Degeneration:*

There was much that bored him, much that he did not look at, but one passage set him reading about Baudelaire and his passion for perfumes, and then the truth came upon him unawares. His wife was a degenerate. She had a morbid, a horrible love of odours. She was a nosophile, a thing that divined the world about her by her scent, as does the dog. (31)

One night Odin returned home late. His wife beckoned to him: "I am mad for your face, your sweet odour." Then, "with a bound like a leopard's, she threw herself on him . . . winding her long ape-like arms about his body." Smelling the scent of another woman on her husband, "she screamed, and bit into his jugular vein, tearing and rending the flesh like a wild beast, blinded with blood, ferocious and growling" (32).

In Huneker's story, the hidden malfeasance of female desire is literalized in the form of an animal. The increasing addiction of Odin's wife to odor, her "nosphilia," transforms her into a monstrous embodiment of her sexuality; or, more precisely, she becomes the expression of women's "always already" animal desires. She is, in Nordau's words, a "degenerate ego-maniac . . . too feeble of will to control [her] own impulsions" (243). Huneker intended this story as a parody of Nordau's theory. Odin's nameless wife, with her alignment to Baudelaire and his love of perfume, her beastly power to smell, kill, and devour, thus emerges as a caricature of the horrors of femininity. The feminine, made into a metaphor for modernity, is a space where perversity runs riot. Like a beast or a vampire, Odin's wife tears her husband's throat out. So goes modernity, or at least a specific modern narrative in which the landscape of modern ruination is easily fitted into an arousing and frenzied femininity. In the story, femininity as such a referential structure stands in for that which cannot be expressed: the irrational experience of desire.[16]

This bears out my first claim: atavism operates as both a policing mechanism and an organizing category of science by which particular groups are marked as less evolved, more chaotic, and more susceptible to modern ills. But like the farce of O. Henry's short story, "The Atavism of John Tom Little Bear," in which the title character suffers a "reversion to type," Huneker's story parodies the fears and anxieties of modern science by producing an exaggerated character with the power to overrun civilization as we know it. This suggests the argument of my second claim: atavism acts as an allegory for modernity. Huneker uses atavism to demonstrate how modern culture has fallen prey to the anxieties that the disciplinary practices of modern science hoped to allay. Atavism becomes, for Huneker, the rhetoric through which modernity has structured itself as a site of the proliferation of anxiety, decay, illness, and perversity. In Huneker's short story, therefore, we have a double allegory: one that references the time of sexual politics, in which the growing visibility of women in the public sphere posed a threat to male dominance and masculinity, and one that uses women's already "mysterious" and "other" sexual inclinations as a way to reference the ruination of the modern subject more generally.[17] Nonetheless, only from an Enlightenment–humanist point of view, one that

devalues monstrosity, do human beasts like Odin's wife appear as solely
negative formations.[18] In a more constructive sense, the atavistic subjects we have encountered in this book have told richly varied stories
about sensation, power, pain, decay, and erotic variation, and the same
might be said of Odin's wife. What happens, for example, when we
take as positive what is assumed to be negative? Odin's wife can then
be viewed as a figure of power—not so much in the clichéd sense of
the monster that designates the sexual power of women, but in the
sense of the power of time that she, as an atavistic body, yields. Her
corporeal clout *is* her temporal embodiment: she is the time of the past,
the time of human prehistory; she does not simply regress, she summons
the past into the present in the enactment of her sexual desires. In her
need to taste and smell and bite, the past returns in menacing conjunction with the present. This conjunction between past and present
allows for a vital, sensual connection to human time, a heightened
sense of touch and smell and even cognition: this is the time of the
animal, and playing itself out in the character of Odin's wife, it is the
time of human being too. Her bifocal engagement with temporality
defies linearity: she is not outside time, but resides comfortably and
securely within it; she does not refuse the multidirectionality of human
history but incarnates it, and thus participates more fully in human
history than any notion of bourgeois individualism possibly could. At
issue here is not simply a thematics of desire, but the rhetorical enactment of time's plenitude—and thus the third claim of the book.

On a pragmatic level, then, what does a project on atavism and
modernity have to offer to the efforts of social change and political
activism? Even the transition I make in this paragraph from an interpretative practice to the idea of social change seems to reinvoke that
notion of progress I have been using the study of atavistic subjectivity
to critique. "Social change" is itself another time phrase, embedded in
a notion of futurity and eventuality. My hope, though, is that the method
I have used in reading atavism offers the opening up of possibilities for
alliance across a number of nonteleological spheres: the convergence of
disparate temporalities, different networks of interpretation, and other
sensuous material collaborations. For this reason, the book has refused
just to track hegemonic forces at work at the fin de siècle. Considering the immensity of modern institutional forms, with their universalizing tendencies and singularizing forces, their extreme poles of private
individual and mass public, I certainly could have. But in tracking the

DJUNA BARNES' VAMPIRE BABY
Belial-baby!
Mouths thus merry, maturing
Madden to murder

ETHEL PLUMMER'S DANGER-GIRL
Girl of the gutter!
Gross, unkempt, you allure by
Links atavistic!

Djuna Barnes's "Vampire Baby" and Ethel Plummer's "Danger-Girl," *Vanity Fair* (1915).

biological and cultural imagination of human being, I have also attempted to explore what other kinds of practices, bodies, desires, and persons become possible when we take the residues of power into account, when we read science against itself. This is not a simple celebration of the proliferation of interpretative possibility, but a belief that by expanding the ways to think the human we expand the capacity for being human.

Along these lines, Djuna Barnes and Ethel Plummer, the latter an artist well known for her popular illustrations of "modern women," embrace the vertiginous fall from humanity that human scientists feared when they published campy portraits of vampire women accompanied by humorous haiku in a 1915 edition of *Vanity Fair*.[19] Ethel Plummer's "Danger-Girl" is described thus:

Girl of the gutter!
Gross, unkempt, you allure by
Links atavistic!

And Djuna Barnes's "Vampire Baby" thus:

Belial-baby!
Mouths thus merry, maturing
Madden to murder

We might understand the meanings of Plummer's danger-girl and Barnes's vamp to coincide with the irreverent and perverse energies of modernity that this book has attempted to chart. The atavistic allure of the modern girl is a perpetual reminder of the expansive time of the human. In the mad merriness of links atavistic, the interdependent contradictions of the modern give rise to a formidable subject.

Notes

Introduction

1. In addition to Maugham and Bagehot, the *OED* makes reference to James Joyce's *Ulysses* (1922), which cites "the sporadic reappearance of atavistic delinquency;" Evelyn Waugh's *Black Mischief* (1932), whose narrator muses, "Was it some atavistic sense of a caste, an instinct of superiority, that held him aloof?"; and E. P. Evans's *Evolutionary Ethics* (1897), in which Evans claims that "the lower classes reflect atavistically the ideas and passions of primitive man." We should also add to this list Marcel Proust's frequent use of the term in *À la récherche du temps perdu* to designate, sometimes interchangeably, his aristocratic and homosexual characters as specters of the ancien régime. For example, in the chapter that ends volume 6, the narrator discovers Robert de Saint-Loup's homosexual predilections and ponders the hereditary nature of this condition: "The Duc de Guermantes, who was wholly innocent of such [homosexual] tastes, had the same nervous trick as M. de Charlus of turning his wrist [. . .] and also in his voice certain shrill and affected intonations, mannerisms to all of which, in the case of M. de Charlus, one might have been tempted to ascribe another meaning, to which he had given another meaning himself, the individual expressing his distinctive characteristics by means of impersonal and atavistic traits which are perhaps simply age-old characteristics ingrained in his gesture and voice. On this latter assumption, which borders upon natural history, it would not be M. de Charlus whom one described as a Guermantes affected with a blemish and expressing it to a certain extent by means of traits peculiar to the Guermantes stock, but the Duc de Guermantes who, in a perverted family, would be the exception whom the hereditary disease has so effectively spared that the external stigmata it has left upon him have lost all meaning." Marcel Proust, *Remembrance of Things Past*, vol. 6, trans. C. K. Scott Moncrieff (New York: Vintage, 1981), 792.

2. Max Nordau, *Degeneration* (1892, English trans. 1895; Lincoln: University of Nebraska Press, 1993), 2.

3. My understanding of history as an absent cause comes from Fredric Jameson, *The Political Unconscious: Narrative as a Socially Symbolic Act* (Ithaca, N.Y.: Cornell University Press, 1981).

4. Lorraine Daston, "Historical Epistemology," in *Questions of Evidence: Proof, Practice, and Persuasion across the Disciplines,* ed. James Chandler et al. (Chicago: University of Chicago Press, 1994), 243–76.

5. Michel Foucault, "Nietzsche, Genealogy, History," in *Language, Counter-Memory, Practice: Selected Essays and Interviews*, ed. Donald Bouchard, trans. Donald Bouchard and Sherry Simon (Ithaca, N.Y.: Cornell University Press, 1977), 80, 81. Need I point out how Foucault himself uses the language of evolutionism and atavism to describe the practice of genealogy here—the "reversals," for instance, that "give birth" to new forms of knowledge in the world?

6. Most recently, Jennifer Fleissner has taken on representative accounts of naturalism that argue the genre is primarily about an unreconstructed masculinism. By contrast, Fleissner suggests that naturalism "is a literature as much (if not more) about domesticity, details, and women's inner lives," and thus is a form of writing squarely attending to the problem of the reproductive role of women in society. See Fleissner, *Women, Compulsion, Modernity: The Moment of American Naturalism* (Chicago: University of Chicago Press, 2004), 28. See also Amy Kaplan, "Romancing the Empire: The Embodiment of American Masculinity in the Popular Historical Novel of the 1890s," *American Literary History*, 2, no. 4 (Winter 1990): 659–90; and Lee Clark Mitchell, *Determined Fictions: American Literary Naturalism* (New York: Columbia University Press, 1989).

7. Madison Grant, *The Passing of the Great Race; or, The Racial Bias of European History* (New York: Scribner, 1916), 112.

8. On Darwin's refusal of Platonism, see Ernst Mayr's introduction to *On the Origin of Species* (Cambridge, Mass.: Harvard University Press, 1964), esp. x–xii.

9. Michel Foucault, "Governmentality," in *The Foucault Effect: Studies in Governmentality*, ed. Graham Burchell, Colin Gordon, and Peter Miller (Chicago: University of Chicago Press, 1991); and *The History of Sexuality*, vol. 1, trans. Robert Hurley (New York: Pantheon Books, 1978), especially the final chapter, "Right of Death and Power over Life," 133–60.

10. See Nicole Rafter, ed. *White Trash: The Eugenic Family Studies, 1877–1919* (Boston: Northeastern University Press, 1988); Daylanne English, *Unnatural Selections: Eugenics in American Modernism and the Harlem Renaissance* (Chapel Hill: University of North Carolina Press, 2004); Laura Doyle, *Bordering on the Body: The Racial Matrix of Modern Fiction and Culture* (New York: Oxford University Press, 1994); and Russ Castronovo, *Necro Citizenship: Death, Eroticism, and the Public Sphere in the Nineteenth-Century United States* (Durham, N.C.: Duke University Press, 2001). On Castronovo's account, the nation fetishizes death as an ideal form of citizenship in such a way as to produce a "mass of depoliticized persons and de-authorized memories" and a "discorporated," abstract body politic at once (xiii).

11. In this regard, see also Susan Gillman, *Blood Talk: American Race Melodrama and the Culture of the Occult* (Chicago: University of Chicago Press, 2003). In this study of the race melodrama in late nineteenth- and early twentieth-century American literature, Gillman argues that representations of race were powerfully informed by a culture of the occult, thus serving to produce race history as a twinned temporal structure of past and present.

12. See Susan Merrill Squier, *Liminal Lives: Imagining the Human at the*

Frontiers of Biomedicine (Durham, N.C.: Duke University Press, 2004); and Laura Otis, *Membranes: Metaphors of Invasion in Nineteenth-Century Literature, Science, and Politics* (Baltimore: Johns Hopkins University Press, 1999).

13. Jack London, *The Sea-Wolf* (New York: Oxford University Press, 1992), 16.

14. Frank Norris, *Vandover and the Brute* (New York: Doubleday, Page, 1914), 310.

15. Jacques Derrida, *Specters of Marx: The State of the Debt, the Work of Mourning, and the New International,* trans. Peggy Kamuf (New York: Routledge, 1994). I am grateful to Jonathan Flatley for suggesting I take up the Derridean idea of spectrality.

16. See especially Walter Benjamin, "On Some Motifs on Baudelaire" and "Theses on the Philosophy of History," in *Illuminations,* ed. Hannah Arendt, trans. Harry Zohn (New York: Schocken, 1969), and *One-Way Street,* trans. Edmund Jephcott, in *Selected Writings, vol. I: 1913–1926,* ed. Marcus Bullock et al. (Cambridge, Mass.: Harvard University Press, 1996).

17. Benjamin, "Theses on the Philosophy of History," 262. See also Gerhard Richter, ed., *Benjamin's Ghosts: Interventions in Contemporary Literary and Cultural Theory* (Stanford, Calif.: Stanford University Press, 2002), especially the essays by Miriam Hansen, "Benjamin and Cinema: Not a One-Way Street," 41–71; and Fritz Breithaupt, "History as the Delayed Disintegration of Phenomena," 191–204.

18. See Matei Calinescu, *The Five Faces of Modernity: Modernism, Avant-Garde, Decadence, Kitsch, Postmodernism* (Durham, N.C.: Duke University Press, 1987); and Reinhart Kosellek, *Futures Past: On the Semantics of Historical Time* (Cambridge, Mass.: MIT Press, 1985).

19. See, for example, the special issue of *Criticism* on enactment culture: "Extreme and Sentimental History," *Criticism: A Quarterly for Literature and the Arts* 46, no. 3 (Summer 2004).

20. For useful accounts of modernity, see Richard Terdiman, *Present Past: Modernity and the Memory Crisis* (Ithaca, N.Y.: Cornell University Press, 1993); Charles Taylor, *Modern Social Imaginaries* (Durham, N.C.: Duke University Press, 2004); Miriam Hansen, "The Mass Production of the Senses: Classical Cinema as Vernacular Modernism," in *Reinventing Film Studies,* ed. Christine Gledhill and Linda Williams (London: Arnold Press, 2000), 332–50; Zygmunt Bauman, *Liquid Modernity* (Oxford: Blackwell, 2000); and Harry Harootunian, *History's Disquiet: Modernity, Cultural Practice, and the Question of Everyday Life* (New York: Columbia University Press, 2000).

21. See Astradur Eysteinsson, *The Concept of Modernism* (Ithaca, N.Y.: Cornell University Press, 1992). See also Peter Osbourne, *The Politics of Time: Modernity and the Avant-Garde* (London: Verso, 1995), in which he offers a compelling account of the dynamic of modernism's "politics of time" as an imagined discontinuity with tradition.

22. See David Harvey, *The Condition of Postmodernity* (Oxford: Blackwell, 1989); and Marshall Berman, *All That Is Solid Melts Into Air: The Experience of Modernity* (New York: Penguin, 1988). See also the Weberian account of the Enlightenment, whereby the triumph of reason forges an "iron cage" of bureaucracy

that diminishes the Baudelairean ideal of aesthetic redemption. Max Weber, *The Protestant Ethic and the Spirit of Capitalism* (1930; New York: Routledge, 2001); and Charles Baudelaire, *The Painter of Modern Life* (1863; New York: Phaidon Press, 1985).

23. In addition to Weber, see John Frow, *Time and Commodity Culture* (New York: Oxford University Press, 1997).

24. In his own reading of the Baudelairean aesthetic ideal, Jürgen Habermas describes modernity as an "incomplete" but "redeemable project." He finds redemption, specifically, by way of a recuperation of reason as separate from the project of capitalist rationalization. Foucault has famously disagreed, arguing instead that the Enlightenment project and its privileging of the category of reason was itself a network of power. See Habermas, "Modernity—An Incomplete Project," trans. Seyla Benhabib, in *The Anti-Aesthetic: Essays on Postmodern Culture*, ed. Hal Foster (Port Townsend, Wash.: Bay Press, 1983), 3–16; and Michel Foucault, *Power/Knowledge*, trans. and ed. Colin Gordon (New York: Pantheon, 1972), 131.

25. See Arjun Appadurai, *Modernity at Large: Cultural Dimensions of Globalization* (Minneapolis: University of Minnesota Press, 1996); Vasant Kaiwar and Sucheta Mazumdar, eds., *Antinomies of Modernity: Essays on Race, Orient, Nation* (Durham, N.C.: Duke University Press, 2003); Dilip Parameshwar Gaonkar, ed., *Alternative Modernities* (Durham, N.C.: Duke University Press, 2001); and Laura Doyle and Laura Winkiel, eds., *Geomodernisms: Race, Modernism, and Modernity* (Bloomington: Indiana University Press, 2005), particularly the essays by Doyle, "Liberty, Race, and Larsen in Atlantic Modernity," 51–76, and Patricia Chu, "Modernist (Pre)Occupations: Haiti, Primitivism, and Anticolonial Nationalism," 170–86.

26. Fredric Jameson, *A Singular Modernity: Essay on the Ontology of the Present* (London: Verso, 2002), 34.

27. For projects that focus on the transition from nonindustrial work routines to the industrial factory system, see E. P. Thompson, "Time, Work-Discipline, and Industrial Capitalism," in *Customs in Common: Studies in Traditional Popular Culture* (New York: New Press, 1993), 352–403; and Herbert Gutman, *Work, Culture, and Society in Industrializing America* (New York: Viking, 1976).

28. Jameson, *Singular Modernity,* 21; Bruno Latour, *We Have Never Been Modern,* trans. Catherine Porter (Cambridge, Mass.: Harvard University Press, 1993).

29. Latour, *We Have Never Been Modern,* 70.

30. Ibid., 2.

31. This is, in part, Terdiman's argument in *Present Past.*

32. Gilles Deleuze, *Cinema 2: The Time-Image* (Minneapolis: University of Minnesota Press, 1995), 100, 82.

33. Although I find an exploration of American nationalism necessary throughout this book, this does not necessarily entail an understanding of the nation as a self-contained unit. As scholars such as John Carlos Rowe and Paul Giles have argued, U.S. nation formation must be thought of as always in

process and therefore always incomplete. U.S. borders are and have always been penetrated by extranational discourse and continental influence (such as the importation of European science). A focus on nation formation does suggest, however, that mechanisms are at work that convert these discourses and influences into something that could be called "American" or that make use of them for specific agendas within U.S. political life. See Paul Giles, *Virtual Americas: Transnational Fictions and the Transatlantic Imaginary* (Durham, N.C.: Duke University Press, 2002); and John Carlos Rowe, *Post-Nationalist American Studies* (Berkeley: University of California Press, 2000). For key accounts of U.S. nationalism and its cultural manifestations, see the work of Gavin Jones, Amy Kaplan, Lisa Lowe, Wahneema Lubiano, and Dana Nelson. See also Donald Pease and Robyn Wiegman, eds., *The Futures of American Studies* (Durham, N.C.: Duke University Press, 2002).

34. See especially the work of Lorraine Daston, Ian Hacking, Donna Haraway, Evelyn Fox Keller, Bruno Latour, Laura Otis, Paul Rabinow, Susan Squier, Isabelle Stengers, Nancy Stepan, and Priscilla Wald.

35. Bruno Latour, *Science in Action: How to Follow Scientists and Engineers through Society* (Cambridge, Mass.: Harvard University Press, 1988), 16.

36. I borrow the term "situated knowledges" from Donna Haraway, "Situated Knowledges: The Science Question in Feminism and the Privilege of Partial Perspective," in *Simians, Cyborgs, and Women: The Reinvention of Nature* (New York: Routledge, 1991), 183–202. Haraway argues that scientific knowledge can only ever be the partial knowledge for which the specific scientist's situation allows. See also Bruno Latour, *Pandora's Hope: Essays on the Reality of Science Studies* (Cambridge, Mass.: Harvard University Press, 1988).

37. I could hardly do justice to the immensity and significance of this field in a footnote. Work that has had powerful consequences for this project includes that of Étienne Balibar, Lauren Berlant, Wendy Brown, Judith Butler, Lee Edelman, Ann Fausto-Sterling, Elizabeth Grosz, Eve Sedgwick, Hortense Spillers, Ann Stoler, Michael Warner, and Kath Weston.

38. See Jenny Reardon, "Decoding Race and Human Difference in a Genomic Age," *differences* 15, no. 3 (Fall 2004): 38–65; and Anne Fausto-Sterling, "Refashioning Race: DNA and the Politics of Health Care," *differences* 15, no. 3 (Fall 2004): 1–37.

39. Elizabeth Grosz, *The Nick of Time: Politics, Evolution, and the Untimely* (Durham, N.C.: Duke University Press, 2004), 2.

40. Ibid.

41. O. Henry, "The Atavism of John Tom Little Bear," in *Rolling Stones* (New York: Doubleday, 1920). Subsequent references are to this edition.

42. I take my understanding of texts as cultural and social agents from the project of cultural studies generally and from Pierre Macherey's argument specifically. Macherey argues that texts do not act as mirrors for history or ideology, but rather participate in the shaping of ideological and historical formations. See Pierre Macherey, *A Theory of Literary Production* (New York: Routledge, 1985).

43. See Frederick Hoxie, *A Final Promise: A Campaign to Assimilate the Indians, 1880–1920* (New York: Cambridge University Press, 1989).

44. For studies on the relationship between race, reproduction, and the family, see Gail Bederman, *Manliness and Civilization: A Cultural History of Gender and Race in the United States, 1880–1917* (Chicago: University of Chicago Press, 1995); Louise Newman, *White Women's Rights: The Racial Origins of Feminism in the United States* (New York: Oxford University Press, 1999); Faye Ginsberg and Rayna Rapp, eds., *Conceiving the New World Order: The Global Politics of Reproduction* (Berkeley: University of California Press, 1995); and Alys Weinbaum, *Wayward Reproductions: Genealogies of Race and Nation in Transatlantic Modern Thought* (Durham, N.C.: Duke University Press, 2004).

45. Rafter, *White Trash;* English, *Unnatural Selections.*

46. Lothrop Stoddard, *The Revolt against Civilization: The Menace of the Under-Man* (New York: Charles Scribner's Sons, 1922), 303–4.

47. Charlotte Perkins Gilman, *His Religion and Hers* (1923; Westport, Conn.: Hyperion Press, 1976).

48. Eugene O'Neill, *The Hairy Ape* (1922; New York: Vintage Books, 1995), 141.

49. In particular, see Harvie Ferguson, *Melancholy and the Critique of Modernity* (New York: Routledge, 1994); and Tom Lutz, *American Nervousness, 1903: An Anecdotal History* (Ithaca, N.Y.: Cornell University Press, 1993).

1. Freud's Menagerie

1. In taking up "The Wolf Man" as my primary text, I join a number of literary critics and social theorists in an endeavor to read this narrative in relation to the condition of modernity. See especially Carlo Ginsburg, "Freud, The Wolf Man, and the Werewolves," in *Clues, Myths, and the Historical Method* (Baltimore, Md.: Johns Hopkins University Press, 1989); Peter Brooks, "Fictions of the Wolf Man: Freud and Narrative Understanding," in *Reading for Plot: Design and Intention in Narrative* (New York: Knopf, 1984); and Lee Edelman, "Seeing Things: Representation, the Scene of Surveillance, and the Spectacle of Gay Male Sex," in *Homographesis: Essays in Gay Literary and Cultural Theory* (New York: Routledge, 1994).

2. Freud's interest in Darwin has been well documented by Lucille Ritvo, *Darwin's Influence on Freud: A Tale of Two Sciences* (New Haven, Conn.: Yale University Press, 1990); and by Frank Sullaway, *Freud: Biologist of the Mind* (New York: Basic Books, 1983).

3. Sigmund Freud, "The Archaic Features and Infantilism of Dreams," in *Introductory Lectures on Psychoanalysis,* trans. James Strachey (New York: W. W. Norton, 1966), 246.

4. Boundary-dependent theory, from Plato to Descartes and beyond, understands the individual as a fixed essence that is not only distinct from the objects and animals with which it coexists but is also fundamentally untouched by interactions with them. In these versions of atomistic individualism, the individual is the prime unit of reality and thus the ultimate standard of value. Accordingly, society is defined as a collection of bounded, autonomous

individuals who act and work together but in such a way that never changes or transforms their basic humanity—that is, their individualism.

5. Bruno Latour, *We Have Never Been Modern*, trans. Catherine Porter (Cambridge, Mass.: Harvard University Press, 1993), 10–12.

6. Isabelle Stengers, *The Invention of Modern Science*, trans. Dan Smith (Minneapolis: University of Minnesota Press, 2000), 114.

7. Ibid., 115.

8. Beginning with Donna Harway's work on the subject, a growing body of scholarship addresses the function of the animal as an index for the human in various ways. In particular, see Haraway, *Primate Visions: Gender, Race and Nature in the World of Modern Science* (New York: Routledge, 1989); Alphonso Lingis, "Bestiality," in *symploke* 6, no. 1–2 (1998): 56–70; Cary Wolfe, *Animal Rites: American Culture, the Discourse of Species, and Posthuman Theory* (Chicago: University of Chicago Press, 2003); Steve Baker, *Picturing the Beast: Animals, Identity, and Representation* (Urbana: University of Illinois Press, 2001); John Berger, "Why Look at Animals?" in *About Looking* (New York: Vintage, 1980); H. Peter Steeves, ed., *Animal Others: On Ethics, Ontology, and Animal Life* (New York: State University of New York Press, 1999); and Akira Lippit, *Electric Animal: Toward a Rhetoric of Wildlife* (Minneapolis: University of Minnesota Press, 2000).

9. Jacques Derrida, *Writing and Difference* (Chicago: University of Chicago Press, 1978), 282.

10. Lorraine Daston, "Historical Epistemology," in *Questions of Evidence: Proof, Practice, and Persuasion across the Disciplines*, ed. James Chandler et al. (Chicago: University of Chicago Press, 1994), 246.

11. On Park's project, see Priscilla Wald, "Communicable Americanism: Contagion, Geographic Fictions, and the Sociological Legacy of Robert E. Park," in *American Literary History* 14, no. 4 (Winter 2002): 653–85.

12. On the popularization of psychoanalysis in American culture, see Joel Pfister and Nancy Schnog, eds., *Inventing the Psychological: Toward a Cultural History of Emotional Life in America* (New Haven, Conn.: Yale University Press, 1997); Nathan Hale, *The Rise and Crisis of Psychoanalysis in the United Sates: Freud and the Americans, 1917–1985* (New York: Oxford University Press, 1995); Ellen Herman, *The Romance of American Psychology: Political Culture in the Age of Experts* (Berkeley: University of California Press, 1995); and Saul Rosenzweig, *Freud, Jung, and Hall the King-maker: The Historic Expedition to America, 1909* (Seattle, Wash.: Rana House Press, 1992).

13. Elaine Hadley, "Thinking in Boxes," in *Living Liberalism: Signature, Citizens and Celebrity in Victorian Britain, 1850–1855* (unpublished manuscript). See also Hadley, "The Past Is a Foreign Country: The Neo-Conservative Romance with Victorian Liberalism," *Yale Journal of Criticism* (Winter 1997): 7–38.

14. Steven Shaviro puts it this way: "The decentered psychoanalytic subject is not something that comes after the Cartesian, bourgeois subject, but something that is strictly correlative with it." Shaviro, "The Erotic Life of Machines," *parallax* 8, no. 4 (October 2002): 29. Here, I seek to describe psychoanalysis as a circulating historical concept in its most popularly understood

forms. There are major differences, therefore, between this description and the one to be found in Lacanian theory, whereby the subject is understood as fundamentally unachieved, not to mention unrestored, such that the "I" and the "it within the I" cannot be so easily resolved.

15. Latour, *We Have Never Been Modern*, 16. Foucault discusses this phenomenon in the context of the examination: "The examination, surrounded by all its documentary techniques, makes each individual a case: a case which at one and the same time constitutes an object for a branch of knowledge and a hold for a branch of power." For Foucault, the examination thus operates "at the centre of the procedures that constitute the individual as effect and object of power, as effect and object of knowledge." Michel Foucault, *Discipline and Punish* (New York: Vintage, 1977), 191, 192.

16. Sigmund Freud, *Three Case Histories: The "Wolf Man," the "Rat Man," and the Psychotic Dr. Schreber* (New York: Collier Books, 1963), 173. Subsequent references are to this edition.

17. In later editions of the case study, Freud suggests that the Wolf Man did not necessarily see his parents having sex but may have inferred as much from his observation of some white sheepdogs copulating on the family's estate. In this later version, the animal becomes a supplement for a supplement.

18. We might see Freud's connections between animality and sexuality as part of a long and diverse history in which that connection operates. Donna Landry, for example, tracks this history at least as far back as the eighteenth century in the literature of English travel narratives in which women's exuberant attachments to their horses becomes both clear and queer. See Landry, "Horsy and Persistently Queer: Imperialism, Feminism, and Bestiality," *Textual Practice* 15, no. 3 (2001): 467–85.

19. Lacan, too, posits a visual event as a critical stage in subject formation. The mirror stage, for Lacan, is the process by which self-perception occurs; here, a child becomes capable of seeing himself as an object and thus a separate individual in the world. At the same time, vision was a vexed category for both Freud and Lacan; in Freud, the analysis of vision in dreams is fundamentally a theory of misrecognition, a theory that Lacan's model of the mirror stage also demonstrates. My point, therefore, is not to posit dreams as ontologically visual events or to overemphasize the role of the visual in subject formation, but rather to suggest that the visual was a central, if unstable, axis through which psychoanalysis conducted its interpretations of the subject. For an account of Lacan's critical stance toward the role of the visual, see Martin Jay, "The Rise of Hermeneutics and the Crisis of Ocularcentrism," *Poetics Today* 9, no. 2 (1988): 307–26, and *Downcast Eyes: The Denigration of Vision in Twentieth-Century Thought* (Berkeley: University of California Press, 1993).

20. Murray Krieger, *Ekphrasis: The Illusion of the Ekphrastic Sign* (Baltimore: Johns Hopkins University Press, 1992), 11. For other studies on the ekphrastic tradition, see Mack Smith, *Literary Realism and the Ekphrastic Tradition* (University Park: Pennsylvania State University Press, 1995); Michael P. Clark, ed., *Revenge of the Aesthetic: The Place of Literature in Theory Today* (Berkeley: University of California Press, 2000); Amy Golahny, ed., *The Eye of the Poet* (Lewisburg,

Pa.: Bucknell University Press, 1996); and Jay Bolter, "Ekphrasis, Virtual Reality, and the Future of Writing," in *The Future of the Book,* ed. Geoffrey Nunberg (Berkeley: University of California Press, 1996), 253–72. For an extended analysis of the sketch of the wolves, see Whitney Davis, *Drawing the Dream of the Wolves: Homosexuality, Interpretation, and Freud's "Wolf Man" Case* (Bloomington: Indiana University Press, 1994).

21. Although the visual aspect of dreams is a key frame of reference for Freud and psychoanalysis more generally, they are not purely visual. Throughout Freud's work on dreams, he provides many examples in which words appear in dreams, with the words themselves acting as signs to be interpreted. Other senses figure prominently in dreams as well, including, crucially, the senses of smell and touch.

22. W. J. T. Mitchell, *Picture Theory: Essays on Verbal and Visual Representation* (Chicago: University of Chicago Press, 1994), 180.

23. Krieger, *Ekphrasis,* 11.

24. Ibid.

25. Mitchell, *Picture Theory,* 70.

26. Mitchell suggests as much himself; ibid., 164 n. 35.

27. Ibid., 83.

28. Gilles Deleuze and Félix Guattari, *A Thousand Plateaus: Capitalism and Schizophrenia,* trans. Brian Massumi (Minneapolis: University of Minnesota Press, 1987), 28.

29. Deleuze and Guattari, *Thousand Plateaus,* 29.

30. Lee Edelman suggests that the scene of parental sex in the Wolf Man evokes the spectacle of gay male sex: "Freud's ambivalence about the vision of his penetration from behind generates, in consequence, a certain defensiveness about the status of his own analytical hypothesis—a defensiveness that may tell us a great deal about the danger posed by the vision of the sodomitical scene." Edelman, "Seeing Things," 179.

31. Sigmund Freud, *Civilization and Its Discontents,* trans. James Strachey (New York: W. W. Norton, 1961); Freud, *Totem and Taboo,* trans. James Strachey (New York: W. W. Norton, 1962).

32. Sigmund Freud and Joseph Breuer, *Studies in Hysteria,* trans. Nicola Luckhurst (New York: Penguin, 2004), 67.

33. Quoted in Lucille Ritvo, *Darwin's Influence on Freud,* 5.

34. Sigmund Freud, *The Interpretation of Dreams,* trans. James Strachey (New York: Basic Books, 1965), 76, 88.

35. Freud, *Three Case Histories,* 27.

36. See Leonard Jonathan Lamm, *The Idea of the Past: History, Science, and Practice in American Psychoanlysis* (New York: New York University Press, 1993).

37. Sigmund Freud, *Beyond the Pleasure Principle,* trans. James Strachey (New York: Norton, 1961), 5. For a reading that stresses Freud's interest in organistic restoration, see Judith Roof, "From Protista to DNA (and Back Again): Freud's Psychoanalysis of the Single-Celled Organism," in *Zoontologies: The Question of the Animal,* ed. Cary Wolfe (Minneapolis: University of Minnesota Press, 2003), 101–20.

38. See Sander Gilman, *Difference and Pathology: Stereotypes of Sexuality, Race, and Madness* (Ithaca, N.Y.: Cornell University Press, 1985); and Siobhan Sommerville, *Queering the Color Line: Race and the Invention of Homosexuality in American Culture* (Durham, N.C.: Duke University Press, 2000).

39. In emphasizing the question of race in Freud's work, I do not mean to dismiss questions of gender and class that are also key to his interpretations of the subject. For an account of gender and class as read through the Wolf Man's relationship to his nurse, see Peter Stallybrass and Allon White, "Below Stairs: The Maid and the Family Romance," in *The Politics and Poetics of Transgression* (New York: Cornell University Press, 1986), 149–70. Because the question of race tends to be deemphasized in readings of Freud, I choose to give it focused attention here.

40. G. Stanley Hall lamented that "overcivilized" men had lost touch with their "savage boyhoods" and "primitive pasts." See Hall, *Adolescence: Its Psychology, Its Relations to Physiology, Anthropology, Sociology, Sex, Crime, Religion, and Education* (New York: D. Appleton, 1904), 59. For an extensive account of ideas and representations of "savage boyhood" in American literature and culture, see Kenneth B. Kidd, *Making American Boys: Boyology and the Feral Tale* (Minneapolis: University of Minnesota Press, 2004).

41. Hall wrote the preface to the American edition of Freud's *Three Sexualities* and in 1909 orchestrated Freud's first visit to the United States for his famous Clark University Lectures, where Hall was president.

42. For an extended treatment of the role of homosexuality as a species of primitivism in Darwin and Freud's work, see Neville Hoad, "Arrested Development and the Queerness of Savages: Resisting Evolutionary Narratives of Difference," *Postcolonial Studies* 3, no. 2 (2000): 133–58.

43. See Josiah Nott, "The Mulatto, a Hybrid," in *American Journal of Medical Science* 5 (1843): 256; and Josiah Nott and George Gliddon, *Types of Mankind* (Philadelphia: Lippincott, 1854). For a discussion of Camper's comparisons, see Stephen Jay Gould, *The Mismeasure of Man* (New York: W. W. Norton, 1996); on the scientific characterization of Sara Bartmann as a Hottentot Venus, see Anne Fausto-Sterling, "Gender, Race, and Nation: The Comparative Anatomy of 'Hottentot' Women in Europe, 1815–1817," in *Deviant Bodies*, ed. Jennifer Terry and Jacqueline Urla (Bloomington: Indiana University Press, 1995), 19–48.

44. Étienne Balibar, "Racism and Nationalism," in *Race, Nation, Class: Ambiguous Identities*, ed. Étienne Balibar and Immanuel Wallerstein (London: Verso, 1991), 56–58.

45. Sigmund Freud, "The Unconscious," in *The Standard Edition of the Complete Psychological Works*, trans. James Strachey (New York: Hogarth, 1961), 115.

46. Lippit, *Electric Animal*, 104.

47. I am influenced here by Robert J. C. Young, *Colonial Desire: Hybridity in Theory, Culture, and Race* (New York: Routledge, 1995).

48. Cannon Schmitt, "Darwin's Savage Mnemonics," *Representations* 88 (2004): 55–80. Schmitt's project theorizes the function of memory in Victorian natural history, especially in expeditions to South America by Darwin, Wallace,

Hudson, and Kingsley. Cannon Schmitt, *Darwin and the Memory of the Human: Evolution, Savages, and South America* (Cambridge: Cambridge University Press, forthcoming).

49. See Judith Butler, *Bodies That Matter* (New York: Routledge, 1993), and *The Psychic Life of Power: Theories in Subjection* (Stanford, Calif.: Stanford University Press, 1997).

50. See the introduction to *Zoontologies*, where Cary Wolfe argues: "The discourse of animality has historically served as a crucial strategy in the oppression of humans by other humans—a strategy whose legitimacy and force depend, however, on the prior taking for granted of the traditional ontological distinction, and consequent ethical divide, between human and nonhuman animals" (xx).

51. To see how this plays out in the context of the debate over gay marriage, see Michael Warner, *The Trouble with Normal: Sex, Politics, and the Ethics of Queer Life* (New York: Free Press, 1999); and Judith Butler, "Is Kinship Always Already Heterosexual?" *differences* 13, no. 1 (Spring 2002): 14–44.

52. Sigmund Freud, *Moses and Monotheism,* trans. James Strachey (New York: Vintage, 1955), 126.

2. Late Modern Morphologies

1. Cesare Lombroso, introduction to Gina Lombroso-Ferrero, *Criminal Man According to the Classification of Cesare Lombroso* (New York: G. P. Putnam and Sons, 1911), xiv–xv.

2. For a study of degeneration theory from various disciplinary perspectives, see J. Edward Chamberlain and Sander L. Gilman, eds., *Degeneration: The Dark Side of Progress* (New York: Columbia University Press, 1985). For an extended treatment of degeneration theory in the French context, see Daniel Pick, *Faces of Degeneration: A European Disorder, 1848–1918* (New York: Cambridge University Press, 1989); in the context of the British gothic novel, see Kelley Hurley, *The Gothic Body: Sexuality, Materialism, and Degeneration at the Fin de Siècle* (New York: Cambridge University Press, 1996).

3. For arguments that stress the visual paradigms that inform modern subjectivity, see John Tagg, *The Burden of Representation: Essays on Photographies and Histories* (Minneapolis: University of Minnesota Press, 1993); and Lorraine Daston and Peter Galison, "The Image of Objectivity," *Representations* 40 (Fall 1992): 81–128. For an account of how nineteenth-century scientific and commercial photography produced a racialized middle-class identity, see Shawn Michelle Smith, *American Archives: Gender, Race, and Class in Visual Culture* (Princeton, N.J.: Princeton University Press, 1999). For an account of the impact of the visual model of subjectivity within Continental philosophy, see Gary Shapiro, *Archaeologies of Vision: Foucault and Nietzsche on Seeing and Saying* (Chicago: University of Chicago Press, 2003).

4. Nancy Armstrong, *Fiction in the Age of Photography: The Legacy of British Realism* (Cambridge, Mass.: Harvard University Press, 1999), 2. When Armstrong claims that "the image supplanted writing as the grounding of fiction,"

her point is not that "writing" as a technique of representation had somehow disappeared at this moment or that it had ceased to matter, but that it was no longer the same because of the advent of visual culture (3). For accounts of how writers approached their subjects in photographic ways, see Carol Schloss, *In Visible Light: Photography and the American Writers: 1840–1910* (New York: Oxford University Press, 1987); and Ralph Bogardus, *Pictures and Texts: Henry James, A. L. Coburn, and the New Ways of Seeing in Literary Culture* (New York: UMI Research Press, 1984).

5. For arguments that emphasize the relationship between visual technology and modernity, see Jonathan Crary, *Techniques of the Observer: On Vision and Modernity in the Nineteenth Century* (Cambridge, Mass.: MIT Press, 1995); Ben Singer, *Melodrama and Modernity: Early Sensational Cinema and Its Contexts* (New York: Columbia University Press, 2001); and Miriam Hansen, "The Mass Production of the Senses: Classical Cinema as Vernacular Modernism," in *Reinventing Film Studies,* ed. Christine Gledhill and Linda Williams (London: Arnold Press, 2000).

6. Cesare Lombroso, *The Female Offender* (London: T. Fisher Unwin, 1895), 93–94.

7. Ibid., 97. Nicole Hahn Rafter and Mary Gibson discuss how Lombroso "urges us to keep in mind that even female born criminals need to be attractive if they want men to invite them to serve as their accomplices or if they want to succeed at such typical crimes as adultery and slander." See Cesare Lombroso and Guglielmo Ferrero, *Criminal Woman, the Prostitute, and the Normal Woman,* ed. Nicole Hahn Rafter and Mary Gibson (Durham, N.C.: Duke University Press, 2004), 10.

8. In undertaking the exploration of the photograph as a social technology, I follow Fredric Jameson's recommendation that we subject the image to historical analysis. See Fredric Jameson, "Reification and Utopia in Mass Culture," in *Signatures of the Visible* (New York: Routledge, 1990). I borrow my understanding of photographs as technologies of meaning from Theresa de Lauretis, who says as much about the cinema in *Technologies of Gender: Essays on Theory, Film, and Fiction* (Bloomington: Indiana University Press, 1987).

9. Building on Foucault's notion of genealogy, Judith Butler argues that in order to fully grasp the notion of the body as a variable boundary rather than an a priori substance, what is required is "a genealogical account of the demarcation of the body as such a signifying practice." Judith Butler, *Gender Trouble: Feminism and the Subversion of Identity* (New York: Routledge, 1990), 130.

10. See Walter Benjamin, "Theses on the Philosophy of History," in *Illuminations,* ed. Hannah Arendt, trans. Harry Zohn (New York: Schocken, 1969); "Little History of Photography," and "On the Image of Proust," in *Walter Benjamin: Selected Writings, Vol. 2, 1927–1934,* trans. Rodney Livingstone et al., ed. Michael Jennings, Howard Eiland, and Gary Smith (Cambridge, Mass.: Harvard University Press, 1999); and "The Work of Art in the Age of Its Technological Reproducibility: Second Version" and "Letter from Paris (2): Painting and Photography," in *Walter Benjamin: Selected Writings, Vol. 3, 1935–1938,* trans.

Edmund Jephcott et al., ed. Michael Jennings, Howard Eiland, and Gary Smith (Cambridge, Mass.: Harvard University Press, 2006).

11. Quoted in Robert Nye, "Sociology and Degeneration: The Irony of Progress," in Chamberlain and Gilman, *Degeneration,* 49.

12. As Sander Gilman summarizes, modern society as a whole came to be considered a locus for infectious disease. He writes, "Societal degeneration contained the seeds for the decay of the individual, just as the degeneration of the individual embodied degeneration of the society." Gilman, *Difference and Pathology: Stereotypes of Sexuality, Race, and Madness* (Ithaca, N.Y.: Cornell University Press, 1985), 204.

13. Max Nordau, *Degeneration* (1892, English trans. 1895; Lincoln: University of Nebraska Press, 1993), 537.

14. Ibid., 1, v.

15. Ibid., 2. Nordau's work especially provoked criticism: William James called it "a pathological book on a pathological subject," and William Dean Howells blasted it as "a senseless and worthless book" whose "insufferable pages" show Nordau to be "a bad-tempered, ill-mannered man" and "a clever quack advertising himself." James, "Degeneration and Genius," *Psychological Review* 2 (1895): 287–94; Howells, "Degeneration," in *W. D. Howells as Critic,* ed. Edwin Cady (London: Routledge, 1973), 217–24. See also George Bernard Shaw's response to Nordau originally published in the American journal *Liberty* in 1895 and later reissued as a pamphlet: *The Sanity of Art: An Exposure of the Current Nonsense about Artists Being Degenerate* (London: New Age Press, 1908).

16. For a more detailed account of Hall's interest in Haeckel and how both of their theories were taken up by Freud, see chapter 1.

17. Thomas Speed Mosby, *Causes and Cures of Crime* (St. Louis, Mo.: C. V. Mosby, 1913), 58.

18. Ibid., 54.

19. On this notion of "racial time," see Michael Hanchard, "Afro-Modernity: Temporality, Politics, and the African Diaspora," in *Alternative Modernities,* ed. Dilip Gaonkar (Durham, N.C.: Duke University Press, 2001), 272–98.

20. Several crucial histories of sexuality demonstrate how fin de siècle concepts of sexuality became vehicles for exercising control and scrutiny over specific populations. Especially see John D'Emilio and Estelle Freedman, *Intimate Matters: A History of Sexuality in America* (New York: Harper and Row, 1988); and Jeffrey Weeks, *Sexuality and Its Discontents: Meanings, Myths, and Modern Sexualities* (New York: Routledge, 1985).

21. Charlotte Perkins Gilman, *The Crux* (New York: Charlton, 1911), 5. I return to Gilman's participation in the discourse on atavism in chapter 5.

22. William S. Sadler, MD, *Race Decadence: An Examination of the Causes of Racial Degeneracy in the United States* (Chicago: McClurg, 1922), 46, 47, 267, 268.

23. James Bryce, "The Relations of the Advanced and the Backward Races of Mankind," in *Racial Determinism and The Fear of Miscegenation, Post-1900, Part II, Anti-Black Thought, 1863–1925: An Eleven Volume Anthology of Racist Writings,* ed. John David Smith (New York: 1993), 8:26.

24. William Benjamin Smith, "The Color Line: A Brief in Behalf of the Unborn," in Smith, *Racial Determinism*, 49.

25. Lothrop Stoddard, *The Rising Tide of Color against White World-Supremacy* (New York: Charles Scribner and Sons, 1920), 309.

26. Lothrop Stoddard, *The Revolt against Civilization: The Menace of the Underman* (New York: Charles Scribner and Sons, 1923), 4.

27. Nancy Stepan, "Biological Degeneration: Races and Proper Places," in Chamberlain and Gilman, *Degeneration: The Dark Side of Progress*, 98.

28. Lombroso, *Criminal Man*, 368.

29. Ibid., 373.

30. John Frow, *Time and Commodity Culture* (New York: Oxford University Press, 1997), 77; and Eric Hobsbawn, *The Invention of Tradition* (New York: Cambridge University Press, 1992).

31. Lisa Cartwright, *Screening the Body: Tracing Medicine's Visual Culture* (Minneapolis: University of Minnesota Press, 1995).

32. Benjamin, "Theses on the Philosophy of History," 255.

33. Bill Brown describes how the Kodak craze "ramified as the massification of the Eye, a new kind of power" that "had the disarming effect of arming the public with sight." See his chapter "Monstrosity," in *The Material Unconscious: American Amusement, Stephen Crane, and the Economies of Play* (Cambridge, Mass.: Harvard University Press, 1996), 236–37. For detailed accounts of photography in America, see Miles Orvell, "Almost Nature: The Typology of Late Nineteenth Century American Photography," in *Multiple Views: Logan Grant Essays on Photography, 1983–1989*, ed. Daniel P. Younger (Albuquerque: University of New Mexico Press, 1991); Alan Trachtenberg, "The Mirror and the Marketplace: American Responses to the Daguerreotype, 1839–1851," in *The Daguerreotype: A Sesquicentennial Celebration*, ed. John Wood (Iowa City: University of Iowa Press, 1989); and William Welling, *Photography in America: The Formative Years, 1839–1900* (New York: Thomas Y. Crowell Company, 1978).

34. See Peter Hales, *Silver Cities: The Photography of American Urbanization, 1839–1915* (Philadelphia: Temple University Press, 1984). Muybridge was well known for his stop-action studies of animals and humans in motion. See Eadweard Muybridge, *Muybridge's Complete Human and Animal Locomotion: Reprint of Original Volumes 1–4* (1887; New York: Dover Press, 1979).

35. Quoted in Hales, *Silver Cities*, 221. Also see Helen Campbell, *Darkness and Daylight: or, Lights and Shadows of New York Life; a Pictorial Record of Personal Experience by Day and Night in the Great Metropolis* (New York: Hartford Publishing, 1897).

36. Brown, *Material Unconscious*, 225.

37. Alan Sekula, "The Body and the Archive," *October* 39 (Winter 1986): 5. Max Nordau, *Degeneration* (1892, English trans. 1895; Lincoln: University of Nebraska Press, 1993), 42; subsequent references are to this edition.

38. Michel Foucault, *The Birth of the Clinic: An Archaeology of Medical Perception*, trans. A. M. Sheridan Smith (New York: Vintage Books, 1994), 114.

39. See Daniel M. Fox and Christopher Lawrence, *Photographing Medicine:*

Images and Power in Britain and America since 1840 (New York: Greenwood Press, 1988).

40. See Sander Gilman, *Seeing the Insane* (New York: John Wiley and Sons, 1982); and Lynn Gamwell and Nancy Tomes, *Madness in America: Cultural and Medical Perceptions of Mental Illness before 1914* (New York: Cornell University Press, 1995).

41. For arguments that focus on different aspects of Charcot's photographs of hysterical women, see Daphne de Marneffe, "Looking and Listening: The Construction of Clinical Knowledge in Charcot and Freud," *Signs* 17, no. 1 (Fall 1991): 71–111; and Ulrich Baer, "Photography and Hysteria: Toward a Poetics of the Flash," *Yale Journal of Criticism* 7, no. 1 (Spring 1994): 41–77.

42. See Alphonse Bertillon, *Signaletic Instructions,* trans. Gallus Muller (Chicago: Werner, 1896). On the rise of scientific theories of individualism, see Ruth Leys, "Types of One: Adolf Meyer's Life Chart and the Representation of Individuality," *Representations* 34 (Spring 1991): 1–28.

43. Francis Galton, *Inquiries into Human Faculty and Its Development* (London: Dent, 1883), 18.

44. Ibid., 125.

45. David Green, "Veins of Resemblance: Photography and Eugenics," *Oxford Art Journal* 7, no. 2 (1984): 12.

46. In the United States, Galton's methods were given a popular forum in an 1886 issue of *Science Magazine* (7:170), which displayed composites of Native American types accompanied by the article "Composite Portraits of American Indians." In 1887, American psychologist William Noyes also put Galton's methods to use in his study of insanity with the intention of proving visually a pathological type. See William Noyes, "Composite Portraiture of the Insane," *Science* 9 (1888): 252–53.

47. Tom Gunning suggests that Galton's attempt to blur the identity of the individual in order to create a knowable type epitomizes one strand of thought at the fin de siècle. He argues, nonetheless, that the photographic process more generally attempted to fix the body as a unique individual identity. Alan Sekula also discusses the differences between Bertillon and Galton, arguing that Bertillon's method does more than simply individualize the subject photographed: "The individual only existed as an individual by being identified. Individuality as such had no meaning. Viewed 'objectively,' the self occupied a position that was wholly relative." See Tom Gunning, "Tracing the Individual Body," in *Cinema and the Invention of Modern Life,* ed. Leo Charney and Vanessa Schwartz (Berkeley: University of California Press, 1995), 15–45. Sekula, "The Body and the Archive," 55, 34.

48. Galton, *Inquiries,* 15.

49. Roland Barthes, *Camera Lucida* (New York: Hill and Wang, 1982), 12.

50. In addition to statistics, the eighteenth- and early nineteenth-century practices of phrenology and physiognomy were important precedents for early twentieth-century medical photography. In the late 1770s, Johann Kasper Lavater systematized the science of physiognomy, arguing that that the surface of the body bears outward signs of internal character. Phrenology emerged in

the first decade of the nineteenth century in the research of Viennese physician Franz Josef Gall, who was highly influenced by Lavater's work. Gall sought to discern correspondences between the topology of the skull and localized mental faculties within the brain. See Johann Kasper Lavater, *Essays on Physiognomy Designed to Promote the Knowledge and the Love of Mankind*, vol. 1 (London: J. Murray, 1792); and Roger Cooter, *The Cultural Meaning of Popular Science: Phrenology and the Organization of Consent* (Cambridge: Cambridge University Press, 1985). For a nineteenth-century text that put Gall's ideas into practice, see Nelson Sizer and H. S. Drayton, *Heads and Faces, and How to Study Them* (New York: Fowler and Wells, 1890).

51. Ian Hacking, "Making up People," in *Forms of Desire: Sexual Orientation and the Social Constructionist Controversy*, ed. Edward Stein (New York: Routledge, 1990), 70.

52. Susan Buck-Morss, "Aesthetics and Anaesthetics: Walter Benjamin's Artwork Essay Reconsidered," *October* 62 (1992): 33.

53. As John Tagg specifies, "The coupling of evidence and photography . . . was bound up with the emergence of new institutions and new practices of observation . . . and to the formation of new social and anthropological sciences," what he refers to, following Foucault, as the "new strategy of governance." *Burden of Representation*, 5.

54. Eugene Talbot, *Degeneracy: Its Causes, Signs, and Results* (New York: Charles Scribner and Sons, 1898), 280–81.

55. Ibid., 361.

56. Mosby, *Causes and Cures of Crime*, 49.

57. Lombroso, *Criminal Man*, 72–73.

58. For a discussion of how photography functions as a mechanism of historical and personal commemoration, see Eduardo Cadava, *Words of Light: Theses on the Photography of History* (Princeton, N.J.: Princeton University Press, 1997).

59. On the calendar as an ideologically charged function of time, see Alison A. Chapman, "The Politics of Time in Edmund Spenser's English Calendar," *Studies in English Literature* 42, no. 1 (Winter 2002): 1–24.

60. Especially see Jonathan Smith, *Charles Darwin and Victorian Visual Culture* (Cambridge: Cambridge University Press, 2006).

61. See Sander Gilman, "AIDS and Syphilis: The Iconography of Disease," in *AIDS: Cultural Analysis, Cultural Activism*, ed. Douglas Crimp (Cambridge, Mass.: MIT Press, 1988), where he argues: "Disease is restricted to a specific set of images, thereby forming a visual boundary, a limit to the idea (or fear) of disease" (88).

62. For the impact of photography on literary realism, see Nancy Armstrong, *Fiction in the Age of Photography*. In a similar vein, Rosalind Krauss discusses how the surrealists used cameras to record "a nature convulsed into a kind of writing," thus blurring the traditionally made distinctions between signs and images. Krauss, *The Originality of the Avant-Garde and Other Modernist Myths* (Cambridge, Mass.: MIT Press, 1985), 113. There is very little work, however, on how medical photographs were themselves shaped by rhetorical and textual media.

63. In his account of the emergence of the "two sex model," Thomas Laqueur has argued that the invention of the female anatomy as separate and distinct from the male only emerged through its pictorial representation in medical texts. Further, he suggests that the anatomy books of the seventeenth and eighteenth centuries are themselves artifacts whose production is part of the history of their epoch, and the female body, or by extension any "typical" medical representation, is an "exercise in a culturally bound aesthetic." See Laqueur, *Making Sex: Body and Gender from the Greeks to Freud* (Cambridge, Mass.: Harvard University Press, 1990), 168.

64. W. J. T. Mitchell argues that the interaction of pictures and texts, or "imagetext," is constitutive of representation as such. See Mitchell, *Picture Theory* (Chicago: University of Chicago Press, 1994). For a discussion of Mitchell's concept of the "imagetext" in the context of Freud's case studies, see chapter 1.

65. Talbot, *Degeneracy,* 103.

66. See David Horn, "This Norm Which Is Not One: Reading the Female Body in Lombroso's Anthropology," in *Deviant Bodies,* ed. Jennifer Terry and Jacqueline Urla (Bloomington: Indiana University Press, 1995), 109–28.

67. Lombroso, *Female Offender,* 89.

68. Ibid., 90.

69. Talbot, *Degeneracy,* 2.

70. As Jacqueline Urla and Jennifer Terry have argued in their introduction to *Deviant Bodies,* "Meticulous techniques of quantification and classification eroded the very possibility of fixing distinctions that researchers assumed were present . . . in the end these efforts actually fueled social and scientific anxieties even further, precisely because science produced no clear demarcation" (7).

71. Judith Halberstam's characterization of the body as a space of "infinite interpretability" has informed my understanding of photographic representational practice here. See Halberstam, *Skin Shows: Gothic Horror and the Technology of Monsters* (Durham, N.C.: Duke University Press, 1995), 31.

72. Paula Treichler, in her study of AIDS discourse, has called the phenomenon of making disease and diseased bodies intelligible through discourse "an epidemic of signification." Treichler, "AIDS, Homophobia and Biomedical Discourse: An Epidemic of Signification," in Crimp, *AIDS,* 31–32.

73. See Judith Butler's discussion, following Nietzsche, on how the body is supposed to function as a guarantee of "the metaphysics of substance." Butler, *Gender Trouble,* 10.

74. The photograph, in this sense, is what Roland Barthes describes as "the advent of myself as other; a cunning disassociation of consciousness from identity." When one is captured by a photograph, Barthes observes, he or she is transformed from a subject into an object, and the resulting image is "a micro-version of death, or parenthesis" that separates the person from the portrayal. Barthes, *Camera Lucida* (New York: Hill and Wang, 1982), 12.

75. Siegfried Kracauer, "Photography," in *The Mass Ornament: Weimar Essays,* trans. Thomas Levin (Cambridge, Mass.: Harvard University Press, 1995), 51.

76. Ibid., 48.

77. Ibid.

78. Ibid.

79. Roland Barthes, *Camera Lucida,* 66.

80. Guy Debord, *Society of the Spectacle* (1967; Detroit, Mich.: Black and Red, 1983), 81.

81. Kracauer, "Photography," 57.

82. Miriam Hansen, "'With skin and hair': Kracauer's Theory of Film, Marseilles 1940," *Critical Inquiry* 19 (Spring 1993): 453.

83. Kracauer, "Photography," 62.

3. "Wolf—wolf!"

1. Djuna Barnes, *Nightwood* (New York: New Directions, 1937). Subsequent references are to this edition.

2. Frank Norris, *Vandover and the Brute* (New York: Doubleday, Page, 1914), 310. Subsequent references are to this edition. Although published in 1914, *Vandover* was written in 1895, with a possible revision in 1896.

3. To see how degeneration theory plays itself out in British gothic novels, see Kelly Hurley, *The Gothic Body: Sexuality, Materialism and Degeneration at the Fin de Siècle* (New York: Cambridge University Press, 1996).

4. W. R. Inge, "Is Our Race Degenerating?" *Living Age,* January 1897, 154, 151.

5. "The Future of America: A Biological Forecast," *Harper's,* April 1928, 529–39.

6. William Monroe Balch, "Is the Race Going Downhill?" *American Mercury,* August 1926, 433.

7. Richard Von Krafft-Ebing, *Psychopathia Sexualis* (New York: Physicians and Surgeons Book Co., 1934), 350, 335, 395; Eugene Talbot, *Degeneracy: Its Causes, Signs and Results* (New York: Charles Scribner's Sons, 1898), 274; and Havelock Ellis, *Sexual Inversion* (1897; New York: Ayer, 1994), 136.

8. See Jennifer Terry and Jacqueline Urla's introduction to their edited volume *Deviant Bodies: Critical Perspectives on Difference in Science and Popular Culture* (Bloomington: Indiana University Press, 1995).

9. For scholarship that addresses both late nineteenth- and early twentieth-century science and its use of race as a determining factor for sexual degeneracy and gender difference, see Sander Gilman, *Difference and Pathology: Stereotypes of Sexuality, Race, and Madness* (Ithaca, N.Y.: Cornell University Press, 1985); Nancy Leys Stepan, "Race and Gender: The Role of Analogy in Science," *Anatomy of Racism,* ed. David Goldberg (Minneapolis: University of Minnesota Press, 1990); and Siobhan Somerville, "Scientific Racism and the Emergence of the Homosexual Body," *Journal of the History of Sexuality* 5 (October 1994): 243–66.

10. Somerville, "Scientific Racism," 247.

11. See my more elaborate development of the construction of queer physiognomies in medical photography: Dana Seitler, "Queer Physiognomies; or, How Many Ways Can We Do the History of Sexuality?" *Criticism* 46 (Winter 2004): 71–102.

12. See Eve Sedgwick, *Epistemology of the Closet* (Berkeley: University of California Press, 1990); Jeffrey Weeks, *Sex, Politics, and Society* (London: Longman, 1981); Edward Stein, ed., *Forms of Desire: Sexual Orientation and the Social Constructionist Controversy* (New York: Garland, 1991); and Jonathan Ned Katz, *Gay American History: Lesbians and Gay Men in the USA* (New York: Harper and Row, 1985).

13. Michel Foucault, "Nietzsche, Genealogy, History," in *Language, Counter-Memory, Practice: Selected Essays and Interviews,* ed. Donald Bouchard, trans. Donald Bouchard and Sherry Simon (Ithaca, N.Y.: Cornell University Press, 1977), 148.

14. Judith Butler, *Gender Trouble: Feminism and the Subversion of Identity* (New York: Routledge, 1990), 129.

15. Ibid.

16. Amy Kaplan, *The Social Construction of American Realism* (Chicago: University of Chicago Press, 1988), 10. Kaplan poses the important question: "Is realism part of a broader cultural effort to fix and control a coherent representation of a social reality that seems increasingly inaccessible, fragmented, and beyond control?" (8).

17. Mark Seltzer, *Bodies and Machines* (New York: Routledge, 1992), 44.

18. Fredric Jameson, *The Political Unconscious: Narrative as a Socially Symbolic Act* (Ithaca, N.Y.: Cornell University Press, 1981), 266.

19. This history includes texts outside the scope of this chapter, from Henry James's sublime tale of hidden sexual knowledge ("the lurking Beast . . . huge and hideous") in "The Beast in the Jungle" to the deeply homoerotic bonds figured through animal exchange and masculine transformation in Jack London's *The Sea-Wolf* (discussed in chapter 6). See Henry James, "The Beast in the Jungle," in *The Turn of the Screw and Other Short Fiction* (New York: Bantam, 1983), 367. We could add present-day incarnations to this list as well: Michael Jackson's donning of a wolf mask in his 1983 "Thriller" video, the uncertain adolescent sexuality of Michael J. Fox's 1985 film *Teen Wolf,* and the queer sensibilities of the film and television show *Buffy the Vampire Slayer*'s brutish demons.

20. Gilles Deleuze and Félix Guattari, *A Thousand Plateaus: Capitalism and Schizophrenia,* trans. Brian Massumi (Minneapolis: University of Minnesota Press, 1987), 241.

21. Carroll Smith-Rosenberg, *Disorderly Conduct: Visions of Gender in Victorian America* (New York: Oxford University Press, 1985), 267. For further discussion, see Lillian Faderman, *Surpassing the Love of Men: Romantic Friendship and the Love between Women from the Renaissance to the Present* (New York: William Morrow, 1981); and John D'Emilio and Estelle B. Freedman, *Intimate Matters: A History of Sexuality in America* (New York: Harper and Row, 1988).

22. See Hubert Kennedy, *Ulrichs: The Life and Works of Karl Heinrich Ulrichs, Pioneer of the Modern Gay Movement* (Boston: Alyson Publications, 1988), 49–51; and Esther Newton, "The Mythic Mannish Lesbian: Radclyffe Hall and the New Woman," *Signs* 9 (Fall 1984): 557–75. Ulrichs, himself a homosexual, thought he was defending same-sex sexual practices. In his view, the homosexual should receive tolerance, not social injustice. In fact, there was ambivalence and even

direct disagreement as to whether homosexuality was pathological. Havelock Ellis infamously wavered on this point, and later work by physicians Iwan Bloch and Magnus Hirschfeld agreed that homosexuality was congenital but rejected Krafft-Ebing's view that linked the homosexual "condition" to pathology.

23. Krafft-Ebing, *Psychopathia Sexualis*, 338–39. See also Arnold Davidson, "Sex and the Emergence of Sexuality," in *Forms of Desire: Sexual Orientation and the Social Constructionist Controversy* (New York: Routledge, 1992). For a study of the anatomical understanding of sex, see Thomas Laqueur, *Making Sex: Body and Gender from the Greeks to Freud* (Cambridge, Mass.: Harvard University Press, 1990).

24. Krafft-Ebing, *Psychopathia Sexualis*, 398–99, 425.

25. Ibid., 399. For an account of how the human sciences defined sexual deviance through signs of gender inversion as opposed to sex acts, see George Chauncey, "From Sexual Inversion to Homosexuality: The Changing Medical Conceptualization of Female 'Deviance,'" in *Passion and Power: Sexuality in History* (Philadelphia: Temple University Press, 1989).

26. Quoted in Ellis, *Sexual Inversion*, 103; see also Sommerville, *Queering the Color Line*, 247–56.

27. See George Mosse, *Nationalism and Sexuality: Middle Class Morality and Sexual Norms in Modern Europe* (Madison: University of Wisconsin Press, 1985).

28. See Ed Cohen, *Talk on the Wilde Side: Towards a Genealogy of Discourse on Male Sexualities* (New York: Routledge, 1993).

29. Talbot, *Degeneracy*, 324; Ellis, *The Criminal* (1890; Montclair, N. J.: Patterson Smith, 1973), 98–102.

30. Frank Norris, "A Case for Lombroso," in *Collected Writings* (New York: Doubleday, 1928), 38. See also Norris's story "A Reversion to Type" in his collection *The Third Circle* (New York: John Lane, 1909), in which an effeminate man's body transforms into a hypermasculine "free-booter seven feet tall, with a chest expansion of fifty inches" as a result of his hereditary destiny (90). For an account of Norris's notions of "race suicide," see Stephanie Bower, "Dangerous Liaisons: Prostitution, Disease, and Race in Frank Norris's Fiction," *Modern Fiction Studies* 42 (Spring 1996): 31–60.

31. Theodore Dreiser, *Sister Carrie* (1900; New York: W. W. Norton, 2006), 54.

32. Frank Norris, *McTeague* (1899; New York: W. W. Norton, 1977), 2, 31.

33. Sherwood Williams, "The Rise of a New Degeneration: Decadence and Atavism in *Vandover and the Brute*," *ELH* 57 (Fall 1990): 711.

34. Seltzer, *Bodies and Machines*, 22.

35. Ibid., 38.

36. Talbot, *Degeneracy*, 17.

37. See George Beard, *American Nervousness: Its Causes and Consequences* (New York: Putnam, 1881).

38. See Tom Lutz, *American Nervousness, 1903* (Ithaca, N.Y.: Cornell University Press, 1991).

39. Ellis, *Sexual Inversion*, 87.

40. I borrow the term *habitus* from Pierre Bourdieu, who describes how

the "habitus is 'put into practice'" whereby the "practices of all agents of the same class . . . owe the stylistic affinity which makes each of them a metaphor of any of the others to the fact that they are the product of transfers of the same schemes of action from one field to another." Bourdieu, *Distinction: A Social Critique of the Judgment of Taste* (Cambridge, Mass.: Harvard University Press, 1984), 173.

41. See Gilman, *Difference and Pathology*, and "AIDS and Syphilis: The Iconography of Disease," in *AIDS: Cultural Analysis/Cultural Activism*, ed. Douglas Crimp (Cambridge, Mass.: MIT Press, 1989).

42. Dana Nelson, *National Manhood: Capitalist Citizenship and the Imagined Fraternity of White Men* (Durham, N.C.: Duke University Press, 1998), 125.

43. Barnes quoted in Cheryl Plumb, "Revising *Nightwood:* 'A kind of glee of despair,'" *Review of Contemporary Fiction* 13 (Fall 1993): 151.

44. For essays that examine *Nightwood*'s relationship to primitivism and anti-Semitic discourse, see Karen Kaviola, "The 'Beast Turning Human': Constructions of the Primitive in *Nightwood*," and Meryl Altman, "A Book of Repulsive Jews? Rereading *Nightwood*," both in *Review of Contemporary Fiction* 13 (Fall 1993): 172–86 and 160–71, respectively.

45. Seltzer, *Bodies and Machines*, 8.

46. Andreas Huyssen, *After the Great Divide: Modernism, Mass Culture, Postmodernism* (Bloomington: Indiana University Press, 1986), vii.

47. Dianne Chisholm, "Obscene Modernism: Eros Noir and the Profane Illumination of Djuna Barnes," *American Literature* 69 (March 1997): 188, 195, 185.

48. Theodore Purdy Jr., review of *Nightwood*, *Saturday Review*, 27 March 1937, 11.

49. Smith-Rosenberg, *Disorderly Conduct*, 282.

50. Irony, writes Naomi Schor, allows an author "both to reject and to reappropriate the discourse of reference." Schor, *Bad Objects: Essays Popular and Unpopular* (Durham, N.C.: Duke University Press, 1995), 105.

51. Joseph Howe, MD, *Excessive Venery, Masturbation and Continence* (New York: Birmingham, 1883), 77, 76, 78.

52. The engagement with wandering as the ground for reimagining queer female sexuality was also taken up by Gertrude Stein: "Melanctha had begun once more to wander. Melanctha did not yet always wander, but a little now she needed to begin to look for others." Gertrude Stein, *Three Lives* (1909; New York: Penguin, 1990), 130.

53. Susan Sniader Lanser, "Speaking in Tongues: *Ladies Almanac* and the Discourse of Desire," in *Silence and Power: A Reevaluation of Djuna Barnes*, ed. Mary Lynn Broe (Carbondale: Southern Illinois University Press, 1991), 158.

54. See Carol J. Allen, "Sexual Narrative in the Fiction of Djuna Barnes," in *Sexual Practice/Textual Theory: Lesbian Cultural Criticism*, ed. Susan J. Wolfe and Julia Penelope (Cambridge, Mass.: Blackwell, 1993); and Jodey Castricano, "Rude Awakenings: What Happens When a Lesbian Reads the 'Hieroglyphics of Sleep' in Djuna Barnes' *Nightwood*," *West Coast Line* 15 (Winter 1994–95): 106–16.

55. Mikhail Bakhtin, *Rabelais and His World*, trans. Hélène Iswolsky (Bloomington: Indiana University Press, 1984).

56. Bonnie Kime Scott, "Barnes Being 'Beast Familiar': Representation on the Margin of Modernism," *RCF* 13 (Fall 1993): 41–52; Jane Marcus, "Laughing at Leviticus: *Nightwood* as Women's Circus Epic," in Broe, *Silence and Power*, 221–51.

57. Leo Bersani, *The Freudian Body: Psychoanalysis and Art* (New York: Columbia University Press, 1986), 38.

58. This last scene has been subject to a series of different readings, especially by feminist critics of *Nightwood* who debate its ability to suggest social change. For instance, Shari Benstock reads the scene as an ultimate act of punishment meted out to its characters that returns "woman as *object* of the patriarchal fiction, robbing [Robin] of a language through which to articulate her passion and anger. . . . Unable, finally, to explain herself, Robin howls like a dog." Judith Lee agrees, discomforted by the narrative's inability to "give voice to (feminine) silence." Conversely, Donna Gerstenberger reads *Nightwood*'s "indeterminate ending" as a reminder that "the desire of Barnes's novel is freedom from the prison of meaning." Bonnie Kime Scott pays attention to the bestiality depicted in the scene but reads Robin's actions more as a matriarchal religious ritual than a theory of sexuality. She writes: "The extended actions of dog and woman are suggestive of ritual healing. . . . [Robin] going down before the dog, as one might in honoring a god." See Shari Benstock, *Women of the Left Bank* (Austin: University of Texas Press, 1986), 266; Judith Lee, "*Nightwood:* The Sweetest Lie," in Broe, *Silence and Power*, 218; Donna Gerstenberger, "The Radical Narrative of Djuna Barnes's *Nightwood,*" in *Breaking the Sequence: Women's Experimental Fiction* (Princeton, N.J.: Princeton University Press, 1989), 138; and Bonnie Kime Scott, *Refiguring Modernism, Vol. 2: Postmodern Feminist Readings of Woolf, West, and Barnes* (Bloomington: Indiana University Press, 1995), 117–18.

59. Here we can see Barnes playing on the analogies made in the human sciences between female sexuality and animality. For example, see Eugene Talbot when he argues, "Degenerate women frequently have supernumerary milk glands arranged on the abdomen as in some lemurs." Talbot, *Degeneracy*, 269.

60. Homi Bhabha, *The Location of Culture* (New York: Routledge, 1994), 12–13.

61. Georges Bataille, *Visions of Excess: Selected Writings, 1927–1939*, trans. Allan Stoekl (Minneapolis: University of Minnesota Press, 1985), 84.

4. Atavistic Time

1. Kath Weston, *Gender in Real Time* (New York: Routledge, 2002), 93, 122.

2. Richard Terdiman has called this a "memory crisis" wherein even as modernity is constituted by way of a forgetting of the past, forms of "involuntary memory" maintain the power of the past on our present lives. See Terdiman, *Present Past: Modernity and the Memory Crisis* (Ithaca, N.Y.: Cornell University Press, 1993), 245.

3. Jürgen Habermas, "Modernity: An Incomplete Project," in *The Anti-Aesthetic: Essays on Postmodern Culture,* ed. Hal Foster (Washington: New Press, 1983), 3–16.

4. David Harvey, *The Condition of Postmodernity* (Cambridge: Blackwell, 1990), 12.

5. Miriam Hansen, "Benjamin and Cinema: Not a One-Way Street," in *Benjamin's Ghosts: Interventions in Contemporary Literary and Cultural Theory,* ed. Gerhard Richter (Stanford, Calif.: Stanford University Press, 2002), 41.

6. Max Horkheimer and Theodor Adorno, *The Dialectic of Enlightenment* (New York: Continuum, 1994).

7. Paul Ricoeur argues that the relationship between time and narrative is of a kind that disables the hierarchization of text over context, and vice versa. Instead, time and narrative presuppose each other: "Time becomes human time to the extent that it is organized after the manner of a narrative; narrative, in turn, is meaningful to the extent that it portrays the features of temporal experience." Ricoeur, *Time and Narrative,* vol. 1 (Chicago: University of Chicago Press, 1984), 29. My argument in this chapter is also influenced by Wai-Chee Dimock's work. See Dimock, "Literature for the Planet," *PMLA* 116, no. 1 (January 2001): 173–88; and "A Theory of Resonance," *PMLA* 112, no. 5 (October 1997): 1060–71.

8. Fredric Jameson (following Althusser) posits various forms of causality in the production of cultural texts, one being "mechanical causality." Jameson writes: "Mechanical causality is thus less a concept which might be evaluated on its own terms, than one of the various laws and subsystems of our peculiarly reified social and cultural life." I am suggesting, however, that serial dime novels are not just (reified) effects of new forms of production, but also ideological agents of the ideas of modern progress in their own right. Jameson, *The Political Unconscious: Narrative as a Socially Symbolic Act* (Ithaca, N.Y.: Cornell University Press, 1981), 26.

9. Richard Ohman, *Selling Culture: Magazines, Markets, and Class at the Turn of the Century* (London: Verso, 1996), 23.

10. See James L. West, *American Authors and the Literary Marketplace since 1900* (Philadelphia: University of Pennsylvania Press, 1988); and Michael Denning, *Mechanic Accents: Dime Novels and Working-Class Culture in America* (London: Verso, 1998).

11. The blockbuster film has capitalized on the promise of narrative recurrence in the form of the sequel, the prequel, and beyond, witnessed so famously in Arnold Schwarzenegger's famous line, "I'll be back," at the end of *The Terminator* (dir. James Cameron, 1984).

12. What would happen, for example, if one began reading in the middle of a series? Entire references to earlier texts would be missed, would indeed necessitate a return to those previous episodes. The dime novel in this sense requires a return to the beginning (the past of the series) while encouraging one to read to the end (the ever-receding horizon of the series's future).

13. Charles W. Burr, "The Prevention of Insanity and Degeneracy," *American Journal of Insanity* 74 (1918): 409–22.

14. Arthur H. Estabrook and Ivan Mcdougle, *Mongrel Virginians: The Win Tribe* (Baltimore: Williams and Wilkins, 1926), 199–201.

15. Quoted in Daniel Kevles, *In the Name of Eugenics: Genetics and the Uses of Human Heredity* (Cambridge, Mass.: Harvard University Press, 1995), 173.

16. Calvin Coolidge, "Whose Country Is This?" *Good Housekeeping* 72 (February 1921): 14.

17. Quoted in Donald K. Pickens, *Eugenics and the Progressives* (New York: Vanderbilt University Press, 1968), 121.

18. For a cogent analysis of Roosevelt's masculinist and racially based ideals, see Gail Bederman, *Manliness and Civilization: A Cultural History of Gender and Race in the United States, 1880–1917* (Chicago: University of Chicago Press, 1995).

19. On Theodore Roosevelt's life and policies, see Edmund Morris, *The Rise of Theodore Roosevelt* (New York: Ballantine, 1979); and Thomas G. Dyer, *Theodore Roosevelt and the Idea of Race* (Baton Rouge: Louisiana State University Press, 1980). For an account of the cultural expressions of imperialism in the United States, see Amy Kaplan, *The Anarchy of Empire in the Making of U.S. Culture* (Cambridge, Mass.: Harvard University Press, 2005).

20. In addition to Kevles and Pickens, for histories of the eugenics movement in the United States, see Ian Robert Dowbiggin, *Keeping America Sane: Psychiatry and Eugenics in the United States and Canada, 1880–1940* (Ithaca, N.Y.: Cornell University Press, 1997); Martin S. Pernick, *The Black Stork: Eugenics and the Death of "Defective" Babies in American Medicine and Motion Pictures since 1915* (New York: Oxford University Press, 1999); and Daylanne English, *Unnatural Selections: Eugenics in American Modernism and the Harlem Renaissance* (Chapel Hill: University of North Carolina Press, 2004).

21. Bruno Latour, *We Have Never Been Modern,* trans. Catherine Porter (Cambridge, Mass.: Harvard University Press, 1993).

22. This is why Latour calls for a governing process constituted by a "Parliament of Things": "In its confines, the continuity of the collective is reconfigured. There are no more naked truths, but there are no more naked citizens either. Natures are present, but with their representatives, scientists who speak in their name. Societies are present, but with the objects that have been serving as their ballast from time immemorial. Let one of the representatives talk, for instance, about the ozone hole, another represent the Monsanto chemical industry, a third the workers of the same chemical industry, another the voters of New Hampshire, a fifth the meteorology of the polar regions; let still another speak in the name of the State; what does it matter, so long as they are all talking about the same thing, about a quasi-object they have all created, the object-discourse-nature-society whose new properties astound us all and whose network extends from my refrigerator to the Antarctic by way of chemistry, law, the State, the economy, and satellites. The imbroglios and networks that had no place now have the place to themselves." Latour, *We Have Never Been Modern,* 144.

23. John Kasson, *Rudeness and Civility: Manners in Nineteenth Century Urban America* (New York: Hill and Wang, 1990). See also Carroll Smith-Rosenberg,

Disorderly Conduct: Visions of Gender in Victorian America (New York: Oxford University Press, 1985); and Mary Douglas, *Purity and Danger: An Analysis of the Concepts of Pollution and Taboo* (London: Routledge, 1995).

24. Kathy Peiss, *Cheap Amusements: Working Women and Leisure in Turn-of-the-Century New York* (Philadelphia: Temple University Press, 1986), 114.

25. Mark Seltzer, *Bodies and Machines* (New York: Routledge, 1992), 150. Bill Brown, in *The Material Unconscious: American Amusement, Stephen Crane, and the Economies of Play* (Cambridge, Mass.: Harvard University Press, 1996), theorizes the intensification of masculine display, especially within American sports culture, as a compensatory practice that replaced images of the war-torn corpses of the Civil War with the intact wholeness of the male athlete's body. See also Anthony Rotundo, *American Manhood: Transformations in Masculinity from the Revolution to the Modern Era* (New York: Basic Books, 1993).

26. For an account of how the work process and the laboring body were reimagined in the late nineteenth century, see Anson Rabinbach, *The Human Motor: Energy, Fatigue, and the Origins of Modernity* (New York: Basic Books, 1990). He explains, "The human organism was considered a productive machine, stripped of all cultural and social relations and reduced to 'performance' which could be measured in terms of energy and output" (183).

27. David Starr Jordan, *The Human Harvest: A Study of the Decay of the Races through the Survival of the Unfit* (Boston: Beacon Press, 1907), 54.

28. As Seltzer puts it, "body building became nation building." Seltzer, *Bodies and Machines*, 149.

29. Donna Haraway, "Teddy Bear Patriarchy: Taxidermy in the Garden of Eden, New York City, 1908–1936," in *Primate Visions: Gender, Race, and Nature in the World of Modern Science* (New York: Routledge, 1989).

30. Victoria Woodhull, *The Rapid Multiplication of the Unfit* (1891), in *The Victoria Woodhull Reader,* ed. Madeleine B. Stern (Boston, Mass.: M and S Press, 1974), 38.

31. Havelock Ellis, *The Problem of Race Regeneration* (New York: Moffat, Yard, 1911), 27.

32. G. Stanley Hall, *Adolescence,* vol. 1 (New York: D. Appelton, 1907), 324.

33. Ellen H. Richards, *Euthenics: The Science of Controllable Environment: A Plea for Better Living Conditions as a First Step toward Higher Human Efficiency* (Boston: Whitcomb and Barrows, 1910), vii.

34. Emma Goldman, "The Social Aspects of Birth Control," *Mother Earth* 11 (April 1916): 469.

35. Cesare Lombroso, introduction to Gina Ferraro Lombroso, *Criminal Man According to the Classifications of Cesare Lombroso* (New York: G. P. Putnam & Sons 1911), xv.

36. See Charles Caroll, *The Negro, a Beast* (Miami: Mnemosyne Publishing, 1900); and F. G. Crookshank, *The Mongrol in Our Midst: A Study of Man and His Three Faces* (New York: Kegan Paul, Trench, Trubner, 1931), 201.

37. This is what Hannah Arendt has called the production of "a natural aristocracy." Hannah Arendt, *The Origins of Totalitarianism* (New York: Harcourt Brace Jovanovich, 1979), 173.

38. As Johannes Fabian argues, "Time is a form through which we define the content of relations between the Self and the Other." See Fabian, *Time and the Other* (New York: Columbia University Press, 1983), ix.

39. William S. Sadler, MD, *Race Decadence: An Examination of the Causes of Racial Degeneracy in the United States* (Chicago: A. C. McClurg, 1922), 1–11.

40. For a good overview of Tarzan's incarnations, see Peter Haining, *The Fantastic Pulps* (New York: Random House, 1975). For a complete biography of Burroughs, see Richard Lupoff, *Edgar Rice Burroughs: Master of Adventure* (New York: Avon Books, 1968); Irwin Porges, *Edgar Rice Burroughs: The Man Who Created Tarzan* (Utah: Brigham Young University Press, 1975); and John Taliaferro, *Tarzan Forever: The Life of Edgar Rice Burroughs, Creator of Tarzan* (New York: Scribner, 1999). Among the many articles and texts that have informed my analysis of the Tarzan series are: Pat Kirkham and Janet Thumin, "You Tarzan," and Walt Morton, "Tracking the Sign of Tarzan: Transmedia Representation of a Pop-Culture Icon," both in *You Tarzan: Masculinity, Movies, and Men,* ed. Pat Kirkham and Janet Thumin (London: Lawrence and Wishart, 1993), 11–46 and 106–25; Pat Kirkham and Janet Thumin, ed., *Me Jane: Masculinity, Movies, and Women* (New York: St. Martin's Press, 1995); Julie Zanger, "Dorothy and Tarzan: Toward a Theory of National Fantasy," in *Contours of the Fantastic,* ed. Michele Langford (New York: Greenwood Press, 1990), 81–88; and Marianna Torgovnick's chapter "Taking Tarzan Seriously," in *Gone Primitive: Savage Intellects, Modern Lives* (Chicago: University of Chicago Press, 1990), 42–74.

41. Edgar Rice Burroughs, *Tarzan and the Golden Lion* (Chicago: McClurg, 1923).

42. Edgar Rice Burroughs, "The Tarzan Theme," *Writer's Digest* (June 1932), quoted in Porges, *Edgar Rice Burroughs,* 135. *Tarzan of the Apes* was first printed serially in the pulp *All-Story Magazine* in 1912; it was later printed in novel form in 1914. Edgar Rice Burroughs eventually wrote twenty-six sequels, and his estate has licensed his narrative to hundreds of other forms and products, including forty-eight films produced between 1917 and 2007, a comic strip (1929), a radio show (1931), and several television series, as well as wrist watches, trading cards, and candy. The 1999 Disney cartoon remake of *Tarzan* was hailed by critics as "a thrilling saga about natural man . . . about agility, instinct, and anthropological appreciation." See Lisa Schwarzbaum, "The King of Swing," *Entertainment Weekly* 491/492 (June–July 1999): 101–2. We could also note that *Tarzan* has a lot of cultural company, including the anthropomorphic King Kong, the primitive and thus virile Rambo (in all three films in the series), the morphing television series *Manimal,* and the blockbuster hits *George of the Jungle* and *Mighty Joe Young,* not to mention the 1999 Anthony Hopkins vehicle, *Instinct,* about an anthropology professor who journeys to Rwanda to study mountain gorillas and ends up reverting to a former ancestral self. See also the 1994 film *Wolf* starring Jack Nicholson, in which, after being bitten by a wolf, the protagonist becomes one, gaining enhanced senses, sexual virility, and corporate success along the way.

43. Quoted in Porges, *Edgar Rice Burroughs,* 462.

44. "I See a New Race" is an unpublished essay by Burroughs, in ibid., 460–62.

45. These passages were taken from the third book in the series, *The Son of Tarzan* (New York: Del Rey, 1992), 3. Subsequent references are to this edition.

46. For a study of U.S. territorial and commercial ambitions in Africa, see Peter Duignan and Lewis H. Gann, *The United States and Africa: A History* (New York: Cambridge University Press, 1987).

47. Similar themes of imperial fantasy exist in Burroughs's Mars novels. See Robert Markley, "Mars at the Limits of the Imagination: The Dying Planet from Burroughs to Dick," in *Dying Planet: Mars in Science and the Imagination* (Durham, N.C.: Duke University Press, 2005), 182–229.

48. See Kirkham and Thumin, *You Tarzan*, 11–46.

49. Even though the Tarzan series was written and published in the United States, Burroughs chooses to give Tarzan the identity of a British aristocrat; this displacement provides a way to recuperate Tarzan's bestiality into one of the most noble of bloodlines. Conversely, it highlights contemporary concerns over the decay and degeneration of those bloodlines.

50. Burroughs, introduction to *Tarzan and the Golden Lion* (1922), xii.

51. G. Stanley Hall, *Adolescence,* vol. 2 (New York: Appleton, 1904), 59–60.

52. Bederman, *Manliness and Civilization,* 221.

53. Torgovnick, "Taking Tarzan Seriously," 45.

54. Edgar Rice Burroughs, *Tarzan of the Apes* (New York: Penguin Books, 1990), 103. Subsequent references are to this edition.

55. Bederman, *Manliness and Civilization,* 231.

56. Burroughs's formulation of the boundaries of humanity is a cogent example of the uses to which fin de siècle human science were put. Burroughs draws on sociobiological claims as the means to negotiate, through narrative, already existing social anxieties and beliefs. For an account of how the biological classification of humans into racial types was emerging as the most acceptable method to understand human identity, see Ann Stoler, "On Politics, Origins, and Epistemes," *Political Power and Social Theory* 11 (Fall 1997): 245–67.

57. Étienne Balibar and Immanuel Wallerstein, *Race, Nation, Class: Ambiguous Identities* (London: Verso, 1991), 99–100.

58. See Michael Hanchard, "Afro-Modernity," in *Alternative Modernities,* ed. Dilip Gaonkar (Durham, N.C.: Duke University Press, 2001), 280.

59. Gayatri Spivak has described this humanizing logic of colonialism as the "terrorism of the categorical imperative." See Spivak, *A Critique of Postcolonial Reason: Toward a History of the Vanishing Present* (Cambridge: Harvard University Press, 1999), especially 112–97.

60. Burroughs, "The Tarzan Theme," quoted in Porges, *Edgar Rice Burroughs,* 135.

61. Mark Twain's novel, *Pudd'nhead Wilson* (1893–94), with which Burroughs was surely familiar, may be an interesting, if unlikely, intertext for Tarzan. In *Pudd'nhead Wilson,* when it becomes impossible to distinguish between Chambers and Tom Driscoll's true racial identity, their fingerprints are used to sort out the difficulty. Twain, like Burroughs, was fascinated by the new sciences

of identification and reportedly owned a copy of Lavater's *Essays on Physiognomy*. Significantly, Francis Galton, founder of the eugenics movement, was also a great popularizer of the fingerprinting technique. See Galton, *The Fingerprint: The Classic 1892 Treatise* (1892; London: Dover Publishers, 2004).

62. Two of the best-known studies suggesting the hereditary nature of various forms of deviance were Richard Dugdale's 1877 study of the Jukes family and Goddard's 1912 study of the Kallikak family. In both studies, the researchers traced the ancestry of each family, whose "inferior heredity" was considered the source of alcoholism, crime, prostitution, feeble-mindedness, poverty, and a host of other ills. See Nicole Hahn Rafter, *White Trash: The Eugenic Family Studies, 1877–1919* (Boston: Northeastern University Press, 1988).

63. Edward Said famously describes the Orient as the source of some of the West's "deepest and most recurring images of the Other," images that offer "not only fecundity but sexual promise (and threat), untiring sensuality, unlimited desire, and deep generative energies." See Said, *Orientalism* (New York: Vintage Books, 1978), 188. A more recent account of the processes of Orientalism argues that Said's formulation can be made even more specific: "Orientalism . . . partakes crucially of one of the key properties of capitalist modernity: the attribution to the hegemonic subject of the notion of exchange value, pure exchangeability—value in the abstract." This argument shifts the focus from portrayals of the Orient as lacking in civilized qualities, and therefore as primitive or temporally backward, to how these portrayals endow the hegemonic subject with universal properties. See Vasant Kaiwar and Sucheta Mazumdar, "Race, Orient, Nation in the Time-Space of Modernity," in *Antinomies of Modernity*, ed. Vasant Kaiwar and Sucheta Mazumdar (Durham, N.C.: Duke University Press, 2003), 273–74.

64. See Ronald Takaki, *Iron Cages: Race and Culture in Nineteenth Century America* (New York: Oxford University Press, 1990).

65. Anne McClintock has named the practice of appropriation and disavowal occurring within the project of empire "commodity racism," an ideology of racial difference by which the mass marketing of empire became possible. McClintock, *Imperial Leather: Race, Gender, and Sexuality in the Colonial Contest* (London: Routledge, 1995), 207–31.

66. Quoted in Kevles, *In the Name of Eugenics*, 97.

67. Throughout the twentieth century, as Lisa Lowe explains, "the Asian immigrant has served as a 'screen' on to which the nation projects a series of complicated anxieties regarding external and internal threats to the mutable coherence of the national body." Lowe, *Immigration Acts: On Asian American Cultural Politics* (Durham, N.C.: Duke University Press, 1996), 18. On the emergence of the legal and social category of the "illegal immigrant," see Mae Ngai, *Impossible Subjects: Illegal Aliens and the Making of Modern America* (Princeton, N.J.: Princeton University Press, 2005).

68. Sax Rohmer is a pseudonym for Arthur S. Ward (1883–1959), who was born in England, where he wrote many of the initial books in the Fu Manchu series, beginning with *The Insidious Dr. Fu Manchu*. All the novels initially appeared in serial form in *Collier's* magazine and were subsequently

published in England and the United States. He lived sporadically in London, Paris, and Cairo, finally settling in White Plains, New York, where he continued to write novels for the series such as *Fu Manchu's Daughter, President Fu Manchu,* and *Emperor Fu Manchu.* In 1955, he sold the film and television rights, at which point several Hollywood films and a television series were produced.

69. Sax Rohmer, *President Fu Manchu* (1936; New York: Pyramid Books, 1963), book jacket.

70. Sax Rohmer, *Yellow Claw* (New York: Mckinlay, Stone, and Mackenzie, 1915). Subsequent references are to this edition.

71. Sax Rohmer, *The Return of Dr. Fu Manchu* (New York: Mckinlay, Stone, and Mackenzie, 1916), 300, 298. Subsequent references are to this edition.

72. Sax Rohmer, *The Hand of Fu Manchu* (New York: McBride, 1917), 65. Subsequent references are to this edition.

73. The anxious reader in this context summons to mind D. A. Miller's *The Novel and the Police* (Berkeley: University of California Press, 1989). Unlike Miller's engagement with the epic narrative holism of the Victorian novel, the dime novel exists in deliberately truncated form, offering a fast-paced, never-ending reading experience.

74. Sax Rohmer, *The Daughter of Fu Manchu* (New York: Doubleday, 1931), 83, 308. Subsequent references are to this edition.

75. Sax Rohmer, *President Fu Manchu,* book jacket. Subsequent references are to this edition.

76. As I discussed in chapter 2, physiognomy and phrenology were the first biological sciences to adapt a metaphysics of race to the emerging materialist methodologies of science; each science privileged the human body as the site at which the intangible (emotions, thoughts, intelligence) might be understood to merge into, or manifest itself as, the physical.

77. See Lowe, *Immigration Acts;* Wahneema Lubiano, ed., *The House that Race Built* (New York: Vintage Books, 1998); Jan Radway, "What's in a Name?" in *The Futures of American Studies,* ed. Donald Pease and Robyn Wiegman (Durham, N.C.: Duke University Press, 2002), 45–75; and Nikhil Pal Singh, *Black Is a Country* (Cambridge, Mass.: Harvard University Press, 2005).

78. Johannes Fabian, *Time and the Other: How Anthropology Makes Its Object* (New York: Columbia University Press, 1983), 32.

79. Max Nordau, *Degeneration* (1892, English trans. 1895; Lincoln: University of Nebraska Press, 1993), 536, 537, 42, 43.

80. Ricoeur, *Time and Narrative,* 7.

81. Latour, *We Have Never Been Modern,* 68, 69, 75.

82. For Gilles Deleuze, this is the time of "becoming" whereby each moment that arises in time becomes the imaginative production of something new and unforeseeable. See Deleuze, *Cinema 2: The Time-Image* (Minneapolis: University of Minnesota Press, 1995).

83. Elizabeth Grosz describes the idea of reversible time by way of her reading of Henri Bergson: "The past is the condition for infinite futures, and duration is that flow that connects the future to the past that gave it impetus."

Grosz, *The Nick of Time: Politics, Evolution, and the Untimely* (Durham, N.C.: Duke University Press, 2004), 184.

84. Lewis Henry Morgan, *Systems of Consanguinity and Affinity of the Human Family,* 356.

85. Theodore Roosevelt, "National Duties," in *The Strenuous Life: Essays and Addresses* (1900; New York: Adamant Media, 2005), 281.

86. Elsie Clews Parsons, "Penalizing Marriage and Child-Bearing," *Independent* 18 (1906): 146–47.

5. Unnatural Selection

1. Anita Loos, "The Force of Heredity, and Nella: A Modern Fable with a Telling Moral for Eugenists," *Vanity Fair,* February 1915, 42. Subsequent references are to this text.

2. For my treatment of *The Sea-Wolf,* see chapter 6.

3. See, for example, Cannon Schmitt, "Mother Dracula," in *Alien Nation: Nineteenth-Century Gothic Fictions and English Nationality* (Philadelphia: University of Pennsylvania Press, 1997), 135–55.

4. The representation of motherhood as either an imperiled or a prescriptive ideal is not new in the context of American history. However, I am arguing that the figure of the mother emerged with new meaning at this time not only for the social world but also for white progressive feminists who could now imagine their value in new ways. For important accounts of cultural representations of motherhood, see Stephanie Smith, *Conceived by Liberty: Maternal Figures and Nineteenth-Century American Literature* (Ithaca, N.Y.: Cornell University Press, 1994); and E. Ann Kaplan, *Motherhood and Representation: The Mother in Popular Culture and Melodrama* (New York: Routledge, 1992). For work dealing with contemporary forms of medical representation, see Rosalind Pollack Petchesky, "Fetal Images: The Power of Visual Culture in the Politics of Reproduction," in *Theorizing Feminism,* ed. Anne Herrmann and Abigail Stewart (Boulder, Colo.: Westview Press, 1994), 416–42. On the particular pressures placed on immigrant women and women of color, see Katrina Irving, *Immigrant Mothers: Narratives of Race and Maternity, 1890–1925* (Urbana: University of Illinois Press, 2000); and Allison Berg, *Mothering the Race: Women's Narratives of Reproduction, 1890–1930* (Urbana: University of Illinois Press, 2002).

5. Charlotte Perkins Gilman, *His Religion and Hers* (1923; Westport, Conn.: Hyperion Press, 1976), 86.

6. Until recently, *The Crux* had been out of print since its original publication in 1911. See my edition of *The Crux* for Duke University Press: Charlotte Perkins Gilman, *The Crux,* ed. Dana Seitler (Durham, N.C.: Duke University Press, 2003), especially the introduction to the edition, 1–22.

7. See, for example, Michelle Birnbaum's analysis of *The Awakening:* "'Alien hands': Kate Chopin and the Colonization of Race," in *Subjects and Citizens: Nation, Race, and Gender from Oroonoko to Anita Hill,* ed. Michael Moon and Cathy Davidson (Durham, N.C.: Duke University Press, 1995).

8. Robyn Wiegman, *American Anatomies: Theorizing Race and Gender*

(Durham, N.C.: Duke University Press, 1995), 202; Louise Newman, *White Women's Rights: The Racial Origins of Feminism in the United States* (New York: Oxford University Press, 1999), 15. The 1998 special issue of *American Literature,* entitled "No More Separate Spheres!" has also called for a reevaluation of how we read early feminist texts. For instance, in the introduction, Cathy Davidson calls into question whether or not the binary characterization of nineteenth-century women's texts within the terms of private and public actually existed, suggesting instead that "the binaric version of nineteenth-century American history is ultimately unsatisfactory . . . for understanding the different, complicated ways that nineteenth-century American society or literary production functioned." Davidson, "Preface," *American Literature* 70, no. 3 (Spring 1998): 445.

9. Anne J. Lane, *To Herland and Beyond: The Life and Work of Charlotte Perkins Gilman* (New York: Pantheon Books, 1990), 18–19.

10. In this chapter, I limit my scope to a particular expression of white progressive feminism at the fin de siècle. This was by no means the only practice of feminism during this period. Other activities at this time by nonwhite women focused on issues of gender oppression, including black clubwomen's organizations and Ida B. Wells's antilynching activism. However, I am wary of simply listing these practices under the larger rubric of feminism because this would subsume them under the very category that I am trying to problematize (precisely because of its historically exclusionary terminologies and tactics). Instead, I would suggest that the political practices of women of color from the turn of the century are deserving of a more contextual and specified understanding of their work around issues of race and gender than I can undertake here. For work that does this, see Paula Giddings, *When and Where I Enter: The Impact of Black Women on Race and Sex in America* (New York: Bantam Books, 1984); Hazel Carby, *Reconstructing Womanhood: The Emergence of the Afro-American Woman Novelist* (New York: Oxford University Press, 1987); and Ann DuCille, *Skin Trade* (Cambridge, Mass.: Harvard University Press, 1996).

11. Daylanne English, "W. E. B. Du Bois's *Family Crisis,*" *American Literature* 72, no. 2 (June 2000): 296.

12. Newman, *White Women's Rights,* 8.

13. Gail Bederman argues that this kind of "racially-based feminism" advocated strongly that women's sexual responsibility was integral to the relative outcomes of either racial survival or racial destruction. She writes: "White, native-born Americans could choose either women's sexual dependence, leading to racial decline and barbarism, or women's sexual equality, leading to racial advance and the highest civilization ever evolved." Bederman, *Manliness and Civilization: A Cultural History of Gender and Race in the United States, 1880–1917* (Chicago: University of Chicago Press, 1995), 136. For a study of how feminism and evolutionism intersected in the British context, see Rita Felski, *The Gender of Modernity* (Cambridge, Mass.: Harvard University Press, 1995).

14. Theodore Roosevelt, "National Duties," in *The Strenuous Life: Essays and Addresses* (1901; St. Clair Shores, Mich.: Scholarly Press, 1970), 280.

15. See Richard Slotkin, *Regeneration through Violence: The Mythology of the American Frontier* (Norman: University of Oklahoma Press, 2000), and *Gunfighter Nation: The Myth of the Frontier in Twentieth-Century America* (Norman: University of Oklahoma Press, 1998), 175.

16. Charlotte Perkins Gilman, *Women and Economics* (1898; New York: Prometheus Books, 1996), 181.

17. Among the many accounts of these shifts and anxieties, see Carroll Smith-Rosenberg, *Disorderly Conduct: Visions of Gender in Victorian America* (New York: Oxford University Press, 1985); Kathy Peiss, *Cheap Amusements: Working Women and Leisure in Turn-of-the-Century New York* (Philadelphia: Temple University Press, 1986); Ruth Rosen, *The Lost Sisterhood: Prostitution in America, 1900–1918* (Baltimore: Johns Hopkins University Press, 1982); and John Haller and Robin Haller, *The Physician and Sexuality in Victorian America* (Carbondale: Southern Illinois University Press, 1974).

18. My understanding of this campaign is informed by Lauren Berlant's work on sex, citizenship, and "the aura of the little girl" in the contemporary United States. She argues: "Sometimes, when the little girl, the child, or youth are invoked in discussions about pornography, obscenity, or the administration of morality in U.S. mass culture, actually endangered living beings are being imagined. Frequently, however, we should understand that these disturbing figures are fetishes, effigies that condense, displace and stand in for arguments about who 'the people' are, what they can bear, and when, if ever." *The Queen of America Goes to Washington City: Essays on Sex and Citizenship* (Durham, N.C.: Duke University press, 1997), 66–67. For a discussion of this campaign within the context of the birth control movement, see Margaret Jones, "Woman's Body, Worker's Right: Feminist Self-Fashioning and the Fight for Birth Control, 1898–1917," in *American Bodies: Cultural Histories of the Physique,* ed. Tim Armstrong (New York: New York University Press, 1996).

19. For extended treatments of eugenics in the United States, see Donald K. Pickens, *Eugenics and the Progressives* (New York: Vanderbilt University Press, 1968); Daniel Kevles, *In the Name of Eugenics: Genetics and the Uses of Human Heredity* (Cambridge, Mass.: Harvard University Press, 1995); Wendy Kline, *Building a Better Race: Gender, Sexuality, and Eugenics from the Turn of the Century to the Baby Boom* (Berkeley: University of California Press, 2001); and Nancy Ordover, *American Eugenics: Race, Queer Anatomy, and the Science of Nationalism* (Minneapolis: University of Minnesota Press, 2003). For Gilman's own record of her eugenic activities, including her speeches on heredity and "Racial Unity" and her involvement with the American Eugenics Society, see relevant entries in Denise D. Knight, ed., *The Diaries of Charlotte Perkins Gilman, Volume 2: 1890–1935* (Charlottesville: University Press of Virginia, 1994).

20. Quoted in Kevles, *In the Name of Eugenics,* 90.

21. Madeleine B. Stern, ed., *The Victoria Woodhull Reader* (Boston, Mass.: M and S Press, 1974), 39. See also "Stirpiculture; or, The Scientific Propagation of the Human Race" in the same volume.

22. Gilman, *Women and Economics,* 295.

23. Ibid., 110.

24. Ibid., 340. These arguments are dramatized in her novel *What Diantha Did* (1910), in which a young woman radicalizes the housework and hotel industry, and a short story called "Making a Change," about a young mother who starts a child care facility on the roof of her apartment building. See also her articles "Kitchen-Mindedness," *Forerunner* 1 (February 1910): 7–11, and "The New Motherhood," *Forerunner* 1 (December 1910): 17–18; and her non-fictional work *The Home: Its Work and Influence* (New York: McClure, Philips, 1903).

25. Charlotte Perkins Gilman, "A Suggestion on the Negro Problem," *American Journal of Sociology* 14 (July 1908): 78, 83. See also Gary Scharnhorst, *Charlotte Perkins Gilman: A Bibliography* (New York: Scarecrow Press, 2003).

26. Charlotte Perkins Gilman, *With Her in Ourland* (1916; Westport, Conn.: Praeger, 1997), 120.

27. Michel Foucault, "Governmentality," in *The Foucault Effect*, ed. Graham Birchell (London: Harvester Wheatsheaf, 1991). For Foucault, the restructuring of power relations in modernity depended on the family as a privileged site of government.

28. Michel Foucault, *The Use of Pleasure: The History of Sexuality*, vol. 2, trans. Robert Hurley (New York: Pantheon Books, 1986), 28.

29. Judith Butler, *Gender Trouble: Feminism and the Subversion of Identity* (New York: Routledge, 1990), 337.

30. Charlotte Perkins Gilman, "The Yellow Wall-Paper," in *The Yellow Wall-Paper and Other Stories* (New York: Oxford University Press, 1995), 3. Subsequent references are to this edition.

31. G. Stanley Hall, *Adolescence*, vol. 1 (New York: Appleton, 1907), 10. See also Alexander Chamberlain, *The Child: A Study in the Evolution of Man* (New York: Scribner's, 1907). For more on Hall and Chamberlain's theories of childhood and recapitulation, see Bill Brown's argument on Crane's "savage boys" in *The Material Unconscious: American Amusement, Stephen Crane, and the Economies of Play* (Cambridge, Mass.: Harvard University Press, 1996). For a different account of Gilman's interaction with fin de siècle medical epistemologies, see Jane Thrailkill, "Doctoring the Yellow Wall-Paper," *ELH* 69, no. 2 (Summer 2002): 525–66.

32. Walter Benn Michaels, *The Gold Standard and the Logic of Naturalism* (Berkeley: University of California Press, 1987), 6.

33. Charlotte Perkins Gilman, *Man-Made World, Our Androcentric Culture* (New York: Charlton, 1911), 179.

34. Charlotte Perkins Gilman, *The Crux* (New York: Charlton, 1911). Subsequent references are to this edition.

35. An interesting addendum to this comparison is that Owen Wister was diagnosed with neurasthenia by the physician S. W. Mitchell (infamous for his "rest cure"), as was Gilman, but Mitchell did not advise him to rest. Rather, Mitchell advised him to take a trip out West for some exercise. In fact, while Gilman wrote "The Yellow Wall-Paper" as a critique of Mitchell's therapy, Wister wrote *The Virginian* in praise of it. See Barbara Will, "The Nervous Origins of the American Western," *American Literature* 70, no. 2 (June 1998): 293–316.

36. For an account of the anxieties over syphilis in the United States, see Alan Brandt, *No Magic Bullet: A Social History of Venereal Disease in the U.S. since 1880* (New York: Oxford University Press, 1987).

37. See Elaine Showalter, *The Female Malady* (New York: Penguin, 1985); and Mary Douglas, *Purity and Danger* (New York: Routledge, 1991). The redescription of disease as a problem of male sexual profligacy was in fact a hallmark of the feminist progressive movement. As Ruth Rosen argues: "Whereas male reformers tended to represent the carriers of sexually transmitted diseases as women, and prostitutes in particular, female reformers represented them as men." *Lost Sisterhood*, 53.

38. Priscilla Wald, "Cultures and Carriers: Typhoid Mary and the Science of Social Control," *Social Text* 52–53 (Fall/Winter 1997): 183. For Wald's larger argument about culture and contagion, see Wald, *Contagious: Cultures, Carriers, and the Outbreak Narrative* (Durham, N.C.: Duke University Press, 2007).

39. Ibid., 210.

40. Laura Doyle, *Bordering on the Body: The Racial Matrix of Modern Fiction and Culture* (New York: Oxford University Press, 1994), 5.

41. Ibid., 5, 4.

42. For a vibrant account of the deheterosexualizing tendencies of otherwise normative gendering practices, see Kathryn R. Kent, *Making Girls into Women: American Women's Writing and the Rise of Lesbian Identity* (Durham, N.C.: Duke University Press, 2003). See especially chapter 1, "'Single White Female': The Sexual Politics of Spinsterhood in Harriet Beecher's Stowe's *Oldtown Folks*," 19–43.

43. Charlotte Perkins Gilman, *The Living of Charlotte Perkins Gilman, an Autobiography* (1935; New York: Arno Press, 1972), 154. See also Lois Magner, "Darwinism and the Woman Question," in *Critical Essays on Charlotte Perkins Gilman*, ed. Joanne Karpinski (New York: Maximillan, 1992).

44. Herbert Spencer, *First Principles of a New System of Biology* (New York: Appleton, 1864), 516.

45. Gilman, *His Religion and Hers*, v.

46. Gilman, *Women and Economics*, 31–32.

47. Ibid., 32.

48. Charlotte Perkins Gilman, *Herland* (1914; New York: Pantheon, 1979), 84, 22, 87. Val Gough characterizes *Herland*'s descriptions of mothers as part of the novel's "lesbian subtext" in which Gilman articulates "a lesbian-feminist vision of the nurturing and collective capacities of women." I, too, am tempted to read *Herland* as a kind of lesbian utopia: its women are strong, assertive, and self-determining in ways that have been important to the development of feminist and lesbian identity formations. To do so, though, would too hastily translate *Herland* into a presentist political currency, one of feminist sexual subversiveness, that places the text in an ideological context that elides the specificities of Gilman's project. Gilman's descriptions may look like an expression of "butch erotics," and her critique of heterosexuality may look like something subversive, but only from a perspective outside the feminism of the period. See Val Gough, "Lesbians and Virgins: The New Motherhood

in *Herland*," in *Anticipations: Essays in Early Science Fiction and Its Precursors,* ed. David Seed (Syracuse, N.Y.: Syracuse University Press, 1995), 197.

49. Gilman's worry over the reproductive consequences of heterosexual sex supports the period's worry, in general, over unrestrained sexual freedom. But Gilman also believed that "responsible" sexual behavior was a necessary component to women's political freedom. I put the word *responsible* in scare quotes because today we associate the term with something positive (as in the practice of safer sex), while for Gilman, responsibility indicated a different set of practices—for example, the self-governance of sexual behavior along class and racial lines. This is precisely why something that initially seems contradictory (feminism and eugenics) is not in the form it is realized in Gilman.

50. T. J. Jackson Lears, *No Place of Grace: Antimodernism and the Transformation of American Culture, 1880–1920* (Chicago: University of Chicago Press, 1981).

51. See Bederman, *Manliness and Civilization,* 142–44.

52. These citations are from Gilman's different fictions: "Bee Wise," 226; *The Crux,* 90; and "Dr. Clair's Place," 297, respectively. Both "Bee Wise" and "Dr Clair's Place" appear in *The Yellow Wall-Paper and Other Stories.*

53. The trope of ascent has appeared throughout American literature, from Little Eva's ascent to heaven in *Uncle Tom's Cabin* (the quasi-religious ascent of sentimental novels) to the theme of capitalist ascent in *Ragged Dick* (the economic mobility of American naturalism). Here I argue that Gilman reformulates the trope of ascent as something feminist and Darwinian at once.

54. See Amy Kaplan, "Manifest Domesticity," *American Literature* 70, no. 3 (September 1998): 581–606; and Jennifer S. Tuttle, "Rewriting the West Cure: Charlotte Perkins Gilman, Owen Wister, and the Sexual Politics of Neurasthenia," in *The Mixed Legacy of Charlotte Perkins Gilman,* ed. Catherine Golden and Joanna Schneider Zangrando (Newark, N.J.: University of Delaware Press, 2000).

6. An Atavistic Embrace

1. Eugene O'Neill, *The Hairy Ape* (1922; New York: Vintage Books, 1995). Subsequent references are to this edition.

2. For Lacan, the process of identification happens in two modes: the transitive mode of identifying the self in relation to the difference of the other, and the reflexive mode of identifying the self in relation to a resemblance to the other. See Jacques Lacan, *Ecrits* (New York: W. W. Norton, 1977). See also J. Laplanche and J. B. Pontalis, *The Language of Psychoanalysis* (London: Hogarth Press, 1983).

3. The Provincetown Players were part of the Little Theater Movement, which formed to support the production of experimental plays as an artistic alternative to the popular melodramas of the commercial theaters on Broadway. See Brenda Murphy, *The Provincetown Players and the Culture of Modernity* (Cambridge: Cambridge University Press, 2005).

4. Bruno Latour, *We Have Never Been Modern,* trans. Catherine Porter (Cambridge, Mass.: Harvard University Press, 1993).

5. For my discussion of a similar use of typography in the Fu Manchu series, see chapter 4. What is interesting in each usage is how a modern system (the technological reproduction of language through typesetting) functions to produce its opposite: the archaic. New technologies, put simply, are drawn on to invent the past.

6. Yank could have been visiting either the Central Park Zoo or the Bronx Zoo. The Parks Commission was authorized to establish the Central Park Zoo (then called the Central Park Menagerie) in 1864. The Bronx Zoo opened its gates to the public in 1899. Another significant historical reference for the play occurs in 1921, the same year that O'Neill wrote *The Hairy Ape,* when the American Museum of Natural History in New York sponsored two well-known events: the first was the Second International Congress of the Eugenics Society; the second, the first public display of a stuffed gorilla (Carl Akeley's "Giant of Karisimbi" from Congo).

7. One of the ways that O'Neill created an on-stage aura of irony and alienation was by using the New Stagecraft method, which emerged to counter the popular use of naturalistic scenery and the attendant notion of detailed authenticity in set design. By contrast, the New Stagecraft movement favored simplicity, using minimal backdrops, black-and-white sets, and abstract scenery. In general, American expressionist playwrights like O'Neill used this method to convey the dehumanizing aspects of modern society. See Julia Walker, *Expressionism and Modernism in American Theater: Bodies, Voices, Words* (Cambridge: Cambridge University Press, 2005).

8. Donna Haraway, *The Companion Species Manifesto: Dogs, People, and Significant Otherness* (Chicago: Prickly Paradigm Press, 2003), 4.

9. See M. Merleau-Ponty, *Phenomenology of Perception,* trans. Colin Smith (New York: Routledge and Kegan, 1962), and *The Visible and the Invisible,* trans. Alphonso Lingis (Evanston: Northwestern University Press, 1968).

10. Ibid., 456.

11. Ibid., 346.

12. Ibid., 410.

13. John Berger, "Why Look at Animals?" in *About Looking* (New York: Vintage Books, 1991), 6.

14. Mark Seltzer, *Bodies and Machines* (New York: Routledge, 1992), 22.

15. See Louis Althusser, *For Marx* (London: Penguin Presss, 1965); and Ernesto Laclau and Chantal Mouffe, *Hegemony and Socialist Strategy: Towards a Radical Democratic Politics* (London: Verso, 1985).

16. Walter Benjamin, *Passagen-Werk,* quoted in Susan Buck-Morss, *The Dialectics of Seeing: Walter Benjamin and the Arcades Project* (Cambridge, Mass.: MIT Press, 1993), 108.

17. Ibid., 59.

18. Yank's misrecognition resonates with Homi Bhabha's reading of Franz Fanon in his discussion of the power of naming practices ("the marking of the subject") in colonial culture. For Fanon, his own "marking" occurs when a young girl, on seeing him on the street, turns to her mother and says, "Look, a Negro . . . Mama see the Negro." Bhabha reads this as "a scene" that fixes

"the seen" within a "totalizing" racist imaginary. Bhabha, *The Location of Culture* (New York: Routledge, 1994), 76.

19. The Bessemer process was one of the first successful procedures for the mass production of steel, named after its inventor, Henry Bessemer. The process involves the oxidation of the impurities in iron. The heat of oxidation raises the temperature of the iron and keeps it molten. The product is then emptied into ladles from which the steel is poured into molds; the slag, or waste, is left behind. I think it is safe to say that O'Neill uses this reference to make a larger point about the various things (and people) produced as waste in capitalist society. On the Bessemer process, see *Sir Henry Bessemer: Father of the Steel Industry*, ed. Colin Bodsworth (London: IOM Communications, 1998).

20. For a Marxist reading (by way of Derrida) of the temporal contingencies of modern capital, see Ernesto Laclau, "'The time is out of joint,'" *Diacritics* 25, no. 2 (Summer 1995): 86–96.

21. Barbara Herrnstein Smith has characterized the human encounter with animals as a "cognitive dissonance," "the sense of a serious disorder or wrongness—and, with it, sensations of alarm, vertigo, or revulsion—that we experience when ingrained cognitive norms are unexpectedly violated." Smith, "Animal Relatives, Difficult Relations," *differences* 15, no. 1 (Spring 2004): 2–3.

22. Bill Brown, *The Material Unconscious: American Amusement, Stephen Crane, and the Economies of Play* (Cambridge: Harvard University Press, 1996), 210.

23. Bhabha, *Location of Culture*, 35.

24. Ibid., 35.

25. Étienne Balibar, "Racism and Nationalism," in Étienne Balibar and Immanuel Wallerstein, *Race, Nation, Class: Ambiguous Identities* (London: Verso, 1991), 45.

26. The word *conspicuous* in relation to *consumption* was made famous by Thorstein Veblen, who used it to describe the activity of "the gentleman of leisure" who "consumes the staff of life beyond the minimum required for subsistence . . . as a means of reputability." Veblen, *The Theory of The Leisure Class* (New York: Penguin Books, 1967), 73–75.

27. As Guy Debord describes it, the spectacle is the capitalist colonization of the image; it subordinates spectators—people in everyday life—to the spectacle's monopoly over appearances. Like the commodity, spectacle disguises what it really is: a dictatorial relationship between persons and classes. For Debord, capitalist ideology itself is spectacular; it operates by luring the "masses" to consume images that express a capitalist hegemonic principle. In the form of spectacle, ideology is cut off from its source; its real relations are mystified by "winking electric lights." Debord, *Society of the Spectacle* (1967; Detroit, Mich.: Black and Red, 1983).

28. Richard Washburn Child, "The Gorilla," *Harper's Monthly Magazine* 130 (January 1915): 223–32. Subsequent references are to this edition.

29. We might want to pause here to consider the use of the word *gorgon*, not least because the Gorgon Pass is a fictional geography. The Gorgon sisters are from Greek mythology, Medusa being the most famous of the three. Instead

of hair, they have live snakes that lend them the power to turn anyone who gazes on them to stone. Like Mildred's power to transform Yank's identity in *The Hairy Ape*, Gorgon Pass seems to reference the destructive power of the feminine gaze.

30. Merleau-Ponty, *Phenomenology of Perception*, 349.

31. Ibid., 316.

32. An understanding of self in the phenomenological sense presented here, of course, may raise a red flag regarding Derrida's critique of the philosophical fetishization of Being as absolute presence. Nonetheless, what is useful about Merleau-Ponty's understanding of self is precisely the way he describes how personhood is shot through with all sorts of nonabsolutes, and the way he pushes a notion of experience to include something other than, even in defiance of, pure consciousness and human exceptionalism.

33. Gilles Deleuze and Félix Guattari, *Anti-Oedipus* (Minneapolis: University of Minnesota Press, 1983), 1.

34. Gilles Deleuze and Félix Guattari, *A Thousand Plateaus* (Minneapolis: University of Minnesota Press, 1987), 240.

35. Deleuze and Guattari, *Anti-Oedipus*, 6.

36. Deleuze and Guattari, *Thousand Plateaus*, 243.

37. Ibid., 245.

38. Ibid., 250.

39. Jack London, *The Sea-Wolf* (1904; New York: Oxford University Press, 1992). Subsequent references to this text are to this edition.

40. See Lee Clark Mitchell, "'And rescue us from ourselves': Becoming Someone in Jack London's *The Sea-Wolf*," *American Literature* 70, no. 2 (June 1998): 317–35.

41. Charles Darwin, *The Descent of Man, and Selection in Relation to Sex* (1892; Princeton, N.J.: Princeton University Press, 1981), 405, italics mine.

42. Ibid., 173.

43. Ernst Haeckel, *Riddle of the Universe* (New York: Harper Bros., 1900).

44. Donna Haraway's understanding of the situatedness of the subject is apropos in this regard; she queries: "Perhaps we can learn from our fusions with animals . . . how not to be man, embodiment of western logos." Haraway, *Simians, Cyborgs, and Women: The Reinvention of Nature* (New York: Routledge, 1991), 173.

45. Walter Benjamin, "Theses on the Philosophy of History," in *Illuminations*, ed. Hannah Arendt, trans. Harry Zohn (New York: Schocken, 1969), 262, 263.

46. Ibid., 262, 261.

47. Ibid., 255.

48. Benjamin, "On Some Motifs in Baudelaire," in *Illuminations*, 155–200. Thus Proust: "But when from a long-distant past nothing subsists, after the people are dead, after the things are broken and scattered, still, alone, more fragile, but with more vitality, more unsubstantial, more persistent, more faithful, the smell and taste of things remain poised a long time, like souls, ready to remind us, waiting and hoping for their moment, amid the ruins of the rest;

and bear unfalteringly, in the tiny and almost impalpable drop of their essence, the vast structure of recollection." Marcel Proust, *Swann's Way, Remembrance of Things Past,* vol. 1, trans. C. K. Scott Moncrieff (1913; New York: Penguin, 1957), 496.

Coda

1. Henry James, *The Portrait of a Lady* (1881; New York: Penguin, 2003).

2. Marcel Proust, *Swann's Way, Remembrance of Things Past,* vol. 1, trans. C. K. Scott Moncrieff (1913; New York: Penguin, 1957), 496.

3. For an account of history as expressed by structures of feeling (like trauma and melancholy) or monumental structures (like buildings, statues, and memorials), see Dominick LaCapra, *History in Transit: Experience, Identity, Critical Theory* (Ithaca, N.Y.: Cornell University Press, 2004); and Andreas Huyssen, *Present Pasts: Urban Palimpsests and the Politics of Memory* (Stanford, Calif.: Stanford University Press, 2003). For an argument about the relation between mass cultural technologies and the collective memory of American experience, see Alison Landsberg, *Prosthetic Memory: The Transformation of American Remembrance in the Age of Mass Culture* (New York: Columbia University Press, 2004).

4. Benjamin was influenced by Freud's work on the indistinction between sleeping and waking, consciousness and unconsciousness. In his own work, he sought to extend Freud's understanding of this indistinction as it operated within the individual to both history and the collective social body. See Margaret Cohen, *Profane Illumination: Walter Benjamin and the Paris of Surrealist Revolution* (Berkeley: University of California Press, 1995).

5. See Walter Benjamin, *The Arcades Project* (New York: Belknap, 2002), and "Paris, Capital of the Nineteenth Century," in *Reflections,* trans. Edmund Jephcott (New York: Schocken Books, 1978), 146–63.

6. W. G. Sebald, *Austerlitz* (New York: Modern Library, 2001), 100–101.

7. Ibid.

8. For an astute reading of Sebald's modernist realism, see Todd Pressner, "'What a synoptic and artificial view reveals': Extreme History and the Modernism of W. G. Sebald's Realism," *Criticism* 46, no. 3 (Summer 2004): 341–60.

9. See Émile Benveniste, *Problems in General Linguistics,* trans. Mary Meeks (Miami: University of Miami Press, 1973).

10. See, among others, the work of David Eng, Roderick Ferguson, Edouard Glissant, Catherine Hall, Jose Muñoz, Jacques Rancière, and Sara Suleri.

11. Wendy Brown writes: "If history does not have a course, then it does not prescribe the future; the 'weight' and contours of history establish constraints but not norms for political action." See Brown, *Politics out of History* (Princeton, N.J.: Princeton University Press, 2001), 116–17. See also Elizabeth Grosz, who, in her analysis of Darwin's theories, argues: "Darwin presents . . . the germs for an account of the place of futurity, the direction forward as the opening up, diversification, or bifurcation of the latencies of the present,

which provide a kind of ballast for the induction of a future different but not detached from the past and present." Grosz, *The Nick of Time: Politics, Evolution, and the Untimely* (Durham, N.C.: Duke University Press, 2004), 91.

12. New and exciting work on time in feminist and queer studies has begun to explore and debate the temporalities of subjectivity, and thus to push us toward a crucial rethinking of the politics of personhood. See especially Lee Edelman, *No Future: Queer Theory and the Death Drive* (Durham, N.C.: Duke University Press, 2004); Carla Freccero, *Queer/Early/Modern* (Durham, N.C.: Duke University Press, 2006); Valerie Rohy, "Ahistorical," *GLQ* 12, no. 1 (Fall 2006): 61–83; "Queer Temporalities," *GLQ* 13, no. 2–3 (Winter 2007): 159–367, special issue edited by Elizabeth Freeman; and Elizabeth Freeman, "Time Binds, or, Erotohistoriography," *Social Text* 84–85 (Fall–Winter 2005): 57–68. In the special issue, Freeman sums up this new engagement when she writes "If we reimagine 'queer' as a set of possibilities produced out of temporal and historical difference, or see the manipulation of time as a way to produce both bodies and relationalities (or even nonrelationality), we encounter a more productively porous queer studies, one shaped by and reshaping not only various disciplines but also studies of race, nation, migration, and postcolony" (159).

13. Here, I follow Kath Weston's argument: "If 'social change' is your business and you want to 'get there,' it's worth your while to attend to what's already there." Weston, *Gender in Real Time: Power and Transience in a Visual Age* (New York: Routledge, 2002), 138.

14. On the logic of the sequence in relation to lesbian representation, see Anamarie Jagose, *Inconsequence: Lesbian Representation and the Logic of Sexual Sequence* (Ithaca, N.Y.: Cornell University Press, 2002). She argues: "The enforcement of sexual sequence is a requirement of the cultural imperative to naturalize heterosexuality as the original or preeminent modality of sexuality itself" (x).

15. James Huneker, "Nosphilia: A Nordau Heroine," in *Decadents, Symbolists and Aesthetes: Fin-de-Siècle American Poetry, An Anthology,* ed. Edward Foster (Jersey City, N.J.: Talisman House, 2000), 30. Subsequent references are to this edition. Huneker's story first appeared in *M'lle New York* 1, no. 6 (October 1895).

16. See Angelika Rauch, "The *Trauerspiel* of the Prostituted Body; or, Woman as Allegory of Modernity," *Cultural Critique* 10 (Fall 1988): 77–88.

17. Martin Amis's contemporary novel *Yellow Dog* inverts this allegorical structure. The main character, who considers himself a liberal and feminist man, suffers from a violent attack, after which he reverts back to a species of primitive masculinity. His wife, before kicking him out, declares: "After you were hit, I thought at first you'd slipped back a generation or two. I now think it's more atavistic than that. If, today, you were to show me around your past, as you once did five years ago, you wouldn't be showing me the pub called the World Upside Down. You'd be showing me your cave—or your treetop." Amis, *Yellow Dog* (New York: Vintage, 2005), 209.

18. Judith Halberstam warns against the traditional humanist paradigm that would "seek refuge in the fully human while abjecting all its monsters." Instead, she imagines "a posthuman monstrosity that is partial, compromised, messy, and queer." See Halberstam, *Skin Shows: Gothic Horror and the Technology of Monsters* (Durham, N.C.: Duke University Press, 1995), 188.

19. *Vanity Fair,* September 1915, 33.

Index

abstraction, embodied, 35–36
acquired characteristics, Lamarckian theory of, 62
Adolescence (Hall), 139, 185
Adorno, Theodor, 130, 265n.6
Africa: African jungle as definitional space of human origin in Tarzan series, 155; Burroughs's interest in African jungle, 142–43; capacity to threaten and regenerate Western civilization, 142–44; imperialist activity in, 142, 155; Tarzan series set in, 141–56
African Americans, Gilman on, 183; *See also* race and racial logic
African Game Trails (Roosevelt), 142
Aggassiz, Louis, 123
AIDS, 259n.72
Akeley, Carl, 278n.6
À la Récherche du temps perdu (Proust), 225, 228–29, 243
alienation: of modern subject, 226; of worker from commodities produced, 212, 215; working-class, 202–3, 207, 226
Allen, Carol J., 263n.54
Allen, Robert, 157
alliance: Deleuze and Guattari's theory of, 217–18; possibilities for, 226, 239
Althusser, Louis, 278n.15
Altman, Meryl, 263n.44
American Eugenics Society, 157
American Journal of Sociology, 183
American Literature, 1998 special issue of, 272n.8

American Mercury (magazine), 96
American Museum of Natural History, 278n.6
American nationalism, 246n.33; strategic practices of, 157
American studies, 17
Amis, Martin, 282n.17
amusement culture, American, 209–10
amusement/knowledge system, 210
anal stage, 46–47
anecdotal evidence accompanying photographs, 86–88
animal and animality: animal as trope of racial other, 139–40; atavism and investigation of human body for signs of, 7, 9; deployed by Freud as sign of atavism, 49–50; discourse of, as crucial strategy in oppression of humans by other humans, 253n.50; generating opportunity for collective experience, 218; hereditary degeneration evidenced in signs of, 139–40; hypermodern machine and precapitalist animal juxtaposed in *The Hairy Ape*, 205; neurasthenia linked to "animal type of brain" in *Vandover*, 105; ontological crisis (and paradox) of human being in modern world and, 201; primitive, 24; psyche as expression of animalism, 31, 32; sexuality and, 38–39, 250n.18, 264n.59; as signal trope of the masculine

Dana Seitler is associate professor of English at the University of Toronto.